The Purification Papers

The Evolution of God and Man

[Revised and Expanded Edition]

Daniel Briggs

To my wife from another life, Karen, my son,
Danny, and all "lovers of the vision of truth"

"Many shall be purified, and made white, and tried; but the wicked shall do wickedly: and none of the wicked shall understand; but the wise shall understand."

(Daniel 12.10)

Copyright © 2008, 2012 Mandala Books, LLC

Preface, Glossary of Terms and Afterword
Copyright © 2018 Mandala Books, LLC

ISBN-13   978-0692156926
ISBN-10   0692156925

BISAC: Mind, Body & Spirit / Prophecy

All rights reserved. No part of this publication may be reproduced, distributed, or transmitted in any form or by any means, including photocopying, recording, or other electronic or mechanical methods, without the prior written permission of the publisher.

Contents

Table of Figures	p. 6
Preface	p. 10

Book I: Purification

Chapter One:	Initiation	p. 12
Chapter Two:	The Bible Code	p. 14
Chapter Three:	Antichrist	p. 21

Book II: Cyclicity

Chapter One:	Precession	p. 33
Chapter Two:	The Maya Calendar	p. 40
Chapter Three:	The I Ching Eschaton	p. 43
Chapter Four:	The Celestial Hierarchy	p. 45
Chapter Five:	Anatomy of a Buddha	p. 49
Chapter Six:	Joseph the Prophet	p. 53
Chapter Seven:	Joshua and Josiah	p. 57
Chapter Eight:	The Trinity	p. 63
Chapter Nine:	The Seat of God	p. 72

Book III: Matriarchy

Chapter One:	Good God, Bad God	p. 77
Chapter Two:	Two Girls for Every Boy	p. 79
Chapter Three:	Necessary Evil	p. 83
Chapter Four:	The Mother Goddess	p. 86
Chapter Five:	Witch or Priestess?	p. 90
Chapter Six:	Shekhinah, the Presence of God	p. 93
Chapter Seven:	Sophia, the Beauty of God	p. 98
Chapter Eight:	Mary, the Glory of God	p. 101

Book IV: Supraliminality

Chapter One:	Return of the King	p. 106
Chapter Two:	The Seventy Weeks	p. 108
Chapter Three:	A Long Dark Night of the Soul	p. 113
Chapter Four:	Zero Point Energy	p. 117
Chapter Five:	Mazzaroth, the Original Myth	p. 125
	Act I: The Fall	p. 130
	Act II: Redemption	p. 136
	Act III: Dominion	p. 142

Chapter Six:	Olam Haba, the World to Come	p. 147
Chapter Seven:	The Pure Land	p. 151
Chapter Eight:	Millennium, Heaven on Earth	p. 155
Chapter Nine:	The Kingdom of Heavens	p. 163
Bibliography		p. 170
Glossary of Terms		p. 174
Afterword		p. 199
About the Author		p. 200

Table of Figures

Book I: Purification

Figure 1:	Kundalini's Path through Shri, a One-Way Valve	p. 13
Figure 2:	Prime Minister Netanyahu trip to Amman ELS	p. 19
Figure 3:	Prime Minister Murdered — Delayed ELS	p. 20
Figure 4:	Third World War, 9th of Av ELS	p. 20
Figure 5:	Caesar Nero	p. 22
Figure 6:	Nazi Swastika	p. 23
Figure 7:	St. Peter's Basilica	p. 27
Figure 8:	Pope John Paul I	p. 28
Figure 9:	Comet — 5772 / 2012 ELS	p. 31
Figure 10:	Comet Crumbled to Pieces ELS	p. 31

Book II: Cyclicity

Figure 1:	Precession of the Equinoxes	p. 38
Figure 2:	The Great Precession Cycle	p. 39
Figure 3:	The Pyramid of the Magician	p. 41
Figure 4:	The Creative and the Receptive I Ching Hexagrams	p. 43
Figure 5:	I Ching Graph Superimposed Upon Itself	p. 43
Figure 6:	McKenna's TimeWave: Target Date 9/11/2001	p. 44
Figure 7:	Tree of Celestial Intelligences	p. 46

Figure 8:	Jerusalem Under Siege	p. 61
Figure 9:	The Living Logos	p. 69
Figure 10:	The Twelve Thrones	p. 75
Figure 11:	The Seven Living Logos	p. 75

Book III: Matriarchy

Figure 1:	Galactic Mandala	p. 78
Figure 2:	Himalayan Yeti Footprint	p. 81
Figure 3:	Lilith	p. 82
Figure 4:	Tarot Card XV: The Devil	p. 84
Figure 5:	The Great Pyramid's Air Shafts	p. 88
Figure 6:	Jeanne D'Arc	p. 93
Figure 7:	K'un / The Receptive	p. 93
Figure 8:	Total Solar Eclipse	p. 94
Figure 9:	Anthropic Tree of Life	p. 96
Figure 10:	Binah — Malkhut	p. 96
Figure 11:	White Buffalo Woman	p. 99
Figure 12:	The Hagia Sophia Cathedral	p. 100
Figure 13:	Madonna Litta, The Hermitage	p. 102
Figure 14:	Miracle Medal: Our Lady of Grace	p. 103
Figure 15:	Tarot Card XIII: Death	p. 104

Book IV: Supraliminality

Figure 1:	1560 Geneva Bible	p. 112
Figure 2:	TimeWave Zero Novelty Graph	p. 115
Figure 3:	The Tzolkin Sacred Calendar	p. 116
Figure 4:	The Persistence of Memory	p. 117
Figure 5:	Teilhard de Chardin	p. 120
Figure 6:	Sunspot Graph — 2012	p. 121
Figure 7-8:	Earth's Magnetic Pole Reversals	p. 122
Figure 9:	Hyderabad Computer Model	p. 123
Figure 10:	Aurora Borealis	p. 123
Figure 11:	Inside the Great Pyramid	p. 127
Figure 12:	The Grand Gallery	p. 129
Figure 13:	The Sphinx	p. 130
Figure 14:	Virgo	p. 131
Figure 15:	Libra	p. 132
Figure 16:	Scorpio	p. 133
Figure 17:	Oannes (Dagon)	p. 134
Figure 18:	Sagittarius	p. 135
Figure 19:	Capricorn	p. 136
Figure 20:	Aquarius	p. 137
Figure 21:	Epic of Atrahasis	p. 138
Figure 22:	Ark on Mt. Ararat	p. 139

Figure 23:	Pisces	p. 140
Figure 24:	Aries	p. 141
Figure 25:	Taurus	p. 142
Figure 26:	Gemini	p. 143
Figure 27:	Denderah Zodiac	p. 143
Figure 28:	Cancer	p. 144
Figure 29:	Leo	p. 144
Figure 30:	The Almagest	p. 147
Figure 31:	Shrine of the Book	p. 149
Figure 32:	Isaiah 53 ELS	p. 150
Figure 33:	Amida Buddha	p. 154
Figure 34:	The Flying Friar	p. 156
Figure 35:	Wudang Temple	p. 157
Figure 36:	Godfrey Hill	p. 157
Figure 37:	Pineal Gland	p. 158
Figure 38:	Cthulhu (Dagon)	p. 165
Figure 39:	The First Death	p. 166
Figure 40:	The Last Judgment	p. 167
Figure 41:	The New Jerusalem	p. 168
Figure 42:	The Jeshua Mandala	p. 169

Preface

"It goes without saying that nobody initiates anyone else, if we understand by *initiation* the Mystery of the Second Birth or the Great Sacrament. This Initiation is operative from above and has the value and the duration of eternity. The Initiator is above, and here below one meets only the fellow pupils; and they recognize each other by the fact that they *love one another* (John 13, 34-35)."   ~*Meditations on the Tarot,* The Magician

The author of *Meditations on the Tarot*, Valentin Tomberg was a student of Anthroposophy, founded by Rudolf Steiner, a former occultist turned mystic Christian. The latter a rare occurrence since knowledge, without a foundation of love, like St. Paul warned, puffs up the pupil until he considers himself peerless. Unless, of course, all those many lifetimes of learning was safeguarded from the ego, like Edgar Cayce's. After years of readings, the sleeping prophet could integrate an enormous akashic canon into his own working philosophy, without losing his love that indeed built up. These two Initiates, Steiner and Cayce, provide the spine that holds this esoteric history of Mankind together. They're a gold standard, against which other occultists can clearly be seen as both puffed up and inferior. It is the second book, *Cyclicity*, where the Cayce material is absolutely indispensible as the past lives of Jesus are elaborated upon. One will see how and why the latter was destined to become the Chosen One, genetically engineered from the purest line of clandestine Anointed Ones. Abraham's profound Initiation as the first messiah consummated with Jesus' own in the Great Pyramid of Giza, yet another amazing revelation from that grandmaster of psychics, Cayce.

In the fourth book, *Supraliminality*, a non-initiated 19th century Biblical scholar from England, Frances Rolleston, reveals nothing less than the Hebrew Messiah as the pivotal figure of our Collective history. The fact that Ms. Rolleston knew nothing of the astrological Forces does not diminish her astonishing discovery that the Zodiacal signs, their images, could also be used to tell a mythological legend so old that it dates back to the antediluvian sons of Adam — Seth in particular. Predating yet augmenting the first book of the Old Testament, a woman's fall from grace begins our gradual descent into this lower dimensional world, the carnal one. After untold generations of genetic breeding and purification, the fallen woman finally reaches her own Omega Point, reincarnating under Her own power, just as Her offspring, the Messiah will do. The righteous role women have played in our drama, misconstrued as miscreant by a misogynistic patriarchal plutocracy, is thoroughly explored in Book III, *Matriarchy*.

A secondary structure weaving through our esoteric study is an integrated compilation of prophecies that point to a grand cyclical consummation, the Great Purification, a *second* mass extinction event — since the 10,900 BC Younger Dryas Event[1] — that will initiate the World into its culminating time cycle, the Messianic Era. This is summarized in Book I, *Purification* and expounded in Book IV, *Supraliminality*, using every shred of evidence, gleaned from every solitary piece of prophecy that points to a soteriological solution to our existential suffering. The scientific foundations supporting sacred Maya and Hindu calendar convergences, establishing precise temporal windows for these eschatological prognostications — are painstakingly presented in Book II, *Cyclicity*, providing rational food for thought.

Furthermore, a wealth of ancient Eastern metaphysics has been utilized to juxtaposition with Western Christianity, creating a sort of symbiotic entity, a "corpus callosum" for the reader's whole brain to incorporate the two primary polar World Religions, Buddhism and Christianity, into one cohesive Truth. Sanskrit, Buddhist, Hebrew *et al.* concepts of transcending intent are highlighted **RED** and explicated in the Glossary of Terms. Many times the reader will be directed to skip forward, where an idea or theme is carried forth. This is *not* recommended until the manuscript has been given an entire read, beginning to end. Upon subsequent readings, one can confidently jump ahead as directed without any danger of being disconnected to the intricate flow of the main storyline.

God forbid any human author taking credit for this empyreal influx of revealed teachings and commentary that came from above. Time and again, the right book appeared at just the right moment, creating a synchronistic event which clarified a convoluted concept. Lest he forget himself at a later date, the author wishes to confess that the Spirit of truth guided the creation of this composition, while the amanuensis may claim credit for his editorial levity (*i.e.,* wise-ass remarks). The sagacious prophecies speak for themselves and, hopefully, have been given a proper container, a powerful book for they who have eyes to read... and *comprehend*.

"Everything a man does hinges on his personal power. Therefore, for one who doesn't have any, the deeds of a powerful man are incredible. *It takes power to even conceive what power is.*"   ~*Journey to Ixtlan*, Juan Matus

---

[1] "On May 23, 2007 a multi-disciplinary team of scientists announced the finding of physical evidence strongly suggesting that, around 12,900 years ago (10,900 BC), a massive Shoemaker-Levy type comet hit the atmosphere, air burst over the Great Lakes region of North America and probably engulfed much of the continent in a fireball and subsequent firestorm with catastrophic effects for life and climate. On September 27, the team officially published their findings as **Evidence for an extraterrestrial impact 12,900 years ago that contributed to the megafaunal extinctions and the Younger Dryas cooling.**"
        ~MetaFilter Network Inc.

Published in the *Proceedings of the National Academy of Sciences*, Vol. 104, no. 41, this highly credible theory behind the abrupt Younger Dryas cooling event supplements the *Great Atlantis Flood Theory* (Eagle/Wind 2005), postulating an unprecedented extraterrestrial impact (evidently where the Grand Canyon, Arizona exists today) as its precursor. See **Book IV: Supraliminality,** page 137, footnote 57.

Book I: Purification

Chapter One: Initiation

"Be on guard so that your hearts are not weighed down with dissipation and drunkenness and the worries of this life, and that day catch you unexpectedly, like a trap. For it will come upon all who live on the face of the whole earth."

"But about that day and hour no one knows, neither the angels in heaven, nor the Son, *but only the* Father." (Matthew 24.36) (Luke 21.34)

The Son of Man's[1] connection with the Spirit was so intimate as to be familiar, referring to the Absolute as "Dad". His ego so sublimated as to fully embody the High Self [*See* p. 14, footnote 9]— "The Father and I are One." (John 10.30)

Of course, the Christ was not unique in this—we've all been there before, either through a near-death experience, illness or fever, an overdose of a powerful psychoactive agent, or death itself. Most of us, though, have to wait until the moment of Transition[2] to once again experience complete Ego transcendence and *yoga* (Skt. union) with the High Self or Oversoul.

For a brief moment, which can be an Eternity, we *clearly* see our life from a detached POV—*as if that person were absolutely someone else*. We fully realize our true nature as God, the Singularity. No illusion of grandeur, no illusion whatsoever. A simple, sad truth that you are all there is, all there was, and all there ever will be—alone, yet filled to the brim and overflowing with Bliss and Light.

For a moment you feel the awesome responsibility that goes with attainment of the Godhead—the Universe, everything that exists, moves and flows through and because of You and only You. Each and every Human Being, from the African pygmy and Mission Street wino to the Pope himself, attains this exalted level of Reality at least once a lifetime.

If someone is lucky enough to reach the Godhead *during* his/her physical incarnation, they are born again [*See* **Book IV**, p. 161] into a new, spiritually ordained life, becoming what used to be called an Initiate.[3] Besides natural psychotropic substances, which have been with us since day one[4], there have been other methods of Initiation. The most extreme of course, is death—the actual severing of the silver cord. Lazarus, the wealthy brother of Martha and Mary from Magdala (on the coast of Lake Galilee), was called upon by Power itself to become History's first full-blown Initiate.

---

1 The noncanonical Book of Enoch is replete with the controversial appellation. Sacrificed to oblivion, an overwhelming number of references to a *Son of Man*—the same unusual moniker appropriated by the "arch-heretic"—left a bad taste in the Sanhedrin mouth.
 "At that hour, that *Son of Man* was given a name, in the presence of the Lord of the Spirits…
 He is the light of the gentiles and he will become the hope of those who are sick in their hearts." (1 Enoch 48.2)
2 A more accurate, less-loaded word than death, which is etymologically derived from Daath (Hbw. knowledge)—a hidden, forbidden gate in Kabbalistic cosmology. This alien dimension leads to complete disintegration of the individual Soul, and therefore true Death.
3 Today's neophytes are feared, shunned as social pariahs. "For he who has been united with the truth has the assurance that all is well with him, even though most people rebuke him for being out of his mind. For, without their being aware, he has moved from delusion to the real faith; and he knows for sure that he is not deranged, as they say, but through truth—simple and always immutably the same—he has been liberated from the fluctuating and fickle turmoil of the manifold forms of illusion." ~*Philokalia II*, St. Maximos
4 The best candidate for the *Tree of Knowledge of Good and Evil* is the enticing, alluring *Datura* plant (*aka* "devil's weed") with its fragrant, trumpet-like flowers. Highly prized among *diableros,* her powerful root a peerless, yet most dangerous *ally*. "In the course of learning about the devil's weed, I realized she was not for me… nearly killed me every time I tried to use her." ~don Juan Matus
 "When the woman saw that the tree was good for eating and a delight to the eyes,
 and the tree was desirable as a source of wisdom, *she took of its fruit* [essence] and ate." (Genesis 3.6)
"This is a beautiful tree, beautiful to view, with leaves so handsome and blossoms so magnificent in appearance." (1 Enoch 24)

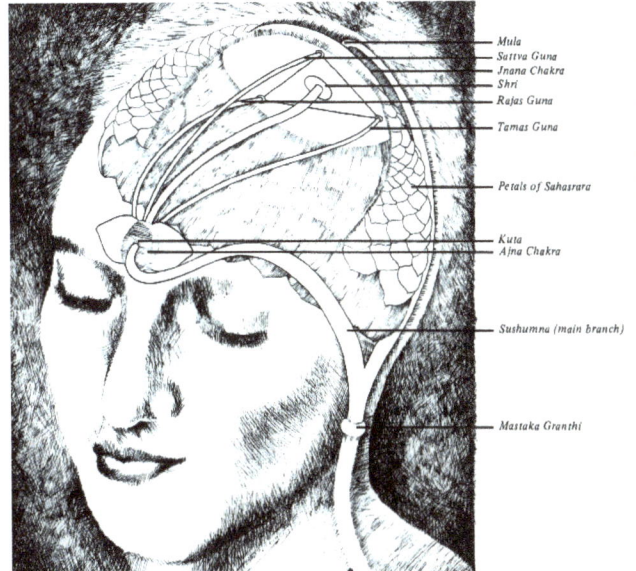

Fig. 1 "*Kundalini* must pass through *Shri* in order to attain the highest stage of knowledge. *Shri* is like a one-way valve— once Kundalini has passed this point, it cannot descend again."
~*Ashtanga Yoga Primer*, Baba Hari Dass

The Christ was careful in delaying His journey to Bethany, Spirit advising Him to let the avaricious young man[5] experience the full three-day Bardo (Tbn. intermediate state). After—and *only* after his Self-realization—was Lazarus ready to receive the whole shocking truth, the perennial, paradoxical mystery teachings of the One and the Many.[6] Once the candidate is "singled-out" by Spirit (many are called, few are chosen) and ascends to the **Most High God**, the Initiate then assumes the role *agent of change*—for either Good or Evil[7]—henceforth retaining the aka cord connection with the Father [*See* **Fig. 1**], ever seeking it out anew life after life.[8]

Another less-extreme method of Initiation— its ancient purposes now long forgotten—utilized the superconductivity generated through a pyramidal point of convergence, a vital manifestation of the massive structure's precise geophysical alignment. Edgar Cayce revealed the original intent of the Great Pyramid (Grk. *Pyro,* fire; O.E. *midd,* center) of Giza, besides preserving Enoch's architectural timeline... [*See* **Book IV**, *Mazzaroth*, pp. 127-129]

"...there began the building of that now called Giza...in the building of this was to be the hall of the initiates of that sometimes referred to as the White Brotherhood. In this same pyramid did the Great Initiate, the Master, take those last of the Brotherhood degrees with John, the forerunner of Him, at that place. John went first to Egypt— where Jesus joined him and both became initiates in the pyramid or temple there." (5748-5)

Other forms of Initiation include the life-long achievement of *samadhi* awakening for the Yogis—both Hindu and Tibetan—as well as the spontaneous *satori* awakening of Chan/Zen in the Chinese/Japanese Schools. Common to all Initiations however is the staggering realization of our true identity as Father/Son/Spirit, the three-in-one nature of the incomprehensible Godhead. The only—yet immensely critical—difference between Jeshua and ourselves is in the *permanence* of the **Cosmic Consciousness** (complete Enlightenment) the former achieved. *And the fact that only one Being (at a time) can sit on the Throne of Power and actualize His Self.* [*See* **Book II**, *The Seat of God*]

---

[5] The same young man *"who went away sad"*—about whom the Master said, **"It is easier for a *rope* to go through the eye of a needle, than for a rich man to enter the kingdom of God."** ~Peshitta Aramaic Bible (Matthew 19.24)

[6] In 1958, while cataloging manuscripts in the library of Mar Saba Monastery twelve miles south of Jerusalem, Columbia graduate student Morton Smith stumbled upon a monk's copy of an ancient letter written by 2nd century Church father Clement of Alexandria. Clement relates that following Peter's death, Mark brought his original gospel to Alexandria and wrote, "a more spiritual gospel for the use of those who were being perfected." He goes on to say, "this text is kept by the Alexandrian Church for use only in the initiation into the great mysteries." Clement then transcribes a fragment of the Lazarus narrative—missing for centuries from the canonized version... **"For he was rich. And after six days Jesus told him what to do and in the evening the youth comes to him, wearing a linen cloth over his naked body. And he remained with him that night, for *Jesus taught him the mystery of the kingdom of God.* And thence, arising, he returned to the other side of the shore."**

[7] Having achieved a permanent *aka* (Hawaiian, *sticky substance*) connection with the Source, the initiate, intoxicated with power, may decide he can use it for personal gain—thus becoming a sorcerer on the Left-Hand Path.

[8] Nobody ever gets "the Power" without initially desiring it—wanting it wholeheartedly. The candidate is succumbed by the promise of power and the caveat *"be careful what you wish for"* is more pertinent here than anywhere! Once the wish for Mastery is declared and granted, it can *never* be revoked in that lifetime. Ironically, one then becomes a *slave* to the Spirit—a slave of God (Love or Hate).

So we see the "Father" is none other than our selves—our truest Self. The third inconceivable part of the triune Being (compounded Soul) that we are.[9] It would be childish to anthropomorphize this aspect of Divinity and picture a geezer with a white beard. The Old World collective unconscious representation of God, exemplified by Michelangelo's Sistine Chapel mural, was seemingly accurate because the original Creator and Galactic Lord, up to the Piscean Age, was indeed the "old man"—**YHVH**. But even Yahweh had to deal with that Unknowable, unpredictable part of Himself which Jeshua called the Father.[10] It *manifests* in the worlds as the Spirit or synchronicity[11]—what the aboriginal Americans call the Great Spirit.[12] As we stood on the precipice of the next Millennium (and annihilation), it is reasonable that the Father, via the vehicle of Spirit[13], chose that most auspicious decade, the 90's, to disclose the *End Time* scenario through an inspired stroke of Jewish ingenuity—or skulduggery?

Chapter Two: The Bible Code

"Go thy way, Daniel: for the words are closed up and sealed til the time of the end." (Daniel 12.9)

---

9 "Trismegistus says: *The monad begot a monad, and reflected upon itself its own heat… Augustine's teaching… namely that God the Father begot another self.*" ~*The Summa Theologica*, Thomas Aquinas *i.e.* The *Trinity* begot a *Trinity*. It replicated itself...

Sigmund Freud's monumental revelation of three different psyches (minds)—id, ego and superego—cooperating as a unity was possibly the single greatest leap forward of the 20th Century. The discovery of the "twin-brain" with its "walnut-like" left and right hemispheres confirmed Freud's hypothesis. Medical research shows how the cognitive, rational "self" resides in the left hemisphere while intuition, memory and feelings take place within the 7 % right-brain half normally in use. Today, almost everyone knows about the dual existence of conscious *(ego)* and subconscious *(inner child* or *id)* yet few are aware of a *third* self: the Superego or *Oversoul*. The Kahuna (Ka =*keeper*, Huna=*secret*) priests of ancient Hawaii had a thorough understanding of the triune psyche they labeled "low (unihipili), middle (uhane) and high self (aumakua)." They learned to manipulate nature and manifest miracles by placating the low self to cooperate with the middle self, and send mana to the High Self or *Utterly Trustworthy Parental Spirit*—empowering her to descend and *overshadow* the two, uniting the three into One. **"Jesus said, If two make peace with each other in a single house, they will say to the mountain, Move from here, and it will move."** (Gospel of Thomas, Logion 48)

"The prevailing view in the Zohar is that the soul consists of three parts, called nefesh, ruah and neshamah. The *nefesh* is attached to the body, preserving it and satisfying its needs. The *ruah* is 'the home of the sensual desires… it controls both good and evil moral conduct'—the *ruah* is the power that enables the *nefesh* to maintain itself in the body. The *neshamah* is a matter of true intellect. It is hewn from the source of life, and from the well-spring of intelligence and wisdom. Glory comes to dwell in the body in order to sustain everything for the service of the Creator, in order to provide him with substance (a Soul)." ~Moses de Leon

"*Neshamah* is called *the highest of all, the most concealed of all the concealed* and *the holy of holies* and whoever is deserving enough to receive the *neshamah* is called *holy*; regarded as if they had become *like holy angels*." ~Isaiah Tishby

10 The "stiff-necked" Hebrews exercised their free will by reverting to Devil worship at the very moment of their final purification and entry into the next level of Awareness: the Kingdom of Heavens. Only Moses' intervention (fully prostrate, forty days!) prevented Yahweh from losing His temper and once again wiping out the Human Race.   [*See* **Book IV**, footnote 6]

11 "*It's a poor sort of memory that only works backwards.*" ~Carl Jung's favorite quote from *Through the Looking-Glass*

"For Jung, a synchronistic event usually involves an archetype (archetypes are nodal points or structural components of the collective unconscious that govern or influence our patterns of behavior). The archetype forms the substructure of the synchronicity, connecting at least two events (an exopsychic one, and an endopsychic one) with a common theme, and acting as a defining quality throughout the experience, thereby intensifying the meaningfulness (Jung. 1960). Synchronicity is not time-dependent in the causal sense where cause must precede effect—the physical event may occur at the same time as an experience in the psyche (an internal image), or even after this experience. Nor is it dependent on spatial determinants (a phenomenon similar in nature to the quantum effect of nonlocality). The relativization of space and time is a hallmark of synchronicity, as indeed it is of paranormal phenomena."

~*Synchronicity, Causality, And Acausality*, Lance Storm, Journal of Parapsychology (1999)

12 "God is a Spirit and they that worship him must worship him in the spirit of Truth."   (Codex Sinaiticus, John 4.24)

13 The Spirit or collective unconscious necessarily works through human agencies to reveal the Father. John Lennon was accused of subtly coding his lyrics with drug references—*Lucy in the Sky with Diamonds* had intense psychedelic imagery—yet the title came from an innocent crayon drawing by his son, Julian. Only later did Lennon (and others) notice that the title was an acronym = **LSD**.

After an onslaught of bogus books claiming to crack a hidden Nostradamus Code, another one in '97, this time declaring a secret cipher embedded within the Bible, seemed ludicrous! A few key differences, however, indicated this book might just be worth taking a second look at...

The author, Michael Drosnin, the very antithesis of a touchy-feely *New Age* writer, has impeccable credentials firmly rooted in the secular world. A top investigative reporter with over 30 years experience at *The Washington Post* and *The Wall Street Journal*, he has shown the rare ability to be in the right place at the right time. Following the death of Howard Hughes, a breach of security at the late billionaire's impregnable Long Beach headquarters—the theft of highly sensitive materials—was an unsolved mystery until Drosnin cracked the case. A clandestine meeting with an informant led the correspondent down a path of collusion and to the cache of stolen materials, boxes containing hundreds of yellow legal pads filled with Hughes' personal instructions and ramblings—a day-by-day diary. Published in 1985, *Citizen Hughes* revealed the world's most famous recluse in all his obsessive-compulsive glory! In 1992, lightning struck a second time as the inquisitive journalist flew to Israel to investigate the claim of a hidden code in the Bible that could reveal current events.

Dr. Eliyahu Rips, an authority in *group theory mathematics* which underlies quantum physics, was only the tip of the prestigious iceberg underwriting this preposterous theory. It had already passed triple hierarchical levels of scrutiny to be published in a U.S. scholarly journal, *Statistical Science* and the indefatigable Drosnin had it independently validated by three qualified scientists at **Harvard**, **Yale** and **Hebrew University**. All they could do was admit the confirmation of something that was seemingly impossible—a 3,000 year-old code weaving through the Pentateuch was accurately pairing modern milestones and personalities to their respective dates of occurrence.

David Kazhdan, Harvard's top-notch number cruncher, said, "I've seen the results. There are no scientific grounds to challenge it. I think it is real."

Yale's leading mathematician Piatetski-Shapiro agreed, "I believe the code is real. I saw the results, and they were quite surprising. Predictions of the future, of Hitler and the Holocaust. There is no way within the laws of mathematics to explain seeing the future. Newtonian physics is too simple to explain a set of predictions this complex and detailed. Quantum physics is also not enough. What we're talking about here is some intelligence that stands outside."

And Israel's most respected mathematician, Robert Aumann concurred, "The Bible code is simply a fact; the science is impeccable. Rips' results are wildly significant, beyond anything usually seen in science. I've read his material thoroughly, and the results are straightforward and clear." [14]

The Bible Code was a shot heard 'round the world when it made its highly publicized debut in 1997. Simultaneous foreign translations immediately broke new records in France, Germany, England, Italy, Portugal, Korea, Australia and South Africa. Then, nearly as quickly as it rose to the top of *The New York Times* bestseller list and declared **"Number 1 in America"** by *The Wall Street Journal*,

---

14 The only scientists who deny the credibility of the code are those who haven't done the math. Australian statistician Avraham Hasofer attacked the code before the mathematical evidence was even published—"Certain types of patterns must inevitably occur in large data sets; you can no more find a patternless arrangement of digits or letters than you can find a cloud without a shape."

Eliyahu Rips, whose paper *Equidistant Letter Sequences in the Book of Genesis* opened the floodgates, defends his work: "Of course you can find random letter combinations in any text—of course, you will find 'Saddam Hussein' in any large enough data base, but you won't find 'Scuds', 'Russian missiles' and the day the war began, all in the same place, in advance. It doesn't matter if we're looking in a text of 100,000 or 100,000,000 letters, you will not find coherent information—except in the Bible."

Book I: Purification

it vanished. What could cause the book that became a new buzzword to suddenly disappear without a trace? *Newsweek's* pithy review provided a clue—"Explosive...No wonder the book is causing a sensation." Drosnin's revelations that **Armageddon** was almost triggered in 1996 and the ***End of Days*** continues with massive earthquakes, economic hardship and World War III—climaxing with a comet nearly annihilating the Earth in 2012—are not exactly sugar-coated! The picture of doom and gloom that the Code painted was simply too depressing for a materialistic country that prides itself on optimism and self-sufficiency. Even the New Agers ran for cover, taking refuge in a slew of "Pollyanna" books like *The Tenth Insight*.[15] Likewise, many Christians, especially the "born-again" fundamentalists, have abandoned rationality with their own *New Age* idea of salvation: the *Rapture*—wherein the Elect are miraculously transported off the planet during the tribulations and returned when the coast is clear. Not that miracles are impossible or even improbable, but the Christ Himself, who laid out the End Time scenario 2000 years ago, declared that *everybody*—the Elect as well as the guilty—will have to experience the "birth pangs". *In fact, it is the precarious situation of those innocent souls that finally summons the Divine Presence.* The Son of Man, seeing in His mind's eye the apocalyptic rescue, spoke in the third person of a future already past—

> **"And if the Lord had not cut short those days, no one would be saved;**
> ***but for the sake of the elect, whom he chose, he has cut short those days."***   (Mark 13.19)

A calmer, less paranoid angle on the End Times can be gleaned from the surviving aboriginal Americans who escaped the genocide. The **Hopi Indians** were set apart from other Pueblo tribes with the appearance of an extraordinary creature around 1100 AD. After migrating to the Black Mesa country of Arizona, the Hopi settled in a remote area called Oraibi—*the place where the roots solidify*. There they encountered a powerful being who gave them the secret of blending with the land and celebrating life, thus establishing a guardianship for Mother Earth. The fearsome entity, called ***Maasaw*** by the frightened Indians, was described in terms that, ever since 1947 Roswell, have become only too familiar—

"His huge staring eyes were like sunken black holes, and his gaping black mouth bristled with sharp white teeth. He had no nose. His entire head was covered with caked blood..."

Apparently not all residents of the **sitra ahra** (Ara. *other side*[16]) are evil and hostile; some are working to rejoin the Human Race (and in the process, bestow an incredible gift of knowledge). This one guided the simple Hopis to live in harmony with Nature and her cycles. The Elders describe the benefits of taking refuge in this sacred way of Life...

---

[15] James Redfield's sequel to his phenomenal bestseller, *The Celestine Prophecy*, expounds a quintessential New Age philosophy that there is no evil and all of us "good people" can together prevent the "polarization of Fear" that has manifested. The author feels the Bible communicates a dangerous "nihilism" and in *The Tenth Insight*, he actually explains his own candy-coated connivance—

"Now we could see why those in the Afterlife felt that our interpretation of these prophecies was key to resolving the polarization. If we decide that these Scriptures mean that the destruction of the world is inevitable, written unalterably into God's plan, the effect of such a belief would be to create this very outcome."

[16] The inorganic beings (aliens) live *outside* the Law (the **anthropomorphic** "Tree of Life")—estranged from the Human countenance.

"The Gerona kabbalists tended to deny the independent existence of evil... they state quite explicitly that evil is nothing but absence of good. In the *Zohar*, we find precise and detailed descriptions that present *evil as an array of powerful forces*."   ~Tishby

"Just as there are ten crowns (sefirah) of faith above, so there are ten crowns of sorcery of uncleanness below."   ~Zohar III, 41b

"All the crowns that are not comprised within a body [That have a body akin to man's. ~Tishby] are abominable and unclean... they left the orbit of the holy body, and were no longer attached to it...they appear to human beings...they move among the mountains and assume corporeal form once a day, and then they dispose with it."   ~Zohar I, 178a-178b

"It was a gentle way for a gentle people; a way to deal effectively with the things that so frequently cause pain in life, and a way to counteract the fulfillment of prophecy. As they repeated day by day, month by month and year by year, the cycle of things Maasaw taught them to do, peace ruled their hearts. ***This peace would achieve its greatest value when the closing of the Fourth Cycle of the world came to pass.***[17]

This was a secret for happiness that was not intended to be a secret, for it was a secret to be shared with all people who truly deserved to hear it."   ~*The Hopi Survival Kit*

The ancient Hopi prophecies that relate to a worldwide catastrophe—the **Great Purification**—were recently given a fresh airing on the nationally syndicated radio program, *Coast-to-Coast with Art Bell*. Single-handedly delving into occult and spiritual issues no other celebrity would dare, Bell is a gifted interviewer, skillful at getting to the heart of the matter. In a rare gathering of Arizonian Hopi Elders (designated *Grandfather One* and *Grandfather Two,* a precaution to protect their identities) on the evening of June 16, 1998, Bell's questions were respectful, direct and to the point:

AB: How does Grandfather feel about the accuracy of the word that has been handed down? Many people dispute the Bible and whether or not IT is accurate. With regard to Hopi prophecy, how does HE feel about the accuracy of the prophecy?

---

[17] "My people await *Pahana*, the lost White Brother, [from the stars] as do all our brothers in the land. He will not be like the white men we know now, who are cruel and greedy. We were told of their coming long ago. But still we await Pahana. He will bring with him the symbols, and the missing piece of that sacred tablet now kept by the elders, given to him when he left, that shall identify him as our True White Brother. *The Fourth World shall end soon,* and the Fifth World will begin. This the elders everywhere know. The Signs over many years have been fulfilled, and so few are left."

This is the First Sign:
> We are told of the coming of the white-skinned men, like Pahana, but not living like Pahana men who took the land that was not theirs. And men who struck their enemies with thunder.

This is the Second Sign:
> Our lands will see the coming of spinning wheels filled with voices. In his youth, my father saw this prophecy come true with his eyes—the white men bringing their families in wagons across the prairies.

This is the Third Sign:
> A strange beast like a buffalo but with great long horns, will overrun the land in large numbers. These White Feather saw with his eyes — the coming of the white men's cattle.

This is the Fourth Sign:
> The land will be crossed by snakes of iron.

This is the Fifth Sign:
> The land shall be criss-crossed by a giant spider's web.

This is the Sixth sign:
> The land shall be criss-crossed with rivers of stone that make pictures in the sun.

This is the Seventh Sign:
> You will hear of the sea turning black, and many living things dying because of it.

This is the Eighth Sign:
> You will see many youth, who wear their hair long like my people, come and join the tribal nations, to learn their ways and wisdom.

And this is the Ninth and Last Sign:
> You will hear of a dwelling-place in the heavens, above the earth, that shall fall with a great crash. It will appear as a blue star. Very soon after this, the ceremonies of my people will cease.

"These are the Signs that great destruction is coming. The world shall rock to and fro. The white man will battle against other people in other lands—with those who possessed the first light of wisdom. There will be many columns of smoke and fire such as White Feather has seen the white man make in the deserts not far from here. Only those which come will cause disease and a great dying. Many of my people, understanding the prophecies, shall be safe. ***Those who stay and live in the places of my people also shall be safe.*** Then there will be much to rebuild. And soon—very soon afterward—Pahana will return. He shall bring with him the dawn of the Fifth World. He shall plant the seeds of his wisdom in their hearts. Even now the seeds are being planted. These shall smooth the way to the Emergence into the Fifth World."   ~Hopi Elder White Feather to minister David Young, 1958

Book I: Purification

GF2: "They were all given this prophecy, so they all had to meet at least once or twice a year, in the Kivas, where they would actually sit down and go back through that. One person would talk about the prophecies, and if he ever so much as added something to it or left something out, then the rest of the group would know that part of the prophecies was missing. So, they would tell him, 'Well, you didn't say this one here,' or 'You added this to it.' So, that is how this was kept alive through word of mouth and everyone had to remember just what those prophecies were about."

AB: Could we please ask why he has decided to share it with the rest of the world?

GF2: [Speaks in Hopi to GF1]
"Through the Elder's teachings and wishes. The Elders wanted to let this become public at a time when we were close to the end times. So, he had decided to take this upon himself to let go of these things, in hopes that there would be a number of people that would understand and realize what is going on and start praying. We ARE very close to it and we are, right now, going through hard times."

AB: If you would ask Grandfather One whether prayer, whether becoming spiritual of nature, can or will change any of what is coming?

GF2: [Asks GF1]
"It's not a matter of quick change. If you wanted to change now and change your life around and do your prayers, it will help a little in the alleviation of much terrible outcome from the cataclysms. There is a lot in store for all of us and the intensity of this will be a lot less if we can all settle down and behave and not be in the way of the actions we have right now… *like we are all being corrupt. That has to be taken care of. We have to keep ourselves from being corrupted by anything from the outside*."

AB: What we would like to do, if it's possible, is to ask Grandfather One if he can give us any details of what is going to happen, here on Earth, with this prophecy. What is coming?
Any specific details at all?

GF2: [Grandfathers One and Two talk back and forth in the Hopi Tongue.]
"Actually, there are a few that he thinks are important things that will be coming up pretty shortly. There's one thing for sure that we are going to come upon is that World War III is… it will take place… and starvation is definitely part of this thing, where we will hit starvation. The weather change, itself, it's erratic, right now, and it's not what it should be. That's part of… you know… leading us into starvation because the crops will not produce."

AB: Now, these are three things: weather change, mass starvation and the third world war. Would you please ask Grandfather if the weather changes are the beginning of these changes…if what we have seen now, with the weather, is the beginning and, of course, we're going to want to ask how soon these other changes, he thinks, will happen.

GF2: [Grandfathers One and Two talk back and forth in the Hopi Tongue.]
"It's been known that this had happened a long time ago but, in our prior world, it happened before, you know, the same things that we had gone through. The teachings were that we were not supposed to follow in the same pattern and try to keep ourselves from going astray from our teachings. These weather patterns that we talked about and cataclysms that take place, are not really set in order…in a fashion that any person could say that, 'Okay, the winds are going to do it this year and the next year will be fires and the following year will be earthquakes, you know.' Also, he's saying that it's not exactly his words that that is the way that it will take place but he knows that these are signs and they are readily available. All the signs are out there. Anyone can see that, that it is taking place and it's only going to get bigger."

While maintaining utmost respect for the wisdom and compassion of the red man, the Elder's *elders* must be acknowledged as well—the **Hebrew Tribes**. Whereas the Hopi Indians' 1000-year-old prophecies are uncertain as to the exact times and places of cataclysmic events, the white man's aboriginal forefathers have unknowingly kept alive an extraterrestrial prophecy of phenomenal predictability for 3200 years! Torah scrolls have always had the strictest guidelines imaginable, ever since Moses himself made 12 identical copies and distributed them to the Tribes.[18] The heavy responsibility that fell to subsequent scribes is echoed in Rabbi Ishmael's admonition to Rabbi Meir—"Be careful in your work, my son, for your work is the work of Heaven. Omit or add a single letter and you can destroy the whole world." We'll see just how critical that scribal effort was and what an invaluable debt the world owes these faithful *Chosen People*. In addition, the importance of the microprocessor computer and its ability to decode the Torah *cannot be overstated*. Dissemination and implementation of the Bible Code will, in the years ahead, be the determining factor in delaying the destruction of the world. Indeed, we came perilously close in 1996.[19]

Months before Netanyahu was elected Prime Minister, journalist Michael Drosnin already knew the outcome because he had consulted the ultimate oracle, the computerized Torah. Only later, when Drosnin heard of the new Prime Minister's plan to visit King Hussein in Amman, Jordan, did the **JULY TO AMMAN** decipher make any sense.

Alarm bells went off when the reporter finally put two and two together. Not only was the year 5756 (1996) ominously encoded with **ATOMIC HOLOCAUST, HOLOCAUST OF ISRAEL** and **END OF DAYS**—but the date chosen for the meeting, July 25th or 9th of Av, happened to be the single most notorious date in the history of the Jewish people!

Fig. 2   Prime Minister Netanyahu—July to Amman

Believe it or not, the following fateful events *all fell on the accursed 9th of Av:*

- The First Temple is destroyed in 586 BC
- The Second Temple is destroyed in 70 AD
- England expels the Jews in 1290
- Spain expels the Jews in 1492
- The first gas chambers begin operation in Treblinka in 1942

---

18 The original codex of exactly 305,805 Hebrew letters remains sequestered in the Ark of the Covenant. According to correspondent Graham Hancock, the latter exists today, carefully guarded by Ethiopian Jews until the time of revelation. In 1986, Hancock traveled to the sacred city of Axum to investigate an ancient legend that the Holy Ark had been surreptitiously transported from Jerusalem to Ethiopia. He learned that St. Mary's of Zion was built in 372 AD to ensconce the relic in her Holy of Holies—subsequently removed to its own fortified chapel in 1965 by Emperor Sellassie. "Haile Sellassie had a special interest in this matter, by the way. He was the two hundred and twenty-fifth direct-line descendant of Menelik, son of the Queen of Sheba and King Solomon. It was Menelik who brought the Ark of the Covenant to our country…" ~*The Sign and the Seal*, Graham Hancock   [*See* **Book II**, footnote 39]

19 As if to cosmically confirm this fact, a previously unknown comet made its spectacular appearance in **1996** (far surpassing the 1986 return of **Halley's**): "…a condensed starlike core brighter than 3rd magnitude and a naked-eye tail 12 degrees long. The comet passes closest to the earth on the night of March 24th **[Exactly 3 years later, on March 24, 1999, NATO bombings began in Yugoslavia]**—no comet has been so intrinsically bright and so near in more than 400 years."   ~*Sky & Telescope*

Book I: Purification

As luck (Divine intervention) would have it, King Hussein got sick at the last minute and had to postpone the meeting. Nevertheless, 1996 was definitely one of the quantum possibilities for limited nuclear exchange, a precursor to WWIII. Drosnin points out that WWI had begun simply enough with the assassination of Archduke Ferdinand of Austria and if Netanyahu had met with foul play so soon after Rabin's assassination, it could easily have fulfilled the Bible Code's warning. While Mike Drosnin and Eliyahu Rips strained to make sense out of an apparent inconsistency in the Code, other messages seemed to pop out of nowhere, each one connected with the word **DELAYED**. [*See* **Fig. 3**]

The 3000-year-old code was (mis) behaving exactly like the Heisenberg *Uncertainty Principle* —the more you measured what, the less you could measure when. But as soon as Drosnin plugged in the *what* of World War, there also appeared a *when*. The shocking result caused most of us to forget we had even read *The Bible Code:* WWIII seemed irrevocably fated to begin in Jerusalem at the end of July, the holy fast of *Tisha B'Av*. The only variable in the equation was the exact year for *Armageddon*.[20] The code revealed two more quantum probabilities: 2000 and 2006. Although the year 2000 matched up with **ATOMIC HOLOCAUST** and **WORLD WAR**, the smart money was on 2006.[21]

Dr. Rips and Drosnin found ELS matches of **ATOMIC HOLOCAUST** and **WORLD WAR** with **END OF DAYS, HOLOCAUST OF ISRAEL** and **GREAT EARTHQUAKE** all linked to **IN 5766 (2006)**. Eli Rips calculated the odds against coincidence at better than a 1000 to 1.

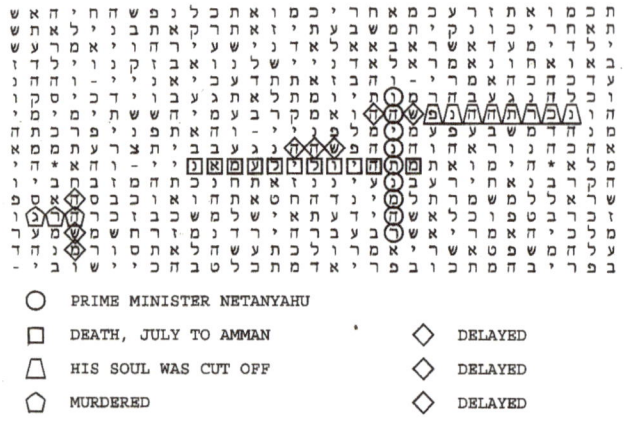

Fig. 3   Prime Minister Netanyahu— Murdered — Delayed

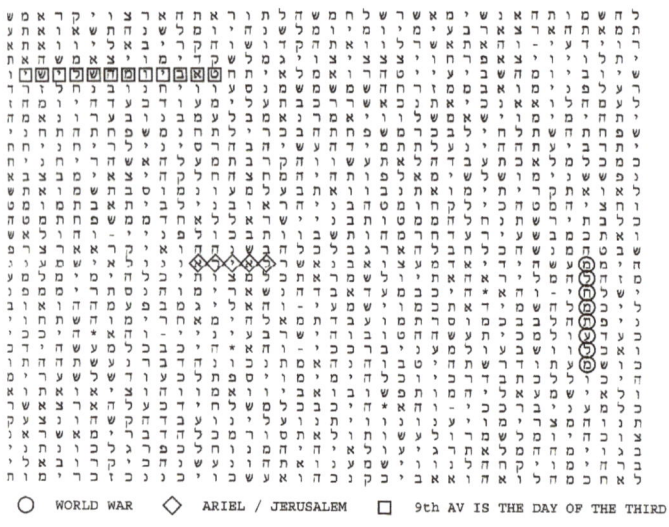

Fig.4   World War — Ariel — 9th Av is the Day of the Third

Every great man, good or bad, leaves a distinctive impression—his particular *modus operandi*—on the sands of time. Certain unique styles of leadership seem to be repeated by different persons throughout history. In **Book II**, *Anatomy of a Buddha*, our sources trace the evolutionary intent of the Messiah through such intense individuals as Enoch, Joseph (son of Jacob), Joshua and Josiah.

Here we begin with the other side of the coin—the *Man of Iniquity* whose havoc, brutality and lust for power can be clearly chronicled, life after life.

---

20 "These are demonic spirits, performing signs, who go abroad to the kings of the whole world, to assemble them for battle on the great day of God the Almighty. And they assembled them at the place that in Hebrew is called Harmagedon."   (Rev. 16.14)
"Scholars generally explain Armageddon as a Greek transliteration of the Hebrew phrase *har Megiddo* (the mountain of Megiddo)."
~*Oxford Companion to the Bible*   Michael Drosnin drove to Megiddo in northern Israel and discovered a clandestine Air Force base, Ramat David. It faces Israel's sworn enemy—Syria.

21 As 2006 passed without incident, skeptics had all the proof they needed to dismiss both God and the whole theory of ELS codes. The fact that **WWIII** was **DELAYED** again simply means the "target date" has been *gracefully* postponed. People have been praying.
"Christians have forgotten they can prevent war and even natural calamities by prayer and fasting."   ~Our Lady of Medjugorje

Chapter Three: Antichrist

Just as the first man was cloned from Yahweh at the dawn of time, his polar opposite, Cain, was subsequently begot by Ba'al—the Dark Lord.[22] Practice makes perfect and the older the soul is—the more experience the entity has accumulated—the more powerful he becomes. Alexander the Great[23] was a culminating incarnation for the Fish-Lord's first born. Tutored by Aristotle and declared "invincible" by the Oracle at Delphi, Alexander seemed to live a charmed life. He quickly gained a chilling reputation for ruthlessness after crushing a rebellion of Greek states by razing Thebes and slaughtering six thousand citizens, women and children included. But his greatest victory and most extensive carnage—capped by a relentless, seven-month siege of Tyre—occurred in 331 BC with the humiliating defeat of Darius and his army, awarding Alexander the Persian Empire. With the seizure of the mighty Kingdom came the idea of creating a *master race* by blending muscular Macedonians with prudent Persians. Alexander and his officers married Persian princesses while ten thousand soldiers were given handsome dowries for taking native wives.

Upon his arrival in Egypt, Alexander is welcomed as a savior and crowned Pharaoh, son of Zeus. Sacrificing in Memphis to the god *Apis*—the sacred Egyptian bull[24], his mounting megalomania now demands others accept him as he sees himself, a god. When he tries forcing the Macedonians and Greeks to imitate the Persian ritual of prostration, they laugh at such a preposterous notion. After surviving life-threatening wounds in battle and several assassination attempts, Alexander the Great dies ignominiously from an extended eating and drinking orgy—he was 32. The vast Empire cannot sustain itself and subsequently splits into four independent Kingdoms with a quartet of generals assuming the crowns:[25]

- Ptolemy 1 — Israel and Egypt
- Seleucus 1 — Syria and Mesopotamia
- Lysimachus — Thrace and Asia Minor
- Cassander — Macedonia and Greece

An influential life will eventually yield one of relative ease and grace. Agrippina the Younger, great-granddaughter of Emperor Augustus, knew her only son was destined to rule and wasted no time in clearing the path to his rightful inheritance. After poisoning her second husband and marrying

---

22 The shape-shifting, draconian Fish-Lord from the dwarf star Sirius B, seeing His opportunity to seize control of the lower world, deceives the mother of Mankind with the promise of God-like power. Upon Eva's brutal *initiation* with a psychotropic aphrodisiac, the serpent resumes His own hideous countenance and rapes her prior to Adam's consummation. The resulting pregnancy and birth of Cain breaches the Creation, generating a second stream of Mankind—the **Sons of Darkness**. [*See* **Book III: Matriarchy**, p. 85]

23 "Hitler, Master continued, **was Alexander the Great**. An interesting point of comparison here is that, in warfare, both Hitler and Alexander employed the strategy of lightning attack or *blitzkrieg*, as Hitler called it. In the Orient, of course, where Alexander's conquests were responsible for the destruction of great civilizations, his appellation, 'the Great,' is quoted sarcastically."

~*Autobiography of a Yogi*, Paramahansa Yogananda

24 Here Alexander pays homage to *his* Father—Ba'al's totem was the bull. "Jeroboam, fresh from his recollections of the Apis worship of Egypt, erected golden calves at Beth-el and Dan, and by this crafty state policy severed effectively the kingdoms of Judah and Israel (I Kings 12:26-33)." ~*Unger's Bible Dictionary*   [*See* **Book II: Cyclicity**, p. 60]

25 Three hundred years before Alexander the Great, *Gabriel* interpreted Daniel's vivid, hallucinatory premonition of the Macedonian.

"The male goat is the king of Greece, and the great horn between its eyes is the first king. As for the horn that was broken, in place of which four others arose, four kingdoms shall arise from his nation, but not with his power."   (Daniel 8.21)

her uncle, the emperor Claudius, she poisons the latter in 54 AD and completes her misanthropic mission the following year by poisoning Britannicus, the son of Claudius and legitimate heir to the throne. The successful *fait accompli* forces the Senate to proclaim a 16 year-old boy, supreme ruler of the Roman Empire.

In a pattern set by Alexander with his mentor Aristotle, young Nero's enlightenment comes through the Stoic philosopher, Seneca. Taught to use his autocratic powers responsibly, Emperor Nero forbids the bloody contests in the circus and reluctantly signs death sentences. He gives greater rights to slaves and tries to limit the extortion practices of the Roman tax collectors. However, his true colors emerge with adulthood when, in 59 AD, he puts his mad mother[26] to death and later has his own spouse Octavia executed—to marry a senator's young wife, Poppaea Sabina.

His obsessive compulsion to emulate Greek architecture (by gutting Rome and rebuilding in the Grecian style) results in the 64 AD Great Fire that nearly devastates the celebrated city. When he blames the "rebellious" Christians for the fire[27], a policy of persecution begins that will continue until Constantine. Squelching an insurrection in Judea, Nero's troops raze Jerusalem and demolish the sacred architectural wonder of the Hebrews—the Temple.[28] But Nero himself was strangely drawn to Greece and spent over a year there, taking in the Greek culture. He even dressed as an ascetic, promenading barefoot with long flowing locks. Upon his return to Rome, Caesar Nero laughs at the report of revolts throughout the Empire. The self-styled rock star whose ego knew no bounds replies, "I have only to appear and sing to have peace once more in Gaul." The rebellion escalates unabated and the Senate condemns Nero to death. He dies at 30 of a self-inflicted wound, leaving the stricken Empire strife with debt, misery and civil war.

Fig. 5 Caesar Nero

From the prison island of Patmos, John the Revelator, an initiate acquainted with Gematria[29], disclosed a secret to ferret out the Antichrist—his name and the autocratic megalomania that he represents is intricately linked to the number six hundred and sixty-six...

---

26 "Cluvius relates that Agrippina in her eagerness to retain her influence went so far that more than once at midday, when Nero, even at that hour, was flushed with wine and feasting, she presented herself attractively attired to her half intoxicated son and offered him her person." ~*The Annals of Imperial Rome*, Cornelius Tacitus (ca. 55-117 AD)

27 "Consequently, to get rid of the report, Nero fastened the guilt and inflicted the most exquisite tortures on **a class hated for their abominations, called Christians** by the populace. Christus, from whom the name had its origin, suffered the extreme penalty during the reign of Tiberius at the hands of one of our procurators, Pontius Pilatus, and a most mischievous superstition, thus checked for the moment, again broke out not only in Judaea, the first source of the evil, but even in Rome, where all things hideous and shameful from every part of the world find their centre and become popular. Accordingly, an arrest was first made of all who pleaded guilty; then, upon their information, an immense multitude was convicted, not so much of the crime of firing the city, as of hatred against mankind. Mockery of every sort was added to their deaths. Covered with the skins of beasts, they were torn by dogs and perished, or were nailed to crosses, or were doomed to the flames and burnt, to serve as a nightly illumination, when daylight had expired. Nero offered his gardens for the spectacle, and was exhibiting a show in the circus, while he mingled with the people in the dress of a charioteer or stood aloft on a car. Hence, even for criminals who deserved extreme and exemplary punishment, there arose a feeling of compassion; for it was not, as it seemed, for the public good, but to glut one man's cruelty, that they were being destroyed." ~Ibid.

28 At Daniel 9.26, the man *Gabriel* nails Nero as the future Antichrist: **"...an anointed one** [Hbw. *Mashiach*] **shall be cut off** [Hbw. *Niphal*, a premature—under 50—death] **and shall have nothing, and the troops of** *the prince who is to come* **shall destroy the city and the sanctuary."**

29 "Their alphabets, which are also numerals, exhibit unexplained features, some of which may be described as mysterious. It is scarcely reasonable to suppose that the element of chance has in any appreciable degree entered into their framing. And this is the more unlikely in that there is evidence of a contrary belief among these peoples, who showed a peculiar reverence for their alphabets, ascribing to each letter its own mystical value, and, to the whole, a body of symbolic teaching in which the principles of Number, Sound, and also Form as connected with each letter, all played their part." ~*Gematria*, Frederick Bond and Thomas Lea

"The identity of the beast is clear; it is the absolutist state as personified in the Roman Emperor Nero. The emperors claimed divine authority and their power seemed invincible. John wanted his readers to understand that the state and its rulers were neither divine nor invincible. They were human and carried the seed of their own destruction: their number is only 666, and does not reach the completion of seven. The number was arrived at by presenting Nero's Greek name Kaisar Neron in Hebrew letters, which also function as numbers: qsr nrwn; q=60, s=100, r=200, n=50, w=6, so qsr nrwn adds up to 666." ~*Oxford Companion to the Bible*, David Van Daalen

The embodiment of Evil nearly reaches its full expression with the most infamous incarnation of all time—Hitler. Unlike Alexander and Nero, young Adolf had already matured into a 30 year-old political activist before meeting the mentor who would empower him. Dietrich Eckhart, independently wealthy financier and publisher of the anti-Semitic journal *In Plain German*, was also an initiated occultist—a member of the inner circle of the *Thule Society*[30] where his path was destined to cross fellow Thulist Adolf Hitler's in 1919. The black magician's influence on the neophyte is echoed by the solitary dedication of *Mein Kampf* to "my teacher Dietrich Eckhart." Master Eckhart proudly molded the monster who would soon be unleashed on an unsuspecting world...[31]

"There can be no doubt that Eckhart—who had been alerted to Hitler by other Thulists—trained Hitler in techniques of self-confidence, self-projection, persuasive oratory, body language and discursive sophistry. With these tools, in a short period of time he was able to move the obscure workers party from the club and beer hall atmosphere to a mass movement. The emotion-charged lay speaker became an expert orator, capable of mesmerizing a vast audience." ~*The Unknown Hitler*, Schwartzwaller

The Thule begat the *German Socialist Party*, which published the *Munich Observer* (renamed the *National Observer*). Hitler's forceful personality soon dominated the Party, which he renamed the *National Socialist German Worker Party*. The new organization needed an intimidating symbol for its flag and fellow Thulist, a dentist named Krohn, suggested a staggered, black *swastika* (Skt. being fortunate). The ancient logo had always been a solar symbol—the sun going through its four-fold seasonal progression. Dr. Krohn conceived the idea of rotating the icon cockeyed, to the left, where it could be envisioned spinning counter-clockwise, invoking the powers of chaos—the *tantric* Left-Hand Path.

Fig. 6   Nazi Party Swastika

Nazi documentary footage of night rallies where soldiers march in a huge human *swastika*, to the left, demonstrate the devolutionary intent of the menacing symbol rotating backwards.

---

30 "Briefly, the creed of the *Thule* society inner circle is as follows: *Thule* was a legendary island in the far north, similar to **Atlantis**, supposedly the center of a lost, high-level civilization. But not all secrets of that civilization had been completely wiped out. Those that remained were being guarded by ancient, highly intelligent beings (similar to the 'Masters' of Theosophy or White Brotherhood). The truly initiated could establish contact with these beings by means of magic-mystical rituals. The 'Masters' or 'Ancients' allegedly would be able to endow the initiated with supernatural strength and energy. With the help of these energies the goal of the initiated was to create a race of Supermen of 'Aryan' stock who would exterminate all 'inferior' races." ~*The Unknown Hitler*

31 "Follow Hitler! He will dance, but it is I who have called the tune! I have initiated him into the *Secret Doctrine*, opened his centres in vision and given him the means to communicate with the Powers. Do not mourn for me: I shall have influenced history more than any other German." ~Dietrich Eckhart on his deathbed, 1923

Book I: Purification

A failed coup against the Bavarian government disables the Nazi Party and sends its leader to Landsberg prison, where he meets his second mentor. General Karl Haushofer not only studied Zen Buddhism as a military attaché in Japan, but upon acquaintance with a Tibetan Lama, became initiated into the secret *tantra*. While writing *Mein Kampf* (My Struggle) in 1924 with the help of Rudolf Hess, the captivated pupil of Karl Haushofer is indoctrinated into the finer Eastern esoteric arts.[32]

Still reeling from the devastating *Treaty of Versailles*, the domino effect of the Great Depression convinced millions of dissatisfied, jobless voters to rally behind the newly reorganized Nazi Party. The dark dictator's unprecedented reign of terror—the *blitzkriegs*—coincided with his crowning achievement as a warrior. In 1938, he seized the legendary Lance of Longinus[33] from the Hofburg museum in Vienna and brought it under armored SS guard to Nuremberg. Hitler believed the Spear was a talisman—the same one that had empowered Emperor Constantine, Charlemagne, five Saxon emperors and seven Hohenstaufen emperors, including Frederick Barbarossa and Frederick II.

In *The Spear of Destiny*, Trevor Ravenscroft recounts an epiphanic moment in young Adolf's life when, visiting the Treasure House in Vienna, he first gazes upon the obscure object of his desire.

"I knew with immediacy that this was an important moment in my life," said Adolph Hitler when he later recounted his first sight of the spear. "And yet I could not divine why an outwardly Christian symbol should make such an impression on me. I stood there quietly gazing upon it for several minutes quite oblivious to the scene of the Schatzkammer around me. It seemed to carry some hidden inner meaning which evaded me, a meaning which I felt inwardly knew yet could not bring to consciousness… The Spear appeared to be some sort of magical medium of revelation for it brought the world of ideas into such close and living perspective that human imagination became more real than the world of sense."

Charlemagne was invulnerable until he dropped the Spear accidentally; Barbarossa was also invincible until he too let the Spear slip from his grasp—he was killed instantly! United States Army Lieutenant Walter Horn took official possession of the Holy Lance on April 30, 1945—the very same day the failed Führer blew his bunkered brains out.

The evil genius that was Hitler's should not be underestimated, regarded as simply uncouth bigotry. On the contrary, his vision merely determined the Jewish race as being the most accessible scapegoat to focus the wrath of German sensibilities. In a 1922 interview with the future Führer, journalist Josef Hell documented a candid moment of cool calculation—

---

[32] "In Berlin, Haushofer had founded the Luminous Lodge or the *Vril Society*. The Lodge's objective was to explore the origins of the Aryan race and to perform exercises in concentration to awaken the forces of 'Vril'. Haushofer was a student of the Russian magician and metaphysician Gregor Ivanovich Gurdyev (George Gurdjieff). Both Gurdjieff and Haushofer maintained that they had contacts with secret Tibetan lodges that possessed the secret of the 'Superman'. The Lodge included Hitler, Alfred Rosenberg, Himmler, Göring, and Hitler's subsequent personal physician Dr. Morell." ~*The Unknown Hitler,* Wulf Shwartzwaller

[33] "Longinus is the centurion who pierced the side of Our Lord while He was hanging on the Cross. Longinus, who was nearly blind, was healed when some of the blood and water from Jesus fell into his eyes. It was then he exclaimed **'Indeed, this was the Son of God!'** [Mark 15:39]. Longinus then converted, left the army, took instruction from the apostles and became a monk in Cappadocia. There he was arrested for his faith, his teeth forced out and tongue cut off. St. Longinus' relics are now in the church of St Augustine, in Rome. His Lance pole is contained in one of the four pillars over the altar in the Basilica of St Peter's in Rome. The spearhead itself is in the Treasure Room of the Hofburg Palace in Vienna." ~Commandery of St. Longinus and the Holy Lance, smotj.org.

"We read in the Gospel of St. John (19:34), that, after our Savior's death, "one of the soldiers with a spear [*lancea*] opened his side and immediately there came out blood and water". Of the weapon thus sanctified nothing is known until the pilgrim St. Antoninus of Piancenza (A.D. 570), describing the holy places of Jerusalem, tells us that he saw in the basilica of Mount Sion "the crown of thorns with which Our Lord was crowned and the lance with which He was struck in the side". In 615 Jerusalem was captured by a lieutenant of the Persian King Chosroes. The sacred relics of the Passion fell into the hands of the pagans, and, according to the "Chronicon Paschale", the point of the lance, which had been broken off, was given in the same year to Nicetas, who took it to Constantinople and deposited it in the church of St. Sophia." ~The Catholic Encyclopedia, 1907-1912

Hitler: "Once I really am in power, my first and foremost task will be the annihilation of the Jews. As soon as I have the power to do so, I will have gallows built in rows—at the Marienplatz in Munich, for example—as many as traffic allows. Then the Jews will be hanged indiscriminately, and they will remain hanging until they stink; they will hang there as long as the principles of hygiene permit. As soon as they have been untied, the next batch will be strung up, and so on down the line, until the last Jew in Munich has been exterminated. Other cities will follow suit, precisely in this fashion, until all Germany has been completely cleansed of Jews."

Josef Hell: When I now broached the question of what the source of his so strongly felt hatred for the Jews was, and why he wanted to destroy this so undeniably intelligent race—a race to which the Germans and all other Aryans, if not the entire world, owes an incalculable debt in virtually all fields of art and knowledge, research and economics—Hitler suddenly calmed down and gave this unexpectedly sober and almost dispassionate explanation.

Hitler: "It is manifestly clear and has been proven in practice and by the facts of all revolutions that a struggle for ideals, for improvements of any kind whatsoever, absolutely must be supplemented with a struggle against some social class or caste. My object is to create first-rate revolutionary upheavals, regardless what methods and means I have to use in the process. Earlier revolutions were directed either against the peasants, or the nobility and the clergy, or against dynasties and their network of vassals, but in no case has revolution succeeded without *the presence of a lightning rod that could conduct and channel the odium of the general masses.*

With this very thing in mind I scanned the revolutionary events of history and put the question to myself against which racial element in Germany can I unleash my propaganda of hate with the greatest prospects of success? I had to find the right kind of victim, and especially one against whom the struggle would make sense, materially speaking. I can assure you that I examined every possible and thinkable solution to this problem, and, weighing every imaginable factor, I came to the conclusion that a campaign against the Jews would be as popular as it would be successful.

There are few Germans who have not been vexed with the behavior of Jews or else have not suffered losses through them in some way or other. Disproportionately to their small number they account for an immense share of the German national wealth, which can just as easily be put to profitable use for the state and the general public as could the holdings of the monasteries, bishops and nobility. Once the hatred and the battle against the Jews have been really stirred up, their resistance will necessarily crumble in the shortest possible time. They are totally defenseless, and no one will stand up to protect them." ~*Adolf Hitler*, John Toland. London 1977

The embodiment of Evil comes full circle with the current incarnation of the AC in the seventh great Empire, America—bringing closure to the Kali Yuga (Fourth World) and ushering in the final Millennium, a glorious Golden Age. Most Biblical scholars worth their salt now agree that the seven heads of Revelation's *Beast* likewise represent the seven autocratic Empires that have arisen...

"This calls for a mind that has wisdom: the seven heads are seven mountains [Empires] **on which the woman is seated; also, they are seven kings** [Reincarnations of the Antichrist], **of whom five have fallen,**

one is living [Caesar Nero], **and the other has not yet come; and when he comes, he must remain only a little while** [Adolf Hitler]. **As for the beast that was and is not, it is an eighth but it belongs to the seven."**[34]
(Revelation 17.9-11)

- Egyptian
- Assyrian
- Babylonian
- Persian
- Grecian
- Roman
- American

---

[34] "The eighth is not merely one of the seven restored, **but a new power or person** proceeding out of the seven, and at the same time embodying all the God-opposed features of the previous seven concentrated and consummated."   ~JFB Bible Commentary

Book I: Purification

This last recycling of Ba'al's boy will be the dénouement—the crowning achievement for the prince of this world. The karmic precedent established in previous lives once again summons the Machiavellian mentors who will mold the new master of manipulation—the latter's intellectual prowess and occult knowledge far exceeding that of Hitler's, whose Taurean characteristics kept him too materialistic and earthbound. In the early 21st century, with a sustained spiritual and intellectual efflux of the Universe emanating from Aquarius, it is more than likely he was born under this sign.[35] Like Ronald Wilson Reagan, another Aquarian, he will exude enormous charisma—a good ol' boy, he'll be perceived as one of the people.

The irony of these times—the darkest days of the darkest Age—is where the good seem bad and the bad appear good. It is, of course, in the best interests of the *Son of Perdition* to keep the planet in one piece until he can cement his position as autocratic ruler. A stock market crash leads to an economic meltdown, the Dollar's destabilizing domino-effect threatening the commercial unity of the World. Establishment of a "G10" Banking Union[36] insures the charlatan's popularity as a global, nonpartisan leader. Initially, he is acclaimed the greatest man of action since Franklin D. Roosevelt.

The bête noire's true colors finally emerge with the belated assassination of Prime Minister Netanyahu, igniting the impending third World War. Like Kennedy with Castro, karma comes around to bite him in the ass when **Mabus** (Nostradamus' anagram) is assassinated. Exactly as the Christ descended to the depths of *Gehenna* (before manifesting to His disciples), the Antichrist plummets to the very bowels to meet *his* "father"—Lord of the Underworld. Three days later and the reborn **beast** revives from an impossibly fatal injury— *initiated* now, **fully embodying the archetype of Evil.**

> "They shall wonder... when they behold the beast *that was, and is not, and yet is*." (Revelation 17.8)

> **"And I saw one of his heads as it were wounded to death; and his deadly wound was healed: and all the world wondered after the beast. And they worshipped the dragon which gave power unto the beast: and they worshipped the beast, saying who is like unto the beast? Who is able to make war with him?'"** (Revelation 13.3-4)

After a very long year of unparalleled warfare culminating in nuclear devastation, Mabus and His *Group of Ten* puppets negotiate a seven-year peace plan[37]—wherein a severely de-populated world acquiesces to the inevitable. An automated, computerized network is the "second beast" the Revelator sees "exercising all the authority of the first beast on its behalf." In an Orwellian nightmare come true, citizens must consent to a constant two-way webcam presence of "big brother" over the ubiquitous Internet. Marshall law enforces a strict curfew—everyone locked in their homes and apartments by 6 PM, reporting to **deadly** flat screen Monitors for retinal identity scans. All business transactions have to pass through His Web portal—credits and debits electronically maintained in the One World economy of a cashless society through a chip interface implanted under the skin.[38]

---

[35] Assuming the AC was born in January/February of 1976 (Year of the Dragon—the strongest sign, bar none. Hitler was born in 1889, Year of the Rat), he turned 33 in 2009, his powers at full strength... From the age of 23 until his Saturn Return in 2004, Uranus (the higher octave of Mercury) and Neptune (the higher octave of Venus) were both traversing the electrifying Aquarian sector (Uranus is now in Taurus, Neptune in Pisces). ***Neptune's powerful presence in Aquarius until 2012*** will inculcate a mesmerizing, messianic quality into the personality of the young Antichrist.

[36] "And the ten horns that you saw are ten kings who have not yet received a kingdom, but they are to receive authority as kings for one hour, together with the beast. These are united in yielding their power and authority to the beast." (Rev. 17.12)

[37] "He shall make a strong covenant with many for one week, and for half of the week he shall make sacrifice and offering cease; and in their place shall be an abomination that desolates..." (Daniel 9.27)

[38] The personal ID chip is linked to the **World Wide Web**—developed at **CERN** (1989) to allow physicists to share data. Today Google indexes 1 trillion unique URLs, each with the obligatory prefix, **www**. Hebrew letters also function as numbers and "**w**" = 6.

> "And he had power to give life unto the image of the beast, that the image of the beast should both speak, and cause that as many as would not worship the image of the beast should be killed. And he causeth all, both small and great, rich and poor, free and bond, to receive a mark in their right hand, or in their foreheads:
>
> And that no man might buy or sell, save he that had the mark, or the name of the beast, or the number of his name. Here is wisdom. Let him that hath understanding count the number of the beast: for it is the number of a man; and his number is Six hundred threescore and six."
> (Revelation 13.15-18)

For his headquarters, the now invincible Mabus[39] chooses the only possible setting for the spiritual/temporal Emperor of a New World Order—the opulent St. Peter's Basilica.[40] Three similar quatrains from Nostradamus seem to indicate both the demise of the Catholic Church and the raiding of Vatican treasures—

> "***Eyes closed, opened by antique fantasy***,
> The garb of the monks will be put to naught:
> The great monarch will chastise their frenzy,
> Ravishing the treasure in front of the temples."
> **CII-12**

Breaching the restricted Vatican Library and looting her art would serve several purposes:

- The general public will see Mabus as a liberator
- A mystical and occult treasure-trove of highly controversial codices come to light after untold centuries of suppression—massive uproar
- The Vatican Bank's Mafia ties are revealed and ensuing schisms sink the great ark of the Church under the weight of Her own karmic convolutions

After opening the world's eyes with the "*antique fantasies*" of Astrology, Reincarnation, etc., Mabus mobilizes the Muslims, Jews and nihilistic New Agers for a Holy Crusade of wiping out any adherents to the "corrupt" religion, Christianity—

Fig. 7   St. Peter's Basilica, Vatican City

---

[39] "He shall prosper until the period of wrath is completed, for what is determined shall be done." (Dan. 11.36) In accordance with *Yang/Yin* principles, the Son of Ba'al must be granted the exact same amount of time allotted the Son of Yahweh—**3½ years**.
[40] Following *Armageddon* and nuclear devastation of the Holy Land—
> "**Jerusalem, Jerusalem which kills prophets and stones those who are sent to thee.
> How often would I have gathered thy children together, as the hen gathers her chickens under her wings,
> but you were not willing: *Behold your habitation shall be left unto you desolate!*"** (Matt. 23.37-38)

the only remaining "temple" of Judeo-Christian heritage resides in Italy. An architectural wonder of the world—U.S. Capital buildings use the massive dome as their prototype—Vatican City's palatial cathedral is surely the most extravagant Temple ever constructed.

Book I: Purification

> "A Killer (Broadsword) with twisted tongue
> Will come to pillage the sanctuary of the gods:
> **For the heretics he will open the gate,**
> Thus reviving the military Church."
> **CVIII-78**

Using Hitler's "scapegoat" tactics from World War II, a nucleus of hatred is organized to combat a common contaminate. Only instead of Jews, it is the "abominable" Christians who once again (à la Nero) become the "lightning rod that could conduct and channel the odium of the general masses."

> "The Church of God will be persecuted,
> And the Holy Temples will be plundered,
> The child will put his mother out in her nightgown,
> Arabs will be allied with the Poles."
> **CV-73**

Reinforcing Nostradamus' myopic outlook for the Holy See, the famous predictions of a 12th century bishop, St. Malachy, have dramatically dwindled down—with eerie precision—to the last man standing. Commencing with Innocent II, the Irish seer used a brief Latin phrase to describe each reigning Pope until the line ends with its beginning, Peter. The 112 prophecies allow but one more Pope following our current Vicar of Christ, Ratzinger—

- **John XXIII**   1958-1963   *Pastor et Nauta*   Pastor and Mariner
- **Paul VI**   1963-1978   *Flos Florum*   Flower of Flowers
- **John Paul I**   1978   *De Medietate lunae*   Of the Half Moon
- **John Paul II**   1978-2005   *De Labaore solis*   From the Toil of the Sun
- **Benedict XVI**   2005-   *Gloria Olivae*   The Glory of the Olive
- ?   *Petrus Romanus*   Peter the Roman

Pope John XXIII (Angelo Roncalli) was appointed Apostolic Visitor to Bulgaria and Bishop of Areopolis in 1925. Pope Pius XII promoted him to Cardinal and titular Patriarch of Venice in '53, thus fulfilling Malachy's prophecy as a "mariner" from the water city. **Pope Paul VI** (Giovanni Montini) was the Vatican Secretary of State, bumped up to Pope by the Conclave of Cardinals in 1963. The Montini family coat of arms portrays three fleurs-de-lis. **Pope John Paul I** (Albino Buciani) served as Pope for 34 days [*See* **Fig. 8**] before his assassination in 1978. The symbolism clear as his ambitious plans to overhaul the corrupt Vatican never reached fruition (full moon).

In 1978, the Apostle Peter's body (positively identified from the torso's missing feet—chopped off after Peter's upside-down crucifixion) was found in a catacomb directly beneath the Basilica, exactly where it was believed to be. Shortly thereafter, **Pope John Paul I** was elected. Over four centuries ago, Michel Nostradamus hit this one dead on...

> "When the sepulchre of the great Roman is found,
> The day after a Pontiff will be elected:
> Scarcely will he be approved by the Senate
> Poisoned, his blood in the sacred chalice."
> **CIII-65**

Fig. 8   Pope Paul I

Pope John Paul II (Karol Wojtyla) came from the common working class of Poland, a laborer toiling under the hot Euro sun. He was born May 18, 1920 during a solar eclipse. (*Lobaore solis* can also be interpreted as *pregnancy*, i.e. *eclipse* of the sun). **Pope Benedict XVI** (Joseph Ratzinger) was appointed Archbishop of Munich in 1977. Trained as a theologian, the dogmatic professor had taught at several German universities when JP II named him *Prefect of the Congregation for the Doctrine of the Faith*, previously known as the Holy Office or Inquisition. An eschatological prophecy by the founder of the Benedictine Order interprets *Gloria Olivae* as signifying this pope must come from them, that is, the *Olivetans*.

Bishop Malachy brings his pithy prophecies full circle with the return of the Apostle Peter...

"In the final persecution of the Holy Roman Church there will reign Peter the Roman, who will feed his flock amid many tribulations, after which the seven-hilled city will be destroyed and the dreadful Judge will judge the people. The End."

And the final nail in the Vatican's coffin comes from Mother Mary Herself. The dreaded third secret of Fatima—a revelation so shocking three reigning popes refused the express instructions of the Queen of Heaven to disclose it—paints a clear picture of the collapse of the Catholic Church.[41] It is here where Paul and Jeshua warn us to heed their "call for the endurance and faith of the saints."

> **"He opposes and exalts himself above every so-called god or object of worship,
> so that he takes his seat in the temple of God, declaring himself to be God."**
> (2 Thessalonians 2.4)

After setting up shop in the world's most hallowed Temple (Basilica), the indomitable despot orders a worldwide ban of the daily "sacrifice" (Mass) in all the "Temples" (Churches)...

> **"When ye therefore shall see the abomination of desolation, spoken of by Daniel the prophet,
> stand in the holy place, (whoso readeth, let him understand:) Then let them which be in Judaea
> flee into the mountains; let him which is on the housetop not come down to take any thing
> out of his house; neither let him which is in the field return back to take his clothes.**
>
> **And woe unto them that are with child, and to them that give suck in those days!
> But pray ye that your flight be not in the winter, neither on the Sabbath day."**
> (Matthew 24.15-20)

---

[41] On June 26, 2000, the Third Secret of Fatima was unceremoniously released to the general public with the "velvet glove" caveat that the prophecy had already been fulfilled by JPII's 1981 assassination attempt.

"After the two parts which I have already explained, at the left of Our Lady and a little above, we saw an Angel with a flaming sword in his left hand; flashing, it gave out flames that looked as though they would set the world on fire; but they died out in contact with the splendor that Our Lady radiated towards him from her right hand: pointing to the earth with his right hand, the Angel cried out in a loud voice: 'Penance, Penance, Penance!' And we saw in an immense light that is God: 'something similar to how people appear in a mirror when they pass in front of it' a Bishop dressed in White 'we had the impression that it was the Holy Father'.

Other Bishops, Priests, men and women Religious going up a steep mountain, at the top of which there was a big Cross of rough-hewn trunks as of a cork-tree with the bark; before reaching there the Holy Father passed through a big city half in ruins and half trembling with halting step, afflicted with pain and sorrow, he prayed for the souls of the corpses he met on his way; having reached the top of the mountain, on his knees at the foot of the big Cross he was killed by a group of soldiers who fired bullets and arrows at him, and in the same way there died one after another the other Bishops, Priests, men and women Religious, and various lay people of different ranks and positions. Beneath the two arms of the Cross there were two Angels each with a crystal aspersorium in his hand, in which they gathered up the blood of the Martyrs and with it sprinkled the souls that were making their way to God."   ~Sister Lucia, Tuy-3-1-1944

Book I: Purification

The eleventh-hour of the tribulation will concentrate all the forces of chaos into one extended period of mass annihilations. The bottoming out of the Kali Yuga postulates unprecedented horror, the likes of which will never recur.

> "For then shall be great tribulation,
> such as was not since the beginning
> of the world to this time, no, nor ever shall be."
> (Matthew 24.21)

The unleashing of repressed anger and jealousy by two-thirds of the population will be enough to upset the balance of Nature. It'll be *time to get out of Dodge* as shifting plate tectonics along the Rim of Fire generate unremitting earthquakes, tsunamis, volcanic eruptions, landslides and other natural disasters à la Edgar Cayce[42]—the wrathful response to unrelenting evil run amok.

The tampering of occult forces[43] and miracles wrought by the *Counterfeit Christ* to quell an unruly populace threaten the very stability of the Universe. The natural consequences of this cosmic imbalance are the same that brought on the *Great Deluge* of 9600 BC and killed the abominable Nephilim[44]—a colossal comet cometh. Curiously, the only key quatrain to outright name *the lawless one* also reveals His termination by the hand of God—

> "Mabus then will soon die, there will come
> Of people and beasts a horrible slaughter:
> Then all of a sudden vengeance will be seen coming,
> **A hundred-hand, thirst, famine when the comet will run.**"
> **CII-62**

Towards the end of Mabus' short reign, a previously unknown comet—*vis-à-vis* Hale-Bopp—is discovered making a beeline for mother Earth. More than likely, the ETA calculated for the emissary of God is **December 21, 2012***, a date reinforced by both the Bible Code and the Maya Calendar. [*See* **Book II**, pp. 41-42] Drosnin's computer search came up with **EARTH ANNIHILATED** a couple of lines

---

[42] The same sordid behavior that preceded the gradual breakup of the great Atlantean Continent, summons the powers of destruction to a modern world— "As to the changes physical again: The earth will be broken up in the western portion of America; the greater portion of Japan must go into the sea; The upper portion of Europe will be changed as in the twinkling of an eye; Land will appear off the east coast of America." (3976-15) And for karmic California—"If there are greater activities in the Vesuvius or Pelee, then the southern coast of California—and the areas between Salt Lake and the southern portions of Nevada—may expect within the three months following same an inundation by the earthquakes. But more in the southern than the northern hemisphere." (270-35)

[43] At Daniel 36.37-39, most Bibles based on the King James Version mistranslate the Antichrist as honoring the *"god of fortresses"*; according to the esteemed **Geneva Study Bible**, the correct translation is *"god of forces"*—

"He shall pay no respect to the gods of his ancestors, or to the one beloved by women [Mary]; he shall pay no respect to any other god, for he shall consider himself greater than all. He shall honor *the god of forces* instead of these; a god whom his ancestors did not know [Astrology was forbidden "sorcery" to the Israelites—Deut. 18.10-14] he shall honor with gold and silver, with precious stones and costly gifts. He shall deal with the strongest forces by the help of a foreign god."

Mabus manipulates the planetary Forces until he reaches the apex of His power—backed by the Dark Lord, the Sun rises at Midnight!
"And it shall come to pass in that day, that the YHVH shall punish the host of the high ones that are on high,
and the kings of the earth upon the earth... *Then the moon shall be confounded, and the sun ashamed...*" (Isaiah 24.21-23)

[44] "Just as it was in the days of Noah, so shall it be in the days of the Son of Man..." (Luke 17.26)

"The sexual mingling with the Sons of God and the daughters of men created a cosmic imbalance and confusion in the cosmic order. The birth of the demigods threatened the fabric of the cosmos... The cosmic imbalance is resolved by a great destruction out of which a new order arises." ~*Understanding the Dead Sea Scrolls*, Ronald Hendel [*See* **Book IV**, pp. 133-134]

* [This date was a *quantum probability*, dependent upon the inception of Antichrist's 3.5 year reign—DELAYED.]

above 5772/2012 and both neighboring **COMET**. However, a second look at the same disturbing prediction turns up a defiant statement that will vindicate the "endurance and faith of the saints". The magnitude of the crisis will *necessitate* the return of the Christ, "for the sake of the elect." [*See* **Fig. 10**]

Similar to *Shoemaker-Levy's* fragmentation prior to final impact with Jupiter, a supernatural light explodes the comet—massive chunks effectively wiping out Italy and outlying areas[45] while leaving the Elect, gathered in parts of the Americas and elsewhere, untouched.

Fig. 9   Comet—5772/2012—Earth Annihilated—Delayed

The resulting shock waves are substantial enough to trigger the periodic reversal of magnetic poles predicted by Cayce[46], sending towering tsunamis across the globe. The awful visual effect of such a pole shift will be the heavenly bodies *apparently* falling out of orbit, while the skies fill with dust and debris from multi-gigaton impacts of gargantuan comet fragments. Thus plunging the earth and her inhabitants into a womb-like darkness lasting a "biblical" forty days and nights...

"Immediately after the suffering in those days the sun will be darkened,
and the moon will not give its light; the stars will fall from heaven,
and the powers of heaven will be shaken.

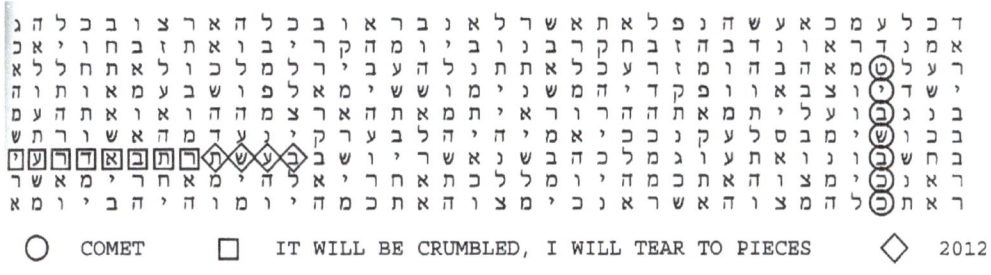

Fig. 10   Comet—It Will Be Crumbled, I Will Tear To Pieces—2012—Delayed

On the forty-fifth day after impact, the billion and a half survivors witness the dawn of a new day unlike any previous one in Human history—visible throughout both hemispheres, an immense *aurora borealis* crisscrosses tens of thousands of miles overhead—[47]

A luminous sign that the tribulation and purification is complete.

---

45   "And then the lawless one will be revealed, whom the Lord Jesus will destroy with the spirit (breath)
of his mouth, *annihilating him by the manifestation of his coming*."   (2 Thessalonians 2.8)

46 Scientists have guestimated the periodic reversal of earth's magnetic fields at one million year intervals, due to a mercurial metal core. A 1963 US Geological Survey concluded the last such flip-flop occurred **980,000** years ago. "By studying lava formations, whose magnetized iron-bearing minerals duplicate the earth's magnetic field, they were able to determine where the north magnetic pole was at that time, testing rock formations from the prehistoric lava flows of Mount Etna and Hawaii."
   One of the more interesting questions put to the Sleeping Prophet was—
   "What great change or the beginning of what change, if any, is to take place in the earth in the year 2000 to 2001 AD?"
   "When there is a shifting of the poles, or a new cycle begins."   (826-8 8/11/36)

47 We explore the scientific properties behind this anomaly and the accompanying "rapture" in **Book IV,** *Zero Point Energy.*

Book I: Purification

Then the sign of the Son of Man will appear in heaven, and then all the tribes of the earth will mourn, and they will see the Son of Man coming on the clouds of heaven with power and great glory."
(Matthew 24.29)

"And yet, when the Son of Man comes, will he find faith on earth?" [48]
(Luke 18.8)

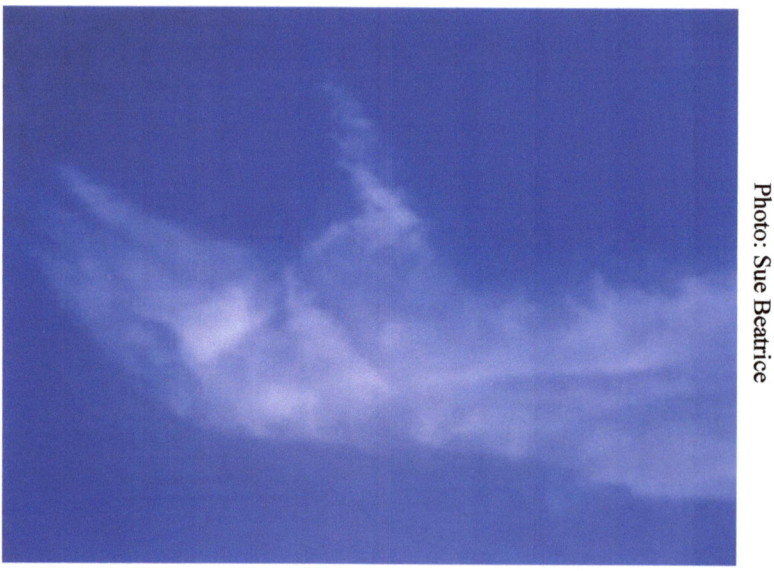

Photo: Sue Beatrice

"May the road rise up to meet you.
May the wind be always at your back.
May the sun shine warm upon your face;
the rains fall soft upon your fields and until we meet again,
May God hold you in the palm of His hand."

---

[48] The common *New Age* belief today, popularized by such books as Matthew Fox's *The Coming of the Cosmic Christ*, is that the Second Coming is merely a metaphor representing Man's fulfillment in reaching the level of Christ Consciousness. Don't believe it.
**"Wherefore if they shall say to you, 'Behold! He is in the desert, go not forth.
Behold! He is in the secret chambers** [the Christ within], ***Believe it not.***"   (Matthew 24.26)

Book II: Cyclicity
Chapter One: Precession

To get a better handle on where we stand in the grand scheme of things, we must determine the historicity of the Platonic Great Year[1]—a definitive Time Cycle of *equinotic precession* wherein four degenerating Epochs (Skt. Yugas) yield seven autocratic Empires within twelve distinct Ages.

The earliest mention of sequential, chronological divisions of Human history comes from the antediluvian Hebrew scripture, the *Book of Enoch*.[2] After a galvanizing tour of the multidimensional Worlds, revealing the hidden forces behind unfailing physical phenomena, the Celestial Commander Uriel instructs Enoch (Hbw. hanak, *initiated*) to read the predestined aftermath of Human folly…

> "So I looked at the tablets of heaven, read all the writing on them, and came to understand everything. I read that book and all the deeds of humanity and all the children of the flesh upon the earth for all the generations of the world… I praised the Lord because of his patience; and I wept on account of the children of the people upon the earth." (1 Enoch 81.2-3)

The grief-stricken patriarch is granted an additional year on earth to instruct all his kith and kin on the architectural symbolism required to record Mankind's schismatic pathways [*See* p. 127], and bequeath to his children *scriptural* warning, a more expansive timeline—an Apocalypse *of Weeks*…

- "I was born the seventh during the first week, during which time judgment and righteousness continued to endure. After me, there shall arise in the second week great and evil things; deceit should grow, and therein the first consummation will take place. But therein also a certain man shall be saved. After it is ended, injustice shall become greater, and he shall make a law for the sinners.
- Then after that at the completion of the third week, a certain man shall be elected as the plant of righteous judgment [Abraham, according to Ethiopian commentators], and after him one shall emerge as the eternal plant of righteousness.
- After that at the completion of the fourth week, visions of the old and righteous ones shall be seen; and a law shall be made with a fence [the *fence* of the tabernacle], for all the generations.
- After that in the fifth week, at the completion of glory, a house and a kingdom shall be built.
- After that in the sixth week, those who happen to be in it shall all of them be blindfolded, and the hearts of them all shall forget wisdom. Therein, a (certain) man shall ascend. And, at its completion, the house of the kingdom shall be burnt with fire; and therein, the whole clan of the chosen root shall be dispersed." [In 70 AD, Roman Legions burn the second Temple—instigating the great *Diaspora*.]
- After that in the seventh week, an apostate generation shall arise; its deeds shall be many, and all of them criminal. At its completion, there shall be elected the elect ones of righteousness from the eternal plant of righteousness, to whom shall be given sevenfold instruction concerning all his flock."

---

[1] "Of the other stars the revolutions have not been discovered by men (save for a few out of the many); wherefore they have no names for them, nor do they compute and compare their relative measurements, so that they are not aware, as a rule, that the 'wanderings' of these bodies, which are hard to calculate and of wondrous complexity [*Precession* as we'll see] constitute Time. Nevertheless, it is still quite possible to perceive that the complete number of Time fulfills the Complete Year when all the eight circuits, with their relative speeds, finish together and come to a head, when measured by the revolution of the Same and Similarly-moving." ~*Timaeus*, Plato

[2] *Nonextant for 1500 years*, Scottish explorer James Bruce donated the long-lost treasure to the Bodleian Library, Oxford in 1773. "Enoch, in large quarto, is amongst the books of scripture that I brought home, standing immediately before the *book of Job*, which is in its proper place in the Abyssinian Canon." These prehistoric scriptures were *already ancient artifacts* when Daniel, studying under King Nebuchadnezzar's wizards during the Babylonian captivity (6th c. BC), quoted an unusual epithet: **"I saw in the night visions, and, behold, one like *the son of man* came with the clouds of heaven, and came to the Ancient of days, and they brought him near before him."** (Daniel 7.13) The peculiar title, *son of man* was sprinkled liberally throughout the "pseudepigraphical" *1 Enoch*. Copies of the latter found among the Dead Sea Scrolls support the theory that young Jeshua also studied the prized antediluvian texts.

Here we have wholly extant, Enoch's original partition of linear time into seven sequential "weeks" (or *Sabbaths*), corresponding directly to John the Revelator's seven-headed Beast of the Apocalypse. Modern Biblical historians concur, seven World Empires can now be distinguished...

1.	(Atlantean—	17,428 BC	——	10,948 BC)
	Egyptian	10,500 BC	——	671 BC
2.	Assyrian	671 BC	——	612 BC
3.	Babylonian	612 BC	——	538 BC
4.	Persian	538 BC	——	331 BC
5.	Grecian	331 BC	——	146 BC
6.	Roman	146 BC	——	476 AD
7.	American	1776 AD	——	

With uncensored access to Yahweh's sacred "script", the unsealed *Book of Life*, the scribe now lays out the entire Timeline, hewn from stone. Three more united Kingdoms will follow the brief post-American, One World Empire of the Antichrist: a righteous eighth, ninth and tenth "Week"—

- "And after that there shall be another week, the eighth week, that of righteousness. And a sword shall be given to it in order that judgment shall be executed in righteousness on the oppressors, and sinners shall be delivered into the hands of the righteous. At its completion, they shall acquire great things through their righteousness. A house shall be built for the Great King in glory for evermore.
- Then after that in the ninth week, the righteous judgment shall be revealed to the whole world. All the deeds of the sinners shall depart from upon the whole earth, and be written off for eternal destruction; and all people shall direct their sight to the path of uprightness.
- Then after this matter, on the tenth week in the seventh part, there shall be eternal judgment; and it shall be executed by the Watchers (angels) of the eternal heaven—the great judgment which emanates from all of the angels. The first heaven shall depart and pass away; a new heaven shall appear; and all the powers of heaven shall shine forever sevenfold.
- Then after that there shall be many weeks without number forever; it shall be a time of goodness and righteousness, and sin shall no more be heard of forever." (1 Enoch 93.3-10, 91.12-17)

Next to the precious *Book of Enoch*, the oldest revealed teachings extant, although corrupt, lie amidst the ancient Vedic scriptures.[3] Here we find evidence that our seven historical Empires have arisen within a much larger archetypal matrix constituting a *four-fold division* of time/space.[4] The esteemed Indian scholar Alain Danielou—personally translating hundreds of Sanskrit records—found among the Puranas detailed information for calculating the duration of the Universe...

---

[3] Some oral knowledge inherited by the Hindus came from the conquering Aryans around 1050 BC, and was incorporated into the existing canon of revealed teachings (*Shaivism*) brought to the Indus Valley by the Dravidians around 9000 BC. Only the Aryan/Dravidian mix survives, and these tainted teachings are revered today as the sacred Vedas. In his recent work, *Practical Kabbalah*, Rabbi Wolf declares the original Dravidian legacy "came from a continent that had been engulfed by the sea. It was to safeguard Isaac that Abraham had cast out his other sons—the sons born to him by his second wife, Hagar. Abraham's gifts would allow them to see the nature of evil—the dark side of higher reality... they departed for the land of the East, biblical code for *Hodu*—India. Their Deity—BRAHMAN—is simply a rearrangement of the basic letters of the father's name—ABRAHAM. Abraham's great-grandson Ashurim was said to have created the spiritual commune known as the *ashram*."

[4] "**A river flows out of Eden to water the garden,** *and from there it divides and becomes four branches*…" (Genesis 2.10)

"Great were the descriptions and the account of how all the sky and earth were formed, *how it was formed and divided into four parts*; how it was partitioned, and how the sky was divided; and the measuring cord was brought, and it was stretched in the sky and over the earth, *on the four angles, on the four corners*, as was told by the Creator and the Maker, the Mother and the Father of Life."

~*Popul Vuh*

Cont. →

Book II: Cyclicity

"**The relative duration of the four ages is respectively 4,3,2,1. Each age is preceded by a period of dawn and followed by a period of twilight. These transition periods (*amsha*) as the beginning and end of each Yuga last a tenth of the duration of the Yuga. The life of Brahma is divided into a thousand cycles called Maha-Yugas, or Great Years.**" ~Linga Purana 1.4.3-7

The scriptures declare the definitive span of the Great Year to be 4,320,000 years and use the *Linga Purana's* scale ratio of 4:3:2:1 to modulate its four inherent cycles, adjusting the pace of gradual, moral decline. The great retrogressive Yugas constituting a Mahayuga are calculated thus:

---

4 *Continued*

The Kabbalah reveres the four basic Elements as creative energies far beyond their simple manifestation here, in the lower world…

"In this, the last tree branch, everything is interrelated and interdependent within the framework of the Four Elements of Life. The four elements, on an archetypal level, represent much more than mere physical states; they constitute Creation through Four successive Worlds—

- *World of Origination*—Fire ascends, expands and transforms. It is hot, radiant, dry and dynamic.
- *World of Creation*—Water descends, purifies, condenses and dissolves to promote germination without manifesting itself in structured forms. It is cold, moist, receptive and absorbing. In shape and color, Water conforms with its receptacle.
- *World of Formation*—Air supports and dispenses. Being so finely divided that it cannot be seen, it scatters in all directions, and moves everything with it. It is hot, moist, expanding and adjusting.
- *World of Manifestation*—Earth confines itself to touchable matter. It is cold, dry, brittle, receptive, passive, concreting, restricting, stable, inert and solid.

YHVH (*Yod*/hand, *He*/window, *Vav*/nail, *He*/window), the sacrosanct name of the Lord God, also known as the *Tetragrammaton*, is another four-world analogy—the correct sound of the holy name is said to contain the immeasurable powers of the Four Elements as they express the Divine Will." ~*Kabbalah, Your Path to Inner Freedom*, Ann Williams-Heller

Primary four-fold divisions in our World are manifold. The good news was locked into History through four distinguished passion narratives, each one taking a slightly different perspective. St. John's (Rev. 4.7-9) and Ezekiel's (Ez. 1.10) four *living beings* came to be symbolized by the four Evangelists (respectively, Aquarius, Taurus, Leo and Scorpio—the *fixed* signs of the Zodiac)…

St. Matthew, **the Man** * St. Luke, **the Ox** * St. Mark, **the Lion** * St. John, **the Eagle**

These four types of men, with their fundamental characteristics, encompass *every possible variety* according to the revealed teachings of the Toltec brujo don Juan Matus, collated by his bumbling apprentice, Carlos Castaneda...

- The first type is the knowledgeable man, the **scholar**; a noble, dependable, serene man, fully dedicated to accomplishing his task, whatever it may be.
- The second type is the **man of action**, highly volatile, a great humorous fickle companion.
- The third type is the **man behind the scenes**, the mysterious, unknowable man. Nothing can be said about him because he allows nothing about himself to slip out.
- The **courier** is the fourth type. He is the assistant, a taciturn, somber man who does very well if properly directed but who cannot stand on his own.

The classic example of the above is the basic Rock n' Roll quartet consisting of rhythm guitar, bass, lead & drums—**John, Paul, George & Ringo**. Women are called the four directions, moods or winds. There are four different female personalities that exist in the Human race—

- The first is the east. **She is called order**. She is optimistic, light-hearted, smooth, persistent like a steady breeze.
- The second is the north. **She is called strength**. She is resourceful, blunt, direct, tenacious like a hard wind.
- The third is the west. **She is called feeling**. She is introspective, remorseful, cunning, sly, like a cold gust of wind.
- The fourth is the south. **She is called growth**. She is nurturing, loud, shy, warm, like a hot wind.

Within a small percentage of Mankind, *mahasiddhas* are reborn with the astounding ability to manifest all four modes of behavior. In the occult Toltec tradition of ancient Mexico, these powerful beings are known as *Naguals*—their luminous "cocoon" containing four energy compartments rather than just the left and right sides of the average Human. "The Nagual man is supportive, steady, unchangeable. The Nagual woman is a being at war and yet relaxed, ever aware but without strain. Both of them reflect the four types of their sex, as four ways of behaving."

The Nagual (nah-**gwahl'**) is a natural leader, the only one capable of organizing large units of temperamentally compatible Initiates and leading them to Freedom. Don Jeshua is the *true* Nagual who will guide us to sure and everlasting Victory—metamorphosis of the carnal body.

Cont. →

- **Krita Yuga**   **A Golden Age**   (1,728,000 years)

  "Neither hate nor envy, care nor fear exist. There is only one God, one law and one ritual. The castes have varying tasks, and each fulfills its duty selflessly."

- **Treta Yuga**   **A Silver Age**   (1,296,000 years)

  "Righteousness declines by one quarter when the performance of sacrifices begins. The sacrifices necessitate rites and ceremonies. The actions of human beings are marked by intentionality; people expect rewards in exchange for their rituals and offerings, and the sense of duty declines."

- **Dvapara Yuga**   **A Bronze Age**   (864,000 years)

  "Righteousness is reduced by one half. Ritual is predominant; only few still abide by the truth. Desires and diseases surface, and injustice grows."

- **Kali Yuga**   **An Iron Age**   (432,000 years)

  "The age of conflict. Righteousness has dwindled to one quarter of its original substance. Spiritual efforts slacken off, knowledge is forgotten, evil dominates. Disease, fatigue, anger, hunger, fear and despair gain ground; ***humanity has no goal***."

---

4 *Continued*

The Vedic Scriptures declare society itself is an organization of four distinct classes *(castes)...*

"The four fold division of society into **Brahmins** (priests), **Kshatriyas** (warriors), **Vaishyas** (cultivators) and **Shudras** (menial servants) has been created by primeval man Purusha. From Purusha's brain have emerged the Brahmins, from his forearms have emerged the Kshatriyas from his abdomen have emerged the Vaishyas and from his feet have emerged the Shudras."   ~*Rig Veda*

In his masterwork, *Pluto: The Evolutionary Journey of the Soul*, Jeffrey Green updates the medieval caste system, a remnant from the archaic Indus Valley civilization—

- "Dimly evolved or de-evolved state: Two or three percent of the human race is characterized by those people who are either just evolving into human consciousness from other kingdoms (such as the animal state), or are in a de-evolved evolutionary condition due to prior-life karmic causes.
- The herd state: Seventy-five percent of the human race exists in this condition, which is characterized by individuals whose identities are a mere extension of societal norms, beliefs, customs and taboos. In fact, this condition is the mainstream of society itself. It is society.
- The individuated state: Approximately twenty percent of the human race exists in this condition, which is characterized by those people who question the beliefs, customs, norms and taboos of society. These people seek to discover their own individuality as distinct from society.
- The spiritual state: Two or three percent of human beings will attempt to understand their own life and others' lives in a universal/holistic context. In fact, these people desire to understand the nature of all Creation in this context and commonly link themselves to spiritual ideas or teachings as the guiding principles of life. This state represents those individuals who have eliminated or are in the process of eliminating all separating or externalizing desires.

These four natural evolutionary conditions are not rigidly delineated classifications. There is movement within and between them."

The Buddha's straight and narrow path to Enlightenment (Kingdom of Heavens) was concentrated into *Four Noble Truths*—

1. **The Reality of Suffering** (*dukkha*)
   Birth, old age, sickness, death, association with unpleasant persons and conditions, separation from beloved ones and pleasant conditions, not getting what one desires, grief, lamentation, distress—all forms of physical and mental suffering.

2. **The Cause of Suffering** (*samudaya*)
   The principle cause of suffering is the attachment to "desire" or "craving", *tanha*

3. **The Cessation of Suffering** (*nirodha*)
   The end of suffering is non-attachment, or letting go of desire or craving. This is the state of *Nibbana*, where greed, hatred and delusion are extinct.

4. **The Eightfold Path to the Cessation of Suffering** (*magga*) →

Widsom (*Panna*)
1. Right Understanding
2. Right Thought

Morality (*Sila*)
3. Right Speech
4. Right Action
5. Right Livelihood

Concentration (*Samadhi*)
6. Right Effort
7. Right Mindfulness
8. Right Concentration

Book II: Cyclicity

Some sages, including Yogananda's mentor Sri Yukteswar, use natural cosmological cycles as a criterion for the Four-Yuga expanse.[5] Suspecting the Epochs *equal* in length, yet *experienced* as growing shorter—time speeding up within each Yuga—Hindu astrophysicists adjusted the *Mahayuga* to align with the astronomical Precession Cycle of 25,920 years. The "Bible" of Western authority, the *Encyclopedia Britannica*, claims the Greeks were the first to discover a previously unsuspected, inconspicuous *third* motion of our sphere, a wobbling dubbed the *Precession of the Equinoxes*.

"In compiling his famous star catalog (completed in 129 BC), the Greek astronomer Hipparchus noticed that the positions of the stars were shifted in a systematic way from earlier Babylonian (Chaldean) measures… This indicated that it was not the stars that were moving but rather the observing platform—the Earth. Such a motion is called precession and consists of a cyclic wobbling in the orientation of the Earth's axis of rotation with a period of almost 26,000 years. Precession was the third-discovered motion of the Earth, after the far more obvious daily rotation and annual revolution. Precession is caused by the gravitational influence of the Sun and the Moon acting on the Earth's equatorial bulge. To a much lesser extent, the planets exert influence as well."

The earliest sources, however, maintain the Egyptians as the original star-gazers, organizing an extensive scientific legacy propagated by subsequent civilizations…

"The Egyptians, taking advantage of the favorable conditions, appropriated to themselves the knowledge of astronomy, which they were the first to study… the Chaldeans of Babylon, being colonists from Egypt, enjoy the fame which they have for their astronomy because they learned that science from the priests of Egypt. The disposition of the stars as well as their movements have always been the subject of careful observation among the Egyptians… they have preserved to this day the records concerning each of these stars over an incredible number of years, this study having been zealously preserved among them from ancient times." ~*Diodoros of Sicily*

The most respected Egyptologist of the 20th century, R. A. Schwaller de Lubicz proved that ancient Egypt not only possessed an intricate knowledge of astronomy, but through observation of discrepancies in the *Sothic cycle*—and their repair—they understood precessional phenomena. De Lubicz explains how the bright star Sirius was preeminent to Egyptian life and cosmology—its annual rising, in perfect tandem with the rising waters of the Nile, kicked off their New Year…

"In order to establish the fixed year, it is a fact that the ancient Egyptians deliberately chose the heliacal rising of Sirius, the only star to return periodically every 365 ¼ days, during the entire Empire. This fact implies exceptional astronomical knowledge as well as a very long period of observation preceding the introduction of the calendar. The first day of the first month of the fixed year, or festival of the New Year, has always been determined by the heliacal rising of Sirius.
Around the year 3400 BC, the Birth of Ra (summer solstice) coincided with the New Year (Sirius Rising)… however, by the year 1320 BC, the Birth of Ra (summer solstice) took place thirteen days before the rising of Sirius or New Year's Day. At that stage, a reform seemed in order for the reckoning of religious festivities: the Birth of Ra was celebrated during the twelfth month instead of the first; this conformed to the true displacement of the solsticial point among the constellations.
For the Pharonic Sothic cycle of 1,460 years, the summer solstice advanced 11.5 days in relation to the rising of Sirius. That this fact was perfectly well known to the ancients is shown by the temporal correction brought to the celebration of the summer solstice of Birth of Ra.
This is the precession of the equinoxes; its discovery was hitherto attributed to Hipparchus."

---

5 In *The Holy Science*, Swami Sri Yukteswar's "opinion is that the Sanskrit scholars were born in the dark age of the Kali Yuga and therefore no longer understood the old traditions. Yukteswar's method is based on astrological cycles." Danielou also warns against the Hindu tendency toward wild exaggeration. "The interpretation of these data poses a few problems as they concern in some cases lunar years (or human years) or ancestral years (years of the various races) or even the years of the gods."

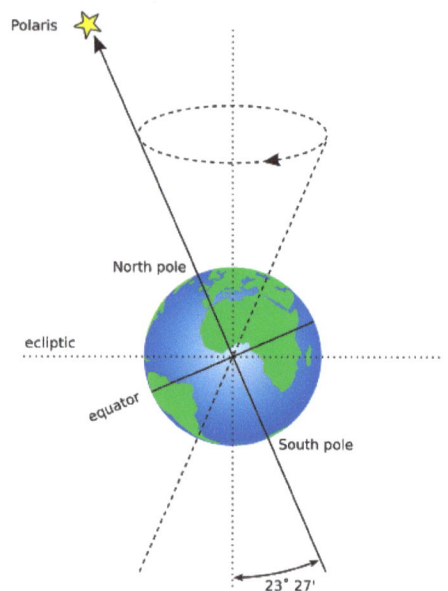

Fig. 1 Precession of the Equinoxes

This precession cycle, known to certain civilizations for millennia, encompasses an apparent 12-fold division analogous to the traditional *zoidia* [See **Book IV**, *Mazzaroth*], seen in retrospect as individual Ages or Eras. Every 2,160 years, the shifting vernal equinox initiates a new *zoidion* Lord with harmonic, historical synchronicities reflecting that particular zodiacal "flavoring". Schwaller de Lubicz demonstrates how certain serendipitous cults, endemic to the **Ages of Gemini**, **Taurus**, **Aries** and present-day **Pisces**, have flourished within respectively corresponding, chronological periods...

"Thus it is that Pharonic prehistory was dominated by the **Twins Shu and Tefnut**, whose nature consists in separating Heaven from Earth. At that time there existed the kingdom of the South with its double capital, Nekhen and Nekheh, and the kingdom of the North with its dual capital, Dep and Pe. The vestiges of this period show a pronounced double character and it is certainly at this time that the Heliopolitan mystery of primordial dualization was revealed.

At Memphis, under the Ancient Empire, there was the domination of **Hap the Bull,** who precipitated celestial fire into terrestrial form. The Bull, the great Neter of the historical period extending from 4380 to 2200 BC, commands the Cretan civilization as well. From the Middle Empire to the beginning of the Christian era, we see the domination of **Amon the Ram**. It is in Thebes, under the predominance of Amon, that the generating fire is 'extracted', so to speak, from its terrestrial gangue-matrix, *Khonsu*, by the grace of *Djehuti* (Thoth), master of Hermaopolis. Finally, toward the year 60 BC, with the end of the political empire of Egypt under Cleopatra, our Christian era of **Pisces** begins. The myth is directly related to the cosmic movements, to cosmic harmony. Because of its calendar, it is possible to situate the essential phases of Pharonic Egypt's history, and by means of it, we are able to understand the modifications brought to the essential cult."

The Ages of **Taurus**, **Aries** and (current) **Pisces** comprise the fourth "Macroseason" of the Mahayuga—the Kali Yuga Autumn, where years/days dwindle down to their minimum length. [See **Fig. 2**]

"***Thus there are cosmic seasons defined by the precession of the equinoxes***, stellar seasons with Sothis (Sirius), planetary seasons through the circuit and particular movements of the planets on the ecliptic, and lastly, the seasons of the luminaries through the sun and the moon. Sun and moon give the essential primary complements. The planets, called the Wanderers, give the qualitative orientations through their situations in different sites of the starry heavens. The groupings of fixed stars tinge the celestial sites and delimit them; through Sothis (Sirius) in coincidence with the sun, they modify the sun's intensities (the eye of Ra), **because Sothis (Sirius) is the great purveyor of energy.**"[6]   ~R. A. Schwaller de Lubicz

Whereas Aryan/Hindu cosmology relies on suspect Vedic scriptures, it is this schema of four *equal* Epochs—each modulating three 2,160-year Ages—that agrees with Natural Law: the Seasons are distinguished by two equinoxes and two solstices, *establishing precise quarterly demarcations...*

- A 2,160-year Age (Macromonth) correlates to one 30-day earthly month
- A 6,480-year Epoch (Macroseason) correlates to one 90-day earthly season

---

[6] The cosmic significance of the Dog Star and its Pup (Sirius B) have yet to be realized. In the last chapter, *The Seat of God*, we will examine Sirius A's pivotal role as headquarters to the Galactic Lord.

The subtle energy signature defining a Yuga "season" is never more apparent than when it wraps the *twilight* stage in preparation for the *dawn* that will initiate the next Epoch. However, the totality of the entire Mahayuga's intent crystallizes when it is the *Kali Yuga* that is closing her twilight phase—since the enormous 26,000-year cycle, the Platonic Great Year, is coming to its dramatic dénouement.

Our little Piscean Era, the third Act in the Kali Triad, is consummating within an increasingly disparate state of confusion: Self-aggrandizing materialists conflict pointedly with the true believers struggling to maintain faith in a Power greater than themselves. One would have to be living in a cave in the Himalayas (or Santa Cruz) not to be aware of the sorry state of affairs in the early 21st century. What used to be just a Generation Gap has polarized into the Great Divide—those *in the know*, the innocent sixties children who indulged in psychoactive substances and glimpsed higher truths, verses the *know-nots*, those unenlightened masters of ignorance, securely blissful within their social moorings. *To those with eyes to see,* we're not only in the Kali Yuga, but have reached the twilight's last gleaming, the *hour of power* where things are literally the opposite of what they appear to be. The struggling good are given black hats, while the insidious bad don white ones. What will eventually prove good, even *essential* to the upward path, is now perceived as evil—while those who appear in the guise of goodness are actually setting up stumbling stones to survival. (*e.g.* by demonizing *any* esoteric learning as "New Age" or Satanic, the Evangelical Right has "**taken away the keys of knowledge**" —hindering both themselves and their innocent congregations.)

The balance of power has stabilized somehow, but the pendulum will soon finish its swing. Of course, it's not considered good manners to point out the obvious infection, the disease, but it's vitally important to see the big picture, so as not to despair when things get ugly. What we don't know *can* hurt us, since we might give up too soon. Castaneda's warrior knew first of all, *that he is waiting*, and secondarily, *what he is waiting for*. Hesse's *Siddhartha* had all the necessary skills for Life: he could think, fast and *wait*. The Kali Yuga must run her fixed course and, as with the Borg, resistance is futile—we must wait, but with absolute certainty of what we are waiting for.

Blind faith won't do in a modern age.

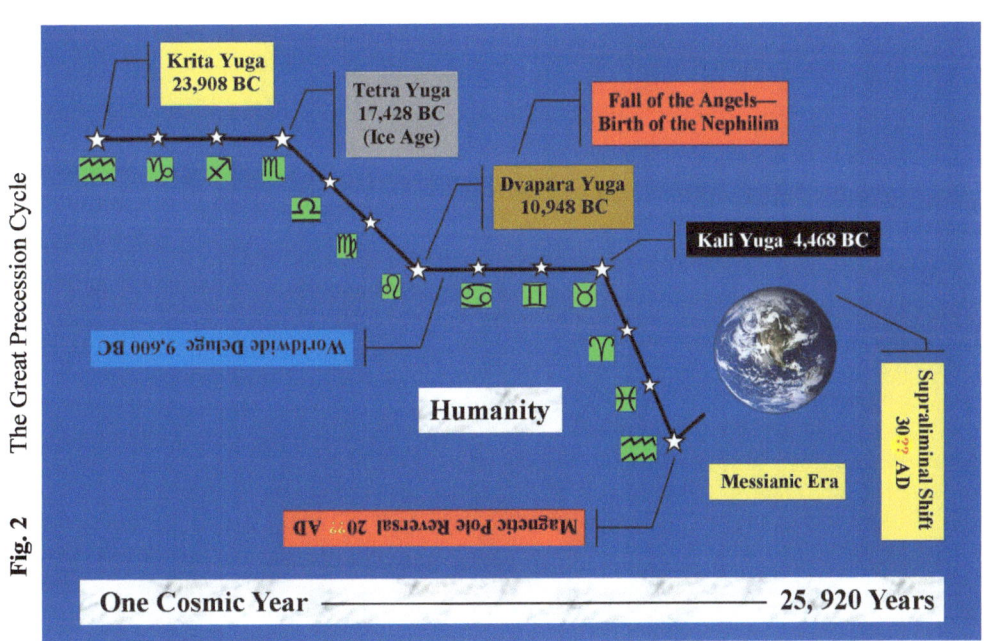

Fig. 2 The Great Precession Cycle

The incredible anxiety that grips our Civilization today is the subconscious knowledge that we are indeed wrapping up the grand Human experiment of free will. The phenomenal success of Cameron's *Titanic* was more than just the result of a good script with CGI cutting-edge technology. The Millennial timing struck a tone of truth within our collective Psyche—the stark symbolism of greedy, materialistic Westerners trapped in a boat that is slowly sinking. And this *should* haunt the vast majority because, contrary to the old adage, we're *not* all in the same boat. Those who have trod upon the straight and narrow, though sidetracking through some colorful landscapes with Lucy in the sky, need not get caught up in the morphic field of fear that is manifesting.   * [*See* **Proverbs 3.25**]
We have but to wait...[7]

"**Another Book of Enoch—which he wrote for his son Methuselah
and for those who will come after him, observing the law in the last days:
You who have observed the law shall wait patiently in all the days until the time
of those who work evil is completed, and the power of the wicked ones is ended.**
As for you, wait patiently until sin passes away..."   (1 Enoch 108.1-3)

Chapter Two: The Maya Calendar

More than striking architectural coincidences (pyramidal temples) link the Egyptian civilization with the Mesoamerican. The Maya's astronomical brilliance, including a unique mathematical constant defining hierarchical, modulated time-cycles, is hinted at in our foreword to their complex calendar. The latter providing an independent verification of the Bible Code's 2012 A.D. probability Date. De Lubicz's theory of "cosmic seasons determined by precessional equinoxes" is further refined, establishing the origin of both the Kali Yuga and the Egyptian Empire circa 4400 BC [*See* **Fig. 2**]— any earlier, and we have only feeble conjecture and fable forgotten in the fog of former freedom. *Thus our entire edifice of human civilization has arisen within this dark cycle, the Kali Yuga.*[8] Seven autonomous Empires have attempted to rule the world—seven beasts have reared their ugly heads.

---

[7] Waiting does *not* mean quitting your job and dropping out of society—it means not giving up hope in the face of futility. Remember Schindler in WWII: "Whoever saves one life, saves the world entire."
"Both renunciation and holy work are a path to the Supreme; but better than surrender of work is the Yoga of holy work."
"...it isn't enough just to have faith. Faith that doesn't show itself by good deeds is no faith at all—it is dead and useless."
(Bhagavad Gita, Chapter 5)   (James 2.17)

[8] "The evil in the world appears for normal mankind as a necessity not only in the causal sense, because it is given as a firm and inextricable part of our world's plan, but also in the final sense, namely as a motive force that facilitates the further evolution of the individual as well as mankind. This evolution would have been impossible in an exclusively positive world without knowledge of evil; such was perhaps that paradisal state of the legendary Golden Age. We find ourselves, however, in the Iron Age, the last and lowest of the four Yugas, and *evil, as a means to an end and a motive force, is part of its destiny.*

Since in this darkest of all ages the veil of Maya is becoming increasingly opaque, and thus the recognition of the good ever less self-evident, religious founders were needed, all of whom appeared just at the onset of the Iron Age, whose moral codes lead us on a path through the valley of darkness... Their indication of the good along with the contrasting evil constitutes the motive force for further evolution as a dialectic principle. It is essential for man's fulfillment that he freely choose the upward path, that is why he has free will."   ~*Harmonics and Sacred Tradition*, Rudolf Haase

"It is the lowest instincts that spur the men of the Kali Yuga on. They do not hesitate to persecute sages. Desire torments them. The sacred books are no longer respected. Men will be without morals, irritable and sectarian. In the age of Kali false doctrines and misleading writings spread. Fetuses will be killed in the stomachs of their mothers and heroes will be assassinated. Priests will degrade themselves by selling the sacraments. Ready-cooked food will be on sale. The sacred books will be sold on street corners. There will be many beggars and unemployed people. Everyone will use hard and vulgar language. No one will be able to trust anyone else. People will be envious. No one will want to return a favor. The degradation of virtues and the censorship of hypocritical and moralizing puritans characterize the period of the end of the Kali Yuga.   *Cont.* →

Book II: Cyclicity

The erudite hypothesis of a 45th century BC Kali Yuga kick-off is the brainchild of MIT Professor Santillana and the University of Frankfort's von Dechend. *Hamlet's Mill: An Essay on Myth and the Frame of Time* affirms that ancient cultures were not only aware of the precession of the equinoxes—evidenced by their myths of an *unhinged*, heavenly Mill—but knew them to be harbingers of Destiny.[9] The two scientists discovered a subtle coincidence in the precession cycle: the solstice and equinox suns lined up with the Milky Way spiral arm at four equidistant time periods—creating, in effect, four distinct 6,480-year Macroseasons, substantiating de Lubicz's speculations. Moreover, Santillana and von Dechend's own pioneering research extrapolates an *Autumn equinox conjunction* with the Milky Way band around 4400 BC. This stable alignment in the heavens reflected a similar harmony on earth. Our Matriarchal society still existed in an age of innocence, relative peace ruled the Collectivity. [*See* **Book III**] Libra, and the first day of Fall, brings a perfect balance of equal days and nights, degenerating thereafter into shorter and shorter days. Santillana and von Dechend conjecture how, century after century, as precession gradually dislodged the autumnal Milky Way conjunction, we began our "descent into history".

In *Maya Cosmogenesis 2012*, John Jenkins picks up where *Hamlet's Mill* left off—the next galactic alignment, the *Winter solstice*, should have a similarly synchronous effect on Humanity…

"I reasoned that one-quarter of a precessional cycle later (6,450 years), the December solstice sun will be conjuncting the bright band of the Milky Way around the year 2012. I studied star charts and proved to myself that a very rare alignment in the precessional cycle will occur on the December solstice of AD 2012—the end-date of the Maya calendar! The alignment involves the December solstice, the traditional 'beginning' point of Earth's yearly cycle.

This was certainly an event worthy of being recognized by the ancient Maya as a rare World Age shift. **The part of the Milky Way that the December solstice sun will conjunct is also where the center of our Galaxy (the Galactic Center) is located.** It is the cosmic womb from which new stars are born, and from which everything in our Galaxy, including humans, came."

Fig. 3   The Pyramid of the Magician—Uxmal, Yucatán peninsula

---

8 *Continued*

There will no longer be any kings. Adventurers will take on the appearance of monks with shaven heads, orange clothing and rosary beads around their necks. People will become inactive, lethargic and purposeless. They will be hungry and sick and will know despair. It is then that some will start to ponder over fundamental values. Heretics will rebel against the principle of the four castes and *the four periods of life*. Unqualified people will pass as experts in matters of morals and religion. People will massacre women, children, cows and one another."   ~Linga Purana, Chap. 40   Yet believe it or not, there is a silver lining to this dark Age—

"The end of the Kali Yuga is a particularly favorable period to pursue true knowledge. Some will attain wisdom in a short time, for the merits acquired in one year during the Tetra Yuga can be obtained in one day in the age of Kali."   ~Shiva Purana 5.1.40

9 "The image of the mill and its owner yielded elsewhere to more sophisticated ones, more adherent to celestial events…This imagery stands, as the evidence develops, for an astronomical process, the secular shifting of the sun through the signs of the zodiac which determines world-ages, each numbering thousands of years. Each age brings a World Era, a Twilight of the Gods. Great structures collapse; pillars topple which supported the great fabric; floods and cataclysms herald the shaping of a new world."   ~*Hamlet's Mill*

The Maya calendar's 2012 AD end-date first gained notoriety via Jose Arguelles' underground bestseller, *The Mayan Factor*. His far-fetched theory that the Maya were ultra-advanced Galactic travelers scouting and mapping sentient solar systems caught on with the gullible seeker/sucker generation. Once we were deemed worthy of attention, the almighty Maya would beam a "synchronization code" through the Sun's periodic solar flare cycle, and the "critical information transduction could occur: the genetic impregnation of the selected planetary field." Arguelles' fantastic assumptions began rationally enough with the 1927 **Goodman-Martinez-Hernandez-Thompson Correlation**, which adjusted the Maya calendar's start-date, 13.0.0.0.0. to the Gregorian calendar's proleptic date, August 11, 3114 BC. The next Great Cycle begins again at 13.0.0.0.0 (12/21, 2012 AD).

Neatly correlating 13 baktun cycles (comprising the calendar's 5,125-year Great Cycle) to historical turning points, Arguelles tweaked the last *baktun* (1618-2012 AD) to ambiguously yield two "crucial resonance" dates: 1863022 and 1863023, August 16-17, 1987. Caught up in his own crackpot ideas, the pseudo-scholar cautioned us:

"The resonant body of Earth, the vibratory infrastructure that literally holds together the sense-perceptible body of Earth, is in a condition of intense 'fever' called resonant dissonance. Remembering that the planets function as gyroscopes holding the frequency pattern of their particular orbits, we see that environmentally impactful events since 1945 have actually set in motion a dissonant vibratory wave affecting the overall spin of the planet. If the dissonance is not checked, then, similar to an uncontrolled nuclear reaction, the end-result would be the development of a wobble in the spin and a consequent shattering of the planetary form. The Earth could be broken up into smaller bodies not unlike the Asteroid belt."

It was up to the ecologically concerned to take those days off and meditate together, so our "DNA infrastructure would interface with the Earth's self-healing processes". **Bing-bodda-bang: crisis over…**

"Such an evocation is in the nature of a planetary mystery, a rite of passage that synergizes hitherto scarcely suspected force-fields into radiant manifestation. This is what is meant by 'harmonic convergence'. Through such an event, the Armageddon script is short-circuited, yet the possibility of a New Heaven and a New Earth is fully present."

And sure enough, come August 16-17, tens of thousands took to the highlands, beaches or back yards and sent blissful vibes to mother Earth. The fact that nothing unusual, astrologically, was going on (except a rather carefree Grand Trine), wasn't the point. We saw it as a *happening* —an opportunity to connect with one another on a spiritual level. So it goes, the ominous end-date of 2012 AD embedded within the collective unconscious. Arguelles believed the calendar's closure would entail the final transformation of Man. He preached of an instant, radical shift into a supernal realm—the Kingdom.

"The Earth itself will be illumined. A current charging both poles will race across the skies, connecting the polar auroras in a single brilliant flash. Like an iridescent rainbow, this circumpolar energy uniting the planetary antipodes will be instantaneously understood as the external projection of the unification of the collective mind of humanity. In that moment of understanding, we shall be collectively projected into an evolutionary domain that is presently inconceivable."

Arguelles' clowning aside, Jenkins' real contribution is in recognizing the fact that the Maya's Great Cycle was established through a precessional artifice, and it is the *Galactic Center* that is being intersected in 2012 AD. In **Book IV**, we penetrate the mystery of the Maya sacred calendar—Tzolkin, expounding upon the esoteric essence of its harmonic fractal 260, the key to cosmic cyclicity.

Chapter Three: The I Ching Eschaton

The late Terence McKenna suspected early on that beneath the apparently arbitrary array of 64 *I Ching* hexagrams[10], there lay a hidden order. Traditionally known as the King Wen (11th c. BC) sequence, 384 solid and broken lines [Based on the Chinese lunation cycle of 13 months (29.53 days X 13 = 383.89 days)] are organized into 32 pairs of hexagrams, with the second member of each pair an *inverse* of the first. The first pair in the oracle is, quite naturally—the Creative, with six *solid* lines, followed by its inverse—the Receptive, hexagram #2 with six *broken* lines...

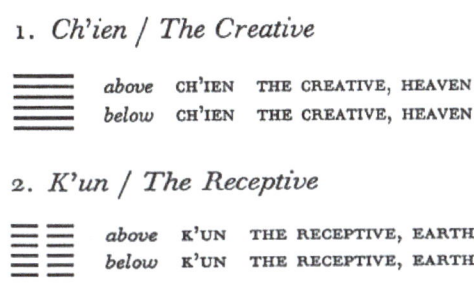

Fig. 4 The Creative (*Ch'ien*) and Receptive (*K'un*)

But the logic ends there. With the exception of the inverted pairing aspect, a willy-nilly order appears to prevail among the 32 pairs. "No known basis exists for determining why pairs are arranged as they are or why one member of a pair precedes another," writes McKenna. However, similar to the *Bible Code*, further investigation revealed an underlying mathematical structure—a method to the madness. The deceptive "randomness" of the hexagram pairs "spells out" a perfect differential ratio pattern of 3 to 1.

---

[10] There are indications that the number 64 represents a numerical perfection–a maxing out within physical reality. The 8 X 8 squares of the mandalic Chessboard appear to symbolize the mathematical maximum inherent in the Galaxy. The game of Chess, like Life itself, seems to be infinitely varied within a fixed structure—

"This is not just a game of complicated strategies but can be seen as a ritual game of life. It can symbolize the conflict between darkness and light, angels and demons, a struggle for the domination of the world. The chequered board is a manifestation of the criss-crossed pattern of life, alternating between good and bad, fortune and ill-fortune. The pieces symbolize aspects of the forces of nature. Not the forces found by science but the symbolic forces of spirituality (the bishop), temporal power (the castle), and so on. The moves themselves are not arbitrary. The knight, who represents the initiate, the force of intellect, moves by jumps of intuition, combining the direct with the diagonal, the rational with the non-rational movement. Pawns are ordinary men, whose path is slow and restricted, whose goal is the state of enlightenment, symbolized by the Queen herself. On the symbolic board, whose eight by eight measure is itself symbolic, all possible moves can be made, all of reality ritualized there, restricted physically to a small field of action. Even time is symbolized by each changing move." ~*On Time*, Michael Shallis

The microprocessor computer will reach its evolutionary peak when the 64-bit chip from Intel makes the current crop of 32-bit computers obsolete. The *I Ching*, with its positive and negative coupling, anticipated computer binary code by several millennia! More recently, enlightened scientists have linked the ancient oracle with the Human Genome—

"The *I Ching* is based on the interaction of the two antithetical principles, Yang (represented by an unbroken line –) and Yin (represented by a broken line – –). Yang and Yin are combined to form four diagrams, Old Yang (=), Old Yin (==), New Yang (– –) and New Yin (===), and the four diagrams are combined three at a time to form $4^3 = 64$ hexagrams. Each hexagram, which is read from bottom to top, represents one of 64 fundamental aspects of life, the nature of each aspect being given by the interaction of the three diagrams of which the hexagram is composed. During the long history of the *I Ching*, the hexagrams have been arranged in several different ways, of which a so-called 'natural' order was worked out during the Sung period about a thousand years ago.

...however surprising may be the anticipation of binary digits by the *I Ching*, the congruence between it and the genetic code is nothing short of amazing. For if Yang (the male, or light, principle) is identified with the purine bases and Yin (the female, or dark, principle) with pyrimidine bases, so that Old Yang and Yin correspond to the complementary adenine (A) and thymine (T) pair and New Yang and Yin to the complementary guanine (G) and cytosine (C) pair, each of the 64 hexagrams comes to represent one of the nucleotide triplet codons. The 'natural' order of the *I Ching* can now be seen to generate an array of nucleotide triplets in which many of the generic codon relations manifest in Crick's arrangement are shown. Perhaps students of the presently still mysterious origins of the genetic code might consult the extensive commentaries on the *I Ching* to obtain some clues to the solution of their problem."
~*The Coming of the Golden Age*, Gunther Stent

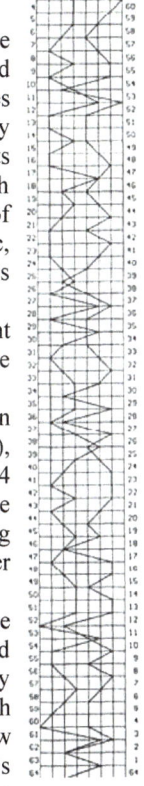

Fig. 5

"The ratio of three to one is not a formal property of any or most sequences but was a carefully constructed artifice achieved by arranging hexagram transitions between pairs to generate fourteen instances of three and two instances of one. Fives were deliberately excluded."

After producing a graph of the sequence, McKenna noticed that if he flipped it upon itself, it would conveniently close at the beginning and end, resembling an alternating current, a conduit running forward and backward. [*See* **Fig. 5**]

"When an image of the graph is rotated 180 degrees within the plane and superimposed upon itself, ***it is found to achieve closure at four adjacent points.*** This construct may best be understood as a reflection on the temporal dimension of the patterns that impart structural order to organisms and their view of the world. Space-time within this idea model is entirely composed of these hierarchically nested waves… Each wave, by itself, contains the entire modular hierarchy through its being a reflection of organization on higher and lower levels in an extensive continuum."

Borrowing a fundamental, philosophical postulate from Alfred Whitehead, McKenna believed that the peaks and valleys of the waves represented two distinct, alternating modes of behavior…

"The universe, or human life or an empire or an ecosystem, any large scale or small scale process, can be looked at as a dynamic struggle between… **habit** and **novelty**. Habit is simply repetition of established patterns, conservation, holding back what has already been achieved into a system, and novelty is the chance taking, the exploratory, the new, the never-before-seen. And these two qualities—habit and novelty—are locked in all situations in a kind of struggle."

McKenna had the modular wave-hierarchy embedded within the *I Ching* programmed by Peter Meyer to produce a time/novelty fractal that could correlate the ebb and flow to any given span of time, from just a few days to millennia. Mapping the highs and lows to key historical moments that might be considered "novel", McKenna's graph displayed an end-date of November, 2012 AD. It seemed a close fit, but when he tweaked the Timewave ahead a month to coincide with the Maya calendar's closure—historical events seemed to line up with eerie precision to the wave fluctuations.

A curious quirk inherent to the *I Ching Eschaton* is the acceleration of resonance at the end. Like the proverbial snowball, the wave is picking up speed, *novelty* increasing exponentially as we near *Supernovelty*.

"This process of novelty is now moving so quickly that within our lifetimes it is going to accelerate essentially so such an intensity that we will be experiencing more novelty in a few weeks or days than we've previously experienced in the whole life of the cosmos. After the turn of the century, the acceleration of the unfolding of these resonances becomes more and more intense and eventually we reach the super-compression of modern times…

We are talking about the dense nesting of concrescent systems. And ultimately, in my own point of view, ***the emergence of a transcendental object at the end of time***. And the end of time is not far off."

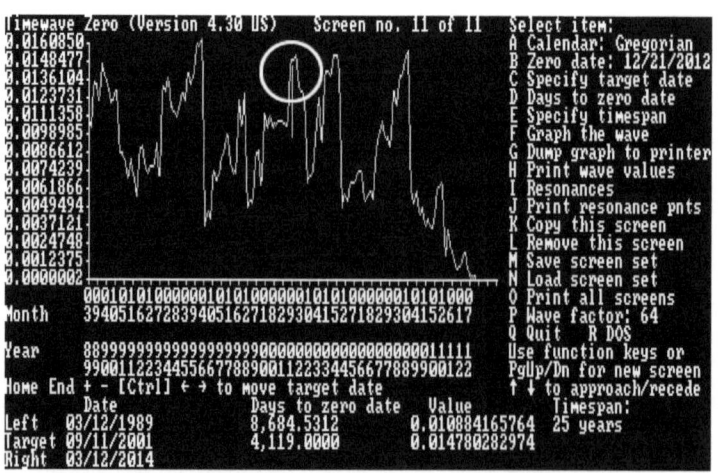

Fig. 6 McKenna's Timewave: Target Date 9/11/2001

Amazingly, the 1985 McKenna/Meyer *I Ching Eschaton* parallels our present experience as we approach the due date, the birth of the next Time Cycle. A new Golden Age (*Krita Yuga*) commences with the "emergence of a transcendental object"—the Tathagata ["Suchness Being", *See* **Book IV**, footnote 81] Christ closing this time frame while simultaneously initializing the next loop. What both McKenna and Arguelles are prematurely proposing is the Eternal Judgment—the last trumpet, the *Second Death* wherein we change "in the twinkling of an eye." As we'll see in **Book IV**, there is a necessary interim period of 1,000 years before Humanity—and Earth herself—can be fully purified by shifting to an untainted, supraliminal Kingdom of Heavens. Then, *for some of us*, time will truly terminate...

Chapter Four: The Celestial Hierarchy

> "A chain likewise extends from on high, as far as to the last of things,
> secondary natures always expressing the powers of the natures prior to them,
> progression indeed diminishing the similitude, but all things at the same time, and
> even such as most obscurely participate of existence, bearing a similitude to the first causes,
> and being co-passive with each other and with their original causes."
> ~*Theology of Plato*, Proclus VI.4

Thanks primarily to Charles Darwin, we observe a hierarchy in the physical realm where Man apparently succeeds as Nature's end-product, the crown of creation, the king of *natural selection*. Yet there's abundant literature, both Western and Eastern, that supports the existence of higher forms of life. Indian scriptures, in fact, preserve a vast nomenclature of deities—male and female with varying characteristics and attributes, known as demigods or Devas. Possessing human qualities and often warring among themselves, the Tibetans subordinate them to the realm of *Jealous Gods*.[11] On the other side of the world, two thousand years of Western theocratic authority whitewashed the entire pantheon, generically reducing them to common servants or messengers—called Angels.

Circa 500 AD, a learned Syrian monk intent upon infusing the Church with Greek wisdom—yet astutely aware of how a 1st century bishop would be more credible—wrote four pivotal treatises using the name *Dionysius the Areopagite*. Clear up to the 15th century, the Areopagitic writings are *highly esteemed*—especially by the Greek Orthodox—and used as a Divinely inspired authority by Thomas Aquinas and Bonaventure, among others, to explain and/or defend matters of faith.[12] Based upon the Neo-Platonic Enneads of Plotinus, augmented with the Judeo-Christian revelation of the "Father"—an *anthropomorphic* Singularity (later morphing into the rabbinic **Holy One, Blessed be He**) —Dionysius arranged a *Tree-of-Life* schematic of the hierarchy of celestial entities above Man...[13]

---

[11] The sophisticated Tibetan cosmology actually assigns *two* levels above the Human: the *Jealous God* and *God* realms. Yet both superhuman realms are still trapped within the *wheel of rebirth* and though nearly immortal, even the gods eventually succumb to death—followed by an ignominious rebirth on the human level. The only permanent release from never-ending suffering is through the extreme sacrificial vehicle of the Bodhisattva—Blessed Buddhahood or *Final* Nirvana, absolute extinguishment from ego-illusion.

[12] "By far the most important document in the case is the report given by Bishop Innocent of Maronia of the religious debate held at Constantinople in 533 between seven orthodox and seven Severian speakers (Hardouin, II, 1159 sq.). The former had as leader and spokesman, Hypatius, Bishop of Ephesus, who was thoroughly versed in the literature of the subject. On the second day, the 'Orientals' (Severians) alleged against the Council of Chalcedon, that it had by a novel and erroneous expression decreed two natures in Christ. Besides Cyril of Alexandria, Athanasius, Gregory Thaumaturgus, and Felix and Julius of Rome, *they also quoted Dionysius the Areopagite as an exponent of the doctrine of one nature."* ~The Catholic Encyclopedia, 1907-1912

[13] The Messiah introduced a unique nomenclature into the Jewish lexicon: *the Kingdom of Heavens*, referring to it over thirty times in Matthew's gospel. A kingdom, whether of Heaven, Hell or Earth, is defined as a natural *hierarchy* of designated authority—

Cont. →

"Theology has given to the Celestial Beings nine interpretative names, and among these our divine initiator distinguishes three threefold Orders. In the first rank of all he places those who, as we are told, dwell eternally in the constant presence of God, and cleave to Him, and above all others are immediately united to Him. And he says that the teachings of the holy Word testify that the most holy **Thrones** and many-eyed and many-winged ones, named in the Hebrew tongue **Cherubim** and **Seraphim**, are established immediately about God and nearest to Him above all others. Our venerable hierarch describes this threefold Order as a co-equal unity, and truly the most exalted of the Hierarchies, the most fully Godlike, and the most closely and immediately united to the First Light of the Godhead.

The name **Seraphim** clearly indicates their ceaseless and eternal revolution about Divine Principles, their heat and keenness, the exuberance of their intense, perpetual, tireless activity, and their elevative and energetic assimilation of those below, kindling them and firing them to their own heat, and wholly purifying them by a burning and all-consuming flame; and by the unhidden, unquenchable, changeless, radiant and enlightening power, dispelling and destroying the shadows of darkness.

The name **Cherubim** denotes their power of knowing and beholding God, their receptivity to the highest Gift of Light, their contemplation of the Beauty of the Godhead in Its First Manifestation, and that they are filled by participation in Divine Wisdom, and bounteously outpour to those below them from their own fount of wisdom.

The name of the most glorious and exalted **Thrones** denotes that which is exempt from and untainted by any base and earthly thing, and the supermundane ascent up the steep. For these have no part in that which is lowest, but dwell in fullest power, immovably and perfectly established in the Most High, and receive the Divine Immanence above all passion and matter, and manifest God, being attentively open to divine participations.

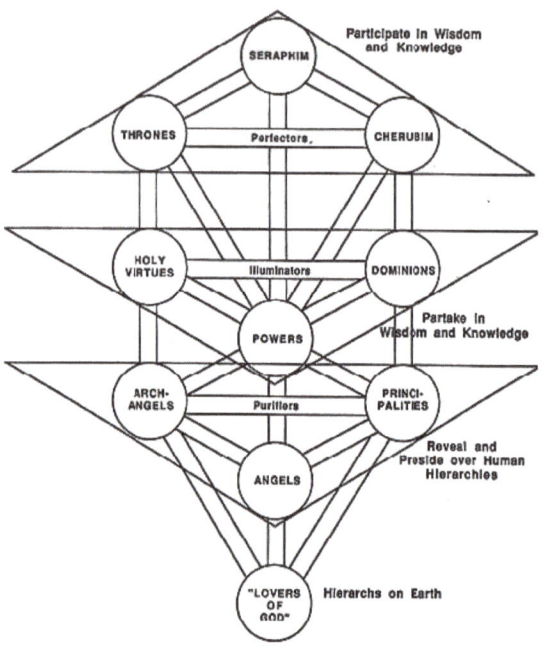

Fig. 7 The Celestial Intelligences

Revealing a thorough grasp of Hebrew oral tradition (*Kabbalah*), the Syrian hermit clearly understood how the sanctified upper triad exists *independently* from the lower triads, the latter receiving the light and warmth (Wisdom and Compassion) of the Sun (Son) as it radiates up and out (spills over).   [*See* Fig. 7—the first Triangle points Upward]

We must recognize that they are pure, not as having been cleansed from stains and defilements, nor as not admitting material images, but as far higher than all baseness, and surpassing all that is holy. As befits the

---

13 *Continued*

a strict chain of command, like that observed in the Marine Corps, Army or Navy. The Hermetic maxim, **"as above, so below"** is the intuitive realization that everything manifesting in the lower world, our world, necessarily originates in the upper Dimensions. All secular governments are natural, subconscious imitations of relegated power structures in higher Worlds. The educated, yet incredibly skeptical (ignorant) Biblical scholar Elaine Pagels tracked this natural process within the embryonic Church:

"Converts from Judaism tended to borrow the structure of the synagogues, where a leader presided over a group of elders, or in the Greek, *presbyteroi,* later translated as 'priests'. Other converts, originally Gentiles, developed a different administrative system adapted from large households, consisting of a group of servants, called in Greek *diakones*, which became the English term 'deacons', headed by an overseer, called in Greek *episcopos,* our word for 'bishop'. Within the next three centuries these bishops came to assume responsibility for specific areas, or dioceses, a pattern modeled on the organization of the Roman army."

After many more centuries of intense opposition from every heretical faction–both within and without—the Roman Catholic Church, with its priests, bishops, archbishops, cardinals and Pope, finally gelled into a precise, microcosmic government reflecting the "Heavenly" macrocosmic hierarchy described by pseudo-Dionysius.

"Whatever is in the earth has its parallel in the world above. There is not a single thing, however small, in the world that does not depend on something else that is higher, that was allocated to it from above, for when the thing below is aroused, that which is allocated to it from above is also aroused, for everything is interdependent."   ~Zohar I, 156a-156b

highest purity, they are established above the most Godlike Powers and eternally keep their own self-motive and self-same order through the Eternal Love of God, never weakening in power, abiding most purely in their own Godlike identity, ever unshaken and unchanging… the imitation of God is granted to them in a preeminent degree, and as far as their nature permits they share the divine and human virtues in primary power… they are wholly perfected through the highest and most perfect deification, possessing the highest knowledge that Angels can have of the works of God; being Hierarchs not through other holy beings, but from God Himself. Now we must pass on to the middle Order of the Celestial Intelligences, contemplating with supermundane sight, as far as we may, the **Dominions** and the truly majestic splendor of the Divine **Virtues** and **Powers**.

    The name given to the **Dominions** signifies, I think, a certain unbounded elevation to that which is above, freedom from all that is of the earth… An exemptness from degrading servility and from all that is low: for they are untouched by any inconsistency. They are true Lords, perpetually aspiring to true lordship, and the Source of lordship, and they providentially fashion themselves and those below them, as far as possible, into the likeness of true lordship.

    The name of the holy **Virtues** signifies a certain powerful and unshakable virility welling forth into all their Godlike energies; not being weak and feeble for any reception of the divine illuminations granted to it; mounting upwards in fullness of power to an assimilation with God; never falling away from the Divine Life through its own weakness, but ascending unwaveringly to the superessential Virtue which is the Source of virtue; perfectly turned towards the Source of virtue, and flowing forth providentially to those below it, abundantly filling them with virtue.

    The name of the holy **Powers**, coequal with the Divine Dominions and Virtues, signifies an orderly and unconfined order in the divine receptions, and the regulation of intellectual and supermundane power which never debases its authority by tyrannical force, but is irresistibly urged onward in due order to the Divine. It beneficently leads those below it, as far as possible, to the Supreme Power which is the Source of Power, which it manifests after the manner of Angels in the well-ordered ranks of its own authoritative power. This middle rank of the Celestial Intelligences, having these Godlike characteristics, is *purified, illuminated* and *perfected*[14] by the divine illuminations bestowed upon it in a secondary manner through the first hierarchical Order… There remains for us the reverent contemplation of that sacred Order which completes the Angelic Hierarchies, and is composed of the Divine **Principalities**, **Archangels** and **Angels**.

    The name of the Celestial **Principalities** signifies their Godlike princeliness and authoritativeness in an Order which is holy and most fitting to the princely Powers, and that they are wholly turned towards the Prince of Princes, and lead others in princely fashion, and that they are formed, as far as possible, in the likeness of the Source of Principality, and reveal Its superessential order by the good Order of the Princely Powers.

    The holy Order of **Archangels**, through its middle position, participates in the two extremes, being joined with the most holy Principalities and with the holy Angels. It is joined with the Princedoms because it is turned in a princely way to the superessential Principality and, as far as it can attain, moulds itself in His likeness, and it is seen to be the cause of the union of the Angels with its own orderly and invisible leadership. It is joined with the Angels because it belongs to the interpreting Order, receiving in its turn the illuminations from the First Powers, and beneficently announcing these revelations to the Angels; and by means of the Angels it shows them forth to us in the measure of the mystical receptivity of each one who is inspired by the divine illumination.

    For the **Angels,** as we have said, fill up and complete the lowest choir of all the Hierarchies of the Celestial Intelligences since they are the last of the Celestial Beings possessing the angelic nature. And they, indeed, are more properly named Angels by us than those of a higher rank because their choir is more directly in contact with manifested and mundane things."   *~The Celestial Hierarchy*

---

14 The theologian explains how the accumulation of Divine Knowledge is always a circular motion (an energy vortex or **chakra**) involving all three governors of any given triad. Beginning with an informed *purification*, followed by its integration or *illumination*, and finally embodiment of that principle, which is indeed *perfection*.

    "The participation in Divine Knowledge is **purification**, an **illumination** and **perfection**. For it purifies from ignorance by the knowledge of the perfect Mysteries granted in due measure; it illuminates through the Divine Knowledge Itself by which it purifies the mind which formerly did not behold that which is now shown to it by the higher illumination; and it perfects by the self-same light through the abiding knowledge of the most luminous initiations."   ~Dionysius

No doubt, future generations will think us medieval to have posited Mankind at the top of the evolutionary pyramid. Yet, even as we have been created "a little lower than the Angels", Humanity is still the most direct path to the superessential Godhead. As offspring of the Elohim, our destiny is to assume the throne of our Father. We are inherently superior to *all the Celestial Intelligences*, and must remember our dignified nature. Fallen and disgraced as we are, it is still wrong to humble ourselves before *any* of God's agents, including the planetary Forces.[15] The anointed priest King David and later, Jeshua Himself, struggled to transmit this truth to their people—

"I have said, 'Ye are gods; and all of you are children of the Most High…'" (Psalm 82.6)

"Jesus answered them, Is it not written in your law, 'I said, Ye are gods?'
If he called them gods, unto whom the word of God came, and the *scripture cannot be broken*;
Say ye of him, whom the Father hath sanctified, and sent into the world,
Thou blasphemest; because I said, I am the Son of God?" (John 10.34-36)

Ironically, our inherently miserable, accursed state—the suffering, purifying turmoil of Human existence—may prove to be a real blessing in disguise. Students of the late, great renaissance man Sri Chinmoy, asked the sage about other inhabited worlds and Man's relative position in the Cosmos…

"If a being from another world wants to achieve God-realization, self-discovery, it has to take a human body… Although we are full of suffering, limitation and ignorance here, this physical world offers the only possibility to realize the Supreme. Beings from every other place must come down into this world if they want to realize God. God is available only here."

Student: Is man unique in the whole universe?

"In the whole Universe, in all of God's creation, man is unique, because next to man is total perfection, complete unveiling consciousness. There are supernatural entities in the vital world with capacities higher that those of ordinary men. These beings are usually good, but they are all finished products. They do not make any progress because they do not care to enter into the world for the transformation of their nature."

Student: So they cannot become God, they cannot reach God?

"No, they cannot. In that world they are stuck at one point. They have to come into a human body and accept human life like us with its bondage, suffering, suppression and humiliation if they wish to evolve. There are some cosmic gods who try, out of jealousy, to prevent human beings from going beyond their [the gods'] own achievements and attaining self-realization, for human beings can have full realization, while the cosmic gods have only a limited consciousness…

We must not give much importance to the cosmic gods, or angels, as we call them in the West. No, we have to go beyond them. They are not human beings; their life process is different than ours."

One can see that when Man/Woman takes the next step in evolution, it's a corker…

From the good graces and merit accumulated through countless lives of interminable suffering, we instantaneously transcend all three celestial Triads, assuming dutiful occupation as a galactic Lord—a CEO, *whose existence the people are barely aware*. Before attempting to define the *Seat of God*, the sacrosanct position above all the Celestials, we should follow the process of God-realization through the *first* man's uphill struggle to embody Reality. In contradistinction to the past-life exploration of the AC in **Book I**, we now have the privilege of portraying the positive component to Power—three influential lives in the evolution of a Western Buddha, the Anointed One…

---

[15] "Even the gods envy those who are awakened and not forgetful, who are given to meditation, who are wise, and who delight in the repose of retirement from the world."   ~*The Dhammapada*, Chapter XIV: The Buddha (The Awakened)

Chapter Five: Anatomy of a Buddha

"The highest type of ruler is one whose existence the people are barely aware.
Next comes one whom they love and praise. Next comes one whom they fear.
Next comes one whom they despise and defy." ~*Tao Te Ching*

Along with the influx of innovative ideas that initiated the 20th century, came one Edgar Cayce—a Kentucky farmer turned photographer whose clairvoyant abilities revealed inexplicable medical knowledge. While sound asleep, his disembodied soul would examine a patient, often hundreds of miles away, and dictate an unorthodox prescription which inevitably cured the malady. However, after 1923 even Cayce was startled by the information coming through—so much so, he began to pray fervently that the source was a Holy one. The devout Sunday-school teacher, with no Eastern mystical or metaphysical edification and a lifetime of fundamental Bible-belt indoctrination, began to elaborate on the past lives of Jesus the Christ, planetary sojourns of the soul between incarnations and karmic, astrological influences coming to bear on his patients' lives!

Cayce's revelations about the entity Jeshua are unparalleled among the prolific clairvoyant or pseudo-psychic channeling of the last century. Around 1908, the damn of ignorance burst open with the appearance of Vivekananda, Sri Yogananda, Madame Blavatsky and the Theosophical Movement, Rudolf Steiner, Gurdjieff and Ouspensky—all high-caliber Initiates dedicated to disseminating the Dharma (Skt. Law, Duty) to the West.[16] Mr. Cayce also began his mission around this time and our debt to the seer magnifies when we realize that *he is the sole source for any occult information concerning the Christ and His Church*. We learned that Jeshua was once an ordinary man like us, with dues to pay within the reincarnational merry-go-round.[17] In fact, he was the first, the one that brought death into the world and started a chain of events that only He, as the *Messiah*, could someday resolve...

Question: "When did Jesus become aware that he would be the Savior of the world?"
Cayce: "When he fell in Eden." (Reading 2067-7)

The Crown of Creation was originally endowed with the same shining countenance as Yahweh...

"Then the YHVH God formed man of the dust of the ground,
and breathed into his nostrils the breath *(neshamah)* **of life;**
and man became a living soul *(nefesh hayyah)***."** (Genesis 2.7)

---

[16] 1908 was the year of a powerhouse planetary opposition between Uranus and Neptune. Oppositions between planets are always a culminating event—releasing the energy accumulated since that planetary pair's previous conjunction. Uranus and Neptune's previous conjunction in 1820 had initiated the Industrial Revolution, a profound change that affected the way men and women work and live. The high-frequency resonation building up to the opposition resulted in the 1906 San Francisco earthquake. Thereafter, certain men and women, feeling a call from on high—impregnated with a powerful spiritual influx—embarked on their holy crusades.

We experienced the beginning of a new Uranus/Neptune cycle with its triple conjunction in 1993. Once again, this unusual conjunction initiated a behavioral transition—the Information Revolution. The Internet, home delivery and automation have reversed the previous trend and people are returning to the home as a base of operations. If you can *truthfully* recall (like Robin Williams said of the 60's—if you remember them, you weren't there), this was a consciousness-raising year that begat an evolutionary impulse that won't be fully realized until the next Uranus/Neptune opposition in 2081 AD.

[17] When a client asked if he would gain perfection within his present lifetime, the Sleeping Prophet shot back with, "Why should you expect to do in one lifetime what it took the Master thirty lives to attain?" In another Reading, Cayce was asked to list the names of the previous incarnations of the Christ—"First, in the beginning, of course as Adam; Then as Enoch, Melchizedek in the perfection. Then in the earth as Joseph, Joshua, Jeshua (Jesus)." (5749-14)

"And when He gave him the *neshamah*, he rose to his feet, and was then like the lower and the upper worlds. His body was like the earth, and his soul was like the upper worlds in form, in honor and glory, in awe and fear." ~*Zohar Hadash*, Bereshit, 16a-16c

The very reflection, *similitude* of the Most High God that, while the protoplast possessed it, **"the fear and dread of you shall rest on every animal of the earth, and on every bird of the air, on everything that creeps on the ground, and on all the fish of the sea…"** (Genesis 9.2)

"In the first, all the creatures of the world trembled and quaked at the sight of man's sublime Upper Holy Image, but after he had committed sin, his image disappeared and was *changed into another similitude*, and a reverse condition, so that the child of man feared and trembled before other creatures." ~*Qabbalah*

What was once freely bestowed upon Man, must now be earned the hard way. Our tenuous connection to the High Self is achieved only after the most strenuous effort imaginable, under extreme conditions of stress, and then gone all too soon. The Judaic exile, Daniel, connected with his higher Soul, the *neshamah*, in a moment of mounting trepidation—facing down a pack of hungry lions. The grateful prophet didn't realize it was his own illuminated countenance that saved him…

"My God sent His angel, and he shut the lions' mouths, and they did not harm me." (Dan. 6.23)

The psychedelicized (self-aware) *adam* is consequently reduced in stature by acquiring yet *another* soul—a grosser similitude to rule over the animal soul, the *nefesh,* and choose between its lower instincts and that of the estranged higher (truest) Self, the numinous *neshamah*. This then is the Ego, the "Jiminy Cricket" middle-self called *ruah*. [*See* **Book I**, footnote 9]

"There are three levels that comprise the soul, and therefore the soul has three names, on the pattern of the mystery above: ***nefesh, ruah*** and ***neshamah***. The **nefesh** is the lowest stimulus. It is close to the body and nourishes it. The body depends upon it, and it depends upon the body. **Ruah** is the power of sustenance, which rules over the nefesh and is a higher level than the nefesh, sustaining it throughout as is fitting. **Neshamah** is the highest power of sustenance, and rules over all, a holy level, exalted above all."   ~Zohar I, 205b-206a

The exile endured his tortured existence—his disconnection from the holy *neshamah*, nearly completing the *Day* allotted him by Yahweh. Jewish midrash maintains the first man lived 930 years. Seven generations later, the prototype reincarnates as the legendary antediluvian patriarch, Enoch…

"I was born the seventh during the first week, during which time judgment and righteousness continued to endure." (1 Enoch 92.4)

According to the fifth chapter of the first Book of Moses, the great-grandfather of Noah lives a well-rounded 365 years before he is "translated". Enoch's upright life leads to a maturity that yields the recapture of his Spirit—he regains the *neshamah* and walks with the countenance of an Elohim! A mistake becomes a sin when it is repeated, and the *adam*, who never sinned again, made great strides within one incandescent incarnation…

"The supernal radiance of Adam's soul, which was taken away from him before its time as a direct consequence of his sin, found a new abode in Enoch, where it could perfect itself in this world. Once it had achieved its full perfection in mortal existence, it ascended and took up its position at the head of the angelic throngs. This means that Enoch in his own life embodied that supernal perfection for which man was destined from the very beginning of his creation."   ~*Wisdom of the Zohar*, Isaiah Tishby

Book II: Cyclicity

Unbeknownst to Enoch, *he* is the chosen one, the *Son of Man*[18], and since the Lord of Spirits needed a mouthpiece, a neutral party who was neither God nor Angel, to relay His harsh judgment to the wayward Watchers, the stunned scribe is snatched away, body and soul, to the 7th heaven of the God of gods, *Y'hovah* (Self-existent).[19] "...then he was no more, because God took him." (Genesis 5.24)

Besides it was a good excuse to keep number one son out of trouble by getting him acquainted with the family business— "Enoch was righteous, but the Holy One, blessed be He, foresaw that he would sin. He therefore took him before he could sin." ~Zohar I, 56b

After doing the Lord's dirty work, the venerable patriarch is returned to his extended family, *living on borrowed time* to draw up blueprints for his "Pillars" [*See* **Book IV**, p. 127] and write the first Scriptures based on the tablets that presage the major turning points of Mankind. The forbidden sorcery of reading and writing, taught by the disgraced Watcher *Pinemu*, had now become unavoidable. Enoch the scribe knew very well how the power of the pen could be used to twist the truth and plant the seeds of doubt—

"And now I know this mystery: For they (the sinners) shall alter the word of truth and many sinners will take it to heart; they will speak evil words and lie, and they will invent fictitious stories and write out my Scriptures on the basis of their own words." [20] (1 Enoch 104.10-11)

The Jesus Seminars, one amongst an onslaught of modern Biblical "debunkers", effectively destroyed the integrity of the Gospels through the judgment of its tribunal, composed of fifty-four Ph.D.'s and twelve Th.D.'s. Their rules of evidence peremptorily dismissed *a priori* all miracle stories and anything suspected of fulfilling OT prophecy. They deemed authentic a few pithy one-liners, principally from the Gnostic *Gospel of Thomas*, as the actual sayings of Jesus. These statements were highlighted in red ink, while pink, gray and finally, black inks prevailed as reliability decreased.

Still, the wise seer understood a primary principle—the fundamental Yang/Yin precepts that balance good and evil. Rare sacred scriptures of astonishing wisdom, first out of the East and later from the Western mystics, would counteract the poisonous ones, bringing light and sustenance to his children—

"Again know another mystery!: that the righteous and the wise shall be given books for joy, truth and great wisdom. So to them shall be given the books; and they shall believe them and be glad in them; and all the righteous ones who learn from them the ways of truth shall rejoice." ~Ibid.

---

18 "Who is this, and from whence is he going as the prototype of the Before-Time? And he answered me and said to me,
'This is the *Son of Man*, to whom belongs righteousness, and with whom righteousness dwells.
And he will open all the hidden storerooms; for *the Lord of Spirits has chosen him*, and
he is destined to be victorious before the Lord of Spirits in eternal uprightness.'" (1Enoch 46.3)

19 Summoned into the terrifying presence of Lord Yahweh Himself, humble Enoch learns he is to be liaison for the Fallen Angels...
"Do not fear, Enoch, righteous man, scribe of righteousness; come near to me and hear my voice. And tell the Watchers of heaven on whose behalf you have been sent to intercede: 'For what reason have you abandoned the high, holy and eternal heaven; and slept with women and defiled yourselves with the daughters of the people, taking wives, acting like children of the earth, and begetting giant sons?' ...Now the giants who are born from the union of the spirits and the flesh shall be called evil spirits upon the earth. Evil spirits have come out of their bodies. They will corrupt until the day of the great conclusion, until the great age is consummated, until everything is concluded upon the Watchers and the wicked ones. You were once in heaven but not all the mysteries of heaven are open to you, and you only know the rejected mysteries. Those ones you have broadcast to the women in the hardness of your hearts and by those mysteries the women and men multiply evil deeds upon the earth. Tell them, *Therefore you will have no peace!*" (1 Enoch 15-16)   We explore this transgression and its consequences in **Book IV**.

20 The well-intentioned but misguided Gnostic initiates of the first centuries, "schooled" in a hodgepodge of Babylonian magic and Judaic mysticism, did exactly that—they rewrote the Gospels, putting their own theological slant on the material. In the section on *The Trinity*, we examine the Gnostic "touch" with the pseudepigraphical *Apocalypse of Peter*.

His prime task of writing out the first complete set of Sacred Scripture accomplished, the weary prophet bids adieu to his offspring—like Moses at Mount Sinai, he gives his final admonition...

"You who have observed the law shall wait patiently in all the days until the time of those who work evil is completed, and the power of the wicked ones is ended. As for you, wait patiently until sin passes away, for the names of the sinners shall be blotted out from the Book of Life and the books of the holy ones; their seeds shall be destroyed forever and their spirits shall perish and die; they shall cry and lament in a place that is an invisible wilderness and burn in the fire—for there exists ground there (as upon the earth)." (1 Enoch 108.2)

The great Initiate is promoted to top dog position in the Sirian hierarchy. The *Sefer Zohar* posits a unique entity at the head of all the Celestial Intelligences—mighty Metatron. His archetypal function: acting Prime Minister for the King, a Riker (#1) to Star Trek's Picard, Sir Lancelot to King Arthur. Despite sitting on the throne of the YHVH as prince and sovereign over the ministering Powers, Metatron is commonly referred to as *na'ar* (Hbw. boy, or lad)—the kid. His most curious characteristic is how he grows old, only to become young again—constantly rejuvenating in tandem with earthly goodness.[21] Isaiah Tishby explains Metatron's vulnerability...

"The relationship between the souls of the righteous and Metatron is a reciprocal one, both in this and in the future world. Metatron's power and authority depend on the deeds of the righteous. This reciprocal relationship between the righteous and Metatron is delineated and explained in a more profound manner in connection with the ascent of Enoch. Both human and angelic perfection are combined in Metatron, and so he is most suited to act as an intermediary between man and God, and to nourish the souls with light from above. But this perfection is not constant and unchanging. It needs to undergo a perpetual renewal. Since his perfection originated in the human state, he needs the assistance of the righteous when the time comes for his rejuvenation."

This then is the secret of Metatron—he is the *translated* Enoch, the recompensed first-born of Yahweh.[22] In his new position, he is reinstated as a cosmic bridge between the celestial and the terrestrial; the *living mold of man*, the ectoplasmic protoplast formed prior to any creature...

"The first of God's creatures...First and foremost among all the hosts of heaven below, and he is the lesser Adam, which the Holy One, blessed be He, made in the celestial image, with no admixture." ~ha-Zohar

Enoch's servitude as Prince of the Presence[23] ensured righteous Mankind would never lose the human countenance, degenerating into the *sitra ahra*—the abominable aliens. [See **Book I**, footnote 16] A necessary sacrifice since as the *adam*, he had changed the entire Human condition.[24]

---

21 "...And the high priest brings it into the Holy of Holies, and [Binah] receives it and brings it to birth as at the beginning, and Metatron is rejuvenated like an eagle and becomes a boy once more." ~Zohar III, 217a-217b

22 Removing Enoch from earthly temptations accelerated his evolution. "In his eternal, spiritual essence, man is very near indeed to the divine realm, and his folly and contamination by sin are no more than manifestations of corruption and degeneration occasioned by his temporal, physical existence. The unique man, Enoch, who was able to achieve the ideal, supernal perfection that was indeed destined for the whole of mankind, but taken from them because of Adam's sin, purified himself of the material defects inherent in corporeal existence, and ascended to the highest levels of the angelic hierarchy. Enoch-Metatron symbolizes the culmination of the ascent for which man is destined to strive, and in this refined image perfect man is superior to the angels." ~Isaiah Tishby

23 **METATRON** "greatest of angels in Jewish myths and legends, variously identified as the Prince (or Angel) of the Presence, as Michael the archangel, or as Enoch after his ascent into heaven. He is likewise described as a celestial scribe recording the sins and merits of men, as a guardian of heavenly secrets, as God's mediator with men, as the 'lesser Yahweh,' as the archetype of man, and as one 'whose name is like that of his master.' The latter appellation is based on Hebrew numerology; i.e., when the consonants that comprise the names *Metatron* and *Shaddai* (Almighty) are analyzed according to preassigned numerical values, each name totals 314."
~Encyclopedia Britannica

24 "...as a result of the snake's deception, human existence was tarnished and this perfect state could no longer be sustained in human form. Therefore Enoch was accorded a special place in the highest reaches of the celestial world." ~Isaiah Tishby

Chapter Six: Joseph the Prophet

With the appearance of Abraham, "the plant of righteous judgment", a genetic course was set to produce the culminating incarnation that would eventually restore Humanity to its original Grace. Upon his victory over the Mesopotamian kings and rescue of his nephew Lot, Abram is greeted by the most enigmatic figure in the OT—Melchizedek (Hbw. *melek*, king; *sedeq*, righteous). Metatron manifests on the gross, earthly plane in full corporeality to establish a clandestine priesthood and initiate the progenitor of the Messianic line, the *friend of God*...

"He was made manifest in Melchizedek by desire alone, not knowing body, not knowing mind—save its own; brought into materialization as of itself; passing from materialization in the same manner." (Cayce 2072-4)

"He is without father or mother or genealogy, and has neither beginning of days nor end of life, but resembling the Son of God he continues a priest forever." (Hebrews 7.1-3)

Even before his enlightening encounter with the king of Salem, Abram was renowned as a great mystic and astrologer.[25] Yet nothing could prepare him for the greatest revelation of all time, to receive (Hbw. *kabbalah*) the keys of knowledge—literally the Divine power of Creation[26]—directly from Enoch/Metatron. The earliest, extant manuscripts of the famed "hidden scroll" bear the title, **"The letters of Abraham our Father, which is called *Sefir Yetzirah*."** Melchizedek taught the patriarch how to use the sacred alphabet of 22 Hebrew letters to create new living souls (*nefesh heyyah*)...

"And when Abraham our father, may he rest in peace, looked, saw, understood, probed, engraved and carved,
He was successful in creation, as it is written, **'And the souls that they had made in Haran.'** (Gen. 12.5)
Immediately there was revealed to him the Master of all, may His name be blessed forever,
He placed him in His bosom, and kissed him on his head, and He called him, 'Abraham my beloved.'"[27]
~Sefir Yetzirah 6.7

Having initiated Abraham into the Mysteries, the minister to the Most High God institutes the sacrament of bread and wine[28], anointing the elder as High Priest in the **Order of Melchizedek**—an exclusive men's club consisting of *messiahs*[29] (Hbw. anointed ones). The same underground lineage that Elijah will sustain through the surreptitious sect of the Essenes, until the Messiah of messiahs can be propagated: Jeshua.[30] The desert hermit monks of Qumran—the sons of Zadok—preserved a prodigious amount of eschatological literature, including the *Books of Enoch* and *Isaiah*. An atypical Dead Sea scroll fragment, **The Heavenly Prince Melchizedek**, echoes Enoch's 10th Week.

---

25 "Abraham had a great astrology in his heart, and all the kings of the east and west arose early at his door." (Bava Batra 16b) Yet even the Cosmic Forces are subject to the Prime Mover. "When God revealed himself to Abraham one of the first things that He taught him was not to be overdependent on astrological predictions." ~*Sefir Yetzirah*, Aryeh Kaplan [See **Book IV**, p. 146]
26 Talmudic legend speaks of an ancient Kabbalistic text, the *Book of Creation* used by medieval Rabbis to create an anthropoid—a *golem*. This living creature, which later inspired Mary Shelly, could not speak, the exact magical formulae distorted over the centuries. "Rava said: If the righteous wished, they could create a world, for it is written, 'Your iniquities have been a barrier between you and your God.' For Rava created a man and sent him to Rabbi Zeira. The Rabbi spoke to him but he did not answer. Then he said: 'You are [coming] from the pietists: Return to your dust.'" ~The Talmud
27 "Abraham was given the letter *he*, which changed his name from Abram to Abraham. This addition can be interpreted as the addition of the name of God as summarized by the letter *he*, it being the letter by which the earth was created." ~Gen. Rabbah
28 **"And King Melchizedek of Salem brought out bread and wine; he was priest of God Most High."** (Genesis 14.18)
29 King David was a *messiah*, descended from this holy line: **"The YHVH has sworn and will not change his mind:
'You are a priest forever according to the order of Melchizedek.'"** (Psalm 110.4)
30 "Your father Abraham was glad to see my day, and he saw it and rejoiced." (John 8.56)

"And the **Day of Atonement** is the end of the tenth Jubilee, when all the Sons of Light and the men of the lot of Melchizedek will be atoned for. And a statute concerns them to provide them with their rewards. For this is the moment of the Year of Grace for Melchizedek. And he will, by his strength, judge the holy ones of God, executing judgment as it is written concerning him in the Songs of David, who said, **ELOHIM has taken his place in the divine council; in the midst of the gods he holds judgment** (Psalms lxxxii, 1).

And he who brings good news, who proclaims salvation: it is concerning him that it is written… To comfort all who mourn, to grant to those who mourn in Zion (Isaiah lxi, 2-3). To comfort those who mourn: its interpretation, to *make them understand all the ages of time*… In truth… will turn away from Satan… by the judgments of God, as it is written concerning him, who says to Zion; your ELOHIM reigns. Zion is…, those who uphold the Covenant, who turn from walking in the way of the people. And your ELOHIM is Melchizedek, who will save them from the hand of Satan. As for that which He said, **Then you shall send abroad the loud trumpet in the seventh month** (Levi xxv, 9)"… ~11QMelch

When the postdiluvian generations had developed to the critical degree where the Twelve Tribes could manifest, Metatron/Melchizedek descends into the womb of Rachel—an eleventh son is born unto the prolific patriarch Jacob—the prophet Joseph.

After a vicarious motherhood through various servants and even fellow-wife, sister Leah, Rachel's patience is finally rewarded, first with Joseph (Hbw. *Jah will add*) and then baby Benjamin. Naturally, the offspring of a true soulmate relationship are esteemed above others, and Jacob, an old man with grown children, doted on his handsome new son… **"Now Israel loved Joseph more than all his children."** (Genesis 37.3) Jacob knew the fruit of his graceful wife's womb was noble born, so he made the seventeen-year-old a fine robe of long *passim*.[31]

One morning while feeding the flock, the boy witnesses his older brothers engaged in what he believes to be a violation of the law—Simeon and Levi, at their whim, cruelly hamstring an oxen and invite the brethren to a barbecue. Ancient Hebrew custom calls for strict guidelines when sacrificing an animal; unsanctified slaughtering of the beast was a felony offense, akin to murder. The shocked young shepherd runs home to tell the no-nonsense patriarch what he saw—little Joe rats on his half-brothers… **"and Joseph brought an evil report of them to their father."** (Gen. 37.2) If this wasn't enough to ignite sibling rivalry, a pair of precognizant dreams that clearly shows Joseph superior, not only to his brothers and sister but parents as well, lights the fuse!

When the naïve child eagerly describes how the Sun, Moon and eleven stars bow down to him, it is the braggart's undoing. The upstart is abducted by his bitter brethren—to avoid bloodshed, prudent Reuben suggests dumping him in a pit—and subsequently sold for twenty silver pieces (foreshadowing His thirty-piece betrayal by Judas) to the next passing caravan. The Ishmaelite traders arrive in downtown Egypt, selling their young slave to Potiphar, captain of the guard.[32]

Adapting to his fate like a fish to water, Joseph is soon running the captain's household. Things are going swimmingly until the handsome helper refuses to betray his master and service Potiphar's horny wife. Framed for his fidelity and thrown into a dungeon, the young seer correctly interprets the diverse dreams of his troubled cellmates, the chief baker and butler—telling the former he will be hanged, the latter, reinstated. Two years later, the prescient talents of the

---

[31] Incorrectly transliterated to the Greek Septuagint, and therefore mistranslated for two thousand years, the coat of *many colors* was actually a full-length robe with *long sleeves*… "The word *passim* means the coat's sleeves reached Joseph's wrists (*pas*). Long sleeves suggest that Joseph was to do no heavy work." ~*Sefer ha-Aggadah*

[32] Knowledge and Compassion being the *two wings of the bird of Enlightenment*, the innocent chosen people needed proper *initiation* into the esoteric realms—knowledge that only the *sitra ahra* (other side) could provide. A harsh Egyptian *purification* spawns the peerless Moses, the Babylonian *illumination* adds the proper seasoning and *voila!* the genetic *perfection* necessary to engender the two perfect adepts of Love and Wisdom: Mariah and Jeshua.

Hebrew slave come to the court's attention when Pharaoh, plagued by a pair of his own puzzling dreams, summons Joseph as a last recourse...

> **"In my dream I was standing on the banks of the Nile; and seven cows, fat and sleek, came up out of the Nile and fed in the reed grass. Then seven other cows came up after them, poor, very ugly, and thin. Never had I seen such ugly ones in all the land of Egypt. The thin and ugly cows ate up the first seven fat cows, but when they had eaten them no one would have known that they had done so, for they were still as ugly as before. Then I awoke..."**
> (Genesis 41.17-21)

When Pharaoh goes on to relate a second, similar dream with good and bad ears of corn, Joseph immediately senses the symbolism—and the double dream means it is fated, fixed by Elohim. Therefore, a wise ruler would gather up grain for storage during the next seven years—to use for the following famine—destined to last another seven years. This same wise king would undoubtedly appoint a trustworthy, capable young man to carry out this urgent task. The not-so-bright Pharaoh is tickled pink with the Hebrew soothsayer. He gives Joseph the royal signet ring, new duds and a personal escort around town with the chariot driver bellowing, "Bow the knee!"

Pharaoh's gifts include a new name, *Zaphenath-paneah*, the High Priest's daughter, Aseneth[33] and absolute authority over the Egyptian Empire. The famine arrives right on schedule and, as fate would have it, so do Jacob's ten sons. Anxious to see his baby brother, the only other son of his noble mother Rachel, Joseph engineers an innovative vengeance worthy of William Shakespeare.

Accusing the brothers of spying on the land, the new viceroy holds Simeon hostage[34] until the others can return with the youngest—to prove their good intent. The gruff Simeon is not sorely missed, but the family gets hungry enough to require a return trip—with Benjamin in tow—to the only food source in the known world, Egypt. Whereupon the governor, emotionally wrought upon meeting his mother's son, nevertheless stays in character, intensifying the head games.[35] Hiding his silver chalice in Benjamin's sack, Joseph loads their donkeys with grain and bids the brothers'

---

[33] The beloved pseudepigraphical tale, *Joseph and Aseneth*, is found extant in sixteen Greek manuscripts at the most hallowed locales, including St. Catherine's Monastery at Mount Sinai, the Vatican Library, Monastery of Konstamonitou at Mount Athos, and the Bodleian Library at Oxford. Believed to be a second century BC *midrash*, the romance fills in some important gaps and explains Joseph's marriage to an Egyptian woman— "Aseneth is a beautiful virgin of eighteen years and the daughter of Pentephres, priest of Heliopolis and Pharaoh's chief counselor. Many princes including Pharaoh's firstborn son, ask for her hand in marriage. She despises them all and prefers to live in her ornate penthouse above Pentephres' palace, where she worships countless idols. One day Joseph, touring Egypt to collect corn, announces his visit to her father. Pentephres tells Aseneth he is going to give her to Joseph in marriage. She refuses flatly, only to fall in love with Joseph when she sees him entering her father's house in royal attire...

"Did I not speak saying that Joseph is coming, the shepherd's son from the land of Canaan? And now, behold, the sun from heaven has come to us on its chariot and entered our house today, and shines in it like a light upon the earth. But I, foolish and daring, have despised him and spoken wicked words about him, and did not know that Joseph is a son of God. For who among men on earth will generate such beauty, and what womb of a woman will give birth to such light?" (Joseph and Aseneth 6.2)

Now it is her time to be repudiated. A Jew who worships God and lives on the bread of life will not kiss a heathen woman who eats food offered to idols. Still Joseph is charitable enough to say a prayer for her conversion, then boards his chariot in order to gather more corn, promising to be back a week later. Utterly shaken, Aseneth destroys her idols, engages in a week of fasting and crying, and repents for both her conceit and idolatry. On the morning of the eighth day, the chief of God's angels comes to see her, declares her reborn, tells her that she is to be a mother city for all who would repent like her, feeds her a piece of honeycomb, which he says is the bread of life, and promises her that Joseph will come to marry her. He does; and the wedding ensues, performed and presided over by Pharaoh himself." ~Intro to the new translation by C. Burchard, *The Old Testament Pseudepigrapha, Volume 2*

[34] "...it was Simeon who had pushed him into the pit; and also Joseph wished to separate him from Levi, lest the two devise a plot against him." ~*Sefer ha-Aggadah*

[35] **"And Joseph saw his brethren, and he knew them, but made himself strange unto them."** (Genesis 42.7)
"He acted like a non-Jew, in that seemingly resorting to divination he took his goblet, tapped it, and said to them, 'I see in the goblet that you are spies...'" ~*Sefer ha-Aggadah*

good journey; then arranges to have them busted, the one with the silver cup imprisoned. With Judah sweating bullets—he had pledged his life to Israel for Benjamin's safety—and the others prostrating flat on the ground before him, Zaphenath-paneah (*revealer of secrets*) lays it on thick...

> "What deed is this that you have done?
> Do you not know that one such as I can practice divination?"   (Genesis 44.15)

Letting his backstabbing siblings squirm at the thought of losing the apple of Jacob's eye, Joseph drops the pretense, breaking down in tears. The once-proud shepherd with the aristocratic robe knew he had important lessons in humility to undergo—and the higher purposes of the Father had to be fulfilled—so genial Joseph forgives unconditionally the dirty, low-down betrayal of his own brethren (as he will do again with James and Jude)...

> "Now therefore be not grieved, nor angry with yourselves, that ye sold me hither: for God did send me before you to preserve life. For these two years hath the famine been in the land: and yet there are five years, in the which there shall neither be earing nor harvest.
>
> And God sent me before you to preserve you a posterity in the earth, and to save your lives by a great deliverance. So now it was not you that sent me hither, but God: and he hath made me a father to Pharaoh, and lord of all his house, and a ruler throughout all the land of Egypt."
> (Genesis 45.5-8)

The remnant (posterity) that Joseph preserves for the future twelve tribes of Israel turns out to be Goshen, the most magnificent, and ultimately, fertile land in the Empire. As the famine wears on, Joseph buys up all the livestock and finally the fields themselves—the territory itself sold for corn. Soon the entire Egyptian citizenry become indentured servants to Pharaoh, while seventy Israelites with their wives and daughters discreetly settle into new, rent-free digs.

After an irregular blessing of Joseph's two sons—the younger Ephraim receiving the right hand and Manasseh the left—the ailing, one hundred forty-seven year old patriarch Jacob Israel, "the one who strives with God" sanctifies the Twelve, revealing their destinies in the Promised Land...

Genesis 49

- **Reuben**— "You are my first born, my might and the beginning of my strength, the excellency of dignity and the excellency of power" yet as "unstable as water." Reuben forfeits his birthright by sleeping with his father's concubine, Bilhah... "You shall not excel."

- **Simeon and Levi**— "in their anger they killed men" when Shechem dishonors their sister Dinah, the bloodthirsty pair kill not only Shechem but also every male in the entire city, "Cursed be their anger, for it is fierce, and their wrath, for it is cruel! I will divide them in Jacob" when Joshua allocates various cities from each tribe for Levi's priestly inheritance, "and scatter them in Israel." Simeon's tribe inherits a section of Judah's vast conquests; they are swallowed up within the immensity of the lion's territory.

- **Judah**— "thy brethren shall praise thee... a lion's whelp." Through courage and strength, Judah's tribe captures the lion's share of the Promised Land. "The scepter shall not depart from Judah... until *Shiloh* (Hbw. He who is to be sent) comes; And to Him shall be the obedience of the people." Levi loses the priestly line. The first *Torah* (Hbw. Law) handed down to Jacob, the *books of Enoch*, promises the God-king, the *Son of Man*.

- **Zebulun**— "shall settle at the seashore; a haven for ships."
- **Issachar**— "is a strong donkey, resting between the sheepfolds… bows his shoulder to the burden." Settling among the Canaanites, they will keep the peace by working the fields for the landowner.
- **Dan**— "shall judge his people as one of the tribes of Israel." Though born of the concubine, his people will have their own Tribe. "Dan shall be a snake by the roadside", crafty and cunning are the Danites. "A viper along the path, that bites the horse's heels so that its rider falls backward." Daniel's destiny is to be a *bodhisattva*—wise as a serpent, postponing Nirvana until the Elect are guaranteed salvation. Dan's tribe will be rearguard, last to break camp… "**The total enrollment of the camp of Dan is 157,600. They shall set out last by companies.**" (Numbers 2.31)
- **Gad**— "shall be raided by raiders, but he shall raid at their heels."
- **Asher**— "food shall be rich, and he shall provide royal delicacies."
- **Naphtali**— "is a doe let loose that gives beautiful words."
- **Joseph**— "is a fruitful bough, a fruitful bough by a spring; his branches run *over the wall*." As the Messiah, He will restore the severed connection to the *neshamah*, breaking down the barrier, the wall, between man and his God. "**The archers fiercely attacked him; they shot at him and pressed him hard. Yet his bow remained taut, and his arms were made strong by the hands of the Mighty One of Jacob, by the name of the Shepherd, the Rock of Israel.**" YHVH tested and then empowered Joseph, the true chief and unshakeable foundation of the Tribes. "**The blessings of your father are stronger than the blessings of the eternal mountains, of my progenitors to the boundaries of the everlasting hills; may they be on the head of Joseph, on the crown of him who was set apart from his brothers.**" The Christ conquers the pull of the ephemeral world.
- **Benjamin**— "is a ravenous wolf, in the morning devouring the prey, and at evening dividing the spoil." The Benjaminites become a rowdy bunch of troublemakers, "a perverse lot."

The forty-day mummification process complete, Joe and the Israelites, with a full entourage of Egyptian high priests and charioteers, carry the great Israel to Abraham's cave in Canaan. With the patriarch dead and buried, the brothers fear Joseph will take revenge for their transgressions. They never did understand this strange son of Rachel; and now, in his maturity, Joey's compassion was beyond the ken of his kin…

> "**Fear not: for am I in the place of God? But as for you, ye thought evil against me; but God meant it unto good, to bring to pass, as it is this day, to save much people alive. Now therefore fear ye not: I will nourish you, and your little ones. And he comforted them and spake kindly unto them.**" (Genesis 50.19-21)

Chapter Seven: Joshua and Josiah

With the Chosen People temporarily transplanted to more fertile ground, the Rock of Israel pledges their deliverance to new lands and at the ripe old age of one hundred ten years, returns triumphantly to the Father. The Israelites, completing their necessary incubation period in the land of idolatry, picked up some bad habits in the process—covering their bases by worshipping the Dark Lord Ba'al, as well as the YHVH Elohim. Believing their deliverer Moses dead upon the mountain, the Tribes resort to Devil worship at the very moment of their final purification. [*See* **Book IV**, footnote 6]

> "**And when Aaron saw it, he built an altar before it; and Aaron made proclamation, and said, Tomorrow is a feast to the YHVH.**" (Exodus 32.5)

They mimicked the Egyptian ritual of invoking both Dark and Light Lords, together.[36] Today they would *get down* and pay homage to Ba'al; tomorrow they'd repent and take care of Yahweh. A nice idea, except the wrath of the YHVH was "waxing hot", and if not for Moses, there wouldn't have been a tomorrow. He reminds the Lord how, after showing His hand by transcending several laws of nature to deliver the People, the Egyptians will claim it was all just a cat and mouse game—a setup, so He could wipe them out at Sinai.

The Lord of our ancestors was a terrible Elohim[37], capable of horrendous acts of vengeance and it is only the rational reprimand of a daring old man that prevents Yahweh from once again (the Flood), losing His cool…

> **"Turn from thy fierce wrath, and repent of this evil against thy people…**
> **And the YHVH repented of the evil which he thought to do unto his people."**
> (Exodus 32.12-14)

The only other man not guilty of participation in Bull/Ba'al worship is Joshua, the magi Moses' young apprentice. Again, the *Son of Man* reincarnates at a pivotal moment—to shepherd the weary Israelites into the new lands. Here Adam/Enoch/Joseph's leadership skills and military prowess (ruthlessness) can be honed and tested. After many learned years at the feet of his mentor, Joshua spends all his time, one-on-one, with his strict but just Father…

> **"So the YHVH spoke to Moses face to face, as a man speaks to his friend.**
> **And he would return to the camp, but his servant Joshua the son of Nun,**
> **a young man, did not depart from the tabernacle."** (Exodus 33.11)

Crossing the miraculously damned Jordan and circling Jericho with the Ark of the Presence, the *exalted one of YHVH* crumbles the wall and wipes out every living creature within—man, woman, child, oxen and sheep. Even the livestock are too tainted to take. However, pockets of postdiluvian descendents of the degenerate *Nephilim* (*i.e.* the *Rephaim* and *Anakim*) remained among the corrupt Canaanites in the land of milk and honey—the abominations a sore reminder of the disobedience and cosmic imbalance (DNA desequencing) inculcated by the lustful Lords. [*See* **Book IV**, p. 134] In a scene reminiscent of *The Godfather*, Yahweh settles all His debts with Ba'al and wipes out the Dark Lord's entire population of worshippers. Joshua and the Tribes are unstoppable. Backed by a mandate from

---

36 The same idea was developing within the Mayan culture, where a balance was maintained by appeasing both Powers, side-by-side.

"The Classic-period is marked with planned cities that had definite astronomical orientations. One of the greatest cities was called Teotihuacan. The city was highly urbanized with a population of two hundred thousand. The prominent feature was the Pyramid of the Sun and the Pyramid of the Moon. During the Post-Classic period, the pyramidal base would have in some cases two temples situated on top. In addition, there were two twin stairways leading to the temples. This style of pyramid would be adapted by the Aztecs and by some of the later Mayan cities." ~*Mesoamerican Sites and World-Views*

37 Six Elohim begotten of the **Self-existent** (YHVH) were *polarized* manifestations: three Light and three Dark Lords. Theoretically, the original, elemental Elohim, the "Manu" YHVH was both Positive *and* Negative—an absolute Power of Good *and* Evil, a Holy terror— **"I form the light, and create darkness: I make peace, and create evil: I the YHVH do all these things."** (Isaiah 45.7)

The Laws of Manu (ca. 500 BC), which codified the caste system, remains the only ancient source extant containing factual evidence of the legendary, Self-begotten Creators of the Universes, the *Seven Elohim*—

"Listen! There are six other Manus in the dynasty of that Manu who was born of the **Self-existent**; they have great souls and great energy and each emitted his own progeny. They are the sons of '**Self-luminous**', '**Uppermost**', '**Dark**', '**Wealthy**', '**Gazing**', and the radiant son of '**the Shining Sun**'. These seven Manus, beginning with the one born of the **Self-existent**, abound in brilliant energy; each one, in his own Epoch, created and pervaded this whole universe, moving and unmoving." (Manu 1.61)

"These Elohim, these Spirits of Light, were seven in number. Six of them united their existence with the actual cosmic sun, and one, known in the Old Testament as Yahweh, separated from them and remained at first united with the earth. He guided and directed the earthly evolution from within, while the others worked upon it from without. That was the position for a time." ~Steiner

the YHVH, a storm of deadly hailstones delivers the Amorites to the Israelites, whereupon Joshua commands the Sun to stop in midheaven[38]—a frenzied finish for the allied forces of the valley Kings.

> **"Then Joshua spoke to the YHVH in the day when the YHVH delivered up the Amorites before the children of Israel, and he said in the sight of Israel: *'Sun, stand still over Gibeon; and Moon, in the Valley of Aijalon.'* And the sun stood still, and the moon stopped, until the people had revenge upon their enemies... So the sun stood still in the midst of heaven, and did not hasten to go down for about a whole day."** (Joshua 10.12-13)

Joseph's dream of commanding the stars becomes a literal reality as Joshua manipulates the fixed laws of nature—a monumental feat eclipsing any previous manifestation, including those of Moses. Yet the greatest miracle of all, Joshua points out in his old age, is how the YHVH delivered His chosen people everything He promised, and more. Just like the Lawgiver before him, Jehoshua (Hbw. *Jah is salvation*) warns his people that the salvation of *Elohim* can turn to destruction if they revert to their old Egyptian habits. The people tell their beloved Joshua that they'll *never* forsake the YHVH to serve other gods. They will never forget His personal intercession; the magnanimous Tribes will always serve the YHVH *as well as* the other Powers!

> **"Ye cannot serve the YHVH: for he is an holy God; he is a jealous God; he will not forgive your transgressions or your sins. If you forsake the YHVH and serve foreign gods, then *he will turn and do you harm, and consume you, after having done you good.* And the people said to Joshua, 'No, we will serve the YHVH!' Then Joshua said to the people, 'You are witnesses against yourselves that you have chosen the YHVH, to serve him.'"** (Joshua 24.19-22)

The lands divvied up and the holy Covenant, promise to serve the One God, revitalized—the good Shepherd goes *the way of all the earth* again at the same ripe old age of one hundred ten. For about 200 years, the People consolidate their power through a tribal confederacy ruled over by Divinely chosen Judges (Hbw. *Elohim*), spiritual/temporal leaders like Deborah, Gideon and Samson. In a psychological setback, the technologically superior Philistines, with state-of-the-art weapons of unbreakable ore, slaughter thousands of Israelites and capture the Ark of the Covenant. When the high priests install it next to their Fish-Lord, Dagon (pronounced: *doggone*), the merman statue falls flat on its face, hands and head severed. The Philistines, breaking out with hemorrhoids and tumors, decide to return the pain-in-the-ass God back to its rightful owners.

Feeling vulnerable and knowing there is strength in numbers, the Israelites demand Samuel, the last of the Judges, appoint a king who will unite their fractured forces. The first King of Israel soon acquires the secret of the Philistine weaponry—iron! However, after failing to wipe out all the Amalekites (Esau's degenerate line)—King Agag and livestock are spared—Saul falls into disgrace

---

[38] "Not many years ago, unpublicized, scientists at the Greenbelt, Maryland Government installation were checking the position of the Sun, Moon and planets out in space, where they would be 1,000 years from today. Such knowledge is necessary so they do not send aloft a satellite and have it bump into something unexpectedly. By means of a computer, they ran the information back and forth over the centuries when it suddenly came to a halt, flashing a red light, a signal that all was not well in their calculations. After much checking they found there was a day missing in space in elapsed time, and there was no immediate answer.

One man in the group got out a Bible and found a statement that appeared ridiculous for anyone who had common sense. It was *Joshua* 10, verses 12 to 14, relating how the Sun stood still. This, the space explorers felt was the missing day, however, it was not close enough. The day missing in Joshua's time was 23 hours and 20 minutes, not a whole day. After rereading the Bible, it was noted the claim was 'about a day'. Next, someone came up with *II Kings*, 20, verses 8 to 10 and read where the Lord brought the shadow backwards ten degrees. Ten degrees is exactly 40 minutes. Twenty three hours and 20 minutes in *Joshua*, plus 40 minutes in *II Kings* makes the missing 24 hours." ~*The Power of the Fixed Stars*, Joseph Rigor

with the merciless YHVH, the latter now regretting making the former king. Samuel surreptitiously supplants Saul by anointing Jesse's son—the musician David—as the *chosen one*, the new priest-king of Israel. When David's hands get too bloody to build the sacred Temple, the honor succeeds to his celebrated son, Solomon—the third and last king to rule the undivided monarchy.

Elevating the Kingdom of the one God to its highest height—implementing the logistically rich seaport of Palestine, consolidating the overland trading routes by marrying the daughters of kings (Solomon's harem boasted 700 wives and 300 concubines, not to mention the Queen of Sheba[39]) and building the crown jewel of the Empire, the glorious Temple upon Mount Moriah—breaks the backs of the overworked Israelites. Nevertheless, the ambitious king had made the one mistake that was *unforgivable*—to placate his pagan princesses and keep them from nagging him to death, the elderly monarch orders a temple built to Moloch[40] (Hbw. King), just outside the city's walls. For David's sake, the YHVH waits until Solomon's death before karmic consequences are considered.

The year 922 BC becomes a major historical turning point when the rabble-rouser Jeroboam encourages an alliance of ten northern Tribes to rebel against the late King Solomon's forced labor policy. Upon secession from the house of David, the neophyte kingdom of Israel, under Jeroboam I, sow the seeds of their destruction by setting up golden calves in competing temples at Beth-El and Dan—ostensibly to wean the People from their habit of worship at the only authorized Temple in Jerusalem. As wicked King Jeroboam lights the incensers for the unholy inauguration of Beth-El's Ba'al shrine, *a man of God* audaciously disrupts the offensive ceremony with an ominous prophecy…

"And he cried against the altar in the word of the YHVH, and said, O altar, altar, thus saith the YHVH: Behold, a child shall be born unto the house of David, *Josiah by name*; and upon thee shall he offer the priests of the high places that burn incense upon thee, *and men's bones shall be burnt upon thee*."
(1 Kings 13.2)

Two hundred years later in 722 BC, the Assyrian Empire assimilates the apostate kingdom of Israel. For centuries of idolatry, culminating with King Ahab's marriage to the notorious Jezebel—her priestly personnel relocated for worship in the new temples of Ba'al and Asherah[41], prompting Elijah's battle of sorcerers on Mt. Carmel—the northern kingdom reaps exactly what it had sown.

---

[39] "Upon her arrival in Jerusalem, she was welcomed into the palace by Solomon, who overwhelmed her with his hospitality and enlightened her with his wisdom. Solomon persuaded her to turn away from the worship of the sun and Makeda became a follower of the one true God… On her last night in the palace, there was a farewell banquet of unprecedented splendor, after which Solomon requested to lie with her. She declined, entreating that he swear not to take her by force. He complied, on the stipulation that she take nothing more from him on that night. She agreed, and so Solomon satisfied himself with her slave. But during the night, she arose to get a drink of water from the cistern in the sleeping chamber, and Solomon, who had been feigning sleep in order to observe her, insisted she had broken her oath by taking such a precious substance in so dry a land. Thus, she had no choice but to submit to his lust. The following morning, Solomon gave her a ring upon which was engraved the seal of the Lion of Judah, instructing her to give it to her firstborn male child, and then to send the boy to him for his education when he came of age. During the long journey back to Ethiopia, Makeda gave birth to a boy she named *Ebna Hakim*, meaning *son of the wise man*."   ~*Catch a Fire*, Timothy White

[40] Yet another alias for Ba'al. The horrific, yet apparently effective custom of the time was sacrificing children upon Moloch's altar, forcing them *to pass through the fire*. "Later kings Ahaz (2 Kings 16:3) and Manasseh (2 Kings 21:6), having been influenced by the Assyrians, worshipped Moloch at the hilled site of Topheth, outside the walls of Jerusalem. This site flourished under Manasseh's son King Amon but was destroyed during the reign of Josiah, the reformer." ~Encyclopedia Britannica
**"And he defiled Topheth, which is in the valley of the sons of Hinnom,
that no one might burn his son or his daughter as an offering to Moloch."**   (2 Kings 23:10)

[41] Literally *"grove"*—a double-entendre indicating the material the "sacred poles" were made from and the groovy goddess herself. All the hilltop temples to Ba'al had these crude phallic symbols (poles) planted nearby. A 1975 excavation in Kuntillet Ajrud unveiled Asherah as the original wife of YHVH, with earthenware inscriptions referring to *Yahweh and his Asherah*. Upon her abrupt exit following the first Creation debacle [*See* **Book III**, p. 80], Asherah aligns with Ba'al and assumes the very archetype of sensual desire. Henceforth known as *Astarte/Ashtoreth* to the Hebrews in Canaan, counterpart to the Babylonian *Inanna/Ishtar*—whereas in Egypt she was *Isis*, the radiant Queen of Heaven. Her pagan deification no doubt a sensitive issue with the YHVH. **"Thou shalt not plant thee a grove** (*asherah*) **of any trees near unto the altar of the YHVH thy Elohim, which… the YHVH thy Elohim hateth."**   (Deuteronomy 16.21-22)

The downsized remnant of the Twelve Tribes, the kingdom of Judah, remains under Assyrian suzerainty, ruled over by good King Hezekiah. The thirteenth successor of David initiates a religious reform that destroys the high places of idolatry and restores Temple worship to its one sanctified location—Jerusalem. When an insurrection mounts against the Assyrian oppressors, Hezekiah prepares for siege by ordering a crawlway carved out—the *Siloam tunnel*—allowing water from the Gihon Spring to flow inside the walled city of Jerusalem. The rebellion, however, is squashed and Assyrian emperor Sennacherib brings the kingdom of Judah to its knees, capturing and looting most of its cities. All along the watchtower, as the great capital's inhabitants are about to be psyched out from the taunts and threats, prophet Isaiah reassures the king that Yahweh has heard his prayer—

Fig. 8   Jerusalem and her Watchtowers under siege

> "By the way that he came, by the same he shall return; he shall not come into this city, says the YHVH. For I will defend this city to save it, for my own sake and for the sake of my servant David."
> (2 Kings 19.33)

Divine intercession saves the City as 85,000 Assyrians are found slaughtered in their sleep. When the cocky king conducts a foreign envoy through his vast treasure house, Isaiah predicts the fated fall of Jerusalem and the Babylonian captivity—Hezekiah nonplussed since it won't happen within his lifetime. Upon Manasseh's succession to the throne, the "high places" for Ba'al are rebuilt, negating the religious reform instituted by his father. The new king and his son's evil ways eventually eclipse even the Philistines', the land's original idolaters—following his dad's decadent lead, Amon burns the sacred scrolls (Torah) and wallows in lust and incest.

At this nadir in Jewish history—Torah forgotten and apostasy run rampant—the *Son of Man* reincarnates to reintroduce the upright path to his wayward people. Three hundred years earlier, when Israel had just begun its downward spiral into Devil worship, King Josiah was predicted, by name, as the Davidic avenger burning the bones of the wicked priests on the altar. As the righteous 18 year-old monarch supervises a repair job on the long neglected Temple, high priest Hilkiah finds something truly precious amidst the dust and debris—the book of the Law (Hbw. *Torah*). Reading the long-lost treasure, especially the baleful book of *Deuteronomy*, the anguished young king rends his clothes—the eye-opening Deuteronomy's 613 regulations showed exactly how far the *Chosen People* had strayed from the Covenant, and what the exacting penalty would be!

Josiah gathers all the people of the kingdom, elders to commoners, and *reads in their ears* the Deuteronomistic record—of one accord, Israel swears anew to abide by the uncompromising laws of their ancestors. The king systematically destroys all the *high places* that had mushroomed throughout the land, like an out-of-control cancer. When he reaches Bethel, the original temple that apostatized the kingdom, Josiah furiously trashes the hilltop (a precursor to his Temple outburst as Jeshua), digging up the bones of the wicked and burning them on the altar—both defiling it and fulfilling the 300 year-old prophecy. Manasseh's pollution, however, had penetrated to the marrow; nobody could undo the generational damage that would reassert itself upon the good king's death.

Realizing the situation hopeless, Josiah settles into fulfilling the main function of his timely incarnation—recording his People's post-Mosaic history in a chronological sextette.[42] The sacred Scriptures properly redacted, King Josiah rides out to mount Megiddo—the same strategic plateau where WWIII (*Armageddon*) is set to erupt—for an unwarranted confrontation with Pharaoh Neco. Mixing it up with the Egyptians costs the king his life when **Josiah the Reformer**, dressed down in a soldier's uniform, takes an arrow meant for the grunts. Back in Jerusalem, songs are sung and legends begun while the mountain of Megiddo is forever accursed…

> **"Before him there was no king like him, who turned to the YHVH with all his heart,
> with all his soul, and with all his might, according to all the law of Moses;
> nor did any like him arise after him."** (2 Kings 23.25)

These are but a few of the more significant lives of *Shiloh*, the Messiah. There are many others such as Akhenaton, instigator of monotheism in ancient Egypt, and Elias, apprentice to the magus Elijah—as a matter of fact there are so many good works accomplished by the first Man…

> **"I suppose that the world itself could not contain the books that could be written."** (John 21.25)

Entropy ensues as the weak-willed sons of Josiah attempt to rule the kingdom. Once again, the hilltop temples are reinstated and the time is ripe for Isaiah's devastating prophecy. In 597 BC, King Nebuchadnezzar destroys the House of the Holy, pillaging the bronze serpentine supports and sanctified altar vessels of silver and gold. The Chaldean army razes the whole city, tearing down the massive wall and herding the Chosen People into the modern metropolis of Babylon. Seventy years later, the greatest Empire the world had ever witnessed adds fabled Babylonia to its impressive list of conquests. As a Zoroastrian, the pious king of Persia subscribed to a dualistic cosmology wherein a Good God is in constant conflict with an Evil One—the former's decisive victory ultimately assured. Cyrus the Great obeys Yahweh, the Good God that put him on top of the world: the people released and the holy Temple rebuilt, all the sacred silver and gold vessels returned.

Under Ezra the reformer, centralization of worship is restored with the rededication of the Temple. However, without the *Holy Presence*—Ark of the Covenant—faith deteriorates and worship

---

42 Since the 19th century, theologians have concluded that the six post-Deuteronomistic books are the products of a single author, displaying a recognizable phraseology and structure. Present-day Biblical scholar Richard Friedman explains their findings…

"The Deuteronomistic historian, in the days of King Josiah, assembled his history out of the texts available to him. The beginning of his history was the book of *Deuteronomy*, and the conclusion was the story of Josiah. He took texts that told the story of his people's arrival in the land—the stories of Joshua, Jericho, and the conquest—and he added a few lines at the beginning and at the end to set the story in a certain light. This became the *book of Joshua*. He did the same with the next set of texts, which told the story of the people's early years in the land: the stories of Deborah, Gideon and Samson. This became the *book of Judges*. Next he placed the stories of Samuel at Shiloh: the stories of Saul and of David, the first kings. This became the *book of 1 Samuel*. After that he set the Court History of David. That became the *book of 2 Samuel*. Then he took several texts that told the stories of the kings who came after David, and he assembled one continuous history out of them that went down to the time of his own king: Josiah. And that became the *books of 1 and 2 Kings*… He was therefore not just recording annals. He was fashioning a history of his people, a history with a purpose and a message."

Friedman, like others before him, believes that the anonymous redactor also penned *Deuteronomy*. This is highly unlikely since the *Torah*, the Five Books of Moses, constitutes one uninterrupted line of dictation from the YHVH at Mount Sinai (the *Bible Code* verifies this; the key factors in the Code's functionality are today's meticulously copied Torah scrolls, absolutely identical clones of the twelve Moses distributed to the Tribes). Friedman's adherence to the theory of a seven-book Deuteronomistic history blinds him to the simple answer: the six-book set, ingeniously grafting off *Deuteronomy*, is the accomplishment of the gifted scribe—King Josiah. The author of *Chronicles* filled in the missing pieces of *2 Kings*: the death of Josiah, the destruction of the Temple and the Babylonian captivity. It seems apparent that Josiah ended his own biography as he did the previous king's histories—**"Now the rest of the acts of Josiah, and all that he did, are they not written in the Book of the Annals of the Kings of Judah?"** (2 Kings 23.28)

is reduced to meaningless repetition of empty ritual. Corruption within the Aaronic priesthood forces the Melchizedek lineage, the Judaic line, underground where Elijah's clandestine school, the Essenes, carry the torch—the Torah. Their *Teacher of Righteousness*, John the Baptizer embarks on his evangelical mission when a rare *triple* conjunction of Jupiter with a most auspicious fixed star (Regulus) announces the imminent birth of the royal God-man, the fulfillment of holy Scripture.[43]

> **"Lo, I will send you the prophet Elijah before the great and terrible day of the YHVH comes.
> He will turn the hearts of parents to their children and the hearts of children to their parents,
> so that I will not come and strike the land with a ban of utter destruction."**
> (Malachi 4.5)

Within forty years of the Christ's execution, though, the land *is* nearly destroyed as Titus—his Roman legions burning the Second Temple—initiates the *Diaspora*, the assimilation of the Tribes throughout the Roman Empire. Nevertheless, the evolutionary intent of the Ten Commandments and Deuteronomistic laws had reached its Omega Point with the parthenogenic birth of Mariah[44], without whose genetic purity (DNA sequence integrity), the *eternal plant of righteousness* could never have been engendered. The Chosen People succeeded in their primary purpose—producing the unbroken bottle that the culminating Messiah could be poured into without cracking.[45]

> "But when the hour of the Divine draws near, The Mighty Mother shall take birth in Time
> and God be born into the human clay. In forms made ready by your human lives."   ~Sri Aurobindo

Chapter Eight: The Trinity

The Son of Man's final incarnation created a conundrum that took over 300 years to unravel. Although He publicly gives credit to the "Father" for the inexplicable healings and manifestations, Jeshua is flabbergasted when His own inner circle doesn't have a clue to the new Godhead…

> **"Philip said to him, 'Lord, show us the Father, and we will be satisfied.'
> Jesus said to him, 'Have I been with you all this time, Philip, and you still do not know me?
> *Whoever has seen me has seen the Father.* How can you say, 'Show us the Father?'**
>
> **Do you not believe that I am in the Father and the Father is in me?
> Believe me that I am in the Father and the Father is in me; but
> if you do not, then believe me because of the works themselves.'"**   (John 14.9-11)

---

[43] See **Book IV**, footnote 51, for the rectified birth date of Jeshua and astrophysical elucidation of the enigmatic *Star of Bethlehem*.
[44] "Thus in Carmel - where there were the priests of this faith [Essenes] - there were the maidens chosen who were dedicated to this purpose, this office, this service…**That was the beginning, that was the foundation of what ye term The Church.** Among them was Mary, the beloved, the chosen one; and she, as had been foretold, was chosen as the channel. Thus she was separated and kept in the closer associations with and in the care or charge of this office…"   (Cayce Reading 5749-7)
  "The Jewish rabbis themselves, at a comparatively late date acknowledged that the four matriarchs *Sarah, Rebecca, Rachel* and *Leah* had occupied a more important position than the three patriarchs, *Abraham, Isaac* and *Jacob*."   ~Briffault
[45] Of all the Hebraic moral and social rules of behavior, the dietary restrictions may have actually turned the tide. The subtle effect of kosher foods, especially the prohibition of pork, did wonders for the thinking processes. For millennia, Moloch/Ba'al kept His people dull-witted and ignorant through the sacrifice of cows, and the addictive craving for bloody carcasses. The Hindu priestly caste made evolutionary leaps of progress through a vegetarian regime, the karmic conundrum of killing weighing heavier on the lower castes…
  "Vegetarianism—a brahminic ideal and a social fact in India—precisely calls into question that fateful dialectic in which every class of being feeds on another. The prohibition of flesh, which became increasingly strict in brahminic society, was one way to break the chain of all this alimentary violence and affirm that it is not really necessary to kill in order to eat."   ~*Jungle and the Aroma of Meats*

The Logo's brief appearance in the Western world was such a mind-boggling event that an entire corpus of fairy-tales was invented to explain the paradox. The educated minority of the first centuries had access to some of the greatest discourses on the nature of God ever assembled, the Neo-Platonic writings of Plotinus. The *Enneads*, like their Eastern equivalent, the *Prajnaparamita*, constantly reiterate the futility of comprehending the **Absolute** with the rational mind. In the final analysis, there is only the One, a Singularity *beyond* number or scrutability—*absolutely* beyond any anthropomorphic conceptualization. God could only be approached *via negativa*—the *Pleroma* defined to the degree of what it wasn't. Contrary to the East where the experience of a living God, Gautama the Buddha, was clear proof of a *Godhead*—to the Gnostics, *any concept*, other than a transcendent Goodness, attributed to the One was heresy. They believed Christ was the *Light-King* (as opposed to the *Demiurge*—a dualism borrowed from Zoroastrianism) but found it impossible to reconcile the fact that He was both man and *Monad*—so they wrote their own gospels, with a trinity of Saviors!

"When he had said those things, I saw him seemingly being seized by them. And I said 'What do I see, O Lord? That it is you yourself whom they take, and that you are grasping me? Or who is this one, glad and laughing on the tree? And is it another one whose feet and hands they are striking?' The Savior said to me, 'He whom you saw on the tree, glad and laughing, this is the living Jesus. But this one into whose hands and feet they drive the nails is his fleshly part, which is the substitute being put to shame, the one who came into being in his likeness. But look at him and me.' But I, when I had looked, said 'Lord, no one is looking at you. Let us flee this place.' But he said to me, 'I have told you, *Leave the blind alone!* And you, see how they do not know what they are saying. For the son of their glory instead of my servant, they have put to shame.'

And I saw someone about to approach us resembling him, even him who was laughing on the tree. And he was <filled> with a Holy Spirit, and he is the Savior. And there was a great, ineffable light around them, and the multitude of ineffable and invisible angels blessing them. And when I looked at him, the one who gives praise was revealed. And he said to me, 'Be strong, for you are the one to whom these mysteries have been given, to know them through revelation, that he whom they crucified is the first-born, and the home of demons, and the stony vessel in which they dwell, of Elohim, of the cross, which is under the Law. But he who stands near him is the living Savior, the first in him, whom they seized and released, who stands joyfully looking at those who did him violence, while they are divided among themselves. Therefore he laughs at their lack of perception, knowing that they are born blind. So then the one susceptible to suffering shall come, since the body is the substitute. **But what they released was my incorporeal body. But I am the intellectual Spirit filled with radiant light. He whom you saw coming to me is our intellectual *Pleroma*, which unites the perfect light with my Holy Spirit.**" ~*Apocalypse of Peter*, Nag Hammadi Library, ca. 150 AD

One can see how the intellectual coupling of Persian-Babylonian syncretism with rudimentary Judeo-Christianity could have posed a serious threat to the neophyte Church. The ingenious allegory even preempted the epiphany of the Age—the Trinity! Paul had planted the seed; he penetrated a mystery that, for many, took two millennia to sink in: Christ was the new Lord *Elohim*.[46] The Gnostic

---

[46] "I am made a minister, according to the dispensation of God which is given to me for you, to fulfill the word of God; *Even the mystery which hath been hid from ages and from generations*, but now is made manifest to his saints." (Colossians 1.26)
"*He is the image of the invisible God*, the firstborn of every creature…" (Colossians 1.15)
To his own people, Paul could delve a little deeper—though he was still giving "milk for children not yet fit to eat whole foods"…
"*He is the reflection of God's glory and the exact imprint of God's very being*, and he sustains all things by his powerful logos.
When he had made purification for sins, he sat down at the right hand of the Majesty on high…" (Hebrews 1.3)
Here Paul gives the biggest clue of all: Even Jeshua had to learn submission to the merciless law of karma—upon His perfection, He *became* the perpetual Creator… the new Light Lord.
"**Though He was the Son, yet He learned obedience by the things which He suffered.
And *having been perfected*, He became the author of eternal salvation** to all who obey Him,
called by God as High Priest "according to the order of Melchizedek." (Hebrews 5.8)

initiates had picked up on St. Paul's insight and the embryonic Church was in danger of losing her authority to a heretical sect sophisticated enough to twist the truth into any shape they desire.[47]

Despite the pagan insurgence, the Church maintained her independent identity and cohesion until the timely deliverance by Constantine in 313 AD. At this juncture she is forced to formalize the untenable sacred tenets into a written doctrine—the *Nicene Creed*.

An inquisitive Alexandrine presbyter—swayed by the Gnostic logic—couldn't imagine a human being existing on the same level as the *First Cause*. Arius thought Jesus was created secondarily, and through the *Pleroma*, begot Creation. The confusion lay in the fact that a *primordial Pattern* was being perceived for the first time. The Egyptian priest couldn't fathom the paradox of how a man can metamorphasize like a butterfly and *become* part of a preexistent Godhead. Of course, with a few exceptions like Greek-wise Origen, neither could the bishops. Nevertheless, the apocalyptic incarnation crystallized the triune hypothesis and the *experience* of a personal, incarnate God had to be reconciled with the accepted Neo-Platonic doctrine of an Inconceivable Absolute. It was necessary to coin a new word at this time, a neologism for the new paradigm that had emerged—Homoousion (Grk. *homos*, same *ousia*, essence), of the same substance of the Father. The First Council of Nicea, in a bold and sublime manner, proclaimed the **Trinity of Godhead** wherein each member functions independently yet they are three modalities of the Supreme One...

---

[47] "When Cyrus entered Babylon in 539 B.C., two great worlds of thought met, and syncretism in religion, as far as we know it, began. Iranian thought began to mix with the ancient civilization of Babylon. The idea of the great struggle between evil and good, ever continuing in this universe, is the parent idea of Mazdeism, or Iranian dualism. This, and the imagined existence of numberless intermediate spirits, angels and devas, as the conviction which overcame the contentedness of Semitism. On the other hand, the unshakable trust, in astrology, the persuasion that the planetary system had a fatalistic influence on this world's affairs, stood its ground on the soil of Chaldea. The greatness of the Seven—the Moon, Mercury, Venus, Mars, the Sun, Jupiter, and Saturn—the sacred Hebdomad, symbolized for millenniums by the staged towers of Babylonia, remained undiminished. They ceased, indeed, to be worshipped as deities, but they remained archontes and dynameis, rules and powers whose almost irresistible force was dreaded by man. Practically, they were changed from gods to devas, or evil spirits. The religions of the invaders and of the invaded effected a compromise: the astral faith of Babylon was true, but beyond the Hebdomad was the infinite light in the Ogdoad, and every human soul had to pass the adverse influence of the god or gods of the Hebdomad before it could ascend to the only good God beyond. This ascent of the soul through the planetary spheres to the heaven beyond (an idea not unknown even to ancient Babylonian speculations) began to be conceived as a struggle with adverse powers, and became the first and predominant idea in Gnosticism. The second great component of Gnostic thought is magic, properly so called, i.e. the power *ex opere operato* of weird names, sounds, gestures, and actions, as also the mixture of elements to produce effects totally disproportionate to the cause. These magic formulae, which caused laughter and disgust to outsiders, are not a later and accidental corruption, but an essential part of Gnosticism, for they are found in all forms of Christian Gnosticism and likewise in Mandaeism.

No Gnosis was essentially complete without the knowledge of the formulae, which, once pronounced, were the undoing of the higher hostile powers. Magic is the original sin of Gnosticism, nor is it difficult to guess whence it is inherited. To a certain extent it formed part of every pagan religion, especially the ancient mysteries, yet the thousands of magic tablets unearthed is Assyria and Babylonia show us where the rankest growth of magic was to be found. Moreover, the terms and names of earliest of Gnosticism bear an unmistakable similarity to Semitic sounds and words.

Gnosticism came early into contact with Judaism, and it betrays a knowledge of the Old Testament, if only to reject it or borrow a few names from it. Considering the strong, well-organized, and highly-cultured Jewish colonies in the Euphrates valley, this early contact with Judaism is perfectly natural.

Perhaps the Gnostic idea of a Redeemer is not unconnected with Jewish Messianic hopes. But from the first the Gnostic conception of a Saviour is more superhuman than that of popular Judaism; their *Manda d'Haye*, or *Soter*, is some immediate manifestation of the Deity, a Light-King, an *Æon (Aion)*, and an emanation of the good God. When Gnosticism came in touch with Christianity, which must have happened almost immediately on its appearance, **Gnosticism threw herself with strange rapidity into Christian forms of thought, borrowed its nomenclature, acknowledged Jesus as Savior of the world, simulated its sacraments, pretended to be an esoteric revelation of Christ and His Apostles, flooded the world with apocryphal Gospels, and Acts, and Apocalypses, to substantiate its claim.**

As Christianity grew within and without the Roman Empire, Gnosticism spread as a fungus at its root, and claimed to be the only true form of Christianity, unfit, indeed, for the vulgar crowd, but set apart for the gifted and the elect. So rank was its poisonous growth that there seemed danger of its stifling Christianity altogether, and the earliest Fathers devoted their energies to uprooting it."

~The Catholic Encyclopedia, 1907-1912

> "We believe in one God the Father Almighty, Maker of all things visible and invisible; and in one Lord Jesus Christ, the only begotten of the Father, that is, of the substance [*ek tes ousias*] of the Father, God of God, light of light, true God of true God, begotten not made, of the same substance with the Father [*homoousion to patri*], through whom all things were made both in heaven and on earth; who for us men and our salvation descended, was incarnate, and was made man, suffered and rose again the third day, ascended into heaven and cometh to judge the living and the dead. And in the Holy Ghost.
>
> Those who say: There was a time when He was not, and He was not before He was begotten; and that He was made out of nothing (*ex ouk onton*); or who maintain that He is of another hypostasis or another substance [than the Father], or that the Son of God is created, or mutable, or subject to change, [them] the Catholic Church anathematizes."

The Church was inadvertently defining an *existential Archetype* while poor Arius was focusing on the human aspect. The latter deduced there was indeed a time when Jesus, like all of us, "was not", but couldn't convince the battle-weary bishops. It would invalidate the eternal Trinity; or so they believed. The Hebrew concept of a *living God* was a foreign one to the assembly of 325 AD. The idea that the Immutable God—in His persona as anthropomorphic Son—evolves and vacates the Seat for the next incumbent, was too advanced for the 4th century (or the 21st century, apparently). *Jesus* became the Logos at His baptism just as the holy dove illuminated Him. The *Christ* emerged from the water, absorbed by the Oversoul yet still retaining a thread of Ego, the Son aspect. From that moment on, His natal astrological chart was superseded for He had become a *Buddha*.[48]

> "(The Spirit of the Lord shall rest upon him) not partially as in the case of other holy men: but, according to the Gospel written in the Hebrew speech, which the Nazarenes read, 'There shall descend upon him the whole fount of the Holy Spirit'... In the Gospel I mentioned above, I find this written: **And it came to pass when the Lord was come up out of the water, the whole fount of the Holy Spirit descended and rested upon him, and said unto him: My son, in all the prophets was I waiting for thee that thou shouldst come, and I might rest in thee. For thou art my rest, and thou art my first begotten son, that reignest for ever."** ~*Gospel of the Hebrews*, Jerome, *On Isaiah*, 4th c.

---

[48] The binding use of Eastern terminology is often the only recourse since an incarnating God, among other cosmic anomalies, is still a foreign concept to the West. Having experienced the *Son of God* in more than one Being (Krishna and Buddha), Hindu Brahmins developed the doctrine of the *Avatar*—an unchanging and eternal Godhead that takes human form when Necessity demands...
"Whenever there is a decline in dharma, O Bharata, and a rise of adharma, I incarnate Myself. For the protection of the good, for the destruction of the wicked, and for the establishment of dharma, I am born in every age." (Bhagavad Gita 4.7-8)

In the 6th century BC, Prince of the Sakyas, Siddhartha Gautama became an *Awakened One* or *Buddha* upon his complete Enlightenment under the Bodhi tree. As a result of the metamorphosis, Siddhartha became God incarnate, an Elohim Lord with no equal. The Asian Shepherd came to re-establish the *Dharma* (Truth) among His pantheistic people. Planting the seeds that took root everywhere *except* India, Lord Buddha was free to go where no mortal can follow—the *Heart Sutra*'s powerful mantra praises the Tathagata upon His final Extinguishment, *Parinirvana*...

OM GATE GATE PARAGATE PARASAMGATE BODHI SVAHA!
"Gone, Gone, Gone Beyond the Other Shore—Hail the Awakener!"

The Eastern Avatar had to leave our Local Universe; two omnipotent Beings cannot occupy the same Time/Space: "Two Buddhas cannot simultaneously arise in one and the same world system, no more than two universal Monarchs can co-exist at the same time."

"This world system of ten thousand worlds can bear just one single Buddha, can bear the virtue of just one single Tathagata. If a second Buddha were to arise, this world system of ten thousand worlds could not bear him. It would shake and tremble, bend, twist, and disintegrate, be shattered, ruined, and destroyed." ~*The Debate of King Milinda,* Chapter 13, The Solving of Dilemmas (VI)

Book II: Cyclicity

Only one fault remained to haunt Him—His fall as Adam. After paying the extreme lawful penalty, the immaculate God-man could ascend as the new Galactic Lord, releasing and replacing the wholly evolved, elemental *Elohim*, Yahweh. The beloved Apostle knew the secret of an ephemeral yet eternal Logos—his familiar "opening statement" put it in a nutshell...

> **"In the beginning was the *Logos*
> and the *Logos* was with God, and the *Logos* was God."**   (John 1.1)

The self-educated *Son of Thunder*, obviously fluent in the Greek language, had the benefit of Greco gleanings to comprehend the Buddha nature of his Master. The 6th century BC philosopher Heraclitus was the first to use the term *Logos* (Divine Reason), revealing the basic substratum of Mind that upholds the everyday world of objective perception. We have few fragments extant, but they point to an unsurpassed intellect—

- "It is wise to hearken, not to me, but to my Logos, and to confess that all things are one."
- "Though this Logos is true evermore, yet men are as unable to understand it when they hear it for the first time as before they have heard it at all. For, though all things come to pass in accordance with this Logos, men seem as if they had no experience of them, when they make trial of words and deeds such as I set forth, dividing each thing according to its kind and showing how it truly is. But other *men know not what they are doing when awake, even as they forget what they do in sleep*."
- "This world, which is the same for all, no one of gods or men has made; but it was ever, is now, and ever shall be an ever-living Fire, with measures of it kindling, and measures going out."
- "God is day and night, winter and summer, war and peace, surfeit and hunger; but he takes various shapes, just as fire, when it is mingled with spices, is named according to the savor of each."
- "It rests by changing."

John had solved the riddle of Buddhahood/Christ Consciousness by going to the root of the enigma—the *Son of God* as a rudimentary impulse from stability to motion. At the first stir of the Singularity, the *Logos* is produced out of Itself—sevenfold [*See* footnote 37]. Each of the self-spawned *Elohim* is the *Monogenes* (Grk. only begotten) Son of God. Since the Galactic cradle can only handle One, there is a process of elimination and/or subordination.[49]

> **"The soul partakes of the Logos which grows out of itself."**   ~Heraclitus

Etymologically, *Logos* is a loaded word—never properly translated into the English language...

"Central to the Prologue is the concept of 'Word', a very inadequate rendering of the original Greek term *Logos*, one of the most important concepts of the Hellenistic world. In ancient Greek, Logos has many meanings, but none of them is 'Word', which is based on a translation of a translation. When the Greek New Testament was translated into Latin, Logos became *Verbum*; and when the English King James translation was made from the Latin version, Verbum became 'Word', twice removed from the original text."   ~David Fideler

---

49 In the struggle for domination, Yahweh's first priority was to separate Leviathan from Behemoth, the male/female nuisance...
Behemoth. "A mythical beast described in Job 40.15–24 as the first of God's creations, an animal of enormous strength that inhabits the river valleys. Although frequently identified with the hippopotamus (as Leviathan is with the crocodile), not all the details of the creature's physiology fit that well-known mammal. In view of the references to Behemoth in the apocrypha and pseudepigrapha, it is more likely that it is a form of the primeval monster of chaos, defeated by Yahweh at the beginning of the process of creation; in fact, according to Job 40.24, the monster is represented as tamed by him and with a ring through his lip, so that like Leviathan he has become a divine pet. According to later Jewish tradition, at the end time Behemoth and Leviathan will become food for the righteous."
~*Oxford Companion to the Bible*, Michael D. Coogan

The great Hungarian epistemologist Georg Kuhlewind delves into the mysterious machinations of the mind-soul (*Logos*) by reflecting back to the *bicameral* days of early antediluvian Mankind…

"Formerly, because of the mixed structure of the mind-soul, the process of thinking was given to people in a dreamlike manner, without clear outlines, and people could not hold their own in this process. Their experience resembled the way we experience ourselves when we dream. Words and concepts were one. They were experienced as they arose, as they entered consciousness. Nowadays, we understand words and concepts in the same way too, but for us their entry into consciousness remains superconscious.

We are clearly conscious only of their result, of what we have understood; of course, by then this has lost its life and become dead. Because of children's dreamlike experience of these processes, their soul life is alive in a way that adults have lost."

Because we are always one step removed from the essence of things, because we must constantly *recollect*, we never experience reality directly. Our inherited superconscious process of thinking about phenomenality in order to perceive has alienated us from direct magical cognition. We now *re*-cognize our surroundings, whereas for early Man each day was a brand new creation. We no longer realize that words and descriptions are *predominant* to the objects they describe—that Plato's Ideas or Archetypes, the names of things, are *more real* than their physical manifestations.

"The world exists entirely of words, of communicability. The world is a transparent, *speaking* world. If I want to make myself understood to a Japanese and we know no common language, I will point to the sky, saying 'sky', and ask him with a gesture what 'that' is called in his language. He understands me and says his word. *What* did he understand, *what* do we have in common? I point to *that*, the sky, and he understands that this *that* is the sky—not the air, not the blue, etc. We understood each other without words: he grasped which that I was pointing to and this *that* was already word, beyond any particular language. He grasped the real word, pure understanding, of which every sign, every spoken word, is only an indication.

This wordless word is not an outer 'name' attached to a thing, it is the thing. Someone who does not have the concept 'book' will perhaps see only paper. It is the word, *i.e.* the concept, the function, that makes something into a *thing*. Words, as earthly representatives of the Word, do not *signify* a thing which would exist just as much without its concept, but the thing becomes through the word. First the idea of the knife, then the knife, even when it is seen; *I see the knife for the first time when its idea dawns in me.*"   ~Kuhlewind

Thus our entire consciousness, our ability to cognize, is wholly dependent upon words, and more specifically, *the* Word or *Logos*.[50] Without the Son, whose presence permeates the Universe, there would be no telling what was what. Just a great jumble of incomprehensible energy patterns. It is His Selfhood, His "I Am that I Am" that keeps the cosmos glued together. We maintain our individual "I Am" *through* Jeshua's Self-awareness. His 24/7 job requires an ever-flowing circular catharsis of Self-absorption, where the egoic *Son* moves into the creator *Father* and generates ceaseless waves of seraphic efflux—the living *Spirit*.[51]

> **"He is the reflection of God's glory and the exact imprint of God's very being,
> and he sustains all things by his powerful *Logos*."**   (Hebrews 1.3)

---

[50] Proof of a personal God is the fact that you are reading these words. The entire intellectual matrix, continually created anew each nanosecond, is absolutely dependent upon the living Logos. "When I speak to someone—in my ability to do so—I *become*, I am. And you—for you I am, and for me you are. The word blossoms between us: cognition, communication, the Logos… I conceive, I form the word and let it go, I send it on its way. It floats to you. It is *truth*. That there is truth, that the word exists, *is* truth. And the word lives, is present, not past. It speaks. And at the same time it says, I am there—I am the I-am-there—and *that* is life." ~Kuhlewind

[51] Though Yahweh was the original Creator God, we now refer to the Christ as our Creator. Isaiah Tishby explains: "*Created* in the Hebrew is a present participle form, and is interpreted to mean its influence continuously renews the sefirot [lower dimensional Worlds] that are emanated from it (*Binah* or the Spirit)."

Book II: Cyclicity

Fig. 9 The Living Logos

Like the lower choirs of triune Celestial Intelligences, the Godhead also participates in His own evolution—the Son *purifies* himself to ascend to the Father (Universal Mind), whereupon He receives nourishment or *illumination*, which is then digested and radiated throughout the entire Galactic body as the *perfecting* Spirit of cognition or gnosis.[52]

Kuhlewind informs us that "to become aware of the Logos is to become aware of the Logos in oneself." The Christ had to leave our lower World so as not to hinder Mankind's development. We needed to become enlightened to the Logos within, and that could only be possible through abandonment by the Godhead—by God *turning His face from us* and allowing the inner Logos to "grow out of itself". After two millennia of evolution, we have nearly caught up to the Great Initiate, realizing our own Buddha nature in the lightning flash of epiphany—the mind-boggling, paradoxical truth of a *personal* Almighty God, Jeshua.[53]

> "Nevertheless I tell you the truth; It is expedient for you that I go away:
> for if I go not away, the Comforter will not come unto you;
> but if I depart, I will send him unto you." (John 16.7)

When the *born again* Jeshua walked the earth, His presence was so over-powering that it was like a contact-high, wiping out the false ego and holding up the mirror of Godhead. Yet the skeptical Jews could not cognize the new Word; with no previous idea or concept, they simply didn't see the "knife"—the miraculous Being in their presence.[54] Mr. Kuhlewind continues his elegant edification...

"The son is the Father's countenance or word, but the ability to see him is the Spirit: the Logos in me. As a visible experience the Son would simply extinguish human I-consciousness. This is what happened to the disciples. Up to the arrest of Jesus, the Logos penetrated them like a luminous enchantment. His essence spread amongst them and spoke through them...

After the ascension of the Logos-being the disciples lose their Comforter forever from the perceptual sphere. The disciples' sadness before Pentecost is part of the Pentecostal miracle, the most significant aspect of which is that, right away, the apostles understood the event in full consciousness."

---

52 A Human Being, the triune, microcosmic equivalent of the Godhead, follows the same circulatory motion of evolution...

The low self animates the body, performing all the subconscious tasks we take for granted—breathing, blood circulation, cell replacement, digestion and elimination. The Ego or middle self depends upon this *Purification* of the organism for its mental and emotional stability—the mind/body connection. Righteous living unites the id/ego duo, allowing the high Self to descend, *Illuminating* the entire Man, now proceeding toward *Perfection*.   [*See* footnote 14]

53 "In His humanity, he is raised above all creatures—and this is a human being! From God he receives all creation as his heritage, just as he himself told his disciples."   ~*Hildegard of Bingen's Book of Divine Works, Vision 7*, Hildegard of Bingen

54 "And the Father himself, which hath sent me, hath borne witness of me. Ye have neither heard his voice at any time, nor seen his shape. *And ye have not His Logos abiding in you*: for whom he hath sent, him ye believe not."   (John 5.38)

"The history of the people of the Old Testament is partly the story of relapses into the worship of idols, symbols of the gods, particularizations of the One, that had to a great extent already lost their meaning at that time. To await the Messiah and to prepare his ways was this people's great task. At the same time, however, the understanding of the Messiah was made difficult for this people. ***Having finally achieved the cult of the invisible, it had to accept the appearance of the Godhead in visible, human form***. After struggling against idolatry in various animal forms, the symbol for which was the golden calf, there comes the appearance of God in a human shape. The Creator of man sends his essence, his creative word, his appearance or revelation, the Man-God, in order to have the living God-Man before men."   ~*Becoming Aware of the Logos*, Georg Kuhlewind

The sacrificial isolation of Jeshua[55] allows the Spirit of Truth to manifest in our world. We had to arrive at the realization of our own Divinity by ourselves, with only the help of an invisible, cognitive emanation from the Christ. His good vibes...

> "**I have yet many things to say unto you, but ye cannot bear them now. Howbeit when he, the Spirit of truth, is come, he will guide you into all truth: for he shall not speak of himself; but whatsoever he shall hear, that shall he speak:** *and he will show you things to come.*" (John 16.12-13)

We see how the Son functions individually as Mind, imparting meaning to an incomprehensible Universe. No small feat, and this is why those *in the know* worship God, send Him love and affection. As Mr. Kuhlewind explained, for an ordinary man to become God was too fantastic for the Jews—the Christ's own relatives found it difficult to believe[56]—and it seems absurd to the unenlightened

---

[55] The greatest sacrifice of Jeshua—far outweighing the callous crucifixion—is to remain behind. Retaining an Ego thread to serve as the living *Logos*, Christ's hard-earned freedom is curtailed. Caught between Extinguishment (Parinirvana) and the phenomenal World, the God-man cannot even indulge in the simplest of Human pleasures: "**But I say unto you, I will not drink henceforth of the fruit of the vine, until that day when I drink it new with you in my Father's kingdom.**" (Matthew 26.29)

    Yet He lovingly chooses to delay His journey to the supramental realm, beyond all conceptuality. Jeshua is truly the Savior, but not because He saved us from our sins—it gets heavier than that—He saves the Human face. Without the *living* God, the very countenance of Goodness— "**So He said to him, 'Why do you call Me good? No one is good but One, that is, God.'**" (Matt. 19.17) —we would lose our individuality and degenerate into the faceless, soulless alien Collective (*sitra ahra*). [*See* **Book I**, footnote 16]

    "What did it mean to be saved, I asked, although I knew the word smacked of Elmer Gantry for both of us. 'I guess it's like discovering you're on the shelf of a pawnshop, dusty and forgotten and maybe not worth very much. But Jesus comes in and tells the pawnbroker, 'I'll take her place on the shelf. Let her go outside again.'" ~*Traveling Mercies*, Anne Lamott

[56] After spiritual discipline in Qumran, initiation in Egypt and perfection in Persia and India, the prodigal son returns to Nazareth, a Superstar—incensing their small-town sensibilities as He declares Himself to be the very anointed one of Isaiah's scripture...

    "**This day is this scripture fulfilled in your ears.**" Jeshua's homies aren't impressed with the big shot from Galilee...

    "**And they said, is this not Joseph's son? And all they in the synagogue, when they heard these things, were filled with wrath, and rose up, and thrust him out of the city, and led him unto the brow of the hill whereon their city was built, that they might cast him down headlong. But he passing through the midst of them went his way.**" ["It was the intention of the mob to push Him over a precipice... then he exerted His occult forces in a proper self-defense. Not a blow struck he—no, he controlled Himself with a firm hand, and merely bent upon them a look. But such a look!" ~*Mystic Christianity*, Yogi Ramacharaka]

    The prophet without honor probably expected as much, having already experienced His own family's impertinence...

"**Behold, the mother of the Lord and his brethren said unto him: John the Baptist baptizeth unto the remission of sins; let us go and be baptized of him. But he said unto them: Wherein have I sinned, that I should go and be baptized of him? Unless peradventure this very thing that I have said is [a sin of] ignorance.**" ~*Gospel according to the Hebrews*, Jerome, 4th century

    Wielding unprecedented power in Galilee creates such a frenzy that His pious family is summoned to restrain the sorcerer. "**And the multitude cometh together again, so that they could not so much as eat bread...**" When His own envious kin deny what Spirit had clearly revealed and blurt out, *he is beside himself*, with betrayal most foul—*he hath an unclean spirit*, the Messiah warns them of unforgivable blasphemy. **Behold, thy mother and thy brethren without seek for thee. And he answered them, saying, 'Who is my mother, or my brethren? And he looked round about on them which sat about him, and said, Behold my mother and my brethren! For whosoever shall do the will of God, the same is my brother, and my sister, and mother.'**" (Mark 3.30)

    Here Jeshua is forced to disown His own mother and siblings. The *Secret Gospel of Mark* [*See* **Book I**, footnote 6] shows just how far that banishment extended. The canonized Mark 10.46 reads, "**And they came to Jericho; [*****] and as he went out of Jericho with his disciples and a great number of people...**" Clement of Alexandria filled in the apparent lacuna: "And after the words, '**And he comes into Jericho**,' the secret Gospel adds only, '**And the sister of the youth whom Jesus loved and his mother and Salome were there,** *and Jesus did not receive them.*'"

    Towards the end of the Passion Play, fallout from Jeshua's disinheritance of His biological family had filtered down to the disciples. By comparing the three synoptic Gospels—each describe the holy Women at Golgotha or after, by the empty tomb—we find such a defiant attitude had arisen amongst the Apostolic boys club that Mary is no longer even acknowledged as the mother of Jeshua. Henceforth she is referred to *as the mother of James and Joses* (or Jude).

- "**And many women were there beholding afar off, which followed Jesus from Galilee, ministering unto him: Among which was Mary Magdalene, and** *Mary the mother of James and Joses***, and the mother of Zebedees children.**" (Matthew 27.55-56)
- "**There were also women looking on afar off: among whom was Mary Magdalene, and** *Mary the mother of James the less and of Joses***, and Salome; (Who also, when he was in Galilee, followed him, and ministered unto him;) and many other women which came up with him unto Jerusalem.**" (Mark 15.40-41)
- "**It was Mary Magdalene and Joanna, and** *Mary the mother of James***, and other women that were with them, which told these things unto the apostles.**" (Luke 24.10)

masses of today. Even those who have become aware of the *Logos* within, have difficulty with the concept of a personal God.[57] Yet it's been an open secret for millennia…

> "The highest secret is the miracle of a supreme Person and apparent vast Impersonal that are one,
> an immutable transcendent Self of all things and a Spirit that manifests itself here
> at the very foundation of cosmos as an infinite and multiple personality."   ~Sri Aurobindo

This Spirit that manifests *here at the very foundation of cosmos*, that we live in as parts of a Group-Soul[58], was known to the Greeks as the **World Soul**—disguised as Nature. Hellenistic scholar David Fideler explains their grand, yet rudimentary (non-anthropic), cosmological structure…

> "In the Neo-Platonic cosmology of Plotinus, the four levels of reality are called the One, Mind, World Soul, and Nature. **The One** is the ultimate, transcendental source of manifestation about which nothing can be said. It is unlimited, and therefore infinite, and because the One is indeterminate, it is 'beyond Being'. **Mind (*Nous*)** is said to be the differentiated 'image' of the One, insofar as the One can be reflected at all. Mind is a perfect, living unity-in-multiplicity of all the universal Forms and individual minds. It is the first level of Being because it is something distinct—it is also eternal and identical with the 'Logos' in its most comprehensive form. **World Soul** is a further differentiated image of Mind, the living dispenser of individual forms and lives, the shaper of organic nature and incarnate form. **Nature**, then, is the living image of Soul."

The third mysterious modulation of Godhead[59], the World Soul or Spirit (Grk. *Pneuma*) seems to be an independent force of the Inconceivable One (Father), yet is intimately tied to the Logos…

> "But the Comforter, which is the Holy Ghost, whom the Father will send
> in my name[60], he shall teach you all things, and bring all things
> to your remembrance, whatsoever I have said unto you."   (John 14.26)

---

57 The Hindus have lost touch with this cardinal rule, despite the fact that their own sacred scriptures clearly understood how a single Being, a *Manu*, stands alone as **Lord of the World**— "This being is the Lord of all things, the Omniscient, seeing instantaneously all effects in their cause; the inner organizer residing at the centre of the world and ruling it from within, directing its movement without participating in it. He is the source of all legitimate power, the beginning and end of all beings that belong to the cyclical manifestation in which he represents the Law."   ~*Mandukya* Upanishad   The revered *Yoga Sutras* refer to a "special Soul" beyond the Atman!
"The Lord Isvara is a special soul. He is untouched by the obstacles, karma, and subconscious predispositions."   ~Patanjali, 1.24
  To put it into modern terms, especially for those familiar with the Toltec revealed teachings—This (and every)Universe is built upon **Intent**. It's up to the reader to decide *whose* Intent upholds *our* Worlds. However, it boils down to *one* Entity, *one* Nagual.
58 All plants, insects and animals belong collectively to their own respective higher Spirit or Deva—
  "Take ants. They are such an intelligent, organized community, but if you examine the nervous system of an ant, it's very simple—there may be six nerve ganglia or so in all. How can they behave so intelligently? It turns out that a single ant is not very smart at all, but the great intelligence of the ant colony is a *deva*, the total consciousness of millions of ants, the god who is a big six-foot-tall ant, and you can ask her to remove her body (the little ants) from your favorite chocolate cookie jar. To negotiate with her, the currency of exchange is love. Just send the ant deva a lot of love, which will stimulate her evolution. Even ant devas need love, in order eventually to know their Creator."   ~*A Cosmic Book*, Itzhak Bentov
  Even with our superior, compounded Soul, Humans are still members of a Group-Soul and without the God-man above, we'd have no existence *whatsoever*— "A single human being has no reality, the existence of 'man' begins with the word that floats between I and you. The Logos connects human beings through the Word—all else is temptation or a temporary connection."   ~Kuhlewind
59 The workings of this *third force* are subtler than the other two—like the discovery of the earth's *third* motion (precession wobble), it has taken centuries to nail down. The 325 AD Ecthesis of Nice avoided the sticky wicket altogether with its pithy statement, "And [we believe] in the Holy Ghost". The first Council of Constantinople (381 AD) embellished with: "And I believe in the Holy Ghost, the Lord and **Giver of Life; who proceeds from the Father and the Son**; who with the Father and the Son together is worshipped and glorified; who spoke by the prophets." We perceive this Conscious web of synchronicity, the Akasha that binds all living things—the Great Spirit—more clearly today than ever before. It's almost impossible to deny its manifestations as we near the end of the Time loop. More magical coincidences seem to pop at every moment as we prepare for the apocalyptic Omega Point of Time/Space.
60 We learned how names are more than mere designations—they can be words of power. All a person has in this world is his good name; it is all he takes with him into the afterlife. The powerful invocation taught by Jeshua, the Lord's Prayer, begins **"Our Father who art in Heaven, Hallowed be thy Name"…** The sanctified name of the Father was the magic word that wrought miracles for the post-Pentecostal apostles. By invoking the name of Jeshua, the *Spirit of Truth* empowered the believer, in the Father's name, to bear witness to the new Elohim. Today, the hallowed name of Christ is the most common cuss word in the world, its effectiveness reduced.

Plotinus compared the World Soul *aka* the Holy Spirit to a great Net, protecting us from the turbulent sea, ever-threatening to engulf its prey...

"The kosmos is like a net which takes all its life, as far as it ever stretches, from being wet in the water; it is at the mercy of the sea which spreads out, taking the net with it just so far as it will go, for no mesh of it can strain beyond its set place: the Soul is of so far-reaching a nature—a thing unbounded—as to embrace the entire body of the All in one extension; so far as the universe extends, there soul is; and if the universe had no existence, the extent of soul would be the same; it is eternally what it is."   ~*The Fourth Ennead, Third Tractate*

Here the Comforter is seen as a *Mae West*, a life preserver in a merciless Sea. The living Soul (Christ) breathes life into His body—the Milky Way Galaxy. The Spirit as breath (in-spiration) not only keeps our physical body alive, but similarly to the Son, we solidify knowledge with every exhale (spiration). Hindu Yoga techniques of concentrated breathing—*pranayama* (Skt. vital breath) can raise the *kundalini* (Skt. coiled) fire all the way up to the seventh *chakra* (Skt. wheel), the "thousand-petalled lotus" where direct knowing is activated. The *arisen* Christ was a Being of pure power—His very breath could awaken the slumbering Logos within the disenchanted disciples...

**"And when he had said this, he breathed on them, and saith unto them,
Receive ye the Holy Ghost: Whosoever sins ye remit, they are remitted
unto them; and whosoever sins ye retain, they are retained."**   (John 20.22-23)

In the annotated version of Augustine's *On the Trinity*, William G. T. Shedd, D.D. clarifies...

"The third person is denominated the Spirit because of the peculiar manner in which the divine essence is communicated to him—namely, by **spiration** or out-breathing: ***spiritus quia spiratus.*** This is supported by the etymological signification of ***pneuma***, which is breath; and by the symbolical action of Christ in John 20.22, which suggests the eternal **spiration,** or out-breathing of the third person."

Chapter Nine: The Seat of God

"God created the sexes, the male and female, from a drop of semen,
and will create all things anew; it is He who bestows and enriches,
He who is the **Lord of Sirius**."   (Koran 33.45)

Having named the One—knowing His handle—we might naturally wonder where the Big Guy hangs out. In His persona as *Spirit*, of course, He is Omnipresent—*everywhere* within the spiral Galaxy, which is as far as Plotinus' net will stretch.[61] Yet His Deitific form (Logos) must be localized, available to the inner circle of celestial *Thrones*. All the scanty evidence points to the Dog Star...

---

[61] Every *Monogenes* [Son of God] is the Elohim [Most High] of the Celestial Intelligences created for its 10-world Cosmos—each a Universe unto itself—completely sealed from its neighboring Galaxies by an impenetrable barrier, a *ring-pass-not*. Physical matter cannot go beyond the Galactic edge. The ethereal sea stretches the cosmic net—World Soul—as far as it will go, "for no mesh of it can strain beyond its set place." Within the last two decades, astrophysicists have observed an unusual phenomenon at the outer edge of our Galaxy—unexpectedly *steady* velocities of hydrogen gas rotations in the outer regions indicate significant matter beyond the Galaxy. An invisible force field seems to surround the entire Milky Way spiral and scientists theorize a "wall" of sheer "dark matter" that is totally undetectable...   "The total mass of the Galaxy, which had seemed reasonably well established during the 1960's, has become a matter of considerable uncertainty. Measuring the mass out to the distance of the farthest large hydrogen clouds is a relatively straightforward procedure. The measurements required are the velocities and positions of neutral hydrogen gas, combined with the approximation that the gas is rotating in nearly circular orbits around the center of the Galaxy. A rotation curve, which relates the circular velocity of the gas to its distance from the galactic center, is constructed.   *Cont.* →

Book II: Cyclicity

Astrophysicists have long suspected a *Sun behind the Sun*, a superior solar generator, whose gravitational pull powers our "puny" satellite system. In his provocative work on advanced Astrology, *The Theory of Celestial Influence*, Gurdjieff and Ouspensky protégé Rodney Collin believes, like Egyptologist R. A. Schwaller de Lubicz, that Sirius may be the power behind the throne...

"The most brilliant object in the heavens, after those within the Solar System itself, is of course the double star Sirius. This consists of **an immense radiant sun, 26 times more brilliant than our own, which circles in a fifty year period with a white dwarf as big as Jupiter and 5,000 times denser than lead.** The mass of the light star being two and a half times that of our Sun, and that of the dark one equivalent to it, the influence upon the solar system of this starry pair, which lie at less than nine light-years remove, must certainly far exceed that of any other extra-solar body that we can think of. By physical distance as by radiance and mass a Sirian system would seem in some way to fill the excessive gap between the cosmoses of the Solar System and the Milky Way. Indeed, the distance from the Sun to Sirius—one million times the distance from the earth to the Sun—falls naturally into the scale of cosmic relationships, and provided nineteenth century astronomy with an excellent unit of celestial measurement, the siriometer, now unfortunately abandoned.

No astronomical data contradict the possibility that the Solar System circles about Sirius, in the course of the latter's circuit of the Milky Way, as Kant believed. For such a circling would only noticeably alter the position in the heavens of Sirius itself and of two or three other near stars, and in a periodicity of some hundreds of thousands of years this could easily pass unnoticed. In fact, we have definite evidence to show that such is the case. As the ancient Egyptians observed, the apparent motion of Sirius—measured by its rising with the sun—is a little less than that of the apparent motion of all the other stars, which is recognized in the precession of the equinoxes. Whereas the general star mass rises twenty minutes later on a given day each year, Sirius rises only eleven minutes later. This corresponds to the difference in apparent motion between points outside a circle and the centre of the circle itself, when observed from a moving point on its circumference—just as, in a landscape seen from a moving car, far and near objects seem to run past each other. From such an observation we have good reason to believe that our Sun does circle about Sirius. And if we suppose the generally accepted figure of 20 kilometres a second for the sun's motion through space to be correct, then this circling would require 800,000 years—in other words, our Sun would make some 250 revolutions about its greater sun for every full circuit of the Milky Way.

Another very striking fact appears to confirm the idea of a local star system with Sirius as centre. If we take the great familiar stars within say forty light-years of the Sun—Sirius, Procyon, Altair, Fomalhaut, Pollux, Vega and so on—we find all but two lie within 15° of the same plane. There is only one likely explanation of this—that all the near stars revolve about a common centre, and that this section is the ecliptic upon which all their orbits lie. Supposing Sirius to be the sun of these suns, then our Sun—curiously enough—appears to

---

61 *Continued*

Velocities are low in the central parts of the system because not much mass is interior to the orbit of the gas; velocities are high at intermediate distances because most of the mass in that case is inside the orbit of the gas clouds and the gravitational pull inward is at a maximum. At the farthest distances, the velocities decrease because nearly all the mass is interior to the clouds. During the 1980's, however, refinements in the determination of the velocity curve began to cast doubts on the earlier results. The downward trend to lower velocities in the outer parts of the Galaxy was found to have been in error. Instead, the curve remained almost constant, indicating that there continue to be substantial amounts of matter exterior to the measured hydrogen gas. This in turn indicates that there must by some undetected material out there that is completely unexpected. It must extend considerably beyond the previously accepted positions of the edge of the Galaxy, and it must be dark at virtually all wavelengths, as it remains undetected even when searched for with radio, X-ray, ultraviolet, infrared and optical telescopes.

Until the dark matter is identified and its distribution determined, it will be impossible to measure the total mass of the Galaxy from the rotation curve... ***The nature of the dark matter in the Galaxy remains one of the major questions of galactic astronomy.*** Other galaxies also appear to have such matter in their outer parts. The only possible kinds of material that are consistent with the nondetections are all rather unlikely, at least according to present understanding in physics and astronomy. Planets and rocks would be impossible to detect, but it is extremely difficult to understand how they could materialize in sufficient numbers in the outer parts of galaxies where there are no stars or even interstellar gas and dust from which they could be formed. It will take considerable effort to identify the dark matter with any degree of certainty. In the meantime it must be said that ***astronomy does not know what makes up much of the universe.***"   ~Encyclopedia Britannica

occupy a similar place in that system to that occupied by the earth in the solar one. And if this is so, then the Sirian system may be regarded as almost exactly a million times greater in diameter that the solar system, as the latter is a million times greater in diameter than the earth, and the earth a million times greater in diameter than an ordinary house. What kind of influence could reach us from the Sirian sun, with its strange combination of a radiance far greater than solar radiation and a density far more appalling than any conceivable in the darkest interior of the densest moon, we cannot know. Such super-heaven and infra-hell[62] are unimaginable for us, nor can we know whether the cosmic rays or any other super-solar radiation is connected with it."

This super-heaven is quite likely the *seventh* heaven, the most rarefied plane of existence vibrating with supernatural pulsations. Only a handful have ever witnessed its glorious splendor…

"Immediately I was in the Spirit; and behold, a throne was set in heaven, and One sat on the throne. And he that sat was to look upon like a jasper and a sardine stone: and there was a rainbow round about the throne, in sight like unto an emerald. And round about the throne were four and twenty seats: and upon the seats I saw four and twenty elders sitting, clothed in white raiment; and they had on their heads crowns of gold. And out of the throne proceeded lightnings and thunderings and voices…"
(Revelation 4.2-6)

The Throne of the Elohim, or *Seat of God*, is where the Son gets high. Simple pranayama breathing induces the transeunt state as the Father *exhales* the perfecting Spirit of perception. The Lord's *at-one-ment* with the Absolute spreads His aural glow to the ends of the Galaxy, filling the "sea" with vital force. Like a great eagle, He unfolds His wings, letting His Holy Spirit soar! Simultaneously, the 24 Thrones rise above themselves, merging into the *Twelve Faces of God*. Their combined luminescence creating a morphic ring-field, the Akashic circle—a synergetic vitalization of the individual, archetypal zones bequeathed to each Pair.

Thrones dwell in fullest power, immovably and perfectly established around the Most High; they energize the ecliptic or *Zodiac* (Grk. animal circle), a 17-degree band of constellations that surrounds and protects the Earth [*See* **Fig. 10**]. The planetary Forces receive and step down the power.

---

[62] An alien assault from the Sirius B system is described in **Book IV**, *Mazzaroth*, pp. 133-134. "First Contact" was in darkest Africa.

"Temple, a highly respected classical scholar and Fellow of the Royal Astronomical Society, was initially fascinated by his discovery that an African tribe called the Dogon appeared to have known for centuries that the dog star Sirius is actually a double-star, a fact finally confirmed by astronomers in 1995. The star's companion, Sirius B, had been invisible to even the most powerful telescopes, although it's existence was suspected as long as 1830.

The Dogon tradition records that knowledge of Sirius B and other astronomical data (such as the fact that the planets revolved around the sun, that the moon was dry and lifeless and that Jupiter had moons and Saturn had rings) had been entrusted to their ancestors by fish-like gods from a third star in the Sirius system almost 5000 years ago. The Dogon called these gods the *Nommo* and had incorporated stories about them and Sirius in their rites and rituals. Temple's interest in a possible Dogon connection with ancient Egypt and Sumeria intensified when he recalled that the Egyptians held Sirius, the dog star, to be sacred and that Isis, the principal goddess of ancient Egypt and sister-wife of Osiris, was often depicted with two minor goddesses, suggesting that the Egyptians might also have known that Sirius was a three-star system. This knowledge was not incorporated in their hieroglyphics as it was reserved for initiates. **He was also impressed by the fact that the Babylonians, who absorbed Sumeria into their empire in 2000 BC, believed that civilization had been founded by fish gods under a leader named Oannes, a name strikingly similar to the Mayan word 'oaana', meaning 'he who has residence in water'.**" ~*Investigating the Unexplained*, Paul Roland

"The Dogon name for Sirius B consists of the word for star, *tolo*, and *po*, the name of the smallest seed known to them. By this name they describe the star's smallness—it is, they say, 'the smallest thing there is.' They also claim that it is 'the heaviest star' (since in it the element earth is replaced by an immensely heavy metal called *sagala*), so heavy 'that all earthly beings combined cannot lift it.' And the color of the star is white. The Dogon thus attribute to Sirius B its three principal qualities as a white dwarf: its smallness, heaviness, and whiteness. They go on to say that the star's orbit is elliptical, with Sirius A at one focus of the ellipse, that the orbital period is 50 years (the actual figure is 50.04 plus or minus .09 years), and that the star rotates on its own axis. The Dogon also describe a third star in the Sirius system, called *Emme Ya* ('sorghum female'). In orbit around this star, they say, is a single satellite. To date *Emme Ya* has not been detected by Western astronomers." ~*The Sirius Mystery*, Robert Temple

So forth down to the earthly domain, the footstool of the *Elohim*. We rechannel the energy back up to the angelic realm immediately above. Water symbolizes this cyclical process—the names for *rain* and *grace* the same in Arabic. Certain mystics can directly perceive the true *logos* or symbols behind the names of the seven upper Realms. One such man was Itzhak Bentov, a remarkable scientific genius whose transcendental bathtub meditations produced some highly intriguing insights.[63]

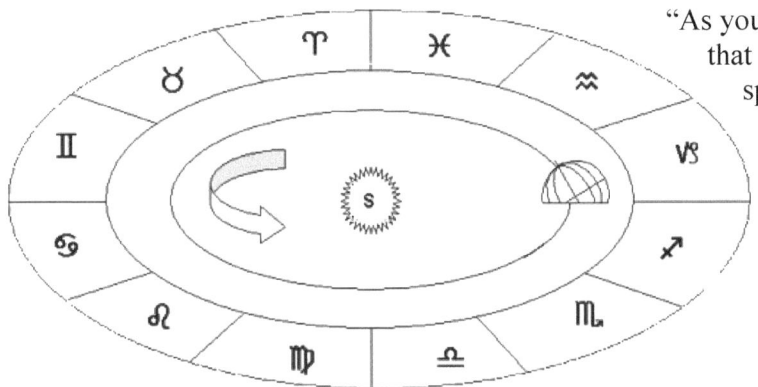

"As you move out of the super-cosmoses, you discover that there are spheres within spheres within spheres: seven levels in all.[64] Each level is represented by a consciousness appearing as an abstract form, and these forms have become the archetypal symbols of mankind: a lily flower for a super-cosmos, an ankh for a super-duper-cosmos, next a cross, then a triangle, followed by an inverted triangle. Then the two triangles are superimposed, forming a star, and finally, on the seventh level, a human form appears, the first to represent a cosmic hierarchy.

Fig. 10 The twelve **Thrones** are represented in Christian iconography around the world as twelve stars upon the crown of Mariah—the Queen of Heaven.

It looks exactly like an Egyptian pharaoh: a rigid figure of golden color, seated on a straight-backed chair, his hands resting on his knees. The Egyptians must have reached this level of consciousness and borrowed this image, in the hope—not without reason—that through a sympathetic resonance with the spiritual hierarchy, they would derive power from their pharaoh, who would act as an antenna for spiritual energies."

Kings of old were *chosen ones*—crowned for exactly that reason. As such, they held absolute power in the kingdom. The people's very prosperity—the fertility of the land and the livestock—were interdependent with that of the King's welfare. His own righteous

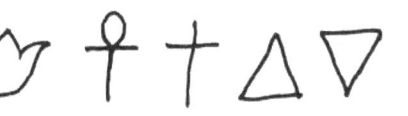

Fig. 11 The Seven Living Logos (Bentov's sketch)

behavior keeps the spiritual influx flowing, while his fall from grace would damn the channels, bringing famine, disaster upon the kingdom. It is the King's mere presence (of mind) on the Throne that keeps the whole enchilada in working order.

Of the manifold planetary systems in this nearly immeasurable Milky Way Galaxy, it may seem unreasonable to suppose our little planet is the only inhabited one—yet that is exactly the case. When we observe how utterly wasteful Nature is, this phenomenon is more readily understood. Pollination carries untold billions of seeds (in pollen sacs) to guarantee *one plant's survival*. Human spermatozoa die by the millions to insure one "man's" job gets done. By the same token, impregnation of the Cosmos results in one living Planet that is perfectly suitable as breeding ground for future *Elohim*—Galactic Lords. When the wheat is separated from the chaff, the cream-of-the-crop will inherit this beautiful blue globe...

---

[63] "On a higher level, a symbol such as a tetrahedron is thrown at you and right away you know and understand all that it would take hours to explain. Our human nervous system can encompass all this and beyond."   ~Bentov
[64] "The seven levels of spheres within spheres represent the seven cosmic hierarchies. The consciousnesses expressing each level are modular; that is, each contains all the consciousnesses below it."   ~Ibid.

> **"And the servants of the householder came and said to him,
> 'Sir, did you not sow good seed in your field? How then has it weeds?'
> He said to them, 'An enemy has done this.' The servants said to him,**
>
> **'Then do you want us to go and gather them?' But he said, 'No; lest in gathering
> the weeds you root up the wheat along with them. Let both grow together until the
> harvest; and at harvest time I will tell the reapers, Gather the weeds first and
> bind them in bundles to be burned, but gather the wheat into my barn.'"**
> (Matthew 13.27-30)
>
> **"The field is the world, and the good seed are the children of the kingdom;
> the weeds are the children of the evil one, and the enemy who sowed them is the devil;
> the harvest is the end of the age, and the reapers are angels.**
>
> *Just as the weeds are collected and burned up with fire,
> so will it be at the end of the age."*
> (Matthew 13.38-40)

Then we will understand how all the insanity, hatred and injustice was necessary for our Spirit's growth; like superfluous sperm, the fallen seeds by the way side will have served their Divine function. The return of the King restores the natural, hierarchical order within the lands as the solemn *eighth week*, the Week of righteousness gets under way. The glory days of Joshua return full circle, with new Promised Real Estate allotted to the neoteric twelve Tribes. After a time of clean-up and rebuilding, the Messianic Age promises the brotherly love and freedom merely hinted at in the heyday of the miraculous '60s...

> *"And a new day will dawn for those who stand long
> And the forests will echo with laughter."*
> ~*Stairway to Heaven*, Led Zeppelin

Book III: Matriarchy

Chapter One: Good God, Bad God

Book II laid a theoretical foundation of hierarchy based upon the world's most reputable and revered sacred texts, somehow still extant. Augmenting Darwinian Nature, our sources established a continuous chain of evolution extending *from* Man, incrementally, up to a Godhead—a pyramid of Lords (gods *and* goddesses), each according to rank and dimension, that culminates with a *supreme* Being. The buck stops with an incandescent Singularity that functions in a Self-sacrificial mode as a source of Unlimited Light—an *anthropomorphic* rock of ages who keeps the entire chain in check within a matrix of inexorable evolution[1]—upwards, toward the Good.

We learned how the living God evolves, with *no end and no beginning*, by continually renewing its Self through the evolutionary thrust of a lower entity's metamorphosis—a perpetual Rose that always smells the same whether the name be Jesus, Yahweh, Buddha, Brahma, Krishna or Allah. The elementary hypostasis simply requires a singular Mind to keep the ongoing, ontological "dream" of Creation in stasis. In the Torah this Overlord is *Elohim,* the Most High God/Goddess, the etymology of the hallowed Hebrew word revealing a polarized, superessential Entity—one Active (dynamic), the other Passive (static). The highest secret, so profound and paradoxical that even the astute Greek mind couldn't wrap itself around the idea of God's dualistic image *co-existing* with the Neo-Platonic One. Extant Eastern teachings, however, still carry a few references to the Judaic revelation of a personal, dynamic God. In the Vedic scriptures of Dravidian India, the Supreme Being was *Manu*. Within the original Theravada Buddhism of two millennia ago, He was acknowledged as the Universal Monarch, *Lord Buddha*. From the land of snows, *Vajrasattva* is the archetypal personification of Power. Persian Zoroastrianism refers to the unbegotten Creator as the Lord of Light, *Ahura Mazda*.

We have seen how the original YHVH Elohim of our Galaxy chose a uniquely qualified tribe of Humans to engender His replacement—how the parthenogenic birth of the Immaculate Mother enabled the preternatural birth of the Avatar. His only remaining task to establish a new contract with the next God (Himself, as it turned out) and pay His dues for the corruption inculcated to the races through sexual misconduct as Adam the protoplast, in the dawn of Time. Thus the Messiah's final incarnation: the great conundrum that awoke the West, bringing the occulted Eastern truth to light as the paradox of the Trinity was finally *grokked* three hundred years later[2] (First Council of Nicea)—through subtle clues left by the enlightened Saul/Paul, together with the cryptic use of Greek terminology employed by the great Initiate, John the Revelator.

Sadly, the epiphany of the One Omnipotent God posited at the peak of a pious pantheon of "pagan" potentates like Zeus and Aphrodite[3] is buried again through centuries of *Endarkenment* (ironically called the Enlightenment), degenerating into a dumbed-down dogma of "the Spirit".

---

[1] The evolutionary impulse descends from the Godhead via the supramundane modules of our Soul-Being not yet fully incorporated: Uranus, Neptune and Pluto. [*See* **Book IV**, p. 114]   "**Now is the judgment of this world: now shall the Prince of this world be cast out. And I, if I were lift up from the earth,** *will draw all men unto me.*"   (John 12.31-32)

[2] It was *fourteen centuries* later when the Spanish Rabbis conceded the hypostatic Trinity, intrinsic to movement within the Godhead: "The Holy One, Blessed be He has Three Heads which are yet One Head. And as the Holy One, Blessed be He is designated by the number three, so also, all the other lights (Sephiroth) with their scintillations, are comprised in the number three."   ~Zohar III, 288b

[3] "Even though there may be so-called gods, whether in heaven or on earth—AS IN FACT THERE ARE MANY GODS AND MANY LORDS—yet for us there is but one god, which is the father, of whom are all things, and we in him: and one lord Jesus Christ by whom are all things, and we by him."   (1 Corinthians 8.5-6)

Book III: Matriarchy

Like the Greeks 3,000 years ago, the simple Native Americans and today's Twelve-Steppers, we acknowledge the ubiquity of Spirit that is ever-present everywhere, verifiable through the magic of synchronicity. Everyday one can see wonder, the ceaseless manifestations of an *apparently* impersonal Higher Power that caters to Good as well as Evil.[4] However, this Great Spirit, One Love doctrine is a vast oversimplification—One Love/Hate is closer to the truth: the Lucas **Force** with its Light and Dark Sides. Twin streams of Mankind, each with their own Lord, feed the amalgamative **Wholly Spirit** with their deeds—good and bad.[5]

Yet today in the 21st century, belief in a pair of *personal* Gods, one Good and the other Evil, is just scientifically ludicrous—a medieval superstition for unsophisticated Third World countries. Or maybe it's the draconic Lord's ace-in-the-hole for a "modern age", the insidious, devilishly simple tactic of laying low for a few centuries.[6] The cost of our technological progress is a Paradigm Lost.

We've also seen how each Galaxy is virtually a Universe unto itself. Bordered by impenetrable dark matter, each galactic Mandala is a self-contained prison with its own benevolent Warden—the latter as much a prisoner of love as the inmates. When we finish our sentences, this Alcatraz, this island Earth, can be transformed back into what it was—an empyreal member of the confederation of Kingdoms. But where does *our* Lord fit into the Empire of the One? Is Jeshua just another Elohim out of countless Buddhas or is He, and by extension us, in the upper echelon? Is there an Elohim of all Elohim, a *capi di tutti i capi*, Godfather of all Godfathers that runs the whole shebang?

These are questions that only the Man Himself can answer. And it won't be that long before we can ask Him, face to face. Meanwhile, we can concern ourselves with more mundane issues—namely, women. Are they all evil and did we make them this way?

Fig. 1 Galactic Mandala

In this third book of the Purification tetralogy, we attempt to corroborate the historicity of the legendary Matriarchy, examine its eventual supersedence by an increasingly megalomaniacal Patriarchy and chart the probable path of its restoration in the coming Golden Age. We will be examining the feminine face of the living God as She exists as an integral archetype of Compassion, and hence the crucial role womanhood is destined to play during the quickened evolution of Humanity in the Messianic Era, now just a few short years away.

---

[4] The surprisingly thorough disintegration of the WTC on 9/11 inspired Bin Laden to declare it an act of God... indeed, it was *his* God.

[5] The Essenes' *Manual of Discipline*, one of a number of valuable documents from the 1947 Dead Sea Scroll cache, declares two distinct divisions of Mankind—the *Sons of Light* and *Sons of Darkness*—shall be governed by two *opposing* Spirits until the end time.

"He created man to have dominion over the world and made for him two Spirits, that he might walk by them until the appointed time of His visitation; they are the Spirits of truth and of error. In the abode of light are the origins of truth, and from the source of darkness are the origins of error. In the hand of the prince of lights is dominion over all sons of righteousness; in the ways of light they walk. And in the hand of the angel of darkness is all dominion over the sons of error; and in the ways of darkness they walk… In these two Spirits are the origins of all the sons of man, and in their divisions all the hosts of men have their inheritance in their generations. *In the ways of the two Spirits men walk.*"

[6] However, the cards are stacked for the Lord of Light. When He moves into the "Father", He becomes Ein-Sof (*Without End, Infinite*), the Inscrutable Source of *everything*, good *and* evil. **The Dark Lord and His Demons exist solely through the will of the Father and function as executors or Lords of Karma.** The Light Lord is Self-limited through a *quid pro quo* "Prime Directive" not to interfere with Mankind's actions: any miraculous intervention on the Christ's part automatically justifies equal and opposite interference from the Dark Lord—a Yang/Yin law of moral metaphysics. Yahweh's empowerment of His Son for 3 ½ years will be counter-balanced by Ba'al's Son for the 3 ½ year tribulation and unholy desecration of the Church. It *appears* the Holy and Unholy Spirits are a single impersonal Force, until *Necessity* summons the Light Lord—overriding the delicate balance. In our everyday misery, we cry wolf: *Quo Vadis Dominus?*, but the Christ loves us too much to interfere with our growing pains, our Self-evolution.

Chapter Two: Two Girls for Every Boy

"We were born before the Wind, ahh so younger than the Son;
Everybody both as One, as we sailed into the Mystic..." ~Van Morrison

According to the Greek father of Western mysticism, Humans were once androgynous beings, male and female united in a single Soul. Upon descent into the world of duality, the singularity polarizes, amoeba-like—splitting into opposites. The entropic effects of degenerative behavior sends the couple spiraling downward until life becomes a desperate, uphill struggle to reunite with our estranged half and re-experience, over and over again, the wonder of true love...

"When one of them meets with his other half, *the actual half of himself*, whether he be a lover of youth or a lover of another sort, the pair are lost in an amazement of love and friendship and intimacy, and will not be out of the other's sight, as I may say, even for a moment: these are the people who pass their whole lives together; yet they could not explain what they desire of one another. For the intense yearning which each of them has towards the other does not appear to be the desire of lover's intercourse, but of something else which the soul of either evidently desires and cannot tell, and of which she has only a dark and doubtful presentiment."
~*The Speech of Aristophanes*

The care-free love of the 60's watered down Plato's poignant revelation of the soulmate to a gross misinterpretation that seemed to justify any lover one desired. The original truth, however, declares there is but *one* destiny, one person whom we have been dancing with throughout the Ages —recognized by that intangible, Harrisonesque quality, *Something* that attracts us like no other lover. Therefore the end of suffering, unification with the High Self, involves integration with our other half. The Creator couple of every Universe is an Aumakua and serving time as Galactic King/Queen will free us from the juvenile *Whee*—l of life and death. Thanks to a 13th century restoration of the sacred oral tradition (*Kabbalah*) by Moses de Leon, we can access Plato's Hebraic source: a five-volume Torah exegesis, *Sefer ha-Zohar* (Book of Splendor)—magnum opus of the rabbinical renaissance in Spain...

"Come and see. All the souls of the world, which are the fruit of the deeds of the Holy One, blessed be He, are all one, and originate in a single mystery. When they descend into the world they all become separated into male and female forms, but the male and female are joined together. After this, when they descend, they become separated, one on one side and one on the other, and the Holy One, blessed be He, unites them subsequently. This union is accomplished by none but the Holy One, Blessed be He, since only He knows how to unite them correctly. Happy is the man whose deeds are meritorious and who walks in the true way, so that soul may be joined to soul as at the very beginning." ~Zohar I, 85b

The first Creation was a wholly act of celestial intercourse, the merging of two supreme Beings.

"Then Elohim said, 'Let us make man in our image, after our likeness...'
So Elohim created man in his own image, in the image of Elohim
he created him; male and female he created them." (Genesis 1.26-27)

Manifestation of the Prototype in the world of polarity instantaneously produces his negative image as well—a powerful creature from the abyss. There are no mistakes in Torah and a broken rule of grammar or textual inconsistency should be carefully examined to find its subtle meaning.

Book III: Matriarchy

"in the image of Elohim he created *him*"—The androgynous protoplast exists in the highest **Atzilut** (Emanation) World— "The monad begot a monad, and reflected upon itself its own heat." ~Trismegistus
The singularity falls into the **Beriah** (Creation) World, one great Soul oscillating from side to side...

"When Adam arose his wife was fastened to his side, and the holy soul that was in him spread to this side and to that, and nourished both sides, because it was comprised of both."   ~Zohar III, 19a

"male and female he created *them*"—the doubled-being is prepared for the **Yetzirah** (Formulative) World, split into positive and negative poles, good and bad Souls—an identical genetic clone of the *Self-existent*: the original (and fiercely ferocious) Elohim couple. [*See* **Book II**, footnote 37]

"...and the female was attached to his side, until God cast a deep slumber upon him and he fell asleep. And the Holy One sawed her off him, and adorned her as they adorn a bride, and brought her to him."   ~Ibid.

With a balance of power achieved on the fifth "day", Elohim pronounces the Creation *very good*—upgraded from just *good* with the crowning touch of the adamic couple to rule over the lower animals. The rough edges are ironed out in the sixth Era (Proterozoic) and during the seventh Cycle (Cambrian Period), as the protoplasmic world of **Malkhut** —the culmination of Creation—gels, They rest. But there is trouble in paradise when Adam's wife, **Lilith**—refusing to be subservient to her equal, the man—flees to the supernal realm of the Cherubim, the "tiny countenances". Mrs. Yahweh (Asherah) walks and the Worlds cannot sustain themselves[7], so there's a Creation Redux, solitary and etheric, as the dynamic Deity—now designated the **YHVH Elohim**—takes the reins...

> "These are the generations of the heavens and of the earth when they were created,
> *in the day* that the Y'hovah Elohim made the heavens and the earth."   (Genesis 2.4)

Skeptical scholars believed that such sloppy editing—a YHVH here, an Elohim there—betrayed a multiple authorship. Several generations were influenced by a solitary 19th c. German hypothesis[8] assigning *four separate authors* to the venerated five-volume anthology credited to Moses.

The Documentary Hypothesis showed little, if any, respect for anything supernatural...

J — (Jehovah redactor) He/she wrote as YHVH from the southern Kingdom of Judah, ca. 950 BC

E — (Elohim redactor) lived in the northern Kingdom of Israel, ca. 850 BC, called himself Elohim

D — (Deuteronomist) wrote Deuteronomy during the religious reform of King Josiah in 622 BC

P — (Levi Priest) filled in many of the holes in the Pentateuch, redacting the entire Torah, ca. 450 BC

Despite three centuries of "Post-Enlightenment" attempts to debunk holy Scripture, the **Five Books of Moses** have recently emerged untainted—scientifically proven to contain a carefully crafted revelation from an *External* (*i.e.* extratemporal), Omniscient Entity. As such, it is Perfect: a sacred document of the highest order with compounded layers of meaning—not the least being a 3,200 year-old quasi-quantum code, time-locked to the 20th century and its supreme technological achievement, the computer. In the world of Biblical scholarship, the Pentateuch has regained some of its dignity with Wellhausen's theory now deemed obsolete...

---

7 According to Kabbalah, the original seven Edomite kings [Genesis 36.31] were created of pure Judgment with no admixture of Mercy (purgatorial Hell). They could not redeem themselves (reincarnate) and just died out, one after the other...   Isaiah Tishby explains: "The system of emanation had not yet been prepared in the image of the supernal Man, which constitutes a harmonious structure by balancing the opposing forces. In the idea of the image of Man even the forces of destruction of *the other side* are able to survive." ~Zohar I
8 Julius Wellhausen's *Documentary Hypothesis*—inspiring Schweitzer's misguided quest for the historical Jesus—influenced millions and led to the general perception of the Bible as a man-made myth, adding fuel to the anti-Semite movement already in motion.

"The evidence presented here points to the following conclusion: there is much more uniformity and much less fragmentation in the book of Genesis than generally assumed. ***The standard division of Genesis into J, E, and P strands should be discarded.*** This method of source criticism is a method of an earlier age, predominantly of the 19th century. If new approaches to the text, such as literary criticism of the type advanced here, deem the *Documentary Hypothesis* unreasonable and invalid, then source critics will have to rethink earlier conclusions and start anew." ~*The Redaction of Genesis*, Rendsburg

Fig. 2 "They seemed to have come over a secondary pass at about 19,500 ft., down to 19,000 ft. where we first saw them, and then went on down the glacier. What it is, I don't know, but I am quite clear that it is no animal known to live in the Himalaya, and that it is big." ~Eric Shipton, 1951 Everest expedition

The ostensible *faux pas* in Genesis hints of something more amazing than simply redaction. The original Creation's prehistoric menagerie included the subhuman simian species, which according to Charles Darwin's brilliant detective work evolved into the cave man—*homo erectus*—over 500,000 years ago. Remnants of the first Creation are evident today in the last living dinosaur, the alligator and Neanderthal man's evolutionary dead-end, the Himalayan Yeti. [*See* **Fig. 2**] Conversely, *homo sapiens* are the product of the *second* Creation, manifesting *fully evolved in the wink of an eye* a mere 26,000 years ago...

"And the Y'hovah Elohim formed man of
the *dust of the ground*, and breathed
into his nostrils the breath of life;
and man became a living soul."   (Gen. 2.7)

The Eloah replicates an etheric double, denser yet not carnal—**dust**, not earth. The new Adam shines in "a glorious light body, like that of the angels, and spirits, and answers to the Yetzirah World." ~*Qabbalah* A miscreant plants an alien flora that is definitely deleterious for the supernal Man. The lower animal matrices are recreated, likewise out of the luminiferous ether. When Adam can find no equal among them as a playmate (alas, no Golden Retrievers yet), his soul is split *again*—the anomalous event engaging our endless search for wholeness. This time, the YHVH Elohim creates a gorgeous creature compared to the spontaneously generated elemental. *Chavvah* (Hbw. life-giver) is a true work of art, a polar *complement* sharing the same good soul as Adam. The YHVH extricates the latter's estranged spouse from her Cherubic haven and brings her down to help govern the lower world. Just one look at Eva's supernal beauty repels the creature and she is dispatched to the deep.

"When she saw Eve, who was attached to Adam's back, and whose beauty was like that of the realms above, and when she saw her perfect image, she flew from there and wished, as at first, to join herself to the tiny countenances. The keepers of the celestial gates did not allow her to approach."   ~Zohar I, 19b

Adam's psychedelic sin of learning right from wrong, his loss of innocence, entails a karmic Fall into an even *lower* dimension of gross materiality—the Assiah (Manifest) World. Adam and Eve are given coats of skin (*i.e.* carnal bodies) for "clothes", viz. ejected from the etheric dimension.[9]

---

[9] Dumbed-down from the Heavenly realm, another medium (the *ruah*) is required to reinterpret the new reality. [*See* **Book II**, p. 50] Here the term "Adam and Eve" is cumulative—their descendents scattered abroad, adapting *organically* to the earthly environments...

"...they became hardened or set—much in the form of the existent human body of the day, with that color as partook of their surroundings much in the manner as the chameleon in the present... [In Atlantis arose] the red or mixture peoples—or colors; known later as the red race." ~*Edgar Cayce on Atlantis*

Book III: Matriarchy

Now turned Demoness and allied with Ba'al (Samael), Lilith is given rule over infants with karmic comeuppances— "Then the Holy One, blessed be He, brought her out of the depths of the sea, and she rules over all infants—'the tiny countenances' of mankind—who deserve to be punished because of the sins of their fathers. She goes to and fro in the world... finding infants who ought to be punished, and she smiles at them and kills them. This happens when the moon is on the wane, as the light diminishes."   ~Zohar I, 19b

Lilith was dreaded during the Middle Ages as the cause of sudden infant death syndrome (SIDS) and protective amulets were fashioned to hang over the baby's crib. Yet the only mention of Adam's first wife in the entire Bible is a *coded* reference in Isaiah's apocalyptic prophecy of a decimated Rome, reinhabited with the dregs of nature...

Fig. 3   Lilith relief, 2000 BC

"The wild beasts of the desert shall also meet with the wild beasts of the island, and the satyr shall cry to his fellow; the screech owl[10] **also shall rest there..."**   (Isaiah 34.14)

Infanticide merely her hobby, the red-headed babe of Babylon's real passion is seducing men through her potent presence in wine yeasts and psychotropic plants. Lilith, *aka* **Mary Jane**, is a tart...

"She dresses herself in finery like an abominable harlot and stands at the corners of streets and highways in order to attract men. When a fool approaches her, she embraces him and kisses him, and mixes her wine lees with snake poison for him. Once he has drunk, he turns aside after her. When she sees that *he has turned aside after her from the way of truth*, she takes off all the finery that she had put on for the sake of this fool...
 She leaves him asleep on the bed and ascends to the realms above, accuses him, obtains authority, and descends. The fool wakes up, thinking to sport with her as before, but she takes off her finery, and turns into a fierce warrior, facing him in a garment of flaming fire, a vision of dread, terrifying both body and soul, full of horrific eyes, a sharpened sword in her hand with drops of poison suspended from it. She kills the fool, and throws him into Gehinnom."   ~Zohar I, 148ab

Drug addiction claims the soul of the fool, enchanted and enslaved by the false *siddhis*. After the honeymoon, the sweet smell of sinsemilla turns fowl as Lily morphs into **Kali the Destroyer**, leaving behind her a shell of the former man—now dependent upon her for sustenance. In Her *tantric* guise, the *lilits* seduce men on the astral planes, inflaming them with lust and collecting their **night seed**. "And she goes and roams the world at night, and makes sport with men and causes them to emit seed. And wherever men are found sleeping alone in a house, they [these spirits] descend upon them and get hold of them and adhere to them and take desire from them and bear from them."   ~Zohar I,19b

Thus we find ourselves at the end of a long line of ancestors begot from the gross, carnal generations of Adam, Ba'al and Eva—polarized through endless struggle into contrary camps of *Light* and *Darkness*. As degenerative offspring, every man has two soulmates[11] to deal with: one true-love, complementary half (à la Plato) and one nasty female who will dedicate her life to ruining yours. The *Zohar* warns that if a man's life is not upright, he'll lose his heaven-sent partner to another...

---

10 liyliyth. *lee-leeth*; a night spectre—screech owl   ~*Strong's Exhaustive Concordance of the Bible*
11 A third polarity type is the twin soul. Growth is usually on parallel paths—but when one falls, the other is always there to pick him/her up again. "Soul mates," John continued, "were actually created for one another at the beginning of time, or what you call at the moment of the Big Bang. They vibrate at exactly the same electromagnetic frequency because they are identical counterparts of one another. Twin souls are more common to find because they have experienced many lifetimes together in one form or another. But soul mates were actually created at the beginning of time as pairs who belonged together."   ~*Out on a Limb*, Shirley MacLaine

"But if a man corrupts his way of life, his prescribed partner is given to another until he corrects his deeds. When he has reformed his way of life, or when the proper time has arrived, one man has to make way for the other, and the latter comes and claims his due."

Not only does one lose his upright soulmate from incorrect living, but she can be replaced by the elemental counterpart from the *sitra ahra*.[12]

"Even though the Holy One, blessed be He, prepares good things to give to a man, nevertheless, if he turns his paths away from the Holy One, blessed be He, and toward 'the other side' (*sitra ahra*), everything that comes upon him, all the evil and disruption, comes from that 'other side' (*sitra ahra*) to which he has committed himself by his evil deeds."   ~Zohar I, 229a

Regrettably, most men these days, at the close of the karmic Kali Yuga, earn the evil woman. Intrigued by an inexplicable sexual compatibility, they mistake the girl/mistress polar *opposite* for the woman/wife polar *complement*—and marry the wrong one! Others succumb to a *Fatal Attraction* with their Glenn Close soulmate, go through a heart-wrenching divorce and generally rue the day they were born. They have found their better half only to lose her later on. It's a delicate balancing act to rise above 26,000 years of aberrant conditioning.

Chapter Three: Necessary Evil

"Might as well face it, you're addicted to love."   ~Robert Palmer

Our lustful nature is our own worst enemy, and *every* act of sexual intercourse reinforces the nasty habit. In this Post-Hefnerian, sexually liberated era, the idea that fornication can be sinful is practically a joke. As long as you're doing it with a consenting adult of the opposite sex, you're way ahead of the pedophiles, rapists and homosexuals, not to mention freakier fans of necrophilia or kinky bestiality. Still, this is only relatively speaking because eventually we have to wean ourselves from the teat before we can evolve into our light bodies.   [See **Book IV**, *The Kingdom of Heavens*]

The catch-22 is we *must* ejaculate to stay healthy and reproduce. Without sexual intercourse or manually "spanking the monkey", the male body falls prey to a host of diseases like prostate cancer. And only the *sweetest taboo* allows a soul to reincarnate and evolve. So we have to give the Devil His due, while consciously reducing our "drug" habit to a minimum.[13] Cold Turkey celibacy only reinforces the craving later on, when the freeze-dried "seeds of desire" thaw.

---

12 Our original, polar opposite is one helluva piece of work, as the promiscuous Solomon knew only too well.
  "And I find more bitter than death the woman, whose heart is snares and nets, and her hands as bands:
    whoso pleaseth God shall escape from her; but the sinner shall be taken by her."   (Ecclesiastes 7.26)
13 In one of the most candid confessions of existential angst ever put to paper, Paul concedes the futility of living a wholly spiritual life while incarcerated in a cursed body…
  "We know that the law is spiritual, but I am carnal, sold under sin. What I will to do, that I do not practice;
    but what I hate, that I do. The good that I will to do, I do not do; but the evil I will not to do, that I practice.
    I delight in the law of God according to the inward man. But I see another law in my members,
      warring against the law of my mind, and bringing me into captivity to the law of sin
        which is in my members. O wretched man that I am! So then, with the mind
          I myself serve the law of God, but with the flesh the law of sin."
                    (Romans 7.14-25)

Book III: Matriarchy

Our perilous climb up the Tree of Knowledge of Good and Evil entails education, especially knowledge of the metaphysical principles behind "making love".[14] Learning how we have unconsciously subjugated women and vise versa is the first step to breaking the insidious chains of addiction that have bound us together since day one...

> "To the woman he said, I will greatly multiply your pain and your conception; in pain you shall bring forth children and you shall be dependent on your husband (*'iysh*), and he shall rule over you."
> (Genesis 3.1)

The original OT word for *husband* was *'iysh*, (Hbw. *eesh;* a man as an individual or a male person ~Strong's). By the time of King Solomon, with the patriarchal Hebrew empire at its material apex, the previous partnership of man and woman had completely degenerated into one of slavery. The new designation for husband became *ba'al*, (Hbw. *bah'–al;* a master; hence, a husband, or *owner* ~Strong's)...

Fig. 4 Live Long and Prosper?

> "A virtuous wife is a crown to her husband *(ba' al)*."
> (Proverbs 12.4)

Indeed, this was also the proper name for the infamous Dark Lord, indicative of the power-tripping that men became accustomed to after millennia of abuse. The addictive properties of sexual intercourse had enslaved both sexes to the critical degree where a compromise from the YHVH became the only feasible answer: humans could have their cake and eat it too provided they limited their lustful appetites to a single partner for life. The institution of Holy Matrimony was sanctified to keep Man from sinking even *deeper* into the carnal, material world. Only choose carefully because—barring infidelity—we can never change dance partners as long as we live.[15]

---

[14] Adam *knew* Eve. Sexual intercourse opens the quasi-quantum eleventh *sefira*, a bottomless abyss of knowledge. The outlawed Tantric practices of Dravidian India were devised to prolong the orgasmic ecstasy, and access this no-man's land. The Kabbalah's most dire warnings concern the tricky Uranian dimension known as *Daath* (Hbw. Knowledge). The rabbis describe a very dangerous door that, once opened, is hard to close again. With good reason, the ancient seers even denied its existence! They warned one another to beware of direct knowledge—use wisdom to understand, become wise through understanding. **"The fear of the YHVH is the beginning of *da'ath*: but fools despise wisdom and instruction."** ~Proverbs 1.7

"Ten Sefirot of Nothingness
Ten and not nine
Ten and not eleven
Understand with Wisdom
Be wise with Understanding

Examine with them
and probe with them
Make [each] thing stand on its essence
and make the Creator sit on His base."
~*Sefer Yetzirah* 11.4

[15] Knowing their own promiscuous nature and the licentiousness of women, the Apostles are aghast to learn how strict that rule is...
"I say unto you, Whosoever shall put away his wife, except it be for fornication, and shall marry another, committeth adultery: and whoso marrieth her which is put away doth commit adultery."

His disciples said unto him: 'If the case of the man be so with his wife, it is not good to marry.' But he said unto them:

"All men cannot receive this saying, save they to whom it [the Power] **is given.** [Celibacy is undertaken by the Chosen, the twice-born] **For there are some eunuchs, which were so born from their mother's womb: and there are some eunuchs, which were made eunuchs of men: and there be eunuchs, which have made themselves eunuchs for the kingdom of heaven's sake.** *He that is able to receive it*, **let him receive it."**
(Matthew 19.9-12)

The original sin of Adam and Eva was not fornication. It was the uncontrollable, superheated sex generated from the alien psychotropics they ingested.[16] Lust came into the world through the first woman *turning on* the first man, infecting the entire line of descent.[17] Instead of a natural function like eating and defecating, reproduction became an ecstatic, orgasmic rush after Eva's tantric initiation (rape) by a *repulsive one* from the Sirian system. [*See* **Book IV,** footnote 52] Simple sex became the single most addictive, insatiable force ever unleashed—an opportunity to experience instant *Nirvana* here on Earth, damning any desire to return to our original, individuated Divinity.

In the '60s, an eager UCLA student shook the academic world with the first-ever revelation to white cultures of carefully guarded, age-old secrets from a *closed* Indian civilization—the Toltec. The controversial, highly praised books[18], culled from copious field notes, faithfully recorded the naïve anthropologist's shamanic initiation from a full-fledged sorcerer, don Juan Matus. The fact that Carlos Castaneda's later writings crossed the lines of decency, morality and Humanity itself doesn't negate the legitimacy of the wisdom teachings. Since the Egyptian exodus and Babylonian captivity, men of God have been *obliged* to acquire hidden (*i.e.* occult) teachings from both Demonic as well as Angelic sources. A cornucopia of psychotropic plants indigenous to old world Mexico enabled the shrewd Toltec *brujos* to unlock the secret of enslaving females, wherein a man becomes their owner or *ba' al*. Florinda Donner and Taisha Abelar, female Castaneda cohorts, disclosed the sorcerer's perception of sex...

"Although the primary function of sexual intercourse is procreation, it also has a secondary and covert function, which is to ensure a continual flow of energy from women to men.

Why do you say it as if it were a one-way street? Isn't the sexual act an even exchange of energy between male and female?

No. Men leave specific energy lines inside the body of women. They are like luminous tapeworms that move inside the womb, sipping up energy.

That sounds positively sinister.

They are put there for an even more sinister reason, which is to ensure that a steady supply of energy reaches the man who deposited them. Those lines of energy, established through sexual intercourse, collect and steal energy from the female body to benefit the male who left them there. I can see the wormlike filaments in women's bodies for myself. You, for example, have a number of them still active. Nature's imperative is to perpetuate our species. In order to ensure that this continues to take place, women have to carry an excessive burden at their basic energy level. And that means a flow of energy that taxes women.

Women are the foundation for perpetuating the human species. The bulk of the energy comes from them, not only to gestate, give birth and nourish their offspring, but also for ensuring that the male plays his part in this whole process. It's bad enough that one man leaves energy lines inside a woman's body, although that is necessary for having offspring and ensuring their survival. But to have the energy lines of ten or twenty men inside her feeding off her luminosity is more than anyone can bear.

---

16 *See* **Book I**, footnote 4. "Toloache (*Datura inoxia*) is still sold in Mexican markets as an aphrodisiac and medicine." ~Grinspoon
17 "When the serpent mounted eve, he injected filth into her." ~Talmud Shab. 146a Eva transferred the fiery infestation to Adam...
"The entire human race that was to pass through woman into offspring was contained in the first man when that married couple received the divine sentence condemning them to punishment, and humanity produced what humanity became, not what it was when created, but when, having sinned, it was punished." ~*City of God*, Augustine
18 The first ground-breaking books were enthusiastically received. "We are incredibly fortunate to have Carlos Castaneda's books. Taken together they form a work which is among the best that the science of anthropology has produced. The story they tell is so good, and the descriptions so vivid, that I was utterly fascinated as I read." ~New York Times   "Makes hypnotic reading. Castaneda is a brilliant, self-mocking and—one assumes, despite the weirdness of the narrative—truthful storyteller." ~Time Magazine

Book III: Matriarchy

Can a woman get rid of those lines?

A woman carries those luminous worms for seven years, after which time they disappear or fade out. But the wretched part is that when the seven years are about to be up, the whole army of worms, from the very first a woman had to the very last one, all become agitated at once so that the woman is driven to have sexual intercourse again. Then all the worms spring to life stronger than ever to feed off the woman's luminous energy for another seven years. It really is a never-ending cycle.

What if the woman is celibate? Do the worms just die out?

Yes, if she can resist having sex for seven years. But it's nearly impossible for a woman to remain celibate like that in our day and age, unless she becomes a nun, or has money to support herself. And even then she still would need a totally different rationale.

Why is that?

Because not only is it a biological imperative that women have sexual intercourse, but it is also a social mandate. You, like every woman, have been tricked and forced into submission. And the sad part is that you're trapped in this pattern, even if you don't intend to procreate. I can only tell you that to wake up, you must break a vicious circle."   ~*The Sorcerer's Crossing*, Taisha Abelar

In just the past few decades, women have, consciously or unconsciously, been breaking their dependencies on men. The cold war has heated up recently with fiercely independent women from all walks of life taking control of their lives. It is fairly routine these days to get married, have a child, get divorced and collect alimony for 18 years. Women aren't getting mad anymore, they're getting even—using men as they have been used and abused for millennia. One should be careful what he wishes for because these ladies are now more advanced than man. After centuries of selfless childbearing, rearing and releasing, her emotional body has evolved exponentially. It's a well-known fact girls mature faster than boys; perhaps less understood is the fact that the entire genus of womanhood is now superior to the male species. The pendulum is swinging back to the prehistoric Matriarchy where the female was venerated, respected and feared—before the very archetype of the Goddess was obliterated from the face of the Earth!

Chapter Four: The Mother Goddess

"She wears an Egyptian ring, it sparkles before she speaks."   ~Dylan

In her lavishly illustrated lifework, *The Language of the Goddess*, Marija Gimbutas brought irrefutable archaeological evidence to bear on her thesis of old-world European society—how it enjoyed a delicate balance of forces until a revolution destroyed every vestige of female veneration.

"The Indo-European social structure is patriarchal, patrilineal and the psyche is warrior. Every God is also a warrior. The three main Indo-European Gods are the God of the Shining Sky, the God of the Underworld and the Thunder God. The female goddesses are just brides, wives or maidens without any power, without any creativity. They're just there, they're beauties, they're Venuses, like the dawn or sun maiden.

So the system from what existed in the matristic culture before the Indo-Europeans in Europe is totally different. I call it matristic, not matriarchal, because matriarchal always arouses ideas of dominance and is compared with the patriarchy. But it was a balanced society, it was not that women were really so powerful that they usurped everything that was masculine."

Before the rise of the Egyptian Empire—the patriarchal civilization that initiated the *Kali Yuga*—magic ruled the Universe, permeated by the feminine in all her multitudinous manifestations...

"Her power was in water and stone, in tomb and cave, in animals and birds, snakes and fish, hills, trees and flowers. Hence the holistic and mythopoeic perception of the sacredness and mystery of all there is on Earth. This culture took keen delight in the natural wonders of this world. Its people did not produce lethal weapons or build forts in inaccessible places, as their successors did, even when they were acquainted with metallurgy. Instead, they built magnificent tomb-shrines and temples, comfortable houses in moderately-sized villages, and created superb pottery and sculptures. This was a long-lasting period of remarkable creativity and stability, an age free of strife. Their culture was a culture of art."

Dr. Gimbutas' *archeomythological* establishment of a Neolithic European matriarchy dominant during the Bronze Epoch[19] corresponds to the *Dvapara Yuga*—as the humble Age of Virgo gave way to the domineering Age of Leo. The portentous Fall of the Angels circa 10,948 BC provided closure to the *Treta Yuga* as the *Dvapara Yuga* dawned—the third 6,480-year cosmic season of Summer, distinguished by the precession of the equinoxes.[20] Naturally, the Virgo Period witnessed a flowering of the virtues inherent in pious womanhood. Leo's Era would carry forth that delicate female presence, adding the will, strength and courage of the lion to the purity of the virgin. And the leonine predilection for creativity would leave a fabulous legacy of art for Ages to come. Not the least being the mysterious Sphinx herself, a Virgo-Leo cusp monument marking a misshapen milestone in prehistory when Mankind took a quantum leap forward in evolution. [*See* **Book IV, Fig. 13**]

The gradual descent into *his*-story was initially a rectification of Yang/Yin polarities. The autumn equinox/Milky Way conjunction circa 4468 BC witnessed the genesis of the first-known organized society, Egypt. This highly advanced civilization, which seemed to spring from nowhere[21], revered above all others the Queen Mother, Isis...

---

19 "Marija Gimbutas has not only prepared a fundamental glossary of pictorial keys to the mythology of the otherwise undocumented era of European prehistory, but has established the main themes of a religion in veneration of both the universe as a living body of Goddess-Mother Creatrix and all the living things within it as partaking in her divinity." ~Joseph Campbell
20 The glacial Ice Age of the *Tetra Yuga* defrosts as frigid Virgo warms up to a brief period of gracious living. [*See* **Book II, Fig. 2**]
21 The peerless psychic Edgar Cayce gave over 2,500 "life readings", many of them delving into the subject's past life in Atlantis. Pooled together, these readings render a remarkable description of self-destruction. Like today, it was out-of-control technology that opened the floodgates and sank the continent. Heads-up refugees poured into the uncivilized Yucatan, Pyrenees and *Egyptian* lands.

"The use of these devices by the Sons of Belial [Hbw. "without a yoke"] brought, then, the first of the upheavals; or the turning of the rays from the Sun—as used by the Sons of the Law of One—into the crystal for the activities of same—produced what we would call a volcanic upheaval; and the separating of the land into several islands—five in number. Poseidia... then became one of these islands."

The massive crystals—just like our nuclear reactors—were initially a great boon to society...

"In Poseidia the entity dwelt among those that had charge of the storage of the motivative forces from the great crystals that so condensed the lights, the forms of the activities, as to guide the ships in the sea and in the air and in conveniences of the body as television and recording voice."

The ambitious Sons of Darkness discovered they could use the crystals' rays as **weapons of mass destruction**...

"In Atlantean land during those periods when there were those determining as to whether there would be the application of the laws of the children of One or of Sons of Belial in turning into destructive channels those influences of infinite power as were being gained from the elements as well as from what is termed spiritual or supernatural powers in the present. Entity wavered between choices and when the destruction came about by the use of those rays as were applied for beneficial forces, entity misapplied ability."

Prior to upheaval, Cayce, a past-life priest in primitive Egypt, sailed for Poseidia to salvage the records of an upright people...

"In Atlantean land before the final destruction—when the priest came from Egypt to Poseidia to gain understanding of the Law of One (or God) that there might be records carried back to Egypt... Entity had charge of records brought to Egypt [and] was one who PERSONALLY cared for the records that were brought by the leaders of that people for preservation in that portion of man's experience in the Earth.... Entity aided the priest in the preparation of the manner of building the temple of records that lies just beyond that enigma that still is the mystery of mysteries to those who seek to know what were the manners of thought of the ancient sons who made man, beast—as part of the consciousness." (Cayce Reading 1792-2)

The devastation of the *first*, and perhaps greatest civilization, Atlantis, forced the evacuation of her leading scientists—the *children of Seth*—to unsophisticated lands… where their ancestors became mythologized as Gods. [*See* **Book IV**, footnote 44]

Book III: Matriarchy

"Isis was the greatest goddess in Egypt and was worshipped for over 3,000 years, from pre-dynastic times—before 3,000 BC—until the second century AD, when her cult and many of her images passed directly on to the figure of Mary."   ~*The Myth of the Goddess,* Baring and Cashford

The mythological tale of the first king of Egypt's resuscitation by Isis demonstrates the initial stabilization, the harmony between Matriarchy and Patriarchy that still existed within the earliest extant civilization. Although Osiris [aka *Oannes*—See **Book IV**, footnote 52] is credited with teaching Egypt the arts of cultivation, including planting wheat for bread, barley for beer and harvesting grapes for wine, he owed his life to his sorceress wife, Isis...

"According to the form of the myth reported by the Greek author Plutarch, Osiris was slain or drowned by Seth, who tore the corpse into 14 pieces and flung them over Egypt. Eventually, Isis and her sister Nephthys found and buried all the pieces, except the phallus, thereby giving new life to Osiris, who thenceforth remained in the underworld as ruler and judge. Isis revived Osiris by magical means and conceived her son Horus by him. Horus later successfully fought against Seth and became the new king of Egypt."   ~Encyclopedia Britannica

That the Feminine still held sway is evident from one of Plutarch's "Five Explanations" for the above story—this, the "Fourth", mythologizes a male monarch to mimic the moon's metamorphosis...

"In § XLII. Plutarch connects the death-day of Osiris, the seventeenth of Hathor, with the seventeenth day of the Moon's revolution, when she begins to wane. The age of Osiris, twenty-eight years, suggests the comparison with the twenty-eight days of the Moon's revolution. The tree-trunk which is made into the shape of a crescent at the funeral of Osiris refers to the crescent moon when she wanes. The fourteen pieces into which Osiris was broken refer to the fourteen days in which the moon wanes."   ~*Legends of the Gods,* E. A. Wallis Budge

Upon his resuscitation, Osiris became Lord of the Underworld—mummification and belief in eternal life a direct result of the king whose body was wrapped in linen and reanimated through words of power.

His infernal realm was the treacherous *Tuat*—unnavigable without a thorough understanding of the "Handbook for the Deceased."[22] Once clear of the *Tuat*, the righteous traveler reached the *Islands of the Blessed*, the circumpolar stars.[23]

Fig. 5   Air shafts of the Great Pyramid, ca. 2500 BC

---

[22] "The object of all the *Books of the Other World* was to provide the dead with a 'Guide' or 'Handbook,' which contained a description of the regions through which their souls would have to pass on their way to the kingdom...

All the principal books relating to the Tuat were profusely illustrated. In the copies of them which were painted on the walls of royal tombs, each division of the Tuat was clearly drawn and described, and each gate, with all its guardians, was carefully depicted. Both the living and the dead could learn from them, *not only the names, but also the forms, of every god, spirit, soul, shade, demon, and monster which they were likely to meet on their way,* and the copious texts which were given side by side with the pictures enabled the traveler through the Tuat—always, of course, provided that he had learned them—to participate in the benefits which were decreed by the Sun-god for the beings of each section of it."   ~*The Egyptian Heaven and Hell,* E. A. Wallis Budge (1905)

[23] "The Pyramid Texts frequently allude to the king's association in his afterlife with the stars and, in particular, with the circumpolar stars and with Orion and Sothis (Sirius)... Once every 24 hours the three stars in Orion's belt passed at culmination over the shaft. [*See* **Fig. 5**] We learn from the Pyramid Texts that Orion and Sirius occupied almost as important positions in the king's plans for his after-life as the circumpolar stars... The Great Pyramid was unique in making provision for the king to associate himself with both the circumpolar stars and the constellation of Orion and Sirius."   ~*The Pyramids of Egypt,* I.E.S. Edwards

> "Thy sacred image, Orion in heaven, rises and sets every day,
> I am Sothis (Sirius) following after him, and I will not forsake him."   ~Ptolemaic Text

The Belt of Orion (Osiris) points directly to the most crucial star in the Egyptian sky, Sirius (Isis), heralding the New Year with her sorrowful inundation of the Nile…

> "The Egyptians say that Isis bewails Osiris when the river begins to rise;
> when it inundates the fields they say that it is the tears of Isis."   ~Pausanias X, 32

Upon the virgin birth of her son, the Queen's maternal instincts are proven exemplary—her devotion to the boy, unconditional. Born from the severed phallus of Osiris, the babe is ensconced in the swamplands until fatally stung by a scorpion. After a day's foraging, Isis returns to the marshes.

> "All day, while I was caring for his needs, I was longing for my little boy. When I returned, expecting to embrace him, I found my beautiful golden Horus, my innocent, fatherless child, lying on and the ground with water streaming from his eyes and saliva dropping from his lips. His body was limp, his heart was weak, the pulses of his body did not beat. I cried out saying, 'Here I am, here I am!' but the child was too weak to reply."
> ~Pyramid Texts

She cries out to the Sun-god, *Ra*, whereupon Thoth descends, giving the breath of life back to the boy. Defeating his mortal enemy Seth, promotes Horus to king of Egypt with mom deified as Mother of the living God.[24] The Egyptian hieroglyph representing Isis was an elevated throne, the female recognized as the *sacred support which empowered the great Pharaohs to rule*. Gradually, over the centuries, the wife of Osiris replaced all the minor goddesses in the pantheon as an existential archetype was acknowledged for the first time in known history—a supreme Female Being, *aka* the *Queen of Heaven*. Her fame continued unabated up to the second century AD, where she takes mercy upon the bewitched Lucius…

> "Behold Lucius I am come, thy weeping and prayers has moved me to succor thee. I am she that is the natural mother of all things, mistress and governess of all the elements, the initial progeny of worlds, chief of powers divine, *Queen of heaven*, the principal of the Gods celestial, the light of the goddesses: at my will the planets of the air, the wholesome winds of the Seas, and the silences of hell be disposed. My name, my divinity is adored throughout all the world in divers manners, in variable customs and in many names… Principally the Ethiopians which dwell in the Orient, and the Egyptians which are excellent in all kind of ancient doctrine, and by their proper ceremonies accustomed to worship me, do call me Queen Isis."   ~*The Golden Ass*, Apuleius

Like the *Son of God*, the *Queen of Heaven* is also an ephemeral echelon—the One continually renewing Itself with the deification of the next polar incumbents. The new Queen, full of grace, took her rightful place as spokesperson for the Lord. In contradistinction to Isis[25], Mary commands

---

[24] See **Book IV**, *Mazzaroth*. This virgin-mother of God story skewed off the *original myth* set in the stars by the third son of Adam.
[25] Isis set Herself apart from the YHVH, granting favors to her retinue. One day, Jeremiah warned the idolaters that jealous Yahweh would not put up with it anymore. The defiant women, however, accustomed to the benefits of Goddess worship, refuse to listen…
'As for the word that you have spoken to us in the name of the YHVH, we will not listen to you! But we will certainly do whatever has gone out of our own mouth, to burn incense to the *queen of heaven* **and pour out drink offerings to her, as we have done, we and our fathers, our kings and our princes, in the cities of Judah and in the streets of Jerusalem.** *For then we had plenty of food, were well-off, and saw no trouble.* **But since we stopped burning incense to the queen of heaven and pouring out drink offerings to her, we have lacked everything and have been consumed by the sword and by famine.'** Furthermore, the hen-pecked men never dared stand up to their wives' idolatrous rituals… **The women also said, 'And when we burned incense to the** *queen of heaven* **and poured out drink offerings to her, did we make cakes for her, to worship her, and pour out drink offerings to her without our husbands' permission?'"**   (Jeremiah 44.15-19)

Power *behind* the Throne, with humility and absolute deference to the Creative Force. Womanhood however, like the old Queen, took a different tack when astounding latent abilities accelerated their evolution—for good and bad.

Chapter Five: Witch or Priestess?

"You say love is a temple, Love a higher law,
Love is a temple, Love the higher law.
You ask me to enter, but then you make me crawl..." ~U2

Women's intuition and empathetic nature are attributed to quasi, reversed hardware wiring—a preponderance of the right-brain, artistic hemisphere over the rational, logical left-brain. In order to compete in a male society, women have been forced to ignore their own natural mechanism and imitate the insipid, "Spock-like" mentality of men. Yet even the most successful will always be second-class citizens, at best. "What good is it that they have access to what men have when they are still considered inferior beings who have to adopt male attitudes and behaviors in order to succeed? The truly successful ones are the perfect converts. They, too, look down on women." ~*The Sorcerer's Crossing*

The close connection that women have with Spirit is considered a liability since it supersedes the dog-eat-dog survival instincts of the male animal. Inspiration or information that is not the practical, putting-meat-on-the-table type is simply of little value. Still, these other methods of knowledge involving abstract thinking were difficult to access and since time immemorial, (male) philosophers from Plato to Jung were obsessed with the process of transcendence—while women effortlessly communed with the Source as their God-given predilection...

"Originally women saw no need to exploit their facility to link themselves broadly and directly to the spirit. They saw no necessity to talk about or intellectualize this natural capacity of theirs, for it was enough for them to put it in action and to know that they had it.

Men's incapacity to link themselves directly to the spirit was what drove them to talk about the process of reaching knowledge, and it is precisely this insistence on knowing how they strive toward the spirit, this insistence on analyzing the process, that gave them the certainty that being rational is a typically male skill. The conceptualization of reason has been exclusively by men, and this has allowed men to belittle women's gifts and accomplishments. Even worse, it has allowed men to exclude feminine traits from the formulation of the ideals of reason." ~Ibid.

Hence, since the 17th century Enlightenment, Humanity has been indoctrinated with a hallowed reverence for the logical mind—a religion of Man far more penetrating and influential than any canon of sacred Scripture thus far revealed, Science[26]... a body of knowledge built one step at a time from strictly empirical observation coupled with uncompromising analysis, dogged resistance to *anything* conjectural. It is the repeatability of the experiment that proves its validity, despite the fact that sacrosanct phenomena of a higher (meta) physical order *cannot be duplicated* at the whim of the secular scientist.

---

[26] "Metaphysics, the first and most glorious of the sciences, has fallen into bad repute and evil times. Even flame-belching Baal was never served by a priesthood more fanatic than now grovels before the altars of mechanistic realism." ~Manly P. Hall

This hierarchical sequencing of thought seeds is peculiar to man, the only possible tool for his linear mind. Women's inverted logic allows them to bypass the analytical process and arrive directly at the solution, without thinking it through.[27]

"Men build knowledge step by step. Men reach up; they climb toward knowledge. Sorcerers say that men cone toward the spirit; they cone up toward knowledge. This coning process limits men on how far they can reach. Women are able to open themselves directly to the source, or rather, the source reaches them directly, in the broad base of the cone. Sorcerers say that women's connection to knowledge is expansive. On the other hand, men's connection is quite restricted. Men are close to the concrete and aim at the abstract. Women are close to the abstract yet try to indulge themselves with the concrete."   ~Ibid.

The capacity for women to access the source or *Intent* directly was a fearsome circumstance for domineering men since the astonishing result of any accumulation of knowledge is occult power—gifts of the Spirit so overwhelming many failed the test. Succumbing to temptation, women abused their *craft* for a little payback by engulfing 15th century Europe in a morphic field of fear. Mal intent supplanted the maternal instinct to heal, forcing the patristic Church to *overcompensate* with the misogynous witch-hunts. Impotent hierarchs were at a loss to deal effectively with this heresy, the empowerment (and *overempowerment*) of women, so in 1486 a complete handbook on the "black arts" was assembled—following the maxim *know thy enemy*—to ferret out, effectively torture and summarily burn any woman suspected of wielding more power than a man... **Malleus Maleficarum**, the notorious Witch-Hammer! Heinrich Kramer and James Sprenger, both dictatorial Dominicans, infused their medieval work with such unmitigated misogyny as to shame all save the utmost bigoted.

"If we inquire, we find that nearly all the kingdoms of the world have been overthrown by women. Troy, which was a prosperous kingdom, was, for the rape of one woman, Helen, destroyed, and many thousands of Greeks slain. The kingdom of the Jews suffered much misfortune and destruction through the accursed Jezebel, and her daughter Athaliah, queen of Judah, who caused her son's sons to be killed, that on their death she might reign herself; yet each of them was slain. The kingdom of the Romans endured much evil through Cleopatra, Queen of Egypt, that worst of women. And so with others. Therefore it is no wonder if the world now suffers through the malice of women... Let us consider also her gait, posture, and habit, in which is vanity of vanities. There is no man in the world who studies so hard to please the good God as even an ordinary woman studies by her vanities to please men...

To conclude. All witchcraft comes from carnal lust, which is in women insatiable. See Proverbs xxx: There are three things that are never satisfied, yea, a fourth thing which says not, It is enough; that is, the mouth of the womb. Wherefore for the sake of fulfilling their lusts they consort even with devils. More such reasons could be brought forward, but to the understanding it is sufficiently clear that it is no matter for wonder that there are more women than men found infected with the heresy of witchcraft. And in consequence of this, it is better called the heresy of witches than of wizards, since the name is taken from the more powerful party. And blessed be the Highest Who has so far preserved the male sex from so great a crime: for since He was willing to be born and to suffer for us, therefore He has granted to men the privilege."

Naturally, the gist of the diatribe centered around the family jewels... sometimes gone astray!

"And what, then, is to be thought of those witches who in this way sometimes collect male organs in great numbers, as many as twenty or thirty members together, and put them in a bird's nest, or shut them up in a box, where they move themselves like living members, and eat oats and corn, as has been seen by many and is a matter of common report?

---

[27] "The crux of our difficulty in going back to the abstract is our refusal to accept that we could know without words or even without thoughts."   ~*The Power of Silence*, Carlos Castaneda

Book III: Matriarchy

It is to be said that it is all done by devil's work and illusion, for the senses of those who see them are deluded in the way we have said. For a certain man tells that, when he had lost his member, he approached a known witch to ask her to restore it to him. She told the afflicted man to climb a certain tree, and that he might take which he liked out of the nest in which there were several members. And when he tried to take a big one, the witch said: You must not take that one; adding, because it belongs to a parish priest."

God forbid a man should ever lose his erection, it was definitely due to devil-driven witches.[28]

"For the devil, being a spirit… can suppress the vigor of that member which is necessary for procreation; just as he can deprive any organ of the power of local motion. He can prevent the flow of the semen to the members in which is the motive power, by as it were closing the seminal duct so that it does not descend to the genital vessels, or does not ascend again from them, or cannot come forth, or is spent vainly."

Any erectile dysfunction constituted interference by *Succubus* (lilits) or *Incubus* devils:

- If he does not find his wife repellent, and yet cannot know her, but can know other women
- If he finds her repellent and cannot copulate with her
- If he does not find her repellent and wishes to have connexion with her, but has no power in his member
- If he has power in his member, yet cannot emit his semen

The sadistic German priests devoted several chapters to "judicial proceedings", *i.e.* torture…

"The method of beginning an examination by torture is as follows:
First, the jailers prepare the implements of torture, then they strip the prisoner (if it be a woman, she has already been stripped by other women, upright and of good report). This stripping is lest some means of witchcraft may have been sewed into the clothing—such as often, taught by the Devil, they prepare from the bodies of unbaptized infants, [murdered] that they may forfeit salvation. And when the implements of torture have been prepared, the judge, both in person and through other good men zealous in the faith, tries to persuade the prisoner to confess the truth freely; but, if he will not confess, he bids attendants make the prisoner fast to the strappado or some other implement of torture.
…the jailers must carry out the sentence, and torture the prisoner according to the accepted methods, with more or less of severity as the delinquent's crime may demand. And, while he is being tortured, he must be questioned on the articles of accusation, and this frequently and persistently, beginning with the lighter charges—for he will more readily confess the lighter than the heavier.
…if the prisoner will not confess the truth satisfactorily, other sorts of tortures must be placed before him, with the statement that, unless he will confess the truth, he must endure these also."

Thus women were taught to fear their natural abilities lest they become a threat to their "lords and masters". Beginning with Eva, a few bad apples spoiled the whole barrel of precious feminine gifts—including Divine prescience. From the virgin oracles at Delphi to the gypsy caravans of Europe, the female's enhanced sixth sense had always been a sought after commodity. However, thanks to overzealous, impotent patriarchs, the very quintessence of the holy woman, seer-priestess was eradicated—the good witch an oxymoron since *any* female with power was bad news.

---

[28] "Their dicks get limp when confronted by a woman of obvious power and what do they do about it? Call them witches, burn them, torture them until every woman's afraid. Afraid of herself, afraid of men—and all for what? Fear of losing their hard-on!"
~*The Witches of Eastwick*, Jack Nicholson

Fig. 6 Jeanne d'Arc, May 30, 1431

If she wished to serve the Lord, she had to change her evil ways by forsaking her Higher Self, renounce possessions and live inconspicuously in the hallowed shadow of man. Only a male priest had the authority to perform Mass magic, transform bread and wine into Holy Eucharist. Re*nun*ciates could not even assist with the sacrifice. In addition to round-the-clock prayer, she could cook, wash the holy vestments and set up the altar, but following St. Paul's aggressive admonition, she had to keep her big mouth shut.[29]

Before moving on to the High Priestess Herself, the successor to Isis, we should walk two moons in the woman's moccasins—use abstract thinking to penetrate the metaphorical aspect of the Feminine mystique. By examining the changing face of wisdom in other cultures, we may prepare for its escalating awareness within this decadent decade pregnant with possibilities. We may even be ready to receive Her saving grace...

Chapter Six: Shekhinah, the Presence of God

*"It's alright, it's alright,
She moves in mysterious ways..."* ~U2

"This hexagram is made up of broken lines only. The broken lines represent the dark, yielding, receptive primal power of yin. The attribute of the hexagram is devotion; its image is the earth. It is the perfect complement of THE CREATIVE—the complement, not the opposite, for the Receptive does not combat the Creative but completes it. It represents nature in contrast to spirit, earth in contrast to heaven, space as against time, the female-maternal as against the male-paternal. However, as applied to human affairs, the principle of this complementary relationship is found not only in the relation between man and woman, but also in that between prince and minister and between father and son. Indeed, even in the individual this duality appears in the coexistence of the spiritual world and the world of the senses.

Strictly speaking there is no real dualism here, because there is a clearly defined hierarchic relationship between the two principles. In itself of course the Receptive is just as important as the Creative, but the attribute of devotion defines the place occupied by this primal power in relation to the Creative. For the Receptive must be activated and led by the Creative; then it is productive of good. **Only when it abandons this position and tries to stand as an equal side by side with the Creative, does it become evil.** The result then is opposition to and struggle against the Creative, which is productive of evil to both."

Fig. 7 K'un / The Receptive

Master K'ung Fu Tzu's (Confucius') renowned commentary on the world's oldest sacred text, the *I Ching*, describes a fundamental paradox at the very root of nature's polarities. Both sexes are equal—Yang cannot exist without Yin—yet the latter must submit to the authority of the former.

---

29   "**Let your women keep silent in the churches, for they are not permitted to speak;
     but they are to be submissive, as the law also says. And if they want to learn something,
    let them ask their own husbands at home; for it is shameful for women to speak in church.**"   (1 Corinthians 14.34-35)

Likewise though, Yang must acknowledge the reverberation he receives from Yin. Even an artist like Paul McCartney, whose musical genius brings comfort and joy to billions of souls around the planet, would soon find his wellspring of inspiration bone dry without us to appreciate his talents. He'd continue to write songs—the Creative *must* create in order to evolve—but it would amount to little more than personal therapy. The Creative needs a devoted stream of feedback from the Receptive, the two spiraling higher and higher through a cosmic, symbiotic dance of give and take…

The twin Lights are Nature's primary polarization—a massive thermonuclear reactor, the Sun and Earth's dead satellite, the Moon. Both bodies are *apparently* identical in mass, verified during a total solar eclipse where the Moon completely, and perfectly, obscures the Sun. Their psychosynergetic forces of complementary positive and negative egoic components are explicated within a mythopoeic "pseudo-science".

Fig. 8   Total Solar Eclipse

The lost science of Astrology, recovered and revitalized in the 20th century, incorporates a non-rational higher system of knowledge that can only be acquired through *subjective* experience, which is then verified communally and disseminated through a body of professional practitioners. After ages of such accumulated information—peaking with Ptolemy and the refined Greek intellect—its psychoanalytic sophistication is unparalleled. Modern astrologers agree that in the next fifty years, the psychiatrist practicing without a Star Chart will be as obsolete as the 18th century astronomer without his telescope. The Sun, Moon and planets are responsible for the psychoactive efflux streaming down to our multidimensional psyche. Without the Sun *and* its psychological counterpart, the Ego—our sense of self that is vital to Life—we'd die. Within our patriarchal society, astrology's acceptance is limited to a common knowledge of Sun signs. Everybody knows his or her Star sign and the qualities associated with it, yet few know their Moon sign and the fact that *it is just as important as the Sun's*.[30] The lower soul, *nefesh* sustains the physical vehicle, the body.

The Moon has always been intimately connected to women through the latter's menstruation cycle. Scientific research control groups have shown that most women have their *monthly* periods at the New and Full Moons. Before jealous Mother Church bumped off the competition (the pantheistic chain), the Moon goddess Diana was known to affect fertility, crops and other natural phenomenon such as ocean tides. Since 1792, faithful farmers that don't give a hoot about Astrology have been using the horticultural gold standard, *The Old Farmer's Almanac* to plant, prune and harvest in strict accordance with the Moon's waxing and waning cycles. Nevertheless, the Moon *cannot shine by herself*—her humble glory is to reflect the splendor of the Sun, the planetary illuminator known to the Egyptians as the "eye of Ra".

Prior to their fall from grace during the medieval ages, womanhood was exalted, personified as the embodiment of wisdom itself: *Sophia*. Socrates, the Greek *philo—sophia* (lover of wisdom), identified the bonafide philosopher by his unrelenting search for the elusive Truth, buried beneath the illusory Manifest…

"He said: Who then are the true philosophers?
Those, I said, who are **lovers of the vision of truth**." ~*The Republic*, Plato

---

30 Or more so because it is subconscious, representing our (over) emotional self and undue attachment to the past. We successfully ignore the embarrassing "inner brat" until it lashes out in an uncontrollable manner, *e.g.* O.J. Simpson. Similar to the extinct race from *Forbidden Planet*—whose technological achievements turned against them when their own "monsters from the id" took over—society's repression of the feminine (emotional) is now close to critical mass.

Slumbering for Ages, the sleeping beauty revealed Herself to the Hellenic-Greco mind in all her naked glory as fine art, music, theogony, astrology and geometry. Claudius Ptolemy formulated standards of astronomy that stood the test of time for centuries; likewise Pythagoras, principles of sacred geometry and mathematics that formed the cornerstone of Western culture. Yet the Greek fathers inherited their passion for Parousia (Grk. *fem*. Presence, Spirit of Truth) from the *original* philosophers who sang praises to an allegorical goddess of Wisdom (Hbw. *Hochmah*)...

> **"Doth not wisdom cry? She crieth at the gates, at the entry of the city, at the coming in at the doors. Unto you, O men, I call; and my voice is to the sons of man. O ye simple, understand wisdom.... and, ye fools, be ye of an understanding heart."**
> (Proverbs 8.1-5)

> **"Counsel is mine, and sound wisdom: I am understanding; I have strength. By me kings reign, and princes decree justice. By me princes rule, and nobles, even all the judges of the earth. I love them that love me; and those that seek me early shall find me. Riches and honor are with me; yea, durable riches and righteousness."**
> (Proverbs 8.14-18)

The Psalmist's son, the wealthiest potentate in the history of Judaism, cherished *Hochmah* as his most precious possession. Like the Christ ["**Lay up for yourselves treasures in heaven, where neither moth nor rust doth corrupt, and where thieves do not break through nor steal.**" ~Matt. 6.20], the sagacious Solomon entreats us to seek the *true* treasure worth dying for...

> **"Receive my instruction, and not silver; and knowledge rather than choice gold. For wisdom is better than rubies; and all the things that may be desired are not to be compared to it."** (Proverbs 8.10-11)

The perks of pleasing a thousand-fold harem inspired the wisest of kings to breathe life into the abstract, resurrecting a vital component to the psyche submerged for centuries—the Goddess.

> **"The YHVH possessed me in the beginning of his way, before his works of old. I was set up from everlasting, from the beginning, or ever the earth was. When there were no depths, I was brought forth; when there were no fountains abounding with water. Before the mountains were settled, before the hills was I brought forth: While as yet he had not made the earth, nor the fields, nor the highest part of the dust of the world. When he prepared the heavens, I was there: when he set a compass upon the face of the depth: When he established the clouds above: when he strengthened the fountains of the deep: When he gave to the sea his decree, that the waters should not pass his commandment: when he appointed the foundations of the earth: Then I was by him, as one brought up with him: and I was daily his delight, rejoicing always before him; Rejoicing in the habitable part of his earth; and my delights were with the sons of men."** (Proverbs 8.22-31)

In the Middle Ages, the Spanish Kabbalists elevated Solomon's concept of the metaphorical goddess to its highest level, casting her as the shy *Shekhinah* (Hbw. Indwelling), Glory of the YHVH. The old Rabbis harkened back to the first manifestations of the YHVH when Moses built the sacred tabernacle with painstaking precision to allow the Holy Presence to dwell in the material world.

> **"And when the cloud was taken up from over the tabernacle, the children of Israel went onward in all their journeys: But if the cloud were not taken up, then they journeyed not till the day that it was taken up. For the cloud of the YHVH was upon the tabernacle by day, and fire was on it by night, in the sight of all the house of Israel, throughout all their journeys."** (Exodus 40.34-38)

Book III: Matriarchy

The masters viewed any visible emergence of Power—in particular the ark's anomalous aura—as feminine, since this *sefirah* (Hbw. enumeration) was identified as *Malkhut* (Hbw. Kingdom), the tenth, culminating Reality that *receives* the influx from all the Upper Worlds. [*See* **Fig. 9**]

Fig. 9 Anthropic Tree of Life

"The last sefirah, Malkhut or Kingdom, the abode of the Shekhinah, does not represent any new attribute, but **symbolizes the harmony of all the others, and the kingdom of that harmony, over the entire universe**. Its name is also Shekhinah, the Divine Presence or Glory of the Deity, which sometimes visibly manifests itself in the universe. Here is the idea of an Ideal Perfect Kingdom, which is in perfect prototype in the highest world and which is to come on earth in the future, in perfection; and in which, the Messiah or Christ, is to govern over all the just or pious…" ~Isaac Meyer

"**Shekhinah** is the divine presence, existing and active in the world and among the people of Israel… In relation to the upper world it is the last link in the chain of emanation, acting as a receptacle for the supernal flow of influence, and representing the extreme limit of the divine being. In relation to the lower world, however, it is the very beginning and highest point, **assuming the role of mother and ruler of the world**..." ~Isaiah Tishby

Malkhut, Shekhinah's shell, reflects and manifests the *upper Shekhinah*, "sefirah **Binah**, the Holy Spirit or Upper Mother."[31] [*See* **Fig. 10**] The Spanish reconstructionists, plumbing the depths of King Solomon's ode to Wisdom, extrapolated subtle references to *Binah*—an idiosyncratic kind of feminine know-how, Intelligence they labeled **Understanding**.

> "Counsel is mine, and sound wisdom: *I am understanding*;
> I have strength. By me kings reign, and princes decree justice."
> (Proverbs 8.14)

"It's the number Three, and its name is Understanding. It personifies the passive, yet always receptive and directing God the Mother, the preserving and reproducing giver of life and form. The third path is called the Sanctifying Intelligence, and it is the foundation of Primordial Wisdom, termed the **Creation of Faith**. It is the mother of Faith, which indeed emanates therefrom." ~Williams-Heller

Here we see that Wisdom (*Hochmah*) is actually the *male* component—#1 Son, become *wholly* through the fruit of feminine Understanding, **Faith**.

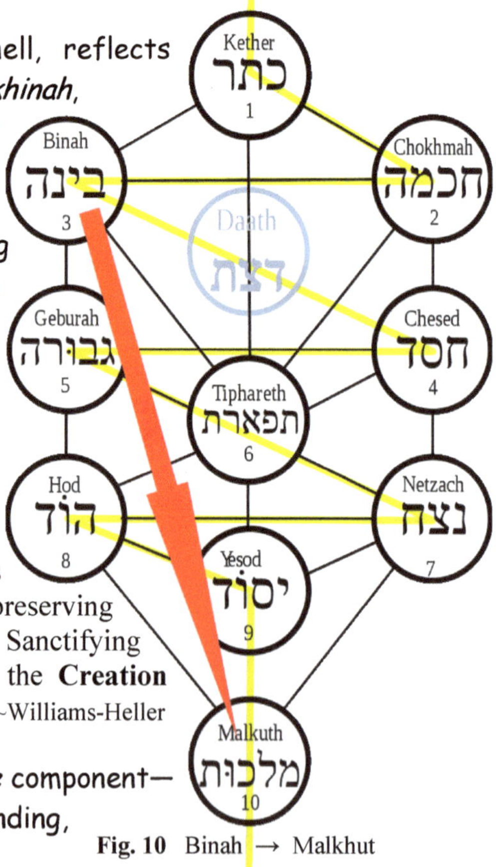

Fig. 10 Binah → Malkhut

---

[31] "Malkhut is also called the Queen, the Matroneethah and the Matron. It represents the World of Matter. Its symbolic sphere is that of the moon, its symbolic color, blue, its ancient metal, silver. It was also called the Church or Congregation of Israel, the Daughter, the Bride of the Spouse, the Shekhinah, *i.e.*, the Glory or Real Presence of the Deity, the Sabbath or Rest day, the Harmony.

It is considered by the Kabbalah, as *the executive energy or power of the sefirah Binah* [Her physical, outershell is Neptune], the Holy Spirit or Upper Mother. Its color is also, blue. Blue is a symbolic color of the Virgin in the Roman Church, who is usually covered with a blue robe, as a red or yellowish-red robe is usually portrayed around Christ." ~*Qabbalah*, Isaac Meyer

Together with *Keter* the Crown, *Hochmah* and *Binah* (Wisdom and Understanding) constitute the upper Triad of Celestial Intelligences. The Original worlds of duality, Yang and Yin, receive from and return to, the Crown in a CCLC-like system[32] that spills over, "watering" the lower worlds. As the *Keter's* "cup runneth over", its exuberant efflux of Love is absorbed and modulated, stepped-down again and again until it reaches our 7th world, the lower *Shekhinah*.   [*See* **Book II, Fig. 7**]

A vital, symbiotic relationship links the two Skekhinahs: Heaven and Earth resonate... [**Fig. 10**]

"There is the Shekhinah below, and the Shekhinah above. The Shekhinah is above in the twelve regions of the holy chariots, and among the twelve supernal *hayyot* creatures; the Shekhinah is below among the twelve holy tribes. Thus the Shekhinah above and below is comprised together, and everything is united at one and the same time. Therefore when Israel is in exile she is in disorder below; and she is also in disorder above because she is in disorder below. And this is the significance of her being in exile with Israel; she shares their exile."

The shy Shekhinah (yet so extremely volatile that the flippant Philistines had to return her to the Israelites) served as a veritable "Oracle at Delphi", inspiring great revelations while the first Temple stood.   "When Israel dwelt in their land, and were engaged in the worship of God, the Shekhinah acted chastely among them, and did not leave the house and show herself outside. Consequently, all the prophets who lived at that time received their prophecy only in her place."

After the death of King Josiah, the Shekhinah is forced into permanent exile as—Babylonian bound—the remaining remnant of Solomon's empire, Judah, is sacked... "When Israel sinned and defiled the land, they immediately forced the Shekhinah, as it were, to leave her place, and she drew near to another place, and then the other peoples began to rule, and permission to rule was granted them."   ~Zohar I

The legendary *exile of the Shekhinah*—the desecrated female—was the very impetus behind all the medieval, mythological gallantry of old: the quest for the damsel in distress, the search for the Holy Grail (the Chalice, a primary symbol of the Receptive). The Hero's Journey will be complete once we bring Mystery (the Feminine) back into the World.

Contrary to popular belief, the Old World patriarchal rabbis were anything but chauvinistic. They saw how the inherent righteousness of a good woman automatically attracts the Shekhinah, whenever the former is united with her husband. Even when separated, the faithful spouse will be protected by the Presence...

"You might object as say that when a man is on a journey, and male and female are not together, the Shekhinah is parted from him. But come and see. When a man is about to set out on a journey he should pray to the Holy One, blessed be He, so his Master's Shekhinah should come down to him before he leaves, while male and female are still together.

Once he has said his prayer and his words of praise, and the Shekhinah has come down to him, he should leave, for then the Shekhinah will be united with him so that male and female may exist together..."

For the duration of his trip, the honorable man's wife is with him in spirit. However, should he succumb to temptation, Lady Luck will flee because his soul has bonded with a strange woman.

> **"Do you not know that whoever is united to a prostitute becomes one body with her? For it is said, 'The two shall be one flesh.'"**   (1 Corinthians 6.16)

---

32 "A Cascading Closed Loop Cycle (CCLC) system is described for recovering power in the form of mechanical or electrical energy from any thermal energy source whose temperature is sufficiently high to vaporize a pressurized light hydrocarbon medium. The liquid medium is then pressurized with a pump and returned to the indirect heat exchangers to repeat the vaporization, expansion, liquefaction and pressurization cycle in a closed, hermetic process."   ~U.S. Patent 6857268

"Come and see. While a man is on a journey he must pay heed to his deeds, to prevent the celestial union (Shekhinah) from deserting him, for then he will be blemished without male and female being together. In town, when his wife is with him, he must do this. How much more important is it here, when the celestial union is bound to him. Furthermore, the celestial union protects him during the journey, and does not leave him until he returns to his home. When he returns to his home he should give his wife great joy [By having intercourse with her ~Tishby], because it was his wife who enabled him to have celestial union." ~Zohar I, 49b - 50a

The husband reengages his wholesomeness as the High Self (upper Shekhinah) resonates with the lower soul halves (lower Shekhinah), momentarily linked together—Divine *coaptation* through orgasmic engagement of luminous filaments bonding the polar, astral bodies. The sacred "mother and son reunion" should be reserved, as discussed above, for *de rigueur* times of recharge[33] and/or procreation—not just for entertainment or the age-old intention of female subjugation.

Chapter Seven: Sophia, the Beauty of God

*"Oh it's rush hour now
On the wheel and the plow,
And the sun is going down
Upon the sacred cow."* ~Dylan

Two of India's greatest saints, Sri Aurobindo (1872-1950) and Sri Ramakrishna (1836-1886) exemplified the yogic path of **Bhakti** (Skt. Devotion) with their absolute trust in, and obeisance to, the Divine Mother. Aurobindo believed our only hope in transforming our battered brigs back to their original, astral (light) condition is to cooperate with the evolutionary impulse—the law of Love.

"The supramental change is a thing decreed and inevitable in the evolution of the earth-consciousness, for its upward ascent is not ended and mind is not its last summit. But that the change may arise, take form, and endure, there is needed the call from below with a will to recognize and not deny the light when it comes. There is needed the sanction of the Supreme from above. The power that mediates between the sanction and the call is the presence and power of the Divine Mother."

To realize a higher order of Being, to *go with the flow*—we must trust *Supermother* Nature and her definitive decree of supramental metamorphosis through the Divine impetus of compassion...

"If we would affirm our independence of Nature, she reveals to us the supreme and omnipresent power of the *Isvara* and ourselves as beings of his being, but that power is herself and we are that in her supernature. If we would realize a higher formation or status of being, then it is still through her, through the Divine *Shakti*, the Consciousness-Force of the Spirit that it has to be done; our surrender must be to the Divine Being through the Divine Mother: for it is towards or into the supreme Nature that our ascension has to take place and it can only be done by the supramental *Shakti* taking up our mentality and transforming it into her supramentality."

~ The Life Divine

---

[33] At the moment of orgasm, partners of *opposite* sex (in homosexual coupling, the life-force is dissipated and healing negated) exchange one another's *chi*. Consummate, energetic healing is accomplished as Yang receives Yin, and vice versa. Contrary to what the Castaneda witches believe, sexual intercourse *is* a two-way street—the psychic connection just as empowering for women, who can use the same luminous lines to enslave men... if they wish.

Sri Ramakrishna understood the merciful Mother as the indispensable mediatrix between us and Omniscience. "One can attain everything through bhaktiyoga. I wept before the Mother and prayed, 'O Mother, please tell me, please reveal to me, what the yogis have realized...' and the Mother has revealed everything to me. She reveals everything if the devotee cries to her with a yearning heart."

Yet the sun is indeed going down upon the sacred cow, the symbol of the bountiful mother.[34] A unique animal held with utmost esteem and reverence in the most spiritual country in the world is prodded against its will into a killing stall, butchered and proudly displayed in Safeways across the carnivorous USA. Ever since Canaan and the good 'ol days of Ba'al worship—gorging on bloody cow carcasses until overwhelmed by a deep, comatose slumber—our bloodthirsty craving has increased exponentially. "Good" parents with the best intentions ["The road to hell is paved with good intentions." ~Johnson] indoctrinate their kids with the All-American, *Sumer*time ritual of BBQ cheeseburgers and steaks. Before they know what's gotten into them, toddlers with parents in tow are demanding their Happy Meals. This gracious creature with four stomachs that gives milk to children, we cannibalize (*carne* of Ba'al, cannibal)—the utter degradation of women nowhere more graphically demonstrated than in the daily slaughter of blessed earth mothers!

Across the pond, a similarly sensitive culture was accidentally (synchronously) dubbed *Indian* by a confused Spanish explorer. The aboriginal Americans, though fiercely macho, have their own version of a Mother Goddess, the White Buffalo Woman. Lakota medicine man Crow Dog relates the single most significant event in the history of the People—the bringing of the sacred Pipe...

Fig. 11 White Buffalo Woman

"The Sioux are a warrior tribe, and one of their proverbs says, 'Woman shall not walk before man.' Yet White Buffalo Woman is the dominant figure of their most important legend. The medicine man Crow Dog explains, 'This holy woman brought the sacred buffalo calf pipe to the Sioux. There could be no Indians without it. Before she came, people didn't know how to live. They knew nothing. The Buffalo Woman put her sacred mind into their minds.' The White Buffalo Woman showed the people the right way to pray, the right words and the right gestures. She taught them how to sing the pipe-filling song and how to lift the pipe up to the sky, toward Grandfather, and down toward Grandmother Earth, to Unci, and then to the four directions of the universe.

The White Buffalo Woman then spoke to the women, telling them that it was the work of their hands and the fruit of their bodies which kept the people alive. 'You are from the mother earth,' she told them. **'What you are doing is as great as what warriors do.'** And therefore the sacred pipe is also something that binds men and women together in a circle of love. It is the one holy object in the making of which both men and women have a hand. The men carve the bowl and make the stem; the women decorate it with bands of colored porcupine quills. When a man takes a wife, they both hold the pipe at the same time and red cloth is wound around their hands, thus tying them together for life.

She told the Lakota that they were the purest among the tribes, and for that reason Tunkashila had bestowed upon them the holy *chanunpa*. They had been chosen to take care of it for all the Indian people on this turtle continent. She spoke one last time to Standing Hollow Horn, the chief, saying, 'Remember: this pipe is very sacred. Respect it and it will take you to the end of the road. The four ages of creation are in me; **I am the four ages.** I will come to see you in every generation cycle. I shall come back to you.'" ~*Lame Deer*, Erdoes

---

34 The Yang/Yin archetypal animals: "The Creative acts in the horse, the Receptive in the cow..." ~*I Ching, Book II: Shuo Kua*
Prior to Isis, the cow-goddess *Hathor* was worshipped for centuries as the Milky Way itself. She embodied her name, the *Mansion of Horus*— "...the closed space through which Horus travels as sun-god… [Hathor] plays the role of protective, regenerative container... represented from ancient periods onwards as a female countenance seen face-on, she symbolizes the face-to-face encounter between the sun and the element in which he appears at the moment of creation." ~*Daily Life of the Egyptian Gods*, Meeks

Sergei Bulgakov, instinctively drawn to the Sophiology of his esteemed Russian predecessor Vladimir Solovyov, worshipped the Trinitarian Godhead in Her feminine expression. An illuminating encounter with the Hagia Sophia Cathedral in Constantinople deeply touched his sensibilities—soaring with epiphanic bliss, Bulgakov knew God could only be comprehended through an open heart, pierced by the indescribable glory of *Presence*. The philosopher-priest Bulgakov had witnessed the Divine's primary avenue of manifestation—*Beauty*.

"This is indeed *Sophia*, the real unity of the world in the Logos, the co-inherence of all with all, the world of divine ideas… Truly, the temple of St. Sophia is the artistic, tangible proof and manifestation of St. Sophia—of the Sophianic nature of the world and the cosmic nature of Sophia. It is neither heaven nor earth, but the vault of heaven above the earth. We perceive here neither God nor man, but divinity, the divine veil thrown over the world."

Bulgakov strived to revitalize the motherland by introducing a feminine constituency to the Holy Trinity. He taught how Spirit could only be perceived in this world by a living quality or principle—a *hyper-hypostatic* truth that can never be nailed down, yet is at the very heart of God, and indeed is the cause of movement within the Divine Triumvirate…

Fig. 12 The Hagia Sophia Cathedral, Istanbul

"But what is it that permeates the life of the Godhead? In other words, what is God? **God is Love**—not love in the sense of a quality or a property peculiar to God, but as the very substance and vigor of his life. The tri-hypostatic union of the Godhead is a mutual love, in which each of the hypostases, by a timeless act of self-giving in love, reveals itself in both the others."

The Russian Orthodox Church censored Bulgakov from teaching his heretical hypothesis that appeared to interject a *fourth* hypostasis into the already crowded Christian creed of the Triune God. The furthest thing from his brilliant mind…

"The Holy Trinity is consubstantial and indivisible. The three persons of the Holy Trinity have one life in common, that is, one *Ousia* (*substantia* or *natura*—substance or nature), one Sophia… neither God nor man, but divinity, the divine One and the same Sophia is possessed in a different way by the Father, the Son and the Holy Spirit, and this threefold 'otherness' is reflected in our definition of Sophia:

The Father represents the transcendental principle within the Holy Trinity, he who does not reveal himself but is revealed insofar as he is immanent in the other hypostases which reveal him… He is the source of beauty, which must exist before beauty can come to be. His is love, although this love is withheld within himself and as yet unmanifested. He is the Father, the source of being and of love, **that love which cannot but diffuse itself.**

The Son is the *Word* of the Father, the image and radiance of his glory, his revelation in the Word.

The Logos is the proper hypostasis of the Word in all the plenitude of the ancient meaning of that term: namely, the Word-thought, Logos-logic, intelligence contemplating itself, both the thinker and the thought, intelligence hypothesized…

Sophia is the love of the divine hypostasis of the Logos for his own self-revelation, for his own divinity. 'Logic' in God does not stand for a cold, compulsory, inevitable link which binds things together (such a conception has its origin in the fallen world), but rather for a **reasonable** love, a special aspect, that is, of love."

The ineffable Truth is most evidently expressed through the visual apparel of the Holy Spirit—beauty, the shy Shekhinah that is witnessed all too fleetingly in today's crass, pop world...

"If in the Old Testament the Holy Spirit is named as 'the Spirit of Wisdom', we find that in the New Testament he is described as the 'Spirit of Truth' (not, that is, as Wisdom or Truth as such, but precisely as Spirit)... As such the Holy Spirit represents the principle of the quickening spiritual reality within the Holy Trinity, the reality and life of the Word of Truth. **But the reality of Truth is Beauty**, the 'good' of Genesis 1.10, 12; the Word becomes adorned by beauty, because the Holy Spirit abides in him... Truth in its own full transparency is beauty, which is the self-revelation of the Deity, **the garment of God**, as it were." [35]

Thus, subtle Sophia must not be confused with *any intrinsic member* of the dynamic Godhead.

"Sophia is not a Hypostasis, but only a quality belonging to a Hypostasis, an attribute of hypostatic being. The Father, *Deus absconditus* (the Hidden God), possesses her as his revelation in the dyad of hypostases which reveals him. The Son possesses her as his own revelation, which is fulfilled, and accomplished through the Holy Spirit. The Holy Trinity possesses her as her triune subject, as it exists in three different hypostases."

Chapter Eight: Mary, the Glory of God

"Well I dreamed I saw the knights in armor
coming, saying something about a Queen..."   ~Neil Young

Continuing our tutelage, the Russian alchemist transmutes the abstract Feminine, Sophia, into the concrete realm of form—revealing how male and female, *together*, personify the image of Elohim. The theologian elegantly threads his transcendental idea of beauty through to the physical, phenomenal embodiment *of all the Goddess metaphors elaborated above*—Mariah.[36]

"Husband and wife, though they differ as two different exemplifications of human nature, **manifest in their unity the fullness of humanity and of the image of God enshrined in it.** Divine-humanity is to be found 'on earth as it is in heaven'—in a double, not only a single, form: not only that of the God-human, Christ, but that of his Mother too. **Jesus-Mary—there is the fullness of Divine-humanity.**

The image of the Mother of God with her child is an expression of this Incarnation of Divine-humanity. To separate Christ from his mother (still more to forget her, as historical Protestantism has done) is in effect an attempted violation of the mystery of the Incarnation in its innermost shrine."

Little did Jerusalem realize the double blessing that was bestowed upon them during the Mother's brief incarnation. Not only did the Avatar walk the Earth, but the exiled Shekhinah once again dwelt amongst Her children—a patriarchal people, unable to accept Her compassion and grace...

"It vanished from the world with the event of the death, resurrection and assumption of our Lady; her glorified likeness is unknown to the world, which cannot yet receive its revelation of the Holy Ghost. It concerns only the age to come and belongs to the last things."

---

[35] "The body should be understood as a revelation of the spirit, of its likeness and of its life. Being informed by intelligence, it provides the outward expression for human individuality—it is, so to speak, an icon of the spirit which dwells in it."   ~Bulgakov
[36] Like Isis before her, Mary, since the kenosis of Christ, supersedes all Goddess figures from Kuan Yin, the Goddess of Mercy to the Divine Mother of Ramakrishna; from White Buffalo Woman of the Native Americans to Marilyn Monroe. She now reigns as the supreme Female Being in whom the entire pantheon of goddesses lives and breathes.

Book III: Matriarchy

Mariah (Hbw. *Mar' ah*—a vision; a mirror, looking glass), an immaculate mirror reflecting the glory of the Lord, fully embodies the Spirit of Truth—Beauty. Her position as Queen of Heaven is relative to the King—"dependent arising" (Skt. *paticca samuppáda*), the good soulmate of Jeshua[37] is deified to the very degree of Her significant Other—Absolutely. As the *authority*, *mercy* and *splendor* of the Christ are matched respectively by Mary's perfect *obeisance*, supreme *compassion* and exalted beauty or *luminescence*—each Divine half completes and complements the other.[38]

"She has been given power, as Queen of Heaven, by virtue of that power over heaven and earth which was granted to her son.
Evidently the two are not identical, for the power of Christ is that which belongs to the divine person of the God-human; while to his Mother power is given corresponding to her complete deification and participation in the glory of her son."

Fig. 13 *Madonna Litta* ca.1490-91
The Hermitage, St. Petersburg

Our Lady's proximity to the dynamic Lord raises Her to the *highest level* in the hierarchy of Celestial Intelligences. Her timely, critical interventions have enlightened at least one body of pious patriarchs—the Orthodox Church of Russia, finally recognizing the Mother as **"more honorable than the cherubim, and incomparably more glorious than the seraphim; who without spot of sin didst bear God the Word; Thee, verily the Mother of God, we magnify."** ~*Axion Esti* (Theotokos), Mt. Athos

"Angels themselves are to be judged [1 Cor. 6.3], apparently upon the execution of their service. Therefore until the glorification of humankind and the full manifestation of its Divine-humanity, even the angels do not enjoy the fullness of their glory, for they have yet part of their course to run. Meanwhile, the holy Mother of God has already attained the fullness of her glory; she is in heaven, set above the angels, who indeed worship her, as sharing with her Son the humanity of the God-human. Nevertheless, in virtue of their holiness the holy angels, with the archangel of the Annunciation at their head, appear to form the immediate entourage of the holy Mother of God... The angels serve the holy Mother of God, recognizing in her the full expression of created Wisdom. For them, too, she is their 'Lady' and the heavenly 'Queen'." ~*Sophia: The Wisdom of God*, Bulgakov

Now let's take Bulgakov's heresy to the next level by deducing a co-existent, *female* Godhead.

- **Sophia** — The Unknowable, Transcendental, All-encompassing Mother of Wisdom: *Faith*
- **Mariah** — The Anthropomorphic Daughter, the Female Countenance or Logos: *Beauty*
- **Shekhinah** — The Holy Spirit of quickening Evolution, Truth and Compassion: *Grace*

Louis de Montfort, an enthusiastic devotee of Mary, founded the Sisters of Wisdom, dedicated to "hospital work and instruction of poor girls", and the Company of Mary, a regiment of missionaries. Moved by his muse, the 17th century saint composed and sang hymns to his holy Lady...

"They both seem to merge; how beautiful their union! Mary wholly in Jesus, her most faithful lover,
Or, better, she no longer lives, for **Jesus alone lives in her**. Let us go within these two hearts,
to warm our coldness and share their ardor, their virtues and their graces.
Let us go, they love sinners, we all find a place there."

---

[37] "Neither Mary nor Jesus had a human father. They were *one* soul as far as the earth is concerned." (Cayce Reading 5749-7)
[38] **"A virtuous wife is a crown to her husband."** The good wife glorifies the righteous man, crowning him with her love. (ty, Sade)

Presently, the Anomalous Woman is beyond our comprehension, *already* existing in the fullness of Grace, the light body that we are guaranteed in the very last days of the Messianic Era—at the **Eternal Judgment**. [*See* **Book IV**, *The Kingdom of Heavens*] In every visitation to this evil world, She has always remained above the ground—either suspended in a cloud or hovering over a tree.[39] Very soon the Purification will be accomplished and our earth once again become a sacred vessel, *Malkhut*, or Kingdom—the ground holy, allowing the *Shekhinah* to permanently dwell in and upon her.

The number of lunar months comprising a solar year is thirteen, inferring a feminine nature to the unlucky digit. The nefarious number, though, has always been to be a favorite one for the first Lady—from the Fatima apparitions, all on the 13th of each consecutive month, to St. John's apocalyptic crown of twelve stars and the oval of twelve pentagrams on the back of the Miraculous Medal. [*See* **Fig. 14**] The twelve ecliptic Thrones, with their Queen, total thirteen. Chances are, we can expect Her majestic presence, with full Angelic entourage, in the year **2013*** ...Jeshua remains the Hidden God[40], available only to the Elect's inner circle. The most powerful piece on the chessboard, Mary, protects our King—She's got His back, inspiring the masses as spokesperson for the Almighty. The antediluvian Matriarchy of the first Golden Age completes a full circle as *Har-mony*, rather than money, once again makes the world go 'round—the natural feminine repose restored on Gaia, the good Earth.

By the 19th century, the patristic pendulum had reached its turning point. The Queen Herself intervened by taking the first steps to reestablish the balance of power. Twenty-eight years prior to the miraculous healing waters of Lourdes, Lady Mary, in Her beloved France[41], materializes before the visionary Zoe Laboure in an apparition of authority. Dwarfing the world, a towering, luminous Goddess lowers Her arms to shower Grace upon the Human race. The Mother commands St. Catherine to have a medal struck of the daunting double-sided hologram with its unusual logo embossed on the reverse—the Cross of Christ securely anchored in, and through, Mariah. Two centuries earlier, Montfort knew the secret of *Jesus living in Mary*.

The power of love is irreproachable, thus it appears that the good Queen—unlike the two Lords—is not bound to the Prime Directive and in 20th century Portugal, She boldly goes where no God would dare. Since Necessity is the mother of miracles, at the height of WWI the Lady of the Rosary commands the sun to dance—zigzag in the azure sky to the open-jawed amazement of 70,000 peasants gathered there. The apocalypse of women had begun, with full blessings from the powers that Be. The mouthpiece for the Omnipotent relays His desire for the Lady's revelation...

Fig. 14   Our Lady of Grace, 1830

> **"Jesus wishes to make me known and loved.**
> **He wishes to establish devotion to my Immaculate Heart**
> **in the world. I promise salvation to those who embrace it."**
> ~Fatima, Portugal, June 13, 1917

---

39 "The Mother of God remains inaccessible to the world, for she is above the world, and if she appears to it, that is only in virtue of her loving condescension, a kind of self-abasement proper to her." ~Bulgakov
40 "Truly You are God, who hide Yourself." (Isaiah 45.15)
41 During her interior locution, St. Catherine heard, **"This globe which you see represents the whole world, *especially* France, and each person in particular."** Descendents of the Lady conceived without sin—the Merovingian kings—settled in parts of old Gaul.

*[DELAYED]

Book III: Matriarchy

The Vatican's anticlimactic release of the dreaded third secret of Fatima [*See* **Book I**, footnote 41] on June 26, 2000 went as planned—unnoticed. Repressed for over eight decades, its final disclosure would have prompted worldwide API/UPI coverage twenty years ago—but the apathy and skepticism of these dark end times obscure even the most crucial revelations. Similar to the devastating *Bible Code*, the prophecy doesn't paint a pretty picture [*See* **Fig. 15**] and the "no worries" philosophy of the materialistic 21st century leaves little room for abject reality. However, the more society ignores the obvious, the more brutally shocking it will be when the truth comes around to bite us in our Collective Ass.

Fig. 15 The 3rd secret graphically represented above. Note the *twin towers* framing the setting sun.

The latest apparitions of the Mother, hailing from the small village of Medjugorje (on the map since Milosevic's Serbian attempted coup of Yugoslavia), bequeathed another disturbing prophecy that, unlike Fatima, *cannot* be changed with prayer and fasting. Mariah tells one of the visionaries, Mirjana—

"Before the visible sign is given to humanity, there will be three warnings to the world. After the first warning, the others will follow within a rather brief period of time... After the visible sign, those who are still alive will have little time for conversion."   ~Mirjana to Father Vlasic, 11/5/83

In **Book IV**, we study the full consequences of the inimitable visible sign, an *aurora borealis* **cross**: "**the sign of the Son of man in heaven.**" The first warning on September 11, 2001 shook our greedy, capitalistic system to its roots. A second similar shock arrived seven years later when the DJIA dropped 777 points on Sept. 29, 2008. One to come.

In summation, we find the sexes are ultimately individualistic.[42] Yet critical, intermediate interaction between the polarities provides the necessary nourishment that eventually enables us to stand alone—together.[43] We both evolve along parallel paths with Jesus and Mary providing the Omega points. While all good men live in the Father Jeshua Group-soul (the Body of Christ), all upright women live in the Mother Mariah Mandala, the suffering, self-sacrificial archetype of Woman.[44]

Like the Native Americans, Negroes and more recently the Tibetan Buddhists, women need to take responsibility for their actions (*karma*) and move on from the victim trip/trap they've fallen into. Using their innate gifts of compassion, females can rise above the evil, prejudicial, feminist male-bashing that has spread, fungus-like, alongside the (overdue) Women's Liberation of the 20th century. Ages of ego sublimation has elevated Womanhood to a much higher pedestal than Man's. Formerly magnificent—riding the crest of the highest cosmic waves—she now plummets to the very depths with the disgraceful aberration of the suit-and-tie female executive.

---

[42] The soulmate essentially belonging to its Self. "But know, the soul is rather the soul-mate of the universal consciousness than of an individual entity." (Cayce Reading 2988-2)

[43]   "Give your hearts, but not into each other's keeping.
   For only the hand of Life can contain your hearts.
      And stand together yet not too near together:
      For the pillars of the temple stand apart,
 And the oak tree and the cypress grow not in each other's shadow."   ~*The Prophet*, Kahlil Gibran

[44] "All women are parts of the Blessed Mother and should be looked upon as mothers."   ~Ramakrishna

It's time she unlearns the artificial mode of cool, left-brain emphasis and returns to her naturally powerful predilection for right-brain analysis—thinking/feeling from the heart. Behind every great man is an even greater woman, the self-deprecating humility paradoxically ennobling her. By swallowing her pride and taking the first step *down* to man's moronic level, she can ascend with her man—all the way *up* to the Heavenly Kingdom on Earth.

In these final years preceding the re-enchantment of the world, male and female must cultivate an enlightened understanding of each other. Working together to prepare ourselves for the incredible rewards of the Messianic Age, we struggle to keep the vision of freedom alive with faith, patience and perseverance. Once upon a time, with a little luck and nothing left to lose, we might find each other again. A true, everlasting love born from aborted lifetimes of trial-and-error will blossom as man and woman look upon each other with a new found sense of *One*der and respect.

And live happily ever after...

December 19, 1996
CLEARWATER, Florida (Reuters) -- Hundreds of people converged on Clearwater Wednesday to see what they believe is a vision of the Virgin Mary on an office building.

"God is giving us a sign," said Sister Martin, a nun of the Order of Saint Anne in Bangalore, India.

The image, two floors high, first emerged last Thursday on the tinted windows of a finance company office. It glows and shimmers, turning from green to blue, to red, and there is a distinct outline of a head, a hooded robe and most of a torso.

Book IV: Supraliminality

Chapter One: Return of the King

If the Western Avatar thought we could handle the truth, He'd have dispatched His disciples with both the Good *and* Bad News. The Good News or Gospel (O.E. *god*, good; *spel*, story, message) being, of course, that the game was over—the ruler of this world, Ba'al (Hbw. *master, owner*) had been defeated for once and for all.[1] Upon relinquishing worldly power to comply with Manifest Destiny, the first creature had become the new Creator, bringing the Most High God and their supernal retinue, the tree of Celestial Intelligences, within Mankind's reach. The Son of Man's victory was our victory.[2] *We're in this struggle together* is the crux of the Christian faith as opposed to the *everyman for himself* motto of today's Western Buddhists.[3]

---

1   "Now is the judgment of this world: *now shall the Prince of this world be cast out.*" (John 12.31)

"And when he is come, he will reprove the world of sin, and of righteousness,
 and of judgment...because *the ruler of this world is judged.*" (John 16.8,11)

"And the seventy returned again with joy saying: Lord, even the very devils are subdued to us through thy name.
And he said unto them: *I saw Satan fall from heaven like a flash of lightening.*" (Luke 10.17)

"Afterward he appeared to the eleven as they reclined at table and reproached them for their unbelief and hardness of heart, for they had not believed those who had seen him after he arose. And they excused themselves with the words, 'This aeon (age) of lawlessness and unbelief is under Satan, who through the unclean spirits does not allow the true power of God to be comprehended. Therefore,' they said to Christ, 'reveal your righteousness now.' And Christ replied to them, '*The measure of the years of Satan's power is filled up.* But other fearful things draw near, also (for those) for whom I, because they have sinned, was delivered to death, that they might turn back to the truth and sin no more in order to inherit the spiritual and imperishable glory of righteousness (preserved) in heaven.'"   ~*The Freer Logion* restores a rare lacuna to **Mark 16.14**, partially transmitted by Jerome (*c. Pelag* II. 15), preserved in whole as Gospel MS W. (4th century), acquired by C.L. Freer in Egypt, 1906 and now heavily guarded in the Freer Gallery of Art of the Smithsonian Institution, in Washington, D.C.

    The usurpation of Satan and inauguration of the Kingdom on Earth were the direct consequences of the birth of the God-man, *wholly dependent* upon the integrity of the Mother's DNA. The Kingdom of Happiness is the Buddha-field (light) emanating from the holy **One** and His Bodhisattva Saints—the Divine Presence *creates* the living Kingdom of Contentment. The good news was indeed that the Kingdom was at hand, if only for 3 ½ years!   "The time is fulfilled, and the kingdom of God is at hand." (Mark 1.15)
"But if I with the finger of God cast out devils, no doubt the kingdom of God is come upon you." (Luke 11.20)
"Then Jesus said unto them, 'Yet a little while is the light with you. Walk while ye have the light...
While ye have light, believe in the light, that ye may be the children of light.'" (John 12.35-36)

2   "These words I have spoken to you, that in me ye might have peace. For in the world shall
 ye have tribulation: but be of good cheer, *I have conquered the world!*" (John 16.33)

3 Conversely, the Eastern Avatar (Skt. *avatara*, "descent"—or incarnation of an Immortal Being), Siddhartha Gautama, sent out His bodhisattvas bearing the Bad News first. His brutally honest Four Noble Truths—the fruit of the bodhi tree vigil condensed to simple "seed-syllable" sentences—laid out the whole situation with its very first Truth: **Life is suffering**. The "pursuit of happiness" is a carrot in front of the donkey; pleasure-seeking ultimately a fruitless, masturbatory activity since we can't get no satisfaction—*ever*. If the principal tenet of Yang/Yin Taoism is true: that every blissful high is *always* accompanied by its opposite, an equally painful low—we are a nation of manic-depressives and don't even know it. The Buddha's diagnosis of the disease was the beginning of the cure.

    And there was a cure, Siddhartha was no anarchist. The third Noble truth carried forth His Good News: There is a way out of suffering. Escape from the inexhaustible Wheel of Becoming is possible and He was living proof! His legacy to the citizens of *samsara* was the Eight-fold Path, a Way of righteous living that guaranteed—at the end of a long "Road to Nowhere"—final *Nirvana* or Full Enlightenment, the equivalent of entering the Kingdom of Heavens with you as King. The Christian promise is identical; just a bigger, chummier picture... "**All who are led by the Spirit of God are children of God... and if children, then heirs, heirs of God, and joint heirs with Christ:** *if in fact we suffer together, that we may be glorified together.*" (Romans 8.17)

    Lord Gautama was an anomaly, the *unconscious* genetic flowering of a righteous people living with God in their hearts. He Himself clearly informed His disciples that He was not *our* Galactic Lord, the Buddha to come. The next Universal Monarch would be recognized by His own Individual essence, the tell-tale characteristic of *loving-kindness*. Sri Siddhartha Gautama prophesied that Maitreya (Skt. *mitra*, "friend")—in Buddhist iconography, a man sitting casually on a throne—will appear after a couple of *kalpas* (millennia) when the Counterfeit Buddhism had finally taken hold... today's Tibetan pseudo-Buddhism, the "fast-track" to Nirvana.

Book IV: Supraliminality

What our Father didn't have the heart to tell us[4]—the Bad News that is only palatable today because we've arrived at the end of the Age (the Kali Yuga's third Act, *Pisces*)—was 2,000 more years of seasoning (suffering) was necessary before the "Bonfire of the Vanities" that will allow the Kingdom of Peace to take root. Two millennia of recycling and perfecting our weary souls laid ahead of us until every single salvageable *self* was prepared for the discarding of the dross. Hence the empathetic patriarch was forced to speak in riddles to His "children", the twelve Initiates.

> **"A little while, and you will no longer see me, *and again a little while*, and you will see me: for I go to the Father."** (John 16.16)

Scripture, both Western *and* Eastern, tells us earthly time is experienced differently in the upper Worlds—especially in the *highest* (7th) heaven.

- **"Thou turnest man to destruction; and sayest, Return, ye children of men. *For a thousand years in Thy sight are but as yesterday when it is past*, and as a watch in the night…"** (Psalms 90)

- **"He rules (all) affairs from the heavens to the earth: in the end will *(all affairs) go up to Him (Allah), on a Day, the space whereof will (as) a thousand years of your reckoning.*"** (Koran 32.5)

- **"Dearly beloved, be not ignorant of this one thing: how that *one day is with the Lord as a thousand years*, and *a thousand years as one day.*"** (2 Peter 3.8)

- **"By human calculation, *a thousand ages taken together is the duration of Brahma's one day.*"** (Bhagavad Gita 8.17)

Assuming the Avatar's POV from the Sirius binary star system approx. 8.7 light years away—the Brigadoon-like edge of time—only a couple of very long days have passed since the Coronation. Indeed, just *a little while*. Ignoring His apostles' perplexity, the Messiah expands upon His cryptic statement to reveal how much He, the Truth shall be distorted and sorely missed in the End Times…

> **"Very truly I tell you, you will weep and mourn, but the world will rejoice; you will have pain, *but your pain will turn into joy.* When a woman is in labor, she has pain, because her hour has come. But when her child is born, she no longer remembers the anguish because of the joy of having brought a human being into the world."** (Jn. 16.20-22)

It may seem evident to the mortal mind of the 21st century that Nietzsche was right and God is dead[5], but just as the nomadic tribes believed Moses dead upon the mountain and backslid as they were about to receive the Kingdom[6], we should understand how close we are[7] and not give up at

---

[4] **"I still have many things to say to you, but you cannot bear them now."** (John 16.12)

[5] **"This first understand, that there shall come in the last days mockers, which will walk after their own lusts and say: 'Where is the promise of his coming?'"** (2 Peter 3.8)

[6] "Now, it is affirmed by the *Zohar* that a change took place in Israel at the foot of Mount Sinai, and this is insisted upon so frequently in terms which never vary as to the alleged fact that one cannot help feeling some principle is involved, some unstated matter of Secret Doctrine. *It is testified that Israel was joined anew to the Tree of Life, so that it beheld the heavenly splendors and realized their lights; it experienced the ineffable joy which fills the hearts of those who desire to know and understand the Supreme Mysteries.*

The serpent could cleave no longer to Israel, and it is affirmed to have disappeared from the world. We must understand all this as a reflection rather of the Divine Intention in its union with the covenant made by the people on their part: **'All that the Lord hath spoken we will do'** (Ex. xix. 8). They were washed also and sanctified… We must remember that in the absence of Moses, and in the uncertainty as to what had become of him, but in the absence otherwise of all temptation, *Israel adored the golden calf, the old evil order was thus reinstated, and I conclude that the serpent returned… It is to be understood further that the riot of the feast which followed the idol-worship signifies a sexual orgy.*" ~*The Holy Kabbalah*, A.E. Waite

[7] "Don't you know? We're as close as can be, man!" ~*Glass Onion*, John Lennon

the very moment of our reward. Unlike the Buddha, the Messiah only hinted around about the awful truth of reincarnation or transmigration of the soul,[8] saying that we'd still be alive to experience His (long overdue, from our POV) return trip...

"Truly I tell you, this generation will not pass away until all these things have taken place." (Matt. 24.34)

Caught in the wheel of time/space, that generation did not pass away; *we are right here*. And exactly as the peripatetic prophet predicted, the Good News (that the Chosen One finally became the new Lord God, cinching our own inevitable Godhood and membership into the elite Kingdom of Celestial Intelligences) has now been spread—and tragically, proselytized—to every nation upon Earth, successfully seeding the Second Coming. What the God-man did *not* sugar-coat was the fact that that supernatural event would climax the greatest natural disasters ever witnessed by the Human Race.[9] Thus the Good News was tempered with a solemn warning of upheaval unparalleled since the previous mass extinction event of 9600 BC. [*See* footnote 57]

The first two books of the **Purification Papers** weaved together an eclectic selection of eschatological prophecies, old and new, to disclose a set chronological pattern of events that are necessary to usher in the Messianic Era. The third installment began to paint a picture of how this glorious Golden Age will be inaugurated with the righteous renaissance of a laid-back, prehistoric matriarchy. The Tetralogy completes itself as we eagerly flesh out the juicy details. But before moving on to those succulent Scriptures that inspired the utopian philosopher states of Plato's *Republic*, Augustine's *City of God*, Hilton's *Shangri-La* or Huxley's *Island*, we should briefly recap the certainty of suffering that shall precede such an amazing antithesis of Joy—the ephemeral birth pangs which, once over, will be like they never happened.[10]

Chapter Two: The Seventy Weeks

Again and again, Gabriel (through the scribe, Daniel), the exiled Evangelist and Jeshua Himself emphasize the fact that, horrible as it may be, the final Tribulation cannot last longer than $3\frac{1}{2}$ years. If the OT Scriptures can be used as a gold standard[11], then the words of a chief Celestial Being[12] should certainly be given some weight. Daniel's pious, counter-culture lifestyle in the midst of Sin City, Babylon is soon rewarded as a God-like entity materializes in answer to his prayer. YHVH's illustrious luminary is sent to dictate a timetable of deliverance, declaring an absolute end to evil and the true beginning of upright living within *Seventy Weeks*.

---

8 "...but I tell you that Elijah has already come, and they did not recognize him..." (Matthew 17.12)
9 "For at that time there will be great suffering, such as has not been from the
  beginning of the world until now, no, and never will be." (Matthew 24.21)
10 "A man should also think in his suffering that God speaks the truth and makes promises in his own name as being the truth. If God forsook his word, his truth, he would forsake his godhead and would not be God, for he is his word, his truth. **Now his word is that our sorrow shall be turned into joy.**" ~*Book of Divine Consolation*, Meister Eckhart
11 "If those to whom the word of God came were called Gods—and *the scripture cannot be broken*—can you say that the one whom the Father has sanctified and sent into the world is blaspheming because I said, 'I am God's Son?'" (John 10.35)
12 Among the ever-vigilant warrior class of archangels, four stood out as exemplary, the chief commanders of the Most High God: "...and I saw four other faces *among them who do not slumber*, and I came to know their names... the third, who is set over all exercise of strength, is Gabriel." (1 Enoch 40) "And Zacharias said unto the angel, Whereby shall I know this? for I am an old man, and my wife well stricken in years. And the angel answering said unto him, *I am Gabriel, that stand in the presence of God*; and am sent to speak unto thee, and to show thee these glad tidings." (Luke 1.18-19)

Book IV: Supraliminality

"Seventy weeks are decreed for your people and your holy city: to finish transgression, put an end to sin, and to atone for iniquity, to bring in everlasting righteousness, *to seal both vision and prophet*, **and to anoint a most holy place."** (Daniel 9.24)

Gabriel's transcript encompasses the entire Human timeline from the end of the Babylonian Captivity (537 BC) to the final decimation of the Dark Prince in the 21st c., sealing both prophecy and prophet in an air-tight container (the *Bible Code*). The Captivity nearly over, the Archangel tells Daniel that in a period of seven weeks' (49 years) time, Jerusalem will be restored and stand tall for another sixty-two weeks (434 years) until the fated sacrifice, "when an anointed one shall be cut off and shall have nothing." This is the *only* Biblical reference, time-wise, to Messiah's manifestation[13] and, believe it or not, theologians using the Decree of King Artaxerxes[14] in 457 BC (Ezra's rebuilding of the holy city) to begin Gabriel's 69 weeks (483 years), arrived at 27 AD, to initiate the last week.

```
Decree of King Artaxerxes    457 BC
Gabriel's 69 "weeks"    =   - 483 Yrs
                            -26  =  27 AD  Baptism at the River Jordan
```

After the Lamb's slaughter, "the troops of the *prince who is to come* shall destroy the city and the Sanctuary." (Daniel 9.26) Aptly documented by the 1st century historian Josephus:

"NOW as soon as the army had no more people to slay or to plunder, because there remained none to be the objects of their fury, (for they would not have spared any, had there remained any other work to be done,) Caesar gave orders that they should now demolish the entire city and temple, but should leave as many of the towers standing as were of the greatest eminency; that is, Phasaelus, and Hippicus, and Mariamne; and so much of the wall as enclosed the city on the west side. This wall was spared, in order to afford a camp for such as were to lie in garrison, as were the towers also spared, in order to demonstrate to posterity what kind of city it was, and how well fortified, which the Roman valor had subdued; but for all the rest of the wall, it was so thoroughly laid even with the ground by those that dug it up to the foundation, that there was left nothing to make those that came thither believe it had ever been inhabited. This was the end which Jerusalem came to by the madness of those that were for innovations; a city otherwise of great magnificence, and of mighty fame among all mankind."   ~*War of the Jews*, Book VII, Chapter 1, Josephus

The end of the 69th week takes us all the way to the present, "…and to the end there shall be war. Desolations are decreed." Then finally, in the last week that shall "put an end to sin", the 70th week, the sentient sentinel again refers to the *prince who is to come*…

**"He shall make a strong covenant with many for one week,
and for half of the week he shall make sacrifice and offering cease;
and in their place shall be an abomination that desolates,
until the decreed end is poured out upon the desolator."**
(Daniel 9.27)

---

[13] Rabbi Moses Abraham Levi: "I have examined and searched all the Holy Scriptures and have not found the time for the coming of Messiah clearly fixed, **except in the words of Gabriel to the prophet Daniel**, which are written in the 9th chapter of the prophecy of Daniel." ~*The Messiah of the Targums, Talmuds and Rabbinical Writers*
[14] "And I, even I Artaxerxes the king, do make a decree to all the treasurers which are beyond the river, that whatsoever Ezra the priest, the scribe of the law of the God of heaven, shall require of you, it be done speedily, Unto an hundred talents of silver, and to an hundred measures of wheat, and to an hundred baths of wine, and to an hundred baths of oil, and salt without prescribing how much. Whatsoever is commanded by the God of heaven, let it be diligently done for the house of the God of heaven: for why should there be wrath against the realm of the king and his sons?" (Ezra 7.21-23)

The counterfeit Christ negotiates a seven-year peace plan on the heels of WWIII. During his decreed time of absolute power (half a week or 3½ years), Mabus sets up flagship headquarters in St. Peter's Basilica and inundates the Catholic Church by opening the occult treasure-trove of the Vatican Library to scholars, declaring a holy war, or *jihad* upon the "corrupt" Christian leaders and banning Mass. With the Prince of Greece waiting in the wings[15], the Kingdom of Hell sics the Prince of Persia on Gabe who has just enough time to fill Dan in on the chronology of the 70 Weeks' Vision...

> "Now I am come to make thee understand what shall befall thy people
> in the latter days: for yet the vision is for many days…" (Daniel 10.14)

The Divine herald now goes into considerable detail as he follows the Usurper through several incarnations of attempted world domination. He begins in 340 BC with the Macedonian who nearly succeeded. The impeccable 1560 *Geneva Bible Commentary*—

> "And a {d} mighty king shall stand up, that shall rule with great dominion,
> and do according to his will." (Daniel 11.3)   {d} That is, Alexander the Great.

> "And when he shall stand up, {e} his kingdom shall be broken, {f} and shall
> be divided toward the {g} four winds of heaven; and not to his {h} posterity,
> nor according to {i} his dominion which he ruled: for his kingdom
> shall be plucked up, even for others beside {k} those." (Daniel 11.4)

{e} For when his estate was most flourishing, he overcame himself with drink, and so fell into a disease: or as some write, was poisoned by Cassander.

{f} For his twelve chief princes first divided his kingdom among themselves.

{g} After this his monarchy was divided into four: for Seleucus had Syria, Antigonus had Asia minor, Cassander had the kingdom of Macedonia, and Ptolemeus had Egypt.

{h} Thus God avenged Alexander's ambition and cruelty, in causing his posterity to be murdered, partly by their father's chief friends, and partly by one another.

{i} None of these four will be able to be compared to the power of Alexander.

{k} That is, his posterity having no part of it.

Next, the indubitable *Book of Truth* finds the AC gutting Rome in 64 and recklessly raising taxes to rebuild in Greco fashion. Mad emperor Nero's assisted suicide an anticlimactic closure…

> "Then shall stand up in his estate a raiser of taxes in the glory of the kingdom:
> but within few days he shall be destroyed, neither in anger, nor in battle." (Daniel 11.20)

Fast-forwarding to the Austrian incarnation, where once again the Man of Perdition nearly achieves his megalomaniacal mission. Hitler's spastic, frothing-at-the-mouth speeches in the Munich beer halls galvanized the sensibilities of the German soul, beat and downtrodden from excessive reparations enforced by the Treaty of Versailles at the end of the First World War—exasperated by the Global, economic melt-down of the Great Depression.

---

[15] "When the Book of Daniel was shown to Alexander the Great (323 BC) wherein Daniel declared that one of the Greeks should destroy the empire of the Persians, he supposed that himself was the person intended."   ~Josephus

Book IV: Supraliminality

> "And in his estate shall stand up a vile person, to whom they shall not give the honour of the kingdom: but he shall come in peaceably, and obtain the kingdom by flatteries." (Daniel 11.20-21)

The remainder of the revelation brings us to the present and final incarnation of the Bastard. Here we reach the eschatological gist of the entire 70 Weeks prophecy—the abomination finally succeeds in his age-old quest for world domination. Yet Gabriel is adamant: the Great Purification is absolutely pre-determined, $3\frac{1}{2}$ years—no more, no less.

> "Then I Daniel looked, and behold, two others stood, one on this bank of the stream and one on that bank of the stream. And I said to the man clothed in linen, who was above the waters of the stream, 'How long shall it be till the end of these wonders?' The man clothed in linen, who was above the waters of the stream, raised his right hand and his left hand toward heaven; and
>
> I heard him swear by Him who lives for ever that it would be for *a time, two times, and half a time*; and that when the shattering of the power of the holy people comes to an end all these things would be accomplished. I heard, but I did not understand. Then I said, 'O my lord, what shall be the issue of these things?' He said, 'Go your way, Daniel, for the words are shut up and sealed *until the time of the end*.'"[16] (Daniel 12:5)

In case there is *any* doubt, Gabriel reiterates the sovereign has but a 42-month window...

> "And from the time that the continual burnt offering is taken away, and the abomination that makes desolate is set up, there shall be a thousand two hundred and ninety days." (Dan. 12.11)

All in all, the unprecedented Book of Daniel reassures us on *five separate occasions*[17] that our birthing process will be as unto an elephant's...

> **1.** "He shall speak words against the Most High, shall wear out the holy ones of the Most High, and shall attempt to change the sacred seasons and the law; and they shall be given unto his power for *a time, two times, and a half a time*." (Daniel 7.25)
> **2.** "And I heard him swear by the one who lives forever that it would be for *a time, two times and half a time*, and that when the shattering of the holy people comes to an end, all these things would be accomplished." (Daniel 12.7)
> **3.** "He shall make a strong covenant with many for one week, and *for half of the week he shall make sacrifice and offering cease*; and in their place shall be an abomination that desolates, until the decreed end is poured out upon the desolator." (Daniel 9.27)
> **4.** "And from the time that the continual burnt offering is taken away, and the abomination that makes desolate is set up, there shall be *a thousand two hundred and ninety days*." (Daniel 12.11)

---

[16] We are clearly in the "time of the end", the auspicious 1997 publication of Drosnin's *The Bible Code* our wake-up call to get on the straight and narrow Path [*See* **Book I**]. Down through the millennia, the Holy Torah has had the reputation of being a "bottomless" text—infinite levels upon which the Scriptures could be contemplated. The 17th century wizard Isaac Newton understood that there was more than met the eye in the Five Books of Moses... "The Bible is a cryptogram set by the Almighty—a riddle of the Godhead of past and future events divinely fore-ordained. This prophecy is called the Revelation, with respect to the Scripture of Truth, which Daniel was commanded to shut up and seal, till the time of the end. Until that time comes, the Lamb is opening the seals."

The general public scoffed at the millennial revelation of the ELS code, **"knowing neither the Scriptures nor the power of God."** Like a dog, they quickly buried the God-sent hypothesis of Dr. Eli Rips and forgot what they had and where they put it. The wise have been getting ready... **"Many shall be purified, and made white, and tried; but the wicked shall do wickedly: and none of the wicked shall understand; but the wise shall understand."** (Daniel 12.10)

[17] In OT Scripture, the repetition of a dream or vision means it is *fixed* by Elohim—a done deal. However, the significance of *this* prophecy is unparalleled in both OT and NT Scriptures. Not only is it repeated *five times*, it is later certified by the Son of Thunder, writing under the influence... **"The beast was given a mouth uttering haughty and blasphemous words, and it was allowed to exercise authority for forty-two months."** (Revelation 13.5) And the Son of Man Himself: **"And if those days had not been cut short, no one would be saved; but for the sake of the elect those days will be cut short."** (Matthew 24.22)

Inexplicably, the fifth and final reference to the fixed time period changes the number, adding 45 days to our trial by fire.

5. "Blessed is he who waits and comes to the *thousand three hundred and thirty-five days*." (Dn 12.12)

Like the Apostles before the Pentecost, we too shall have a 40+ day waiting period before the blessings from Above; a month and a half for the sky to clear after a renegade rock breaks the feet of Nebuchadnezzar's Icon. Dan's diversity of soteriological themes includes the king of Babylon having precognitive dreams—one rattles his cage so bad he can't go back to sleep. Summoning the clueless Chaldean conjurers who can't begin to guess the grave nature of his night vision, King Nebuchadnezzar is POed to the point of killing every wise man in Babel when Danny boy comes to the rescue with not only the details of the dream, but its interpretation as well...

"Thou, O king, sawest, and behold a great image. This great image, whose brightness was excellent, stood before thee; and the form thereof was terrible. This image's head was of fine gold, his breast and his arms of silver, his belly and his thighs of brass, His legs of iron, his feet part of iron and part of clay.

Thou sawest till that *a stone was cut out without hands, which smote the image upon his feet that were of iron and clay, and brake them to pieces.* Then was the iron, the clay, the brass, the silver, and the gold, broken to pieces together, and became like the chaff of the summer threshing floors; and the wind carried them away, that no place was found for them: and the stone that smote the image became a great mountain, and filled the whole earth." (Daniel 2.31-35)

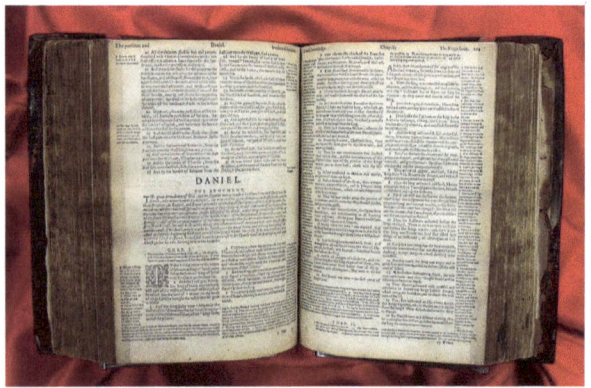

Fig. 1 1560 Geneva Bible, the event of verse divisions

The pentamerous statue represented the five great Empires predestined to arise... [Excluding the Egyptian and Assyrian, already history at that time. Daniel substantiates both Revelation's seven-headed Beast and Enoch's seven "weeks". *See* **Book II**, p. 34]

"Daniel above all others had most special revelations of such things as would come to the Church, even from the time that they were in captivity, to the last end of the world, and to the general resurrection, as of the four Monarchies and empires of all the world, that is, of the **Babylonians, Persians, Grecians, and Romans.**" ~*The Geneva Bible*

The fifth part, the feet of iron and clay, refers to U.S., the new holy American Empire, the great melting-pot of the world. The final world monarchy soon to come into absolute power with the benign acquiescence of ten International Allies (toes).[18] Old Nebuchadnezzar's nightmare ends with an enigmatic stone, *not cut by human hands*, breaking the "feet" into smithereens.

---

18 "The ten kingdoms do not arise until a deterioration (by mixing clay with the iron) has taken place; they are in existence when Christ comes in glory, and then are broken in pieces. The ten have been sought for in the invading hosts of the fifth and sixth century. But though many provinces were then severed from Rome as independent kingdoms, the dignity of emperor still continued, and the imperial power was exercised over Rome itself for two centuries. So the tenfold divisions cannot be looked for before A.D. 731. But *the East is not to be excluded, five toes being on each foot*. Thus no point of time before the overthrow of the empire at the taking of Constantinople by the Turks (A.D. 1453) can be assigned for the division. **It seems, therefore, that the definite ten will be the ultimate development of the Roman empire just before the rise of Antichrist, who shall overthrow three of the kings, and, after three and a half years, he himself be overthrown by Christ in person.** Some of the ten kingdoms will, doubtless, be the same as some past and present divisions of the old Roman empire, which accounts for the continuity of the connection between the toes and legs, a gap of centuries not being interposed, as is objected by opponents of the futurist theory. The lists of the ten made by the latter differ from one another; and they are set aside by the fact that they include countries which were never Roman, and exclude one whole section of the empire, namely, the East [TREGELLES]."   ~Jamieson Fausset Brown Bible Commentary

Book IV: Supraliminality

Referring to the scenario in **Book I**, our Savior returns in the nick of time to blast the cursed comet about to consume the world.[19] The shattered "stone" showers mammoth mountains of fiery debris, wiping out all major centers of the unholy "Roman Empire". Both stumbling stone and Rock of Ages, our Messiah and His Church[20] "became a great mountain and filled the whole earth."

"…and at that time thy people shall be delivered, every one that shall be found written in the book. And many of them that sleep in the dust of the earth shall awake, some to everlasting life, and some to shame and everlasting contempt." (Daniel 12.1-2)

Chapter Three: A Long Dark Night of the Soul

"There is an incessant influx of novelty into the world,
and yet we tolerate incredible dullness."
~Henry David Thoreau

With minor skirmishes around the world, but nothing full-blown, the only real confirmation of any apparent "End-Time Scenario" is a subjective one. The peaceful suffering we are experiencing today is the raising of consciousness as we approach the Galactic Center, a humongous, cyclopean matter/antimatter reactor assembly (M/ARA) à la Star Trek. In **Book II** we learned how every 6,480 years, the solstice and equinox suns line up with the Milky Way Galactic plane, defining four distinct Macroseasons (*Yugas*)—each quarterly Epoch emanating a subset of three 2,160-year Ages which appear to resonate (synchronize) with History.

John Jenkins is credited with publishing the fact that the *next* Yuga, *i.e.* "Winter"—since the 4468 BC Autumnal equinotic conjunction/initiation of the "Fall" Yuga—commences portentously with the solstice sun occulting the **GC** (27° Sagittarius). This momentous revelation originally germinated in a legendary, entheogenic primer by the late psychonaut Terence McKenna and his brother, Dennis.

"Dennis and Terence McKenna… in their book *The Invisible Landscape* mentioned the eclipse of the Galactic Center by the solstice sun in 2012. The McKennas arrived at the 2012 date using sources that did not involve the Maya calendar. This book was an underground classic upon publication in 1975, and was revised and republished in 1993. The McKennas write that the alignment in 2012 could 'implicate the galaxy as a major formative influence upon the structure of the molecules that maintain and define life.' I can trace my interest in precession back to my encounter with this book in 1984. *The Invisible Landscape* and *Hamlet's Mill* are the two earliest sources that recognized the impending alignment of the solstice sun with the Milky Way Galaxy."
~*Maya Cosmogenesis 2012*, John Jenkins

---

[19] This fireball's been coming for a long time; the Adam's fall from grace created a *determinate* timeline—written in stone—that concludes with OT "fire and brimstone" (sulfuric meteorites) raining from heaven...
"Likewise also as it was in the days of Lot; they did eat, they drank, they bought, they sold, they planted, they builded: But the same day that Lot went out of Sodom it rained fire and brimstone from heaven, and destroyed them all. Even thus shall it be in the day when the Son of man is revealed." (Luke 17.28-30)

[20] Stone—Messiah and His kingdom (Gen 49:24; Ps 118:22; Isa 28:16).
"In its relations to Israel, it is a 'stone of stumbling' (Isa 8:14; Act 4:11; 1Pet 2:7, 8) on which both houses of Israel are broken, not destroyed (Mt 21:32). In its relation to the Church, the same stone which destroys the image is the foundation of the Church (Eph 2:20). In its relation to the Gentile world power, the stone is its destroyer (Dan 2:35, 44; compare Zec 12:3). Christ saith (Mt 21:44, referring to Isa 8:14, 15), **'Whosoever shall fall on this stone** (that is, stumble, and be offended, at Him, as the Jews were, from whom, therefore, He says, **'The kingdom shall be taken')** shall be broken; but (referring to Dan 2:34, 35) on whomsoever it shall fall (referring to the world power which had been the instrument of breaking the Jews), it will (not merely break, but) **grind him to powder'** (1Cor 15:24). The falling of the stone on the feet of the image cannot refer to Christ at His first advent, for the fourth kingdom was not then as yet divided—no toes were in existence (see Dan 2:44)." ~Jamieson Fausset Brown Bible Commentary

As mentioned above, the increasing energy efflux is affecting *everyone*, subjectively. Every year, during the window of opportunity (November through June), our consciousness is getting higher and higher—time escalating as we close in on the GC. In **Book II** we proposed that the ebb and flow in McKenna's *Novelty Theory*[21] (static verses dynamic temporal progression) are directly linked to the Retrograde and Direct motions of the upper Worlds, Uranus, Neptune and Pluto. This most auspicious decade has all three working in tandem to release and regulate the evolutionary intent of Spirit that should eventually empower us to reclaim our rightful Godhood.

The first planet to kick in is ultra-subtle, yet powerful Pluto[22] in September. We hardly even notice its evolutionary force—maybe we decide it's time to clean up our act—when Neptune comes back online in late October. Ok, this is feeling freakin' familiar, but we're not ready to concede anything unusual is happening until Uranus—the higher octave of Mercury (higher Mind)—goes online in November. Our holographic mind is now able to grasp how Habitual life is transforming into Novelty living: what's up is anybody's guess as we are brought completely into the Now. As the trio takes us forward again, back along the same energy path we traveled the previous year, we begin to remember the urgency of the situation we're in.

By February, we are entering new terrain, energetically speaking. We're not ready to admit it to others, but we can feel, without a doubt, that time is increasing exponentially. During this stimulating month, the Sun transits Aquarius and we are so completely in the Now that we can feel the future as well—how each year speeds up, relentlessly. The evolutionary pressure continues until the graceful retrograde of Pluto in early April. Here we once again take a deep breath and give thanks to the perfect wisdom and mercy of the Father. We are still thanking our lucky stars when, in May, Neptune stops beaming down her delusions of grandeur, her dream-promises of Godlike nobility. And then by July, when Uranus goes offline and the long, dog days of Summer arrive, our regression from Novelty to Habit is complete.[23]

---

[21] McKenna's innovative application of the 64 binary hexagrams "randomly" sequenced by King Wen in the 12th century BC for an oracle, the *Book of Changes (I Ching)*. Discredited by British mathematician Watkins in 1996, McKenna's *Novelty Theory* gained new credibility from physicist John Sheliak's impressive revision...

"This work has served to clarify and formalize the process by which the 384 number TimeWave data set is generated. This has been done by showing that the process is describable within the framework of piecewise linear mathematics in general, and vector mathematics in particular. Each step has been delineated and formalized mathematically, to give the process clarity and continuity. The formalized and revised data set serves as the foundation of the TimeWave generated by the TimeWave Zero software, which is viewed as a graphical depiction of a process described by the ebb and flow of a phenomenon called Novelty. Novelty is thought to be the basis for the creation and conservation of higher ordered states of complex form in nature and the universe."

While Dr. Sheliak has removed some of the tarnish from McKenna's name, he also makes it clear that the accuracy of the TimeWave software as a reliable indicator of historical processes has yet to be verified...

"...It does show that the proper mathematical treatment of the FOD number set produces a TimeWave that appears to be more consistent with known historical process. This consistency is general, however, and more work needs to be done to examine the specific reflections or projections that the TimeWave may be revealing. If *Novelty Theory* is a valid hypothesis, reflecting a real phenomenon in nature, then one would expect that it is verifiable in specific ways." ~John Sheliak

[22] From 2006-2008, Pluto occulted the Galactic Center at 27° Sagittarius—maximizing the former's evolutionary intent. Ironically, on August 24, 2006, the International Astronomical Union chose this most tempestuous time to downgrade Pluto to a new category: dwarf planet (the scientists' pet peeve being the "unplanet-like" behavior of its highly elliptical orbit, which intersects Neptune's periodically)—a knee-jerk reaction triggered by the 2005 (official) discovery of transplutonian object, **2003 UB313**...

"Aptly named after the Greek goddess of conflict, the icy dwarf planet, Eris, has rattled the general model of our solar system. The object was discovered by astronomer Mike Brown of Caltech in the outer reaches of the Kuiper belt in 2005. So if Pluto qualified as a full-fledged planet, then Eris certainly should too. Astronomers attending the International Astronomical Union meeting in 2006 worked to settle this dilemma. **In the end, we lost a planet rather than gaining one.** Pluto was demoted and reclassified as a dwarf planet along with Eris and the asteroid Ceres, the most massive member of the asteroid belt." ~Science Daily (June 18, 2007)

[23] Like Cliff Robertson's award-winning performance in *Charly* (Best Actor, 1969), we slowly revert to our old habit patterns of greed and ignorance. Through monotonous repetition of dull routine—our higher centers deactivated—we eventually fall asleep again.

Book IV: Supraliminality

Since the annual evolutionary window is a subjective one, we can easily lie to one another; act like nothing was out of the ordinary. The fact that we were all intellectual *savants*—high as a kite for six months[24]—is something civilized people don't discuss since it's out of our control. Are we living in the medieval ages when illiterate people believed in magic, higher powers and gods? As a result of the 17th century Enlightenment, we can scientifically explain anything in this mundane, mechanistic world. There must be some concrete clarification of what is affecting us the way it is. Maybe the CIA is putting LSD in the water? Or the pharmacist is dicking with our meds. While there are innumerable conspiracy theories, the simple truth is: it is us—the unknowable, Divine part of ourselves, the Father, whom we have to learn to trust.[25]

Scientifically sound or not, McKenna's Novelty graph does represent what linear time would look like when the *I Ching's* 384 integer values are applied as a "fractal transform". It matches up with historical events while providing a solid blueprint to our subjective experience of time's periodical acceleration and condensation, synchronized to the Direct and Retrograde motions of the planetary Forces as they release and retract the raw evolutionary efflux emanating from the GC.

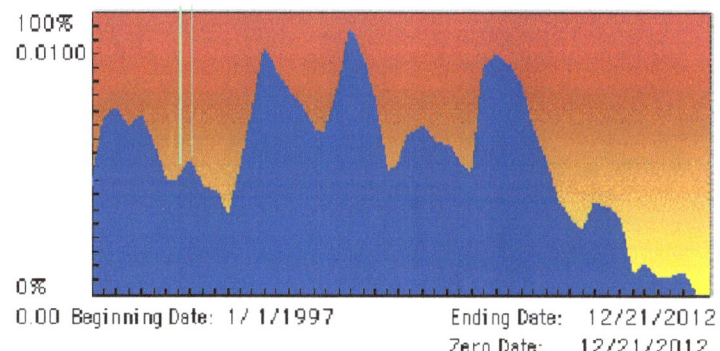

Fig. 2   TimeWave Zero

For a *scientific* corroboration of the cyclical nature of time, also terminating with the Winter solstice of 2012 AD, we have to go back five thousand years. Recently, a new appreciation of the Maya techies has brought their sacred calendar onto center stage. Supporting McKenna's hypothesis of a time wave, *this* harmonic fractal is the real McCoy, the digital key to our Anthropic Cosmos—260, gestation period of the Human (260 days) and Humanity (26,000 years)…

"The Tzolkin can be regarded as a periodic table of galactic frequencies, because it is a fractal of the vague count of the 26,000-year precession of the equinoxes. The 26,000-year cycle of the sun's revolution around the Pleiades, the 26,000,000-year periodicity of extinctions reported in an extensive literature related to comet showers, and possible pole shift, as Earth recurrently passes through the Oort cloud, and other celestial cycles related by periods of time, the factor of which is 260."   ~*Beyond Prophecies and Predictions*, Moira Timms

The Maya's uncanny knowledge of the fractal loop within our space/time continuum begot a meticulous mathematical system integrating three disparate calendars: the *Long Count* comprising 13 baktuns, the *Haab*, a 365-day solar calendar and the *Tzolkin*, a sacred calendar of 260 days.

"The Maya had three calendars. All three calendars were based on the vigesimal mathematical system (times twenty) which is the refinement of the calendar by the Maya over other similar systems in Mesoamerica.

---

[24] Of course, getting high is old hat to the GAS (Great Awakening of the Sixties) survivors. Bob Dylan and some of us don't feel so all alone now that everybody gets stoned—metaphorically speaking.
[25] To trust the Father is to trust His holy agents. **"There is one glory of the sun, and another glory of the moon, and another glory of the stars: for one star differeth from another star in glory."** (1 Corinthians 15.41)

If Pluto is the pressure cooker, Neptune the water and Uranus the fire, one by one, the pressure is reduced. First the clamp is released, the water continues boiling but it can "breathe" now, and finally it cools down completely when the fire is turned off. The best analogy is that of climbing Mt. Everest. Since 1993's initiatory jump to "Base Camp" (17,600 ft.), we've been slowly ascending the highest mountain in the world. Each June, we return to Camp for acclimatization before ascending higher. We get comfortable enough, bored even, when it's time to continue the trek. **Leaving** "Camp 3" in 2009—**we'll reach** the Summit (29,029 ft.) in 2012-13.

The calendars were designed to harmonize actual time, the solar year and the revolutions of the various heavenly bodies. The first calendar called the Long Count was used for looking back in time and recording events. The Maya spoke of eras of 5,125.40 years each equaling 13 baktuns of 144,000 days each. Each cycle of 13 baktuns was reckoned as an Age or Great Cycle, a specific historical epoch. In addition to the Long Count, the Maya employed two cyclical calendars. The Maya intermeshed a solar exoteric calendar Haab with a sacred esoteric calendar, Tzolkin. The solar calendar, used primarily for practical and agricultural reasons, consisted of 365.242129 days and is actually more precise than our Gregorian calendar of 365.242500 days.

The Maya year was divided into 18 months of 20 days each. This left five days without names or unlucky days at the end of the year. Each of the 18 uinals was dedicated to a specific deity and his corresponding festivals which related to the season of the year, the work to be done during the season and the nature of the season itself. The days were designated in groups of 13. Each day had its specific omens, used for astrological divination.

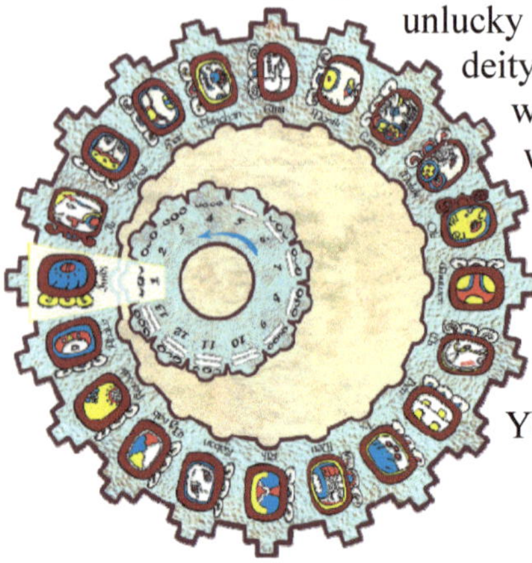

The Tzolkin, the sacred year calendar, used for ceremonial and ritualistic purposes, lasted 260 days. The Tzolkin consisted of a smaller wheel of 13 glyphs rotated with a larger wheel of 20 days, resulting in the 260-day sacred year. Any given day represented a particular intermeshing of the Haab Solar Year and the ritualistic Tzolkin resulting in a specific forecast."
~*Uncovering the Secrets of the Mayan Calendar*, Kathie Garcia

Fig. 3   The Tzolkin

Using the Maya system, we are consummating a challenging 20-year cycle (1993-2012) known as 13 Reed/20 Ahau.[26] The last *katun* of the final *baktun* (1618-2012) within the Great Cosmic Year (26,000 years)—a **Long Dark Night of the Soul**.

"April 6th, 1993 is the beginning of the last katun period of the Mayan Great Cycle. A katun is about 20 years in length, and there are 260 katuns in a Great Cycle of 13 baktuns (about 5125 years)."   ~John Jenkins

During the next few months, as we approximate the *Tula* (Mayan GC), the magical aspects of Reality, the synchronicities, will become too apparent to ignore. The subjective state become *objective* when "mass hallucinations" like UFOs pop into *our* existence. By the end date of the fractal loop, our little blue ball conjuncts the awesome forces of the GC and time will stand still as we breathlessly await the immanent revelation (Gk. apocalypse) of Dark and Light Lords. We've come full circle, around to the same Alpha point—now the Omega point—where the Human protoplast popped into existence 25,920 years ago, our previous alignment with the Galactic Center. It was the beginning of a Golden Age, bodies dressed of light at play in the fields of the Lord.

1993's closing *katun* was inaugurated by a cosmic meeting of the gods, Uranus and Neptune.[27] 1993 and 1994 were strange years in many respects, initiating the World into a locked pattern of evolution, a quickening that will climax with a temporal Singularity igniting the Heavens.

---

26 In **Book III**, we observed the Queen of Heaven's affinity with the number 13, a key figure in Maya astrophysics. Their Great Cycle (5,125.40 years) began **13.0.0.0.0**—the Goodman-Martinez-Thompson (GMT) correlation is **August 11, 3114 BC** (Julian Day #584,283). The end date of the 13-baktun cycle is also written **13.0.0.0.0** and correlates to **December 21, 2012 AD**. Moira Timms explains the significance of the 13th Galactic "tone" *Reed*, as well as their 20th day sign, *Ahua*—bound to be an Aha! moment.

"Thirteen Reed synchronizes cycles. In order to do this, it brings transformation and new beginnings by means of destruction or renewal, breakdown or breakthrough... Planetary alignments and evolutionary shifts occur during 13-Reed periods. Twenty Ahau as the last glyph of the day calendar, and heart of the calendric system, unifies and completes all natural, cultural, religious and prophetic time cycles. **The tail end of the Age of Pisces is upon us, as is the close of the Mesoamerican Fourth World, and the Kali Yuga of the Hindus, all nested within the culminating revolution of the precessional Great Year.**"

27 "The key to Mayan cosmo-conception is the 260-day cycle, which allowed the Maya to predict eclipses and at least the movements of Venus and Mars. Because the 260-day cycle is an ingenious key to many if not all cycles of the solar system, *it can also be used to find the conjunction cycles of Uranus and Neptune.*"   ~Jenkins

Book IV: Supraliminality

It would have been easy to forget those two years if not for the surreal scene right out of *Blazing Saddles* broadcasting over Coast-to-Coast television. As O.J. Simpson rolled down the L.A. freeway with a gun to his head—threatening to kill himself if the police didn't back off—thousands of fans lined the highway to cheer. The farcical murder trial only added to the capricious thrust of the previous year. In the heavens of 1993, something really extraordinary had occurred: a *triple* conjunction of the outer planets, Uranus and Neptune. A single conjunction of this odd couple would have given sufficient reason to wonder, considering the weird energies involved. Our true sense of Individual awareness, coupled with the *higher* truth of Oneness, created an ambiguity that was mind-boggling. Three times that year, you could feel—*for a fact*—how you were you but they were you too. Or you were them. The influx of information (via Uranus) was more than we could assimilate, and throughout 1993 *all* the New Age "gurus" cancelled their agendas. It was impossible to continue the intent of Separateness (Uranus) while simultaneously glued to the living, *higher* reality of Unity (Neptune). In the next year, we could deny it ever happened—and get back to our game of Me vs. You. But thanks to Orenthal and a cast of characters including Judge Ito surrounded by an escalating collection of clocks and hourglasses, we could never completely forget how time seemed to **stretch...**

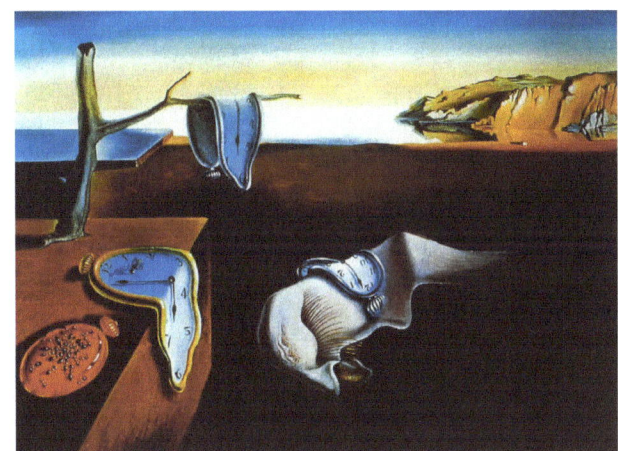

Fig. 4   *The Persistence of Memory*, Salvador Dali

Chapter Four: Zero Point Energy

Such was our *initiation* into the wonderful world of Oneness; a group initiation[28] that will peak or culminate at the Apocalyptic Singularity. McKenna speculates about that magical moment and the years leading up to it:

"There is only one point in the entire cycle where the level of habit drops to zero; effectively then novelty becomes infinite. And that point occurs on this solstice date in 2012. Now it's very interesting... There are some people on the net called singularists, and they're hard-headed engineering types, and they take rates of energy release and rates of data storage, this sort of thing, and draw all their curves out, and they can see that some time between 2008 and 2020 everything will produce infinite amounts of energy."

IT consultant and "hard-headed engineering type" Patrick Salsbury, explains McKenna's model...

---

[28] "Astronomically, we are not yet functioning fully within the influence of Aquarius; we are only just emerging from the Piscean influence, and the full impact of the energies which Aquarius will set loose has not yet been felt. Nevertheless, each year carries us closer to the center of power [**GC**], the major effect of which will be to induce recognition of man's essential unity, of the processes of sharing and of cooperation and of the emergence of that new world religion whose keynote will be universality and initiation.

If the word 'initiation' signifies the processes of 'entering into,' then it is indeed true today that humanity is undergoing a true initiation as it enters into the new age of Aquarius; it will then be subjected to those energies and forces which will break down the barriers of separation, and which will blend and fuse the consciousness of all men into that unity which is distinctive of the Christ consciousness."   ~*The Reappearance of the Christ* (1948), Alice Bailey

"Essentially, if we take a look at some of the really species-changing events in our history, we see 3 really MAJOR developments that changed the entire course of human history.

    1) The Agricultural Revolution   2) The Industrial Revolution   3) The Information Revolution

30,000 years ago, we learned how to farm. 350 years ago, we learned how to mass-produce machines. About 50 years ago, we learned how to build computers. As you can see, the rate of change is increasing, as is the ability afforded by the change. With computers, we have the ability to build more efficient things, fly planes and spaceships, educate more people, etc. Each of these enabling technologies will build further development, and at a faster rate. According to the mathematical model, we should see approximately *61* more of these species-changing developments before 12/21/2012! All of the same magnitude as the three noted above! Again, it's only a model, but they predict 18 of those changes on the last day, and 13 of those to happen in the last FRACTION OF A SECOND, as things accelerate towards that infinity point." ~Novelty Theory and the Singularity

This will be a moment out of time, experienced as an Eternity. When the many become One, even for the briefest moment, a situation of *zero-point energy* (ZPE)[29] is achieved, obliterating every known law of physics. Mathematician/philosopher Alfred North Whitehead coined a neologism, *concrescence*, to describe the incomprehensible synergy produced within a theoretical ZPE field...

"The ultimate metaphysical principle is the advance from disjunction to conjunction, creating a novel entity other than the entities given in disjunction. The novel entity is at once the togetherness of the 'many' which it finds and also it is one among the disjunctive 'many' which it leaves; it is a novel entity, disjunctively among the many entities which it synthesizes. The many become one, and are increased by one. In their natures, entities are disjunctively 'many' in process of passage into conjunctive unity... Thus the 'production of novel togetherness' is the ultimate notion embodied in the term *concrescence*. These ultimate notions of 'production of novelty' and 'concrete togetherness' are inexplicable either in terms of higher universals or in terms of the components participating in the concrescence. The analysis of the components abstracts from the concrescence. **The sole appeal is to intuition.**"   ~*Process and Reality*

---

29 Zero-Point Energy. "Vibrational energy retained by molecules even at a temperature of absolute zero. Since temperature is a measure of the intensity of molecular motion, molecules would be expected to come to rest at absolute zero. However, if molecular motion were to cease altogether, the atoms would each have a precisely known location and velocity (zero), and the uncertainty principle states that this cannot occur, since precise values of both position and velocity of an object cannot be known simultaneously. Thus, even molecules at absolute zero must have some zero-point energy." ~Encyclopedia Britannica

    The fifth element of the ancients, the *Ether* provided a "substratum" to the Universe, a glue that held everything in its place. "Proven" obsolete by Newton, the mysterious ether has recently been making a comeback as *Akasha*, a living ZPE field.

    "Ervin Laszlo in his book, *Science and the Akashic Field—An Integral Theory of Everything* describes what he refers to as the A-field, which is a universal-wide holographically distributed information field that is actively involved in the evolutionary process. It provides the basis for a universal mind or memory. Jung recognized this field and called it the collective unconscious. A-field refers to the Akashic field. Akasha is an ancient Sanskrit word meaning ether or all-pervasive space. In Indian philosophy it was considered to be the first and most fundamental of the five elements, four of which were recognized by the early Greeks to include fire, water, earth, and air; Laszlo indicates that **a new paradigm is emerging in science that describes an informed universe rooted in the rediscovery of the Akashic or A-field.** This A-field is a vacuum based holofield that permeates the entire universe.

    Within this A-field information is generated throughout, conserved and conveyed by and among all of its parts. It is strongly interconnected and builds on the information that it has already generated. *Space is not empty but is the origin and the memory of all things that exist or have ever existed.* This cosmic information field connects all organisms and minds in the biosphere, as well as all particles, stars and galaxies throughout the universe. The A-field continuously interacts with matter at every level from the subatomic to the cosmic, to influence the way that every living thing grows, adapts and evolves." ~Dr. Roger D. Blomquist

    Quantum physicist David Bohm's theory of the *Implicate and Explicate Order* was also based upon the idea of ZPE...

    "Bohm's understanding of physical reality turns the commonplace notion of 'empty space' completely on its head. For Bohm, space is not some giant vacuum through which matter moves; space is every bit as real as the matter that moves through it. Space and matter are intimately interconnected. Indeed, calculations of the quantity known as the zero-point energy suggest that a single cubic centimetre of empty space contains more energy than all of the matter in the known universe! From this result, Bohm concludes that *'space, which has so much energy, is full rather than empty.'* For Bohm, this enormous energy inherent in 'empty' space can be viewed as theoretical evidence for the existence of a vast, yet hidden realm such as the implicate order." ~Will Keepin

Book IV: Supraliminality

Soon this "ultimate metaphysical principle" of a higher conjunctive Self will be realized by all; science will have the supersensible proof it has always demanded. Just as astronaut Edgar Mitchell experienced on his return trip to the Earth, we will personally verify *Samadhi* awakening, once the exclusive realm of mystics, saints and psychonauts...

"The place where Mitchell claims to have gone during his space flight is *Samadhi*, in which one can observe things as separate from self, yet recognize that they are all connected with one another and to self; that separation is an illusion. It is also accompanied by the experience of ecstasy and eternity. Creating additional dualisms (illusions) that separate self from the purest state of awareness forms the states below *Samadhi*.

These include the existential state, in which individuals perceive things as separate from self but sense the eternal nature of being; the ego state, in which most of us are usually present, and where we lose our sense for the eternal and ecstatic; and finally, the subconscious state, in which instincts, archetypes, and most animals reside. With these definitions as a backdrop, scientists have set out to define the nature of human consciousness.

In the past half-century, science has begun to recognize that consciousness is not a byproduct of physics and biology. Rather, consciousness structures the universe, and matter is a byproduct of mind. Scientists discovered this by probing deep into the structure of matter. There, they found only empty space, and labeled it the 'zero-point' field of energy. It has been ascertained that all matter arose from this field, the stuff of the 'Big Bang.' Here, structure disappears into dynamic exchange of energy with the zero-point field, non-locality prevails, and space/time ceases to exist as all exchanges of energy are reversible, continuous, and unpredictable.

The zero-point field is subatomic and also hypothesized as being macro (beyond universe). It can be found at the limits of speed (time becomes meaningless), heat (matter disappears), and cold (matter combines as coherent mass). It provides the quantum potential for all physical structure and the potential for awareness to exist, inextricably tied together."   ~*The Prophets Conference*, NYC, 2001, Chris Butterfield

One of the few geniuses of the 20th century capable of combining science with religion, Pierre Teilhard de Chardin[30] referred to this atemporal, dynamic state of ZPE as the *Omega Point*, Alfred Whitehead's concrescence in more personal terms.

"All our difficulties and repulsions as regards the opposition between the All and the Person would be dissipated if only we understood that, by structure, the noosphere (and more generally the world) represent a whole that is not only closed but also centered. Because it contains and engenders consciousness, space-time is necessarily of a convergent nature. Accordingly its enormous layers, followed in the right direction, must somewhere ahead become involuted to a point which we might call Omega, which fuses and consumes them integrally in itself."

Lest one misconstrue convergence as a *loss* of ego, the truth is quite the contrary...

"The concentration of a conscious universe would be unthinkable if it did not reassemble in itself all consciousnesses as well as all the conscious; each particular consciousness remaining conscious of itself at the end of the operation, and even (this must absolutely be understood) *each particular consciousness becoming still more itself and thus more clearly distinct from others the closer it gets to them in Omega*. Egoism, whether personal or racial ...feels right.

---

30 TEILHARD DE CHARDIN (Pierre)
"French Jesuit paleontologist (Sarcenat, Puy-de-Dôme, 1881—New York 1955). The scientific work of Teilhard de Chardin is situated primarily in Asia: discovery of the Peking Man (1929), explorations in India, in Java, participation in the Yellow Crossing (1931, etc.). His theological and philosophical writings, *banned from publication during his lifetime*, have been disseminated since his death.

Enlightened by a synthesizing vision of the universal unfolding of evolution, they give validity to the phenomenon of the cerebral complexification of the human phylum, ending in the abrupt appearance of the consciousness of self (the 'threshold' of reflection), then in a worldwide communication network of human thought, the noosphere, at the heart of which is acting 'Christ, the capstone of evolution', who is conducting humanity, in a simultaneously immanent and transcendent fashion, towards the 'Omega point' (the Kingdom of God). His principal work, the *Phenomenon of Man*, appeared after his death."
~Le Grand Larousse Universel, Tome 14, p.10095

Its only mistake, but a fatal one, is to confuse individuality with personality. In trying to separate itself as much as possible from others, the element individualizes itself; but in doing so it becomes retrograde and seeks to drag the world backwards toward plurality and into matter. In fact it diminishes itself and loses itself.

To be fully ourselves it is in the opposite direction, in the direction of convergence with all the rest, that we must advance—towards the 'other'. The peak of ourselves, the acme of our originality, is not our individuality but our person; and according to the evolutionary structure of the world, we can only find our person by uniting together. There is no mind without synthesis… *The true ego grows in inverse proportion to 'egoism'.* Like the Omega which attracts it, the element only becomes person when it universalizes itself."

To achieve this evolutionary goal, it was necessary for a real Person (a true Ego, a Christ) to become element again in order to "superanimate the general ascent of consciousness".

"As early as in St. Paul and St. John we read that to create, to fulfill and to purify the world is, for God, to unify it by uniting it organically with himself. How does he unify it? By partially immersing himself in things, by becoming 'element', and then, from this point of vantage in the heart of matter, assuming the control and leadership of what we now call evolution. Christ, principle of universal vitality because sprung up as man among men, put himself in the position (maintained ever since) to subdue under himself, to purify, to direct and superanimate the general ascent of consciousnesses into which he inserted himself."

The paleontologist priest was appalled at the staggering ignorance of his fellow scientists (*i.e.* psychologists). He knew the most powerful force in the Universe, the elementary particle or gluon in the General Unified Theory was anthropological in nature: our *gut* feeling of Love.

"How can we account for that irresistible instinct in our hearts which leads us towards unity whenever and in whatever direction our passions are stirred? A sense of the universe, a sense of the all, the nostalgia which seizes us when confronted by nature, beauty, music—these seem to be an expectation and awareness of a Great Presence. The 'mystics' and their commentators apart, how has psychology been able so consistently to ignore this fundamental vibration whose ring can be heard by every practiced ear at the basis, or rather at the summit, of every great emotion? Resonance to the All—the keynote of pure poetry and pure religion; ...the severed particle which trembles at the approach of the 'rest'."

"We have only to believe. And the more threatening and irreducible reality appears, the more firmly and desperately we must believe. Then, little by little, we shall see the universal horror unbend, and then smile upon us, and then take us in its more than human arms."

Fig. 5 Teilhard de Chardin

"And the third angel sounded, and there fell a great star from heaven, burning as it were a lamp, and it fell upon the third part of the rivers, and upon the fountains of waters." (Rev. 8.10)

Toward the end of the Beast's reign, astrophysicists ascertain an asteroid's fixed course has *apparently* sealed our fate. A year later, with scant hours to Impact counting off around the world, every face is turned heavenward—some resigned to certain annihilation from the rogue planetoid, while others, with mounting trepidation and exhilaration, manage to suspend their disbelief.

Times such as these call for extraordinary courage, a faith that defies rational analysis. Necessity summons the Divine Presence as a cosmic Singularity ignites the heavens. The temporal shock from a transcendental Being's quantum manifestation in our time/space[31] smashes the death comet into pieces, hailing megalithic, flaming asteroid-chunks down to the earth.

---

31 **"And then shall that Wicked be revealed, whom the Lord shall consume with the spirit of his mouth, *and shall destroy with the brightness of his coming.*"** (2 Thessalonians 2.8)
The exodus of the God-man created a similar ZPE anomaly in the space/time continuum, opening a temporal window (wormhole) for Himself and some of the pious Elect, a ticket to Paradise for a care-free, extended vacation. *Cont.* →

Book IV: Supraliminality

Anybody dumb enough to still be in Dodge, better get out fast...

**"In that day, he which shall be upon the housetop, and his stuff in the house,
let him not come down to take it away: and he that is in the field,
let him likewise not return back. Remember Lot's wife."** (Luke 17.31-32)

As multi-gigaton detonations cremate hapless millions at every major center of commerce, volumes of smoke and soot fill the skies, plunging Earth and her inhabitants into nuclear winter.[32]

**"Immediately after the tribulation of those days shall the sun be darkened,
and the moon shall not give her light, and the stars shall fall from heaven,
and the powers of the heavens shall be shaken."** (Matthew 24.29)

**And the fourth angel sounded, and the third part of the sun was smitten,
and the third part of the moon, and the third part of the stars;
so as the third part of them was darkened, and the day
shone not for a third part of it, and the night likewise."** (Revelation 8.10)

Following the Bruce Willis-like heroics of the God-man, the billion and ½ survivors begin a 45-day "Pentecostal" vigil as the darkness slowly dissipates. Enveloped in a womb-like atmosphere, the Elect pray together in humble silence, grateful for another day of life. Mindfulness meditation techniques keep us calm and centered as the earth tremors continue unabated...The relentless pounding of Mother Earth is triggering her overdue Pole Shift.

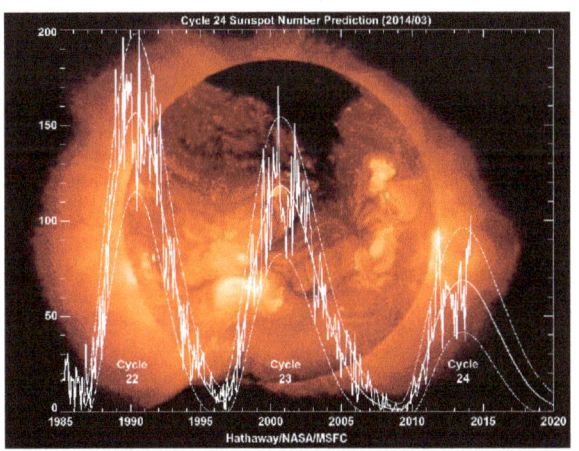

Fig. 6 Cycle 23-24 Sunspot Number Prediction

Of more immediate attention is the relatively minor reversal of the Sun's magnetic poles, scheduled for this year, peaking its 11-year Sunspot cycle.

"The Sun's magnetic poles will remain as they are now, with the north magnetic pole pointing through the Sun's southern hemisphere, until the year 2012 when they will reverse again. This transition happens, as far as we know, at the peak of every 11-year sunspot cycle— like clockwork."   ~NASA

---

31 *Continued*
"And the graves were opened; and many bodies of the saints which slept arose, and came out of the graves
after his resurrection, and went into the holy city, and appeared unto many." (Matthew 27.52-53)
"...that there might be undeniable evidence of their own resurrection first, and through it of their Lord's. Thus, while it was not deemed fitting that He Himself should appear again in Jerusalem, save to the disciples, provision was made that the fact of His resurrection should be left in no doubt. It must be observed, however, that the resurrection of these sleeping saints was not like those of the widow of Nain's son, of Jairus' daughter, of Lazarus, and of the man who 'revived and stood upon his feet,' on his dead body touching the bones of Elisha (2 Kings 13:21)—which were mere temporary recallings of the departed spirit to the mortal body, to be followed by a final departure of it 'till the trumpet shall sound.' But this was a resurrection once for all, to life everlasting; and so there is no room to doubt that they went to glory with their Lord, as bright trophies of His victory over death."   ~Jamieson Fausset Brown

The *Parousia* or second supernatural manifestation of the Tathagata (the Supreme Being) brings back the same great saints, the "bright trophies" that left the world at His previous departure, as luminous signs of His immanent return—to walk the earth again and guide us through the last 45 days. **"For the Lord himself shall descend from heaven with a shout,
with the voice of the archangel, and with the trump of God: and the dead in Christ shall rise first."** (1 Thes. 4.16)
32 "The fragments of Shoemaker-Levy 9 were traveling at an impact speed of 60 km/sec when they struck Jupiter with a kinetic energy equivalent to 600 times the world's estimated nuclear arsenal."   ~amazingspace.org

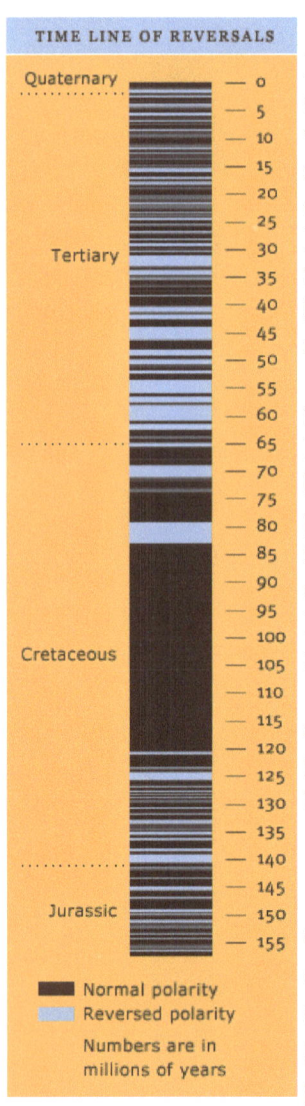

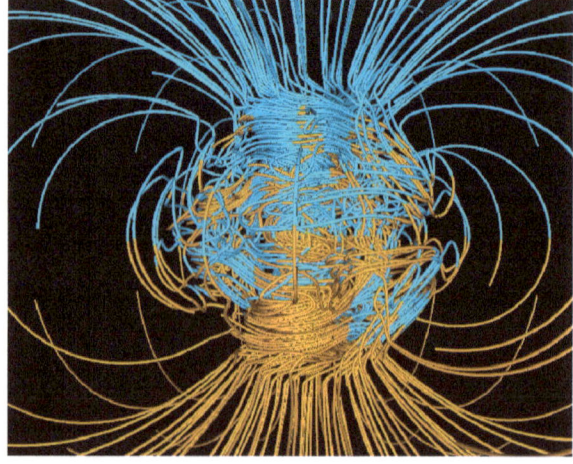

Figs. 7-8 Earth's periodic magnetic pole Reversals

"The strength of the Earth's magnetic field is known to drop during 'magnetic reversals', when the north and south poles swap places. Records of the field direction, frozen into sediments laid down on the seabed, show that the magnetic field has reversed hundreds of times in the past 400 million years.

In normal circumstances, the magnetic field protects the Earth's surface from dangerous high-energy particles, including particles from the sun and cosmic rays from deep space. But as the field switches polarity, it can drop to below 10 per cent of its normal strength for thousands of years. Such a weakened field would allow lethal radiation to reach the Earth's surface, with potentially disastrous consequences for the atmosphere, the climate and particularly for life.

The Earth's magnetic field is showing worrying signs that it is about to reverse again. Not only has the magnetic north pole wandered by 1100 kilometres in the past 200 years, but its strength is dropping at a rate of 5 per cent a century 'This is the fastest decrease since the last reversal 730,000 years ago,' Lesch says."

~*New Scientist Magazine*[33]

With Earth's magnetism dropping close to zero Gauss, Sun flare activity at its peak, and both coinciding with a Galactic conjunction—we can only expect the unexpected. Even under normal conditions, erupting sunspots wreak havoc on Earth.[34] Dwelling on a worse-case scenario, some astronomers have conjectured a catastrophic "Perfect Storm" scenario should the Earth's Poles also chooose this most ominous date to do their own mischievous tango.

---

[33] Yet it appears our *conscious* Universe has a self-preservation instinct: "In a paper to be published in the journal *Astronomy and Astrophysics*, Guido Birk and Harald Lesch of the University of Munich, Germany, and Christian Konz of the Max Planck Institute for Plasma Physics in Garching report an investigation of exactly what happens when the field is drastically reduced or vanishes altogether. Their simulations show that the solar wind—the million-kilometre-an-hour stream of hydrogen and helium nuclei from the sun—wraps itself around the Earth in a way that induces a magnetic field in the ionosphere as strong as the original field. 'We were quite surprised about its effectiveness,' Lesch says."   ~New Scientist Magazine (2004)

[34] Sept. 12, 2005— "A rowdy sunspot cluster hurled a record-breaking flare into space on Wednesday, blacking out all high- and low-frequency radio communications on both American continents, causing power surges, blinding satellites and lighting up aurorae, and more trouble is likely on the way, say experts. A massive initial X-ray flare on Sept. 7 was immediately followed by an eruption of solar material that broke free from the sun at a speed of 5.8 million miles per hour, the speediest seen in 20 years of CME observations by the National Center for Atmospheric Research's High Altitude Observatory in Hawaii. Earth and near-Earth space was first hit with X-rays, followed by an ongoing magnetic storm and hard radiation."   ~Discovery News

   * [Indeed, a potential disaster was slated for 2012. Few knew how close we came. "In the December 2013 issue of the journal *Space Weather*, a paper entitled *A major solar eruptive event in July 2012*, describes how a powerful coronal mass ejection (CME) tore through Earth orbit on July 23, 2012. Fortunately Earth wasn't there. 'I have come away from our recent studies more convinced than ever that Earth and its inhabitants were incredibly fortunate that the 2012 eruption happened when it did,' says Daniel Baker of the University of Colorado. 'If the eruption had occurred only one week earlier, Earth would have been in the line of fire.' Analysts believe that a direct hit by an extreme CME such as the one that missed Earth in July 2012 could cause widespread power blackouts. Before 2012, when researchers talked about extreme solar storms their touchstone was the iconic Carrington Event of Sept. 1859, named after English astronomer Richard Carrington. A series of powerful CMEs hit Earth head-on with a potency not felt before or since. Intense geomagnetic storms ignited Northern Lights as far south as Cuba and caused global telegraph lines to spark, setting fire to telegraph offices, thus disabling the Victorian Internet. 'In my view the July 2012 storm was in all respects at least as strong as the 1859 Carrington event,' says Baker. The only difference is, it missed."   ~**Near Miss: The Solar Superstorm of July 2012**, NASA Science]

Book IV: Supraliminality

"Magnetic Pole reversal is a process when North Pole and South Pole reverse positions. When this happens, at some point of time Earth's magnetic field reaches zero Gauss which simply means, Earth at that point of time has zero magnetism. When this coincides with an eleven year cycle of Sun's Polar reversal, a major problem arises. According to the Hyderabad Computer Model, the polar reversal of Earth and Sun can cause the following serious problems other than electronic malfunction, migrating birds losing sense of direction and so on:

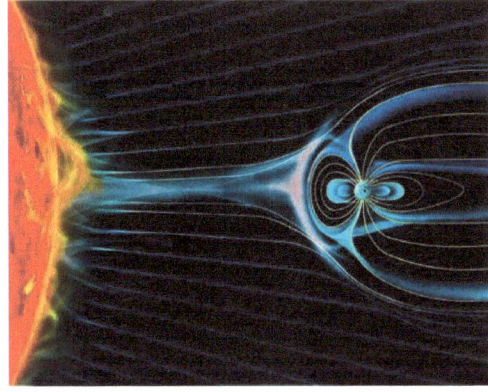

- The earth's crust will experience increasing volcanoes, tectonic movements, earthquakes and landslides.
- The Earth's gravitational field will experience a change though no one knows how it will change." ~IndiaDaily.com

However, only the Apocalypse itself can trigger such a portentous planetary rectification as Polar reversal...

Forty-five days and nights later, the soot-stained skies suddenly clear to reveal a marvel of nature — a crisscrossing *aurora borealis*, leagues in length, is all that remains of Earth's magnetic field. Mary's *visible* sign... the ubiquitous logo of the **Son of Man**.

Fig. 9   Hyderabad Computer Model

"And then shall appear the sign of the Son of man in heaven:

Like postdiluvian Noahs, an unnatural calm claims the land as the People walk warily in the first light of a new day. The multitudes are brought to their knees upon witnessing a sight too good to be true—enveloped within a majestic, cumulous cloud, surrounded by a congregation of Celestial Beings, the Lord Christ appears jubilant as tear-stained millions look on in utter disbelief.

...then shall all the tribes of the earth mourn, and they shall see the Son of man coming in the clouds of heaven with power and great glory."
(Matthew 24.30)

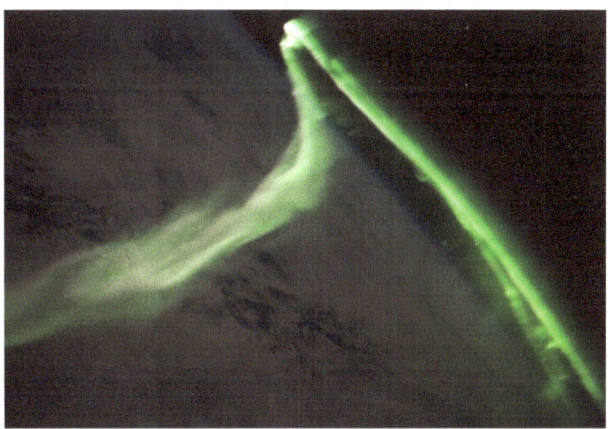

Fig. 10   Aurora Borealis

Momentarily a powerful X-ray pulse, preceding a monumental sun flare, strikes the earth with such an *uninhibited* mega-g force concussion that we *ricochet* off the ground. Zero Gauss magnetism occurring within the Pole shift induces a gravity-free condition, assisting the pulse to repel us skyward at terrific velocity...

"Then we which are alive and remain shall be caught up together with them in the clouds, to meet the Lord in the air..."   (1 Thessalonians 4.17)

Expelled miles above the earth, resigned to certain death, we are suddenly transfixed in space as well as time—escalating explosions of consciousness bring on the *Samadhi* experience of ecstasy and eternity... Concrescence achieved at the Omega Point of Time, the disjunctive many coalesce into a conjunctive Novelty, creating novel togetherness, the One.

Meanwhile Gaia, a self-correcting organism, has renewed her magnetic field, flip-flopping poles. As miraculously as we ascended, we gently descend to the good Earth, her gravitational flux returning at just the right instant. The (re) birth pangs over, the Great Purification is complete. The Teacher has come now that the students are ready.

After experiencing the apex of raw energy emanating from the GC occultation at the Zero Point of Time, the psychoactive influx will diminish, gradually, as the new Golden Age, the *Krita Yuga* or 6,480-year Macroseason of "Winter" commences. What goes up must come down—the long, dark Age of heroes and villains yields to a new Era of cooperation and hope where every "day" (year) gets longer and brighter.[35] Our descent back down the mountain will seem as precarious as the climb up, with the major difference that each year will get a bit easier, antithesis of the previous 20-year *katun*. The next 20 years completely dislodge us from the center of Power[36], life returning to a level of normality in the 2030s as Habit (stasis) once again counterbalances Novelty (dynamism).

However, life down here will never be the same again. Thank God. A numinous Being, with His retinue of *mahasiddha*[37] saints living in the natural world (*Malkhut*), changes the laws of physics by His very presence. Within 20 years time, daily life will literally evolve into the unimaginable...

> **"But as it is written, Eye hath not seen, nor ear heard, neither have entered into the heart of man, the things which God hath prepared for them that love him."** (1 Corinthians 2.9)

The first order of business will be to round up the war criminals and underlings of the evil seventh Empire who survived the Purification. Prosecution procedures drag on for years while the minions of Mammon are hunted down and arrested...

> **"And after that there shall be another week, the eighth week, that of righteousness, and a sword shall be given to it that a righteous judgment may be executed on the oppressors, and sinners shall be delivered into the hands of the righteous."** (1 Enoch 92.13)

The guilty are delivered up to the God-Emperor Himself for impenitent Judgment...

> **"When the Son of man shall come in his glory, and all the holy angels with him, then shall he sit upon the throne of his glory: And before him shall be gathered all nations: and he shall separate them one from another, as a shepherd divideth his sheep from the goats: and he shall set the sheep on his right hand, but the goats on the left."** (Matt. 25.31-33)

---

35 Psychologically, the last weeks of autumn produce a spiraling down effect; energy in the biosphere is rock bottom on the shortest day, the Winter Solstice, but at the same time there is a feeling of anticipation. We know from experience that *this too shall pass*. In the old days we had less faith in Nature's Way...

"In pre-Christian times the solstice was an important time when the sun miraculously alters its course and the days shift to becoming longer, the nights shorter. In a World without electric light this was a profound reason for thanksgiving. People got nervous as the days got shorter, because they could see perpetual night coming. They didn't understand the rotation of the earth and how it makes the days shorter and longer. The Celtic priests and other leaders of early faiths in Northern Europe would promise to use their 'power' to re-ignite the sun. In the old Celtic tradition the evening of the longest night involved the local 'priest' ordering the burning of a pine tree on the nearest 'high hill'—a precursor to 'beacon fires'. Local people would be told to drag a pine tree to the top of the highest hill around December 21st. With great ceremony the priest would assert his power and control over the sun by commanding it to return to full brilliance in the following days, and firing the tree. In this way he was assured that his power was also recognized by the people he controlled." ~simonthescribe.co.uk

36 Our local Solar System/GC conjunction (SS ☌ GC) is an astrological aspect with distinct degrees of influence, cusps, preceding and succeeding the actual alignment. Since this cycle is so huge—every 26,000 years—it has an unusually extended cusp of influence: 20 years or one *katun*. All in all, a typical, Biblical purification process—40 years wandering through the wilderness (1993-2033 AD).

37 Mahasiddha. "...in the Tantric, or esoteric, traditions of India and Tibet, a person who, by the practice of meditative disciplines, has attained *siddhas* (miraculous powers); a great magician. Both the Shaivites (followers of Shiva) of Hindu India and the Tantric Buddhists of Tibet preserve legends of 84 mahasiddhas who flourished up to the 11th century." ~Encyclopedia Britannica

Book IV: Supraliminality

After two thousand years of unconditional love, mercy and forgiveness, there is no chance of reprieve for the guileful "goats". Sentenced to death, Capital Punishment delivers them—male and female—down to the desperate depths of damnation. A very real world, make no mistake.[38]

> "And these shall go away into everlasting punishment: but the righteous into life eternal."
> (Matthew 25.46)

A caste system based on merit is enacted as elected ones of the Elect are chosen to receive the hierophantic teachings, the mysteries of the *Kingdom of Heavens*[39], directly from the Teacher.

> **"At its completion, there shall be elected the elect ones of righteousness from the eternal plant of righteousness, to whom shall be given *sevenfold* instruction (learning, knowledge) concerning all His creation."** (1 Enoch 92.12)

> "But who can conceive, not to say describe, what degrees of honor and glory shall be awarded to the various degrees of merit? Yet it cannot be doubted that there shall be degrees."
> ~*The City of God*, Book 22, Augustine

While worker classes salvage the cities' infrastructures, the chosen representatives are assembled to learn the Quantum Metaphysics of a seven-tiered, interlaced Universe, the hierarchy of luminous Lords (Forces) that delimit the Unlimited Light of the Godhead—the first science given to Mankind before they were ready to receive it: Astrology.[40]

Chapter Five: Mazzaroth, the Original Myth

Thanks to the painstaking research of Frances Rolleston, we have access to the true origin of the twelve zodiacal signs or *zoidia* (Grk. *zoidion*, a living space or locus)[41], comprising an ancient Myth occulted by the sands of time. The earliest storytellers taught the synergy of heavenly influence by using simple connect-the-dots imagery, weaving the chronicle of Mankind's Fall and Redemption through a patchwork of starry constellations. Hardly a pagan construct as we'll see...[42]

Mazzaroth: The Constellations, Parts I-IV, magnum opus of a pious 19th century Englishwoman, Rolleston, went unnoticed until the 1893 publication of E.W. Bullinger's, *The Witness of the Stars*.

---

38 "...they shall cry and lament in a place that is an invisible wilderness and burn in the fire—for there exists ground there (as upon the earth)." (1 Enoch 108) Without the Daughters of Darkness, Ba'al's bastards cannot reincarnate for a thousand years—Evil put under lock and key: **"And he laid hold on the dragon, that old serpent, which is the Devil, and Satan, and bound him a thousand years, And cast him into the bottomless pit, and shut him up, and set a seal upon him, that he should deceive the nations no more, till the thousand years should be fulfilled: and after that he must be loosed a little season."** (Rev. 20.2-3)
39 "Heaven" (Hbw. *Shamayim*, plural form of the unused singular *Shameh*) is always translated in the plural, Heavens. In the Greek NT, Jeshua always refers to the kingdom of *heavens*—mistranslated as *Ouranos* (singular), a mistransliteration of *Shamayim*.
40 The 10,948 BC *Fall of the Angels* unleashed an "evil impulse" unto the naïve, antediluvian children of God—higher knowledge. We'll see how 200 Fish-Lords (Watchers) from the dwarf star system, Sirius B, descended upon the delightful daughters of men and taught them the "rejected mysteries". **"Barak-el taught the Astrologers."** (1 Enoch 8.5)
41 "[Hellenistic] astrologers called these [signs] the twelve *zoidia*, a word that has several interesting meanings. A *zoidion* is a living thing, also the seat of a god, also a picture or icon." ~*Astrological Roots: The Hellenistic Legacy*, Joseph Crane
42 "Josephus informs us that the twelve tribes of Israel bore the twelve signs on their banners; and the Chaldee paraphrase, of a still earlier date, asserting the same, adds that the figure of a man was borne on the standard of Reuben, a bull on that of Ephraim, a lion on that of Judah, an eagle on that of Dan. The Targums also attribute to Dan a crowned serpent, or basilisk. Libra was not borne on any of the standards, Simeon and Levi being included together under Pisces, and the place of Libra and of Levi in the encampment of Israel being that occupied by the Tabernacle." ~*Mazzaroth*, Rolleston

A direct descendant of Johann H. Bullinger, the Swiss reformer, E.W. was a lifelong scholar, Doctor of Divinity whose secular credentials added considerable credibility to the amateur Rolleston's thesis. Yet the latter's impeccable Biblical scholarship laid the entire edifice—albeit haphazardly—that Bullinger merely edited and commented upon. In her preface, Rolleston states her objective:

"The object of this work is to show, by the combined testimony of tradition and of ancient writers, and from the meaning of the yet extant ancient names of stars and emblems, that they were invented to transmit the earliest and most important knowledge possessed by the first fathers of mankind."

This imperative knowledge was the Messianic Plan—engraved in stone since the Adam's fall—that had to be preserved in as simple a manner as possible; a myth that could be easily memorized and repeated from generation to generation. And to guarantee its survival, the story would disclose the various characteristics embodied by each of the twelve Thrones, while synchronistically meshing with the Redemption legend itself. An ingenious artifice, arbitrary pictographs[43] in the stars taught the ABCs of Astrology by linking the archetypal energies to the story of Mankind's Enlightenment.

Several inveterate cultures assert a legendary sage, Seth—*aka* the Egyptian god Thoth or **Hermes Trismegistus**—invented astrology.[44] Prolific 1st century historian, Josephus confirmed the primordial buzz that the third son of Adam had imparted a precious legacy to his progeny.[45]

---

[43] The error of sidereal (*Jyotish*) astrology is to assume the physical, fixed constellations are responsible for their respective Akashic fields' emanations. The locomotive engine of the Zodiac begins its surge at 0°Aries, the precise moment of the Vernal Equinox as viewed from Earth. The *symbolic* signs progress according to their own inherent, dynamic combustion, building an increasingly vital *link* connecting all twelve Thrones. The subtle circle of Forces operate on the etheric level, fundamental to the physical world. The constellations themselves are merely arbitrary constructs created to teach Astrology and preserve the YHVH's Salvation Plan.

The primordial mythmaker's genius was to *tweak* these Primary patterns to reveal the inherent synchronicities binding the twelve Thrones (Judges) to the Messianic prophecy: Virgo as the *fallen* woman, the *off-balance* Scales, the Scorpionic *lust* of the fallen Angels, the war of the *Centaurs* (Sagittarius), the *cutting off* of the Fish-Lords (Capricorn), and so forth...

[44] We learned in **Book III**, footnote 21, how the gifted children of Seth settled in Egypt prior to the final destruction of Poseidia—the Atlantean refugees' forefathers, Adam, Seth and Enoch immortalized as *Creator Gods* by the primitive aboriginals.

"Jewish, Persian, and Arabian ancient writers preserve the tradition, that 'the family of Seth,' Adam, Seth, and Enoch, 'invented astronomy,' the Egyptians attributing it to **Seth or Thoth, said to be the same as *Hermes Trismegistus*, the thrice-great.** Plutarch mentions Seth, 'to whom the third day of the five of the epact was dedicated,' as worshipped in Egypt. He was said to be the third son of Set and Netphe, the father and mother of the gods, whose names are given by Bunsen as Seb and Nutpe." ~Rolleston

"The dependence of the early Egyptian star (sun) worship (the basis of the worship of Osiris) upon early Chaldaic influences belongs to the still unsettled question of the origin of early Egyptian civilization. But undoubtedly the priests of the Pharaohs were the docile pupils in astrology of the old Chaldean priests. **The mysterious Taauth (Thoth), the *Hermes Trismegistus* of antiquity, was regarded the earliest teacher of astrology in Egypt. He is reputed to have laid the foundation of astrology in the 'Hermetic Books'; the division of the zodiac into the twelve signs is also due to him.** In classic antiquity many works on astrology or on occult sciences in general were ascribed to this mythical founder of Egyptian astrology. The astrological rule of reckoning named after him, 'Trutina Hermetis' made it possible to calculate the position of the stars at the time of conception from the diagram of the heavens at the time of birth. The Egyptians developed astrology to a condition from which it varies but little today. The hours of the day and night received special planets as their rulers, and high and low stood under the determinative influence of the stars which proclaimed through the priestly caste the coming fate of the land and its inhabitants. *It is significant that in ancient Egypt astronomy, as well as astrology, was brought to an undoubtedly high state of cultivation.*

The astoundingly daring theories of the world found in the Egyptian texts, which permit us to infer that their authors were even acquainted with the helio-centric conception of the universe, are based entirely on astrologico-theosophic views. The astrology of the ancient inhabitants of India was similar, though hardly so completely developed; they also regarded the planets as the rulers of the different hours. Their division of the zodiac into twenty-eight houses of the moon is worthy of notice; this conception like all the rest of the fundamental beliefs of Hindu astrology, is to be found in the Rig-Veda. In India both astrology and the worship of the gods go back to the worship of the stars. Even today, the Hindus, especially the Brahmins, are considered the best authorities on astrology and the most skilful casters of horoscopes." ~The Catholic Encyclopedia, 1907-1912

[45] "There is nothing, then, improbable in the report of Josephus, when he says that the descendants of Seth were skilful astronomers, and seems to ascribe to them the invention of the cycle of which Cassini has developed the excellence. The Jews, Assyrians, and Arabians have abundance of traditions concerning the antediluvian astronomical knowledge, especially of Adam, Seth, Enoch, and Ham. It was asserted in the book of Enoch, as Origen tells us, that the constellations in the time of that patriarch were already named and divided. The Arabians say that they have named Enoch, Edris, on account of his learning." ~*The Zodiacs*, Sir W. Drummond

Book IV: Supraliminality

"The children of Seth were the inventors of that peculiar sort of wisdom which is concerned with the heavenly bodies, and their order; and that their inventions might not be lost before they were sufficiently known, upon Adam's prediction, *that the world was at one time to be destroyed by the force of fire, and at another time by the violence and quantity of water,* **they made two pillars, the one of brick, the other of stone**. They described their discoveries on them both, that in case the pillar of brick should be destroyed by the flood, the pillar of stone might remain, and exhibit those discoveries to mankind, and also inform them that there was another pillar of brick erected by them. Now this remains in the land of Syria or Seirad to this day." ~*Antiquities*

Known in Freemasonry as the Pillars of Enoch, the Great Pyramid (stone) and the Ziggurat[46] (brick) were the antediluvian Temples erected by Enoch's ancestors to preserve our predetermined timeline engraved on the Tablets of Heaven—the prophecy *built into their very structures...*

"Then there began the building of that now called Gizeh... the Hall of the Initiates... This, then, receives all the records from the beginnings of that given by the priest... to that period when there is to be the change in the earth's position and the return of the Great Initiate to that and other lands for the folding up of those prophecies that are depicted there. *All changes that came in the religious thought in the world are shown there, in the variations in which the passage through same is reached, from the base to the top—or to the open tomb and the top. These are signified by both the layer and the color [and] in what direction the turn is made.*"   (Cayce Reading 5748-5, 1932)

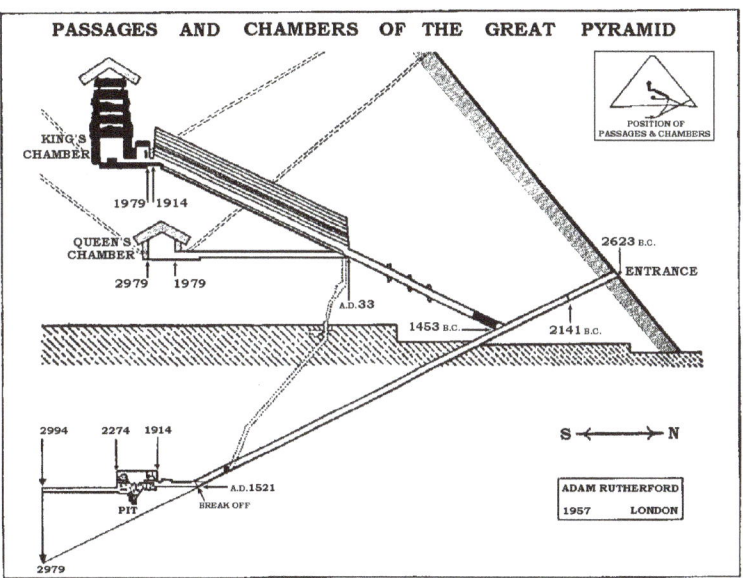

Fig. 11   Inside the Great Pyramid of Giza

"The discovery of several unique features determined the chronological starting point in the Great Pyramid. Down the Descending Passage, at a distance of about 40 feet from the entrance, there are found, on the side wall, straight knife-edge lines cut from roof to floor, one on each side and exactly opposite each other. Their appearance on the otherwise smooth walls of the passage certainly suggests that they are intended as a clear zero line, or "datum line" from which to take measurements. They are called the 'Scored Lines'. Prof. Piazzi Smyth was the first person to realize the full significance of the Scored Lines. He surmised that if the elevation of the Descending Passage represented what, for want of a better term, might be called the plane of the Dragon Star, then it was clear that the Scored Lines could represent the intersection of that astronomical plane by another equally significant plane. Calculations soon confirmed the suspicion. It turned out that at one time—and at one time only—during the third millennium B.C. (3000-2000 B.C.) the plane denoted by the Scored Lines passed directly through Alcyone (chief star of the Pleiades, or Seven Sisters, in the constellation of the Bull) at the same time as the axis of the Descending Passage was locked directly onto the Dragon Star (Draconis). The Dragon Star, sometimes referred to as the Devil Star, symbolically shone down the Great Pyramid's Descending Passage marking man's descent into materialism, and for those who continued on this path, death and damnation.

---

46 By 2500 BC, The Great Temple of Dagon in Mari, Syria dominated Mesopotamia, her legendary ziggurat already *dust in the wind*. "**ZIGGURAT**, form of temple common to the Sumerians, Babylonians and Assyrians. The earliest examples date from the end of the 3rd millennium BC, the latest from the 6th cent. BC. The ziggurat was a pyramidal structure, built in receding tiers upon a rectangular, oval, or square platform, with a shrine at the summit. The core of the ziggurat was of sun-baked bricks, and the facings were of fired bricks, often glazed in different colors, which are thought to have had cosmological significance. Access to the summit shrine was provided by a series of ramps on one side or by a continuous spiral ramp from base to summit. The number of tiers ranged from two to seven. Notable examples are the ruins at Ur and Khorsabad in Mesopotamia."   ~The Columbia Encyclopedia

The Scored Lines provided an exact astronomical fix—and that fix, as it turns out, occurred precisely at noon of the vernal equinox, 21 March, 2141 B.C. It was clear, then, that noon of 21 March, 2141 B.C., was the starting date for the Great Pyramid's internal chronograph. And with this dating now suitably confirmed it only remained to discover the symbolic time-scale.

The dimensions of the Great Pyramid are based on a single unit—the Pyramid inch. The Pyramid inch is equal to 1.001 British inches that happens to be equal to a 500,000,000 part of the Earth's Polar Diameter. The Pyramid inch is the universal measurement that the engineers used in the construction of the Great Pyramid. It was only logical, then, that the Pyramid inch be used in the chronological time-scale. This is how it works: Measurements in P.(Pyramid) inches, backward or forward from the Scored Lines, represent the corresponding number of years before or after that astronomically fixed date of 2141 B.C.

Measuring 688 P. inches beyond the Scored Lines, down the Descending Passage, an aperature appears in the roof. This aperature is the entrance to the Ascending Passage, which leads into the Grand Gallery. Progressing 688 years from 2141 B.C. gives the date 1453 B.C., or to be more precise as tests and calculations can prove, the 30th of March, 1453 B.C. [*See* **Fig. 11**]

The significance of this date to the early pyramidologists was clear: It marks the date of the Exodus of the Israelites from Egypt, and their receiving the Law, through Moses. A granite plug, at this very point, fills the Ascending Passage. Measuring up the Ascending Passage, at the given scale of one P. inch per year, we find that the entrance of the Grand Gallery is marked 1485 P. inches away. Remembering 1 A.D. immediately follows 1 B.C., 1485 years after 30 March, 1453 B.C. brings us to 1 April, 33 A.D. This is nothing less than the traditionally recognized date of the Crucifixion of Jesus the Christ and the sudden 'raising of the roof' at this point refers to human enlightenment, the release of cosmic power, which flowed from that event.

The Well-Shaft was created top-down, almost as if it was ripped apart. Its rocky and steep incline is in stark contrast to the other well-formed passages. The placement appears intentional. **The Well-Shaft adjoins both these passages offering a type of bridge between two divergent paths—a redemptive route, centering on the events of the period immediately following AD 33.**

Pyramidologists interpreted the Well-Shaft to symbolize the path opened by the teachings of Jesus to the travelers of the lower path or Descending Passage. To Christians it obviously represents the saving grace of Christ, the possibility of redemption for errant humanity.

Modern pyramidologists, in particular Peter Lemesurier, discovered that *the scale changes when a step is encountered*. The designer of the Great Pyramid with mathematical certainty makes it clear we change the scale according to the depth of the step. Corresponding to the year 1845, the Great Step, three feet high at the end of the Grand Gallery [*See* **Fig. 12**], marks a 'lifting up' of those traveling the highest road. Many of today's modern religious movements began at this time, effecting the destinies of millions ever since:

- The Adventists. The leading prophet of the Second Coming of Christ during this period was a man called William Miller, who predicted the Second Coming would take place in 1844. Miller's North American followers numbered close to 100,000 in the years prior to 1845. Today, several churches trace their origins to Miller's group, the largest being the Seventh Day Adventists.

- The Mormons. The 1830s saw the formation of a unique religious movement that was to have a profound effect on North America, and is known today as the Church of Jesus Christ of Latter-Day Saints (or Mormons). The founder of the Church, Joseph Smith, claimed that a Messenger of God had appeared before him and told him that the covenant between God and Israel was about to be fulfilled and to prepare for the Second Coming. Smith eagerly accepted this mission but met a sudden end in 1844, when an angry mob murdered him because of his beliefs. Smith had predicted his own death three days beforehand.

- The Ba'hai faith. In the East, Mirza Ali Mohammed from Persia, after a long period of prayer and meditation became convinced in the year 1844 that God had chosen him as a prophet. He declared himself the Bab and a manifestation of God and from that the Ba'hai faith grew to become one of the most active international movements in the world today.

Book IV: Supraliminality

The period around 1845, spiritually speaking, manifested new religions and sprung new branches upon older faiths. The effect shows in two ways: the souls of the higher path in this actual period (1845) were touched by a religious outpouring resulting in prophetic visions and revelations. Secondly, the subsequent establishment of the new religious movements effects all who travel the higher path to this very day.

1914 is a very important date, according to our prophetic chronology, marked on both the lowest and highest paths. The 'lower' path descends into the Great Subterranean Chamber in the Summer of 1914, plunging into a chaotic nightmare and symbolically named in the *Egyptian Book of the Dead*, the 'Egyptian Chamber of Ordeal.' The beginning of 'Hell on Earth'—is how the Great Pyramid seems to portray this period.

Returning our attention to the top chambers, the year 1914 marks just prior to a narrow constricted passage that leads into the Ante-Chamber. Significantly, it represents the finish of the Grand Gallery and the entry into the upper chambers of the pyramid. According to the chronology, 1914 heralds a period of absolute war, carnage and chaos, and, apparently, the beginning of the end of this Age. The travelers of the highest road now enter the final stages of their journey.

Our chronology has led us from the year 2623 B.C. right up to the significant date of 1914. The 'lower' path emerges into a chamber of chaos and the 'Pit', while the 'upper' path enters the Ante-Chamber and moves toward the King's Chamber.

The beginning of the Ante-Chamber marks the date 1979. History now starts to 'speed' up. Still in the Ante-Chamber, 1999 registers a change in floor masonry from limestone to granite. Since granite is usually accorded with spirit, it characterizes the purifying and perfecting of the souls of the higher path before they enter the Father's Kingdom (King's Chamber)."

~*Prophecy and the Great Pyramid*, Jason Jeffrey

Fig. 12 The Grand Gallery
The Ante-Chamber and King's Chamber is straight ahead, under the ladder.

Pyramidologist Peter Lemesurier conjectured how a return to the P.inch per year scale *inside the King's Chamber*—superseding the Great Step's adjustment—would calibrate the Messianic Event to exactly 2012 AD. In his 1977 landmark classic, *The Great Pyramid Decoded*, Lemesurier inadvertently tapped into the Maya's Great Cycle end-date...

"It might still be argued that the scale of 1" per year should apply throughout the King Chamber's Passage and right into the King's Chamber, since no actual 'step' has intervened... Application of such a thesis would date the first Messianic advent at A.D. 2012."

The symbolic architecture, a *Bible in stone*, bestowed upon Mankind a living diagram displaying our God-given choice of free will between two directions: **Descending Passage** to the Subterranean Chamber and damnation or **Ascending Passage** through the Grand Gallery and redemption. [*See* **Fig. 11**]

"See, I have set before thee this day life and good, and death and evil." (Deuteronomy 30.15)

The Sphinx, a woman (**Virgo**) with a lion's (**Leo**) body[47], sat guard before the Temple of Giza to demarcate the disastrous *Fall of the Watchers* in 10,948 BC (the **Virgo-Leo** cusp), a ghastly

---

47 "In Greek mythology the most famous sphinx was that of Thebes in Boeotia. According to Apollonius, she was the daughter of Typhon and Echidna, and had the face of a woman, the feet and tail of a lion and the wings of a bird." ~Encyclopedia Britannica

reminder of Azazel's abominable DNA manipulations (mermaids, centaurs, sphinxes). The polysymbolic landmark also provided an important clue to commence Seth's circular symbolism, *The Hero with a Thousand Faces*.[48]

"The word 'Sphinx' is from the Greek, to bind closely together. It was therefore designed to show where the two ends of the Zodiac were to be joined together, as where the great circle of the heavens begins and ends."
~E.W. Bullinger

The Great Sphinx indicates the *zoidion* legend begins with a Virgin and ends with the Lion. On the first day of Spring—the vernal equinox—

Fig. 13 The Woman/Lion (Virgo/Leo cusp) Sphinx, ca. 10,500 BC[49]
We are now exactly 180° from the prehistoric turning point. Light (Truth) emerging as we round the circle these last days of the *Pisces-Aquarius* cusp.

our ancestors would solemnly wait until dark when **"night unto night reveals knowledge."** (Psalm 19.2) In the primordial, crystal-clear night sky of *Sham El Nessim*—a sacred festival celebrating the beginning of Creation—with the constellation Virgo illustriously illuminated above, the aboriginal Atlanteans first beheld the world's oldest myth, *Mazzaroth*.[50]

Act I: The Fall

Virgo	THE WOMAN, the Branch
Libra	THE SCALES, the Imbalance
Scorpio	THE SCORPION, the Corruption
Sagittarius	THE ARCHER, the Hunting Down

---

48 Perhaps Jungian mythologist Joseph Campbell's subconscious knew that his thousand mythological faces were based upon the real historical hero encoded in the *Mazzaroth*—the true, original mythos of the redeeming Messiah preserved in the constellations.
49 "In my book *The Orion Mystery*, I demonstrated that the best fit for the Giza Pyramids/Nile pattern with the Orion's belt/Milky Way pattern occurred when the sky was pushed back in time (i.e., precessed) to the epoch of 10,500 BC. There were good reasons for doing so. The ancient Egyptians, for example, constantly referred to a remote golden age they called *Zep Tepi*, the 'First Time' of Osiris, which they believed had long predated the Pyramid Age. Osiris was Orion, and the Great Pyramid had a shaft directed to Orion at the meridian. In his *Fingerprints of the Gods*, Hancock pointed out that the First Time date of 10,500 BC denoted the beginning or First Time of the Age of Leo. This was when the Lion constellation would have risen heliacally (at dawn before the sun) on the day of the vernal (spring) equinox. This event brought the celestial lion to rest due east, thus in perfect alignment with the Sphinx. The Sphinx, in other words, was made to look at his own image in the horizon—and consequently at his own 'time'." ~Robert Bauval
50 "Canst thou bind the sweet influences of Pleiades, or loose the bands of Orion? Canst thou bring forth *Mazzaroth* in his season or canst thou guide Arcturus with his sons?" (Job 38.31-32)
"*Mazzaroth*, though sometimes in modern lexicons differently interpreted, is here used as meaning the constellations. In Job 38.32, it stands in the text of the English Bible untranslated: in the margin it is rendered 'the twelve signs.' *Mazzaroth* is a feminine or neuter plural noun, applied to separate chambers of divisions, such as the constellations. *Mazaloth*, a word with which it is sometimes identified, means a way through which any thing goes, as the sun through the zodiac, and the moon through the lunar mansions, or *Manzil al Kamar*, the Arabic appellation of the lunar zodiac still used in the East. It occurs in the sacred Scriptures only in 2 Kings 23.5, probably in the same sense." ~*Mazzaroth*, Rolleston

Book IV: Supraliminality

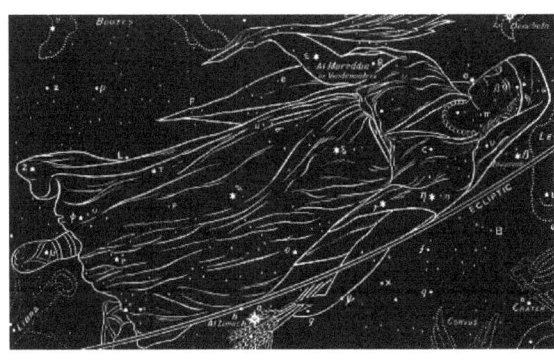

Fig. 14   Virgo ♍

Latin: VIRGO, a virgin[51]
  or VIRGA, a branch
Hebrew: BETHULAH, a virgin
Arabic: BETHULAH, a branch

"And I will put enmity between thee and the woman, and between thy seed and her seed; it shall bruise thy head, and thou shalt bruise his heel."
(Genesis 3.15)

"Therefore the Lord himself shall give you a sign; Behold, a virgin shall conceive, and bear a son, and shall call his name Immanuel." (Isaiah 7.14)

"The brightest star in Virgo (1st magnitude) has an ancient name, handed down to us in all the star-maps, in which the Hebrew word *Tsemech* is preserved. It is called in Arabic *Al Zimach*, which means *the branch*. This star is in the ear of corn which she holds in her left hand. Hence the star has a modern Latin name, which has almost superseded the ancient one, *Spica*, which means, an ear of corn (seed).

There are twenty Hebrew words translated *branch*, but only one of them (*Tsemech*) is used exclusively of the Messiah, and this word only four times."   ~E.W. Bullinger

---

[51] From time immemorial, the Constellation Virgo held the key to the Messianic "myth". The 6th century BC exile, Daniel learned the ancient legend of the *Mazzaroth* from his Chaldean teachers, including the fact that an astronomical anomaly appearing in the sign of the *fallen woman* would indicate the birthplace of the anticipated *Son of Man*, "**the eternal plant of righteousness**."

"Thomas Hyde, an eminent Orientalist, writing on the ancient religion of the Persians, quotes from Abulfaragius (an Arab historian, 1126-1286), who says that Zoroaster, the Persian, was a pupil of Daniel the Prophet, and that he predicted to the Magians (who were the astronomers of Persia), that when they should see a new star appear it would notify the birth of a mysterious child, whom they were to adore. It is further stated in the *Zend Avesta* that this new star was to appear in the sign of the Virgin." ~E.W.

Theologian Ernest L. Martin builds a strong case for a September 11, 3 BC (Virgo) nativity of the baby Jesus, beginning with an unusual *triple conjunction* of Jupiter/Regulus—and punctuated by a visually spectacular Venus/Jupiter conjunction a year later, the fabled "Star" of Bethlehem: **"Where is he that is born King of the Jews? for we have seen his star in the east..."**   (Matthew 2.2)

"Regulus is the chief star in the constellation of Leo, the Lion, and because it lay practically on the path of the Sun, it was reckoned as a 'Royal Star' [*See* **Fig. 29**]. Jupiter and Regulus came into juxtaposition on September 14, 3 B.C. and as viewed from earth they were only .33 degrees from each other. Here was the 'King planet' (Jupiter) now coming in contact with the 'King star' (Regulus) and in the 'Royal Constellation' (Leo the Lion).

Jupiter first united with Regulus and then it continued on its normal course in the heavens. On December 1, 3 B.C., Jupiter stopped its motion through the fixed stars and began its annual retrogression. In doing so, it once again headed toward the star Regulus. Then on February 17, 2 B.C., the two were reunited, .85 degrees apart. Jupiter continued in its motion (still in retrogression) another 40 days and then it reverted to its normal motion through the stars. Remarkably, this movement placed Jupiter once again into a third conjunction with Regulus on May 8, 2 B.C. They were then .72 degrees from each other. **The visible effect of these three conjunctions of Jupiter (the King planet) with Regulus (the King star) would have shown Jupiter making a circling effect over and around Regulus. Jupiter was 'homing in' on Regulus and pointing out the significance of the King star as it related to the King planet...**

It was the early evening of June 17, 2 B.C. All the cities around Babylon in Mesopotamia were aglow with talk about a spectacular astronomical event being witnessed in the western sky. What had been monitored for several weeks was the planet Venus moving eastward among the stars on what appeared to be a collision course with the planet Jupiter. Now the expected event had happened right in front of their eyes. This astronomical drama being enacted in the western part of the sky showed the 'collision' of the two brightest planets in the heavens. *So small was the separation between them that to the naked eye they would have appeared not as two stars, but as one brilliant star shining far brighter than any other star or planet.* Though the two planets were millions of miles away from one another, to observers in Babylon in the year of 2 B.C., they appeared as a single star dominating the twilight of the western sky in the direction of Palestine...

On December 25, 2 B.C., when the King planet Jupiter came to its stationary point in mid-Virgo the Virgin, it would have been seen 'stopped over Bethlehem' as viewed from Jerusalem. The Magi then went to Bethlehem and gave the child the gifts they brought from the east. Jesus was now a *paidion* (Greek: toddler) not a *brephos* (Greek: infant, as in Luke). He was old enough to stand and to walk. In the papyrus codex Bodmer V of the *Proto-Evangelium of James* written in Egypt in the 4th century, it even states that the Magi were able to see Jesus 'standing by the side of his mother Mary' (21:3)."   ~*The Star That Astonished the World*, E. Martin

> "Behold, the days come, saith the YHVH, that I will raise unto David a righteous *tsemech*, and a King shall reign and prosper, and shall execute judgment and justice in the earth." (Jeremiah 23.5)
>
> "Hear now, O Joshua the high priest, thou, and thy fellows that sit before thee: for they are men wondered at: for, behold, I will bring forth my servant the *tsemech*." (Zechariah 3.8)
>
> "And speak unto him, saying, Thus speaketh the YHVH of hosts, saying, behold the man whose name is the *tsemech*; and he shall grow up out of his place, and he shall build the temple of the YHVH." (Zechariah 6.12)
>
> "In that day shall the *tsemech* of the YHVH be beautiful and glorious, and the fruit of the earth shall be excellent and comely for them that are escaped of Israel." (Isaiah 4.2)

The desecrated Eva eventually reincarnates as the Lotus-Born Mary, a pure genetic branch from the tree of Abraham capable of generating the promised seed, as only Her Buddha-matrix womb could do. Mariah's immaculate conception and cloistered life as a temple virgin, an orthodox Essene dedicated to the YHVH [*See* **Book II**, footnote 44], ensures the preternatural nativity of the Davidic Branch. Temporal degeneracy (devolution) began with a *fallen woman* and so proceeds Seth's mythopoeic prophecy, dubbed *Our Ladye's Waye* by the Celtic Anglo-Saxon's of the 15th century.

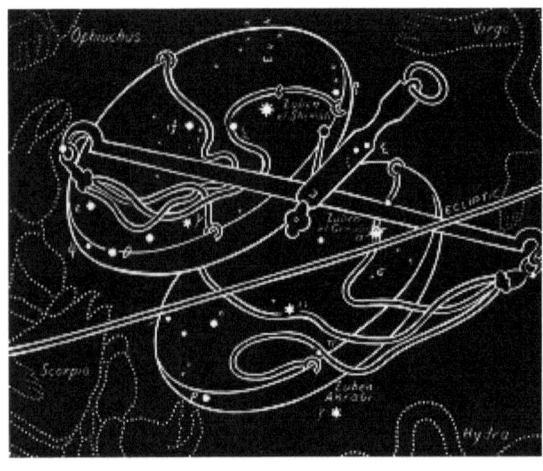

Fig. 15   Libra ♎

Latin: LIBRA, weighing
Hebrew: MOZANAIM, the scales, weighing
Arabic: AL ZUBENA, purchase

> "You have been weighed in the balances, and found wanting…" (Daniel 5.27)
>
> "None of them can by any means redeem his brother, Nor give to God a ransom for him; For the redemption of their soul is costly, And must be let alone for ever." (Psalm 49.7)
>
> "That we should be to the praise of his glory, who first trusted in Christ. In whom ye also trusted, after that ye heard the word of truth, the gospel of your salvation: in whom also after that ye believed, ye were sealed with that holy Spirit of promise, which is the earnest of our inheritance *until the redemption of the purchased possession*, unto the praise of his glory." (Ephesians 1.12-14)

"The brightest star (in the lower scale), is named *Zuben al Genubi*, which means the purchase, or price which is deficient. This points to the fact that man has been utterly ruined. In the upper scale we have another bright star with the name *Zuben al Chemali* —The Price Which Covers." ~Bullinger

The Fall into the carnal world tips the scales, forever damning Mankind into endless cycles of birth and death until the 26,000-year *Mahayuga* is completed. The upper scale indicates the hefty karmic sacrifice (of the Adam as the Lamb) that shall rectify the imbalance. The redemption of our souls was costly indeed, the ransom paid in full. As the *purchased possession*, we must wait until His return—the servants alert and on best behavior, not knowing (exactly) when the Master arrives.

Book IV: Supraliminality

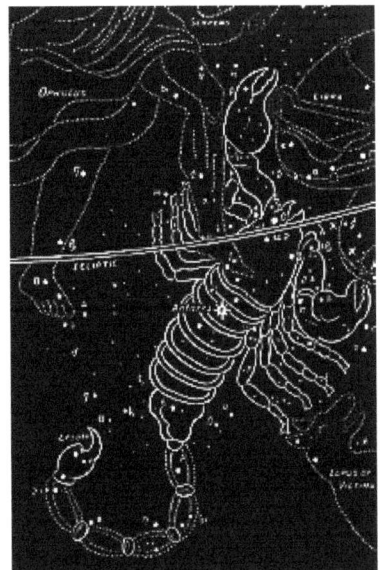

Fig. 16 Scorpio ♏

Latin: SCORPIO, scorpion
Hebrew: AKRAB, the scorpion, the conflict or war
Arabic: AL AKRAB, the scorpion, wounding

"And there was *war in heaven*: Michael and his angels fought against the dragon; and the dragon fought and his angels, and prevail not; neither was their place found any more in heaven. and the great dragon was cast out, that old serpent, called the Devil, and Satan, which deceiveth the whole world: he was cast out into the earth, and his angels were cast out with him." (Rev. 12.7-9)

"And it came to pass when the children of men had multiplied that in those days were born unto them beautiful and comely daughters. And the angels, the children of the heaven, saw and lusted after them, and said to one another: 'Come, let us choose us wives from among the the children of men and beget us children.' And Semjaza [*Samael*], who was their leader, said unto them: 'I fear ye will not indeed agree to do this deed, and I alone shall have to pay the penalty of a great sin.' and they all answered him and said: 'Let us all swear an oath, and all bind ourselves by mutual imprecations not to abandon this plan but to do this thing.' Then sware they all together and bound themselves by mutual imprecations [*sodomy*] upon it. And they were in all two hundred who descended in the days of Jared on the summit of Mount Hermon." (1 Enoch 6.1-7)

"The brightest star (1st magnitude, in the heart), bears the ancient Arabic name of *Antares*, which means the wounding. It is called by the Latins *Cor Scorpii*, because it marks the scorpion's heart. It shines ominously with a deep red light." ~Bullinger

Corruption enters the natural world when Watchers from the dwarf-star system, Sirius B[52]—behaving more like voyeurs—succumb to lust and travel over eight light-years (the long-distance record for *poontang*) to plunder the enchanting earth women. As in the days of Adam and Eva, the Fish-daemons seduce the innocent Atlantean females with intoxicating, psychotropic aphrodisiacs.

---

52 **Book II**, footnote 62 introduced an impossibly learned African tribe who worshipped Fish-Lords that came from the sky in an "ark".
"The descriptions of the landing of the ark are extremely precise. The ark is said to have landed on the earth to the north-east of Dogon country, which is where the Dogon claim to have come from (originally, before going to Mande) and that is, of course, the direction of Egypt and the Middle East in general. The landing of the ark is visually described: 'The ark landed on the Fox's dry land and displaced a pile of dust raised by the whirlwind it caused. The violence of the impact roughened the ground... it skidded on the ground... The great ark came out of the sky and came down. In the center the Nommo was standing, he came down. Then he returned to the water... with respect men call him *di tigi*, master of the water'." Temple traced the fishy story back to the famed Sumerian legend of amphibian extraterrestrials—the **Annunaki**—who jump-started civilization. 3rd century BC Babylonian historian, Berossus refers to the **Annedoti**, the ***Repulsive Ones***, Fish-Lords that apparently started off on the right foot (or fin), only to fall from grace...
"At Babylon there was (in these times) a great resort of people of various nations, who inhabited Chaldæa, and lived in a lawless manner like the beasts of the field. In the first year there appeared, from that part of the Erythræan sea which borders upon Babylonia, **an animal destitute of reason**, by name **Oannes**, whose whole body (according to the account of Apollodorus) was that of a fish; that under the fish's head he had another head, with feet also below, similar to those of a man, subjoined to the fish's tail. His voice too, and language, was articulate and human; and a representation of him is preserved even to this day. [the Bishop's MITRE]
This Being was accustomed to pass the day among men; but took no food at that season; and he gave them an insight into letters and sciences, and arts of every kind. He taught them to construct cities, to found temples, to compile laws, and explained to them the principles of geometrical knowledge. He made them distinguish the seeds of the earth, and showed them how to collect the fruits; in short, he instructed them in every thing which could tend to soften manners and humanize their lives. From that time, nothing material has been added by way of improvement to his instructions. And when the sun had set, this Being Oannes, retired again into the sea, and passed the night in the deep; for he was amphibious. After this there appeared other animals like Oannes, of which Berossus proposes to give an account when he comes to the history of the kings." ~*Fragments of Chaldaean History*, Berossus

Cont. →

Fig. 17   Oannes (Dagon)

> "And all the others together with them took unto themselves wives, and each chose for himself one, and they began to go in unto them and to defile themselves with them, and they taught them charms and enchantments, and the cutting of roots, and *made them acquainted with plants*." (1 Enoch 7)

Impudent Azazel teaches metallurgy and the art of warfare to the men, cosmetics to the women. Other Repulsive Ones instruct their concubines in astronomy, astrology, sorcery and *tantric* "swinging" (free love). Knocked up in the process, the little girls beget abominable, 450-ft. tall offspring—the *Nephilim* (Hbw. *fallen ones*), aka the *Rephaim* (Hbw. *dead ones*).

> "And they became pregnant, and they bare great giants, whose height was *three thousand ells*:[53] Who consumed all the acquisitions of men. And when men could no longer sustain them, the giants turned against them and devoured mankind. And they began to sin against birds, and beasts, and reptiles, and fish, and to devour one another's flesh, and drink the blood." ~Ibid.

> "And the sons of men in those days took from the cattle of the earth, the beasts of the field and the fowls of the air, and taught the mixture of animals of one species with the other, in order therewith to provoke the YHVH." (Jasher 4.18)

Genetic manipulation was another "forbidden" mystery taught to the naïve Atlantean peasants. Eventually, complete chaos ensues when mermaids, minotaurs, centaurs and other victims of crossed chromosomes mate and create new AIDS-like plagues. The ogres eventually run out of food, and start slaughtering people. Soon the whole Earth is covered in blood and debauchery, cries of the oppressed reaching up to heaven...

> "Then the earth laid accusation against the lawless ones." (1 Enoch 7)

---

52 *Continued*

Thus we have a modern tribe from darkest Africa, the *Dogon*, that continue to kowtow to Fish-Demons—their notorious name inherited from the Philistine Dark Lord, **Dagon**. "Unlike the Baals, who, among the Canaanites, were essentially local deities, Dagon seems to have been considered by the Philistines as a national god (1 Chronicles 10:10). To him they attributed their success in war; him they thanked by great sacrifices, before him they rejoiced over the capture of Samson (Judges 16:23); into his temple they brought the trophies of their victories, the Ark (1 Samuel 5:1, 2), the armour, and the head of Saul (1 Samuel 31:9-10; 1 Chronicles 10:10)."
~The Catholic Encyclopedia, 1907-1912

The mythological **Dragon** is also an etymological descendant of the first Dark Lord's dreaded *nom de plume*...

"Oannes, the Annedotus, reminds us of the 'Dragon' and 'Snake-Kings'; the *Nagas* who in Buddhist legends instruct people in wisdom on lakes and rivers, and end by becoming converts to the good Law and Arhats." ~*Encyclopedic Theosophical Glossary*

In 1928, French archeologists unearthed myriad cuneiform tablets dating from the fifteenth to the thirteenth century BC. On a par with the Dead Sea Scrolls bonanza, the **Ugaritic Texts** revealed a rare title for the shape-shifting tempter of Eva—*son of Dagon*.

"Baal is prominent in the great complex of fifteenth century BC Ugaritic epics, where he is called son of Dagon and is named 250 times, sometimes interchangeably with Hadad, the widely know Semitic storm god, whose symbol, like Baal's, was the bull."
~*Oxford Companion to the Bible*, David Burke

Ba'al subdues His homey from Sirius B prior to the Second Creation. Oannes (Dagon), the *Leviathan* is retired as Dark Lord.

"In the Ugaritic texts, Baal defeats Lothan (ltn, a linguistic variant of Leviathan), described as a seven-headed serpent, apparently identified with Baal's adversary Prince Sea. In the Bible, Leviathan is also identified with the Sea (Job 3.8) and has many heads (Psalm 74.14), and his defeat by God is a prelude to creation (Psalm 74.15). According to apocalyptic literature, that battle will be rejoined in the end time when the evil Leviathan will be finally defeated (Isaiah 27.1; Revelation 12.3; Revelation 17.1-14; Revelation 19.20; Revelation 21.1). In Job 41, Leviathan is described as fully under God's control, a divine pet. Many commentators have equated the Leviathan of Job 41 with the crocodile, and some elements of the description seem to fit this identification."
~*Oxford Companion to the Bible*, Michael D. Coogan

Losing the battle, but not the war, Daddy *Dagon* is due for a deadly resurrection at the end of the thousand years of peace...

"He will be sacrificed for the purification and reorganization of the universe... Then he will take on his original form, will rule from the waters and will give birth to many descendants." ~*Dogon* Testimony   [*See* **Cthulhu**, p. 165]

53 The original 1821 translation of the Ethiopian texts by Reverend Richard Lawrence reads "300 cubits", approximately 450 feet tall.

Book IV: Supraliminality

"And God saw the whole earth and it was corrupt, for all flesh had corrupted its ways upon earth, all men and all animals.[54] And the YHVH said, I will blot out man that I created from the face of the earth, yea from man to the birds of the air, together with cattle and beasts that are in the field for I repent that I made them." (Jasher 4.18-19)[55]

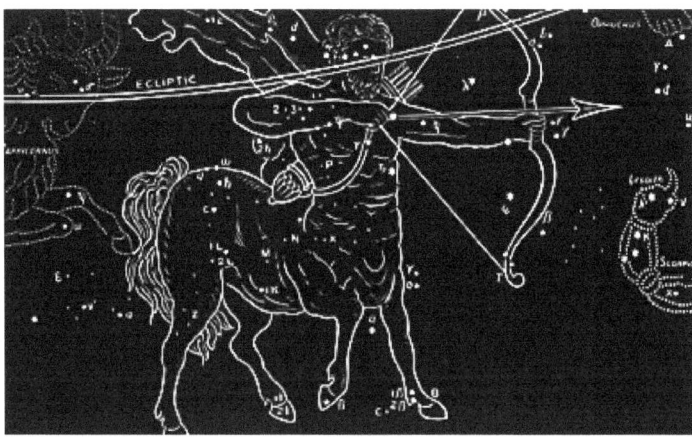

Fig. 18   Sagittarius ♐

Latin: SAGITTARIUS, the archer
Hebrew / Syriac: KESITH, the archer
Arabic: AL KAUS, the arrow

"The brightest stars (all in the bow) are significant: Hebrew, *Naim*, which means the gracious one. Hebrew, *Nehushta*, **the going or sending forth.** We see the same in the Arabic names which have come down to us: *Al Naim*, the gracious one; *Al Shaula*, the dart; *Al Warida*, **who comes forth**; *Ruchba er rami*, the riding of the bowman." ~Bullinger

The YHVH *sends forth* the swift Uriel to warn Noah, the gracious Michael to bind Semyaza for the defections and fornication, the healer Raphael to bind Azazel for teaching the unnatural sciences and repair the damages wrought by the monstrous manipulation of DNA, the warrior Gabriel to hunt down the Watchers' dinosaur children and wipe out the abominable half-breeds by instigating a civil war of *Nephel* against *Nephel*. The Greek epic, **War of the Titans** preserves our racial memory as myth: Atlas, Heracles, Prometheus and Epimetheus "mighty men which were of old, men of renown." (Genesis 6.4)

"Then spoke the Most High, the Holy and Great One! And he sent Uriel to the son of Lamech, and said to him: 'Go to Noah and tell him in my name 'Hide thyself!' and reveal to him the end that is approaching: that the whole earth will be destroyed, and a deluge is about to come upon the whole earth, and will destroy all that is on it. And now instruct him that he may escape and his seed may be preserved for all the generations of the world.'

And again the Lord said to Raphael: 'Bind Azazel hand and foot, and cast him into the darkness: and make an opening in the desert, which is in Duda 'el, and cast him therein. And place upon him rough and jagged rocks, and cover him with darkness, and let him abide there for ever, and cover his face that he may not see light. And on the day of the great judgment he shall be cast into the fire. And heal the earth which the angels have corrupted, and proclaim the healing of the earth, that they may heal the plague, and that all the children of men may not perish through all the secret things that the Watchers have disclosed and have taught their sons. *And the whole earth has been corrupted through the works that were taught by Azazel: to him ascribe all sin.*'

---

54 The interbreeding of Humans and animals begot "things"—trained to serve as beloved "pets" that took care of all the menial tasks.
  "We find that in those periods there was not a laboring for the sustenance of life (as in the present), but rather individuals who were children of the Law of One—and some who were the children of Belial (in the early experience)—were served by automatons, or THINGS, that were retained by individuals or groups to do the labors of a household, or to cultivate the fields or the like, or to perform the activities of artisans. And it was concerning these 'things' about which much of the disturbing forces grew to be factors to be reckoned with, between the children of the Law of One and the Sons of Belial." (Cayce Reading 1928-2)
55 The nonextant *Sefer HaYashar* (Book of the Upright) resurfaced in Venice, 1625. **"And the sun stood still, and the moon stayed, until the people had avenged themselves upon their enemies. Is not this written in the *book of Jasher*?"** (Joshua 10.13) **"Also he bade them teach the children of Judah the use of the bow: behold, it is written in the *book of Jasher*."** (2 Samuel 1.18)

And to Gabriel said the Lord: 'Proceed against the bastards and the reprobates, and against the children of fornication: and destroy [the children of fornication and] the children of the Watchers from amongst men [and cause them to go forth]: send them one against the other that they may destroy each other in battle.'

And the Lord said unto Michael: 'Go, bind Semyaza and his associates who have united themselves with women so as to have defiled themselves with them in all their uncleanness. And when their sons have slain one another, and they have seen the destruction of their beloved ones, bind them fast seventy generations in the valleys of the earth, till the day of their judgment and of their consummation, till the judgment that is for ever and ever is consummated.' "

(1 Enoch 10. 1-13)

Act II: Redemption

Capricornus	THE GOAT FISH, cut off
Aquarius	THE WATER URN, deluge
Pisces	THE FISHES, bound
Aries	THE LAMB, slain

Fig. 19   Capricorn ♑

Latin: CAPRICORNUS, the horned goat
Hebrew: GEDI, the kid, cut off
Arabic / Syriac: AL GEDI, the kid, cut off

"And he shall take the two goats, and present them before the YHVH at the door of the tabernacle of the congregation. And Aaron shall cast lots upon the two goats; one lot for the YHVH, and the other lot for the scapegoat. And Aaron shall bring the goat upon which the YHVH's lot fell, and offer him for a sin offering.

But the goat, on which the lot fell to be the scapegoat, shall be presented alive before the YHVH, to make an atonement with him, and to let him go for a scapegoat into the wilderness." [56]

(Leviticus 16. 7-10)

"In all the ancient Zodiacs, or Planispheres, we find a goat with a fish's tail. In the Zodiacs of Denderah and Esneh, in Egypt, it is half-goat and half-fish, and it is there called *Hu-penius*, which means the place of the sacrifice. The Goat is bowing its head as though falling down in death. The right leg is folded underneath the body, and he seems unable to rise with the left. The tail of the fish, on the other hand, seems to be full of vigour and life. The star named *Al Gedi*, means the kid or goat, while the star called *Deneb Al Gedi*, means the sacrifice cometh. Other star-names in the sign are *Dabih* (Syriac), the sacrifice slain; *Al Dabik* and *Al Dehabeh* (Arabic) have the same meaning; *Ma'asad,* the slaying; *Sa'ad al Naschira*, the record of the cutting off."   ~Bullinger

---

[56] *Yom Kippur* (Day of Atonement) is arguably the holiest day in Judaism, an annual purification of sins committed within the past year. In memoriam of the antediluvian debauchery, the iniquities of Israel are ritualistically transferred to a scapegoat, the latter sent out into the desert, to Azazel. Bathing, fasting and prayer coupled with sexual abstinence is the norm.

Book IV: Supraliminality

With the Repulsive Ones imprisoned and most of their Nephilim kids slain, the entire genetic line of mermen is completely cut off, with no seed left to regenerate. The racial cleansing provides the atonement necessary to appease the YHVH. Yet the Tribes' hopelessly degraded DNA leaves the Father no choice but to purge the earth, starting over again with a pure remnant of the original root race, the great-grandson of Enoch. "...perfect in his generations, Noah walked with God." (Gen. 6.9)

Fig. 20   Aquarius ♒

Latin: AQUARIUS, the water bearer
Hebrew / Arabic: DELI / DELU,
    the water-urn, bucket
Coptic: HUPEI TIRION,
    the station of pouring out

"In the six hundredth year of Noah's life, in the second month, the seventeenth day of the month, the same day were all the fountains of the great deep broken up, and the windows of heaven were opened. And the rain was upon the earth forty days and forty nights."
(Genesis 7.11-12)

"The star (in the right shoulder) is called *Sa'ad al Melik*, which means *the record of the pouring forth*. The star (in the other shoulder) is called *Saad al Sund*, who goeth and returneth, or *pourer out*. The bright star (in the lower part of the right leg) is well-known today by its Hebrew name *Scheat*, which means who *goeth and returneth*. The bright star in the urn has an Egyptian name—*Meon*, which means simply an urn."   ~Bullinger

The disastrous Deluge[57] (DELU) is memorialized in the heavens as the *place of pouring out*. The extinction event left a permanent "rent" in the time/space continuum, the psyche of Mankind. In a single day (Nov. 1, All Soul's Day), countless millions were *poured out*. Every ethnographically advanced society around the old world records a titanic Flood that wipes out all civilization. The world's oldest literary composition—18th century BC tablets unearthed in Nippur, Iraq—bespeaks a Sumerian myth where Enki (god of waters) warns Zi-ud-sura of an impending flood; the latter rewarded for "preserving the animals and the seed of mankind". A marvelously intact version survives on

---

[57] "An abrupt climate change happened about 11,600 years ago at the termination of the Younger Dryas cold event, which was the last blast of cold climate at the end of the last Ice Age. (NOAA) Ice core records from Greenland show in less than a decade there was a sudden warming of around 15 degrees Celsius (27°F) of the annual mean temperature. **The Great Atlantis Flood Theory** (Eagle/Wind 2005) correlates this event with destruction of Atlantis as reported in the dialogues of Plato, which state that Atlantis disappeared beneath the sea 11,600 years ago.

    Scientific evidence reveals that about 11,600 BP, an impulse rupture earthquake hit Kerch, Crimea, Ukraine. Eagle/Wind propose that this earthquake caused the Manych-Kerch Gateway to fracture, allowing the Caspian Sea, which was already overflowing from glacial melt waters, to spill into the area of the present Sea of Azov. The earthquake also caused the area of the present Sea of Azov to sink 8 to 10m and fill with water from the overflowing Caspian Sea (Tchepalyga, Andrey). The Kerch Peninsula did not sink because it is located on Orogene formation. The earthquake generated a tsunami in the Black Sea, driving waves inland, further inundating the Sea of Azov and sending waves up the river channels, which were already swollen from the glacial melt waters.

    One third of Europe drains into the Black Sea, which had risen to 20m below its current level. The tsunamis broke over the Sakarya River Delta, into Lake Sapanca and Izmit Basin. This accounts for the presence of Caspian Sea mollusks in the Black Sea, Sea of Marmara and the Dardanelles. The increased hydraulic pressure, aided by the earthquake and aftershocks, fractured a proposed subterranean outflow channel from the Black Sea into the Mediterranean Sea, which ran beneath the Bosporus land bridge and the Sea of Marmara. A series of three magnificent fountains, as geysers, broke through the fractures and erupted in the area of the present Sea of Marmara. The mixture of churning water and debris inundated the fertile plains of the northern Aegean Sea area; leaving only the bare bones as islands, as recorded by Plato."   ~*Atlantis Motherland*, L. Eagle and M. Wind

an Akkadian cuneiform tablet, the *Epic of Atrahasis* [58], also circa 1700 BC—same storyline, the titular hero now Atrahasis (Akk. *Extra-wise*). A thousand years later, the *Epic of Gilgamesh* blatantly plagiarizes the Akkadian account, exchanging Enki and Atrahasis for Ea and Utnapishtim, the latter offering King Gilgamesh immortality—which he fails to possess. Plato's story of Atlas and the destruction of the Atlantean culture preserves the primeval record of Athen's golden age...

"...afterward there occurred violent earthquakes and floods, and in a single day and night of rain all your warlike men in a body sunk into the earth, and the island of Atlantis in like manner disappeared, and was sunk beneath the sea. And that is the reason why the sea in those parts is impassable and impenetrable, because there is such a quantity of shallow mud in the way; and this was caused by the subsidence of the island."   ~*Critias*, Plato

Fig. 21 Epic of Atrahasis, British Museum

The Norse version holds Odin responsible for the Deluge, a frost giant, Belgelmir, its only survivor. The Maya-Kiché natives of pre-Columbian Guatemala recorded their *Popul Vuh* for posterity...

"Then by the will of Hurakan, the Heart of Heaven, the waters were swollen, and a great flood came upon the mannikins of wood. They were drowned and a thick resin fell from heaven... Because they had not thought on Hurakan, therefore the face of the earth grew dark, and a pouring rain commenced, raining by day and by night... Then ran the mannikins hither and thither in despair.

They climbed to the roofs of the houses, but the houses crumbled under their feet; they tried to mount to the tops of the trees, but the trees hurled them from them; they sought refuge in the caverns, but the caverns closed before them. Thus was accomplished the ruin of this race, destined to be overthrown."   ~*Popul Vuh*, Spence

---

[58] "The story outlines the structure of the universe according to Babylonian beliefs. Heaven is ruled by the god Anu, the earth by Enlil and the subterranean sweet water by Enki. The text then explains how the minor gods work in the fields but then rebel. As a result, humans are made from clay, saliva and divine blood to act as servants of the gods. This does not prove a perfect solution, as the humans reproduce and their noise disturbs Enlil's sleep. He decides to destroy them with plague, famine, drought and finally a flood. However, each time Enki instructs one of the humans, Atrahasis, to survive the disasters.

The god gives Atrahasis seven days warning of the flood, and he builds a boat, loads it with his possessions, animals and birds. He is subsequently saved while the rest of humankind is destroyed. However, the gods are unhappy as they no longer receive the offerings they used to. There is a gap in the text at this point but it does end with Atrahasis making an offering and Enlil accepting the existence and usefulness of humans. Copies of this story have survived from the seventeenth to the seventh century BC showing that it was copied and re-copied over the centuries. This is the most complete version. There are clear similarities between this Flood story and others known in Mesopotamian literature, for example, the *Epic of Gilgamesh*."   ~The British Museum

Zecharia Sitchin's theories of Human origination, based on the above Sumerian myth and published in his 1976 bestseller, *The 12th Pla*net, gave nihilistic New Agers—weary of the old "One God, first Man" Judeo-Christian scenario—all the debunking they needed. The fact that Robert Temple presents a completely rational account of extraterrestrial interference in his painstaking research into the *Sirius Mystery*, doesn't faze the "I want to believe" X-file enthusiasts... the Russian-born skeptic Sitchin spins a much more tantalizing tale of lazy gods from planet-X who create Human slaves—"in their image"—to take over the mining of precious minerals.

"Sitchin's claim to fame is announcing that he alone correctly reads ancient Sumerian clay tablets. All other scholars have misread these tablets which, according to Sitchin, reveal that gods from another planet (Niburu, which orbits our Sun every 3,600 years) arrived on Earth some 450,000 years ago and created humans by some genetic engineering with female apes... Sitchin stands alone, on nobody's shoulders, as a scholar nonpareil... He alone knows how to correctly translate ancient terms allowing him to discover such things as that the ancients made rockets...

Like [Erich] von Däniken and [Immanuel] Velikovsky, Sitchin weaves a compelling and entertaining story out of facts, misrepresentations, fictions, speculations, misquotes and mistranslations."   ~Robert Todd Carroll, *Skeptic's Dictionary*

Writer Ian Lawton (*Genesis Unveiled*) enlisted the aid of a Sumerian linguist to analyze Sitchin's so-called scholarship. "[Sitchin] demonstrates a consistent lack of appreciation of even some of the most basic fundamentals of Sumerian and Akkadian grammar, even to the extent of regularly failing to distinguish between the two entirely different languages, and mixing words from each in interpreting the syllables of longer compound words."

Book IV: Supraliminality

The original inhabitants of Mexico traced their ancestral heritage back to survivor/immigrants of a worldwide cataclysm.

"It is found in the histories of the Toltecs[59] that this age and first world, as they call it, lasted 1716 years; that men were destroyed by tremendous rains and lightning from the sky, and even all the land, without the exception of anything, and the highest mountains, were covered up and submerged in water fifteen cubits (*caxtolmolatli*); and here they added other fables of how men came to multiply from the few who escaped from this destruction in a *toptlipetlocali*; that this word nearly signifies a close chest; and how, after men had multiplied, they erected a very high *zacuali*, which is to-day a tower of great height, in order to take refuge in it should the second world (age) be destroyed.

Fig. 22 Mt. Ararat anomaly, **USAF** 1949

Presently their languages were confused, and, not being able to understand each other, they went to different parts of the earth. The Toltecs, consisting of seven friends, with their wives, who understood the same language, came to these parts, having first passed great land and seas, having lived in caves, and having endured great hardships in order to reach this land; ...they wandered 104 years through different parts of the world before they reached *Hue Hue Tlapalan*, which was in *Ce Tecpatl*, 520 years after the Flood."
~*Ixtlilxochitl Relaciones*, Kingsborough's "Mex. Ant.", vol. ix, pp. 321-322

India's sacred text, the *Matsya Purana* was recited by the God Vishnu himself, as a fish…

"Vishnu then revealed that it was indeed he who had adopted the form of a fish. He told Manu that the earth would soon be flooded with water. Vishnu had a boat built by the gods. When the earth was flooded, Manu was to place all living beings in the boat and thus save them. Vishnu would himself arrive in his form of the fish and Manu was to tie the boat to the fish's horn. Thus the living beings would be saved. And when the waters of the flood receded, Manu could populate the world and rule over it."

This multitude of myths, dating back to the 18th c. BC, cast dispersions upon the authenticity of the 12th c. BC Semitic scriptures, scribed by Moses. Yet modern scholarship is beginning to grasp the possibility that the original records from the universal Deluge may be older than imagined…

"Both the older Babylonian account (Atrahasis) and the Hebrew account belong to larger compositions passing from the creation of human beings to later history, the flood and its aftermath. Scholars often claim that the Hebrew flood story depends on the Babylonian, with modifications in the interest of Israel's monotheistic faith. **Consideration of certain differences, however, makes it more likely that both depend upon a common original.**"   ~*Oxford Companion to the Bible*, Alan Milard

The established Hebrew narrative, of course, depicts the YHVH drilling Noah—in meticulous detail—on the master Masonic erection of an enormous 300 cubit (450 ft.) closed-roof houseboat. Its final resting place high upon a dormant volcano—Mount Ararat, Turkey. [*See* **Fig. 22**]

---

[59] Interestingly enough, Lewis Spence informs us that the Toltec-Maya-Aztec Dark Lord (Ba'al) was known as **Quetzalcoatl**.

"The name is compounded from two Kiché words signifying **'Feathered Serpent,'** and its meaning in the Nahuatl is precisely the same. Concerning the nature of this deity, there is probably more difference of opinion than in the case of any other known to comparative mythology. Strangely enough, although unquestionably an alien in the mythology of the Aztecan branch of the Nahuatlacâ, he hulks more largely in the myths of that people than in the legends of the Kichés.

To the Aztecâ he seems to have appeared as a half-friendly Baal, to worship or revile according to the opportunism of national fortune. Although unquestionably the same god to both Mexicans and Kichés, he had acquired a significance in Aztecan eyes quite out of all proportion to his Kiché or Mayan importance. To the Aztecan mind he was a culture-hero, unalterably associated with the sun, and with the origins of their civilization. To the Toltecs he was the Man of the Sun, the traveler, who, with staff in hand, symbolized the daily journey of the Sun-god. In all likelihood *Quetzalcoatl* was evolved upon Mexican soil by the Toltecs, perhaps adopted from some older cults by them."   ~*Popul Vuh*, Lewis Spence

"**Now all the writers of barbarian histories make mention of this flood, and of this ark**; among whom is Berossus the Chaldean. For when he is describing the circumstances of the flood, he goes on thus: 'It is said there is still some part of this ship in Armenia, at the mountain of the Cordyaeans; and that some people carry off pieces of the bitumen, which they take away, and use chiefly as amulets for the averting of mischiefs.'

Hieronymus the Egyptian also, who wrote the *Phoenician Antiquities*, and *Mnaseas*, and a great many more, make mention of the same. Nay, Nicolaus of Damascus, in his ninety-sixth book, hath a particular relation about them; where he speaks thus: 'There is a great mountain in Armenia, over Minyas, called Baris, upon which it is reported that many who fled at the time of the Deluge were saved; and that one who was carried in an ark came on shore upon the top of it; and that the remains of the timber were a great while preserved. This might be the man about whom Moses the legislator of the Jews wrote.'" ~*Antiquities*, Josephus

Fig. 23 Pisces ♓

Latin: PISCES, fish, multiplying
Hebrew: DAGIM, the fishes (multitudes)
Arabic: AL HAUT, the fish
Coptic: PI-COT ORION,
  fish of him that cometh

"Look now toward heaven, and tell the stars, if thou be able to number them: and he said unto him, So shall thy seed be." (Gen. 15.5)

"And Isaac called Jacob... God Almighty bless thee, and make thee fruitful, and multiply thee, that thou may be a multitude of people."
(Genesis 28.3)

"The Sign is pictured as two large fishes bound together by a Band, the ends of which are fastened separately to their tails. One fish is represented with its head pointing upwards towards the North Polar Star, the other is shown at right angles, swimming along the line of the ecliptic, or path of the sun. The names of two of the stars in the sign are *Okda* (Hebrew), the united, and *Al Samaca* (Arabic), the upheld." ~Bullinger

Both genetic lines survive the first Purification, the *Sons of Light* and *Sons of Darkness*—the superior seed of Adam, the poor pips from Cain's kids. The tribes are fruitful, multiplying quickly and in no time the planet is repopulated. Good and bad seeds struggle for dominance, the former treading the vertical path (upwards, toward the North Star[60]), the latter the path of least resistance (ignorantly trapped within the Wheel of Delusion). Inextricably bound together, we are one Humanity with two diametrically opposed agendas. [*See* **Fig. 23**] Only the atoning sacrifice of the Adam, as the Anointed One, will break Ba'al's bonds.

---

[60] The Elect (**Sons of God**) are a predetermined number—153 "fish", indicating the final population count of End Time survivors: 1,530,000,000—give or take a few hundred thousand who may wise up. **"Then Jesus saith unto them, Children, have ye any meat? They answered him, No. And he said unto them, Cast the net on the right side of the ship, and ye shall find. They cast therefore, and now they were not able to draw it for the multitude of fishes... Simon Peter went up, and drew the net to land full of great fishes,** *an hundred and fifty and three*: **and for all there were so many, yet was not the net broken."** (Jn. 21.5-6, 11)

"The Apostles caught 153 fish, a number Augustine and other Church Fathers found significant. 153 is cabalistically the number of the Sons of God. This expression, 'Sons of God' (Hebrew: *Bene Elohim*) occurs several times in scripture, and per gematrium it counts up 153. Hengstenberg found in this number the fullness of the Gentiles indicated according to 2 Chronicles 2.17, where Solomon reckons the strangers in Israel at 153,600. **'They had toiled all night on unproductive soil in Israel, and now the Light of Day shall begin to rise and spread o'er all the earth, and the Gentiles shall walk in it.'** *Cont.* →

Book IV: Supraliminality

Fig. 24   Aries ♈

Latin: ARIES, the ram
Hebrew: TALEH, the lamb
Syriac: AMROO, the lamb
Arabic: AL HAMAL, the sheep, gentle, merciful

"The next day John seeth Jesus coming unto him, and saith, Behold the Lamb of God, which taketh away the sin of the world."
(John 1.29)

"Worthy is the Lamb that was slain to receive power and riches, and wisdom, and strength, and honor, and glory, and blessing."
(Revelation 5.12)

"Its chief star (in the forehead), is named *El Nath*, or *El Natik*, which means wounded, slain. The next (in the left horn), is called *Al Sheratan*, the bruised, the wounded. The next is called *Mesarim* (Hebrew), the bound."

"HERODOTUS tells us how the ancient Egyptians, once a year, when it opened by the entrance of the sun into ARIES (TAURUS then marked the Spring Equinox), slew a Ram, at the festival of **Jupiter Ammon**; branches were placed over the doors, the Ram was garlanded with wreaths of flowers and carried in procession.

Owing to the precession of the equinoxes, the sun, at the time of the Exodus, had receded into this sign of ARIES, which then marked the Spring Equinox. But by the time that the antitype—the Lamb of God, was slain, the sun had still further receded, and on the 14th of *Nisan* [the sun's entrance into Aries], in the year of the Crucifixion, stood at the very spot marked by the stars *El Nath*, the pierced, the wounded or slain, and *Al Sheratan*, the bruised or wounded! God so ordained 'the times and seasons' that during that noon-day darkness the sun was seen near those stars which had spoken for so many centuries of this bruising of the woman's Seed—the Lamb of God." ~Bullinger

Game over. The man without blemish, upright and exemplary in the Buddha's indispensable qualities: Right view, intention, speech, action, livelihood, effort, mindfulness and concentration—voluntarily lays down His life, balancing the scales again as *Zuben al Chemali*—The Price Which Covers. Actions speak louder than words and only such a heinous crime, the slaying of a Buddha[61], could echo thunderously down through the centuries—even the Father of Lies has had His hands full with the Crucifixion. From the counterfeit Gnostic "scriptures" to Dan Brown's cheesy thriller, one single fact still lingers on: an innocent man who was either a religious fanatic, sorcerer or Avatar died an excruciating, ignoble death. Judging the tree by its fruit, even the dilettante historian can do the aftermath—the dynamic consequences of the sacrifice witnessed the birth and maturation of the greatest universal (catholic) Church in known history.

---

60 *Continued*
   Petrus Bungus (16th century) wrote 'It was shortly after our Lord's Resurrection that the wonderful draught of fishes is related, and therein was a reference to a new and eternal life for all who were safely brought 'out of the deep' into the ship; therefore there were no reprobate sinners taken in the net, for all these were on the left side. The net was not broken; heresy and schism had not yet done damage.'" ~*Biblia Cabalistica*, Walter Begley (1903)
61 "If a Buddha is in the world and you injure him and shed his blood, you fall into the Avici hell. *Avici* means 'unspaced.' In this hell, if there are many people, it's full; if there is just one person, it's still full. It's called 'unspaced' because there is no space there. What kind of people fall into the Avici hell? Those who commit the Five Rebellious Acts:
   1. Killing one's father 2. Killing one's mother 3. Killing an Arhat **4. Shedding a Buddha's blood**
   5. Breaking up the Sangha. 'Shedding a Buddha's blood' also includes damaging or destroying Buddha images."
   ~*The Lotus Sutra*, Chapter Nineteen: The Merit and Virtue of a Dharma Master

Act III: Dominion

Taurus	THE BULL, Rule of Antichrist
Gemini	THE TWINS, Egalitarian Kingdom
Cancer	THE CRAB, Mankind secure, growth
Leo	THE LION, the eternal Sons of God

Fig. 25   Taurus ♉

Latin: TAURUS, the Bull[62]
Hebrew / Arabic: SHUR / AL THAUR, the Bull, coming, ruling
Coptic: APIS, who cometh

"I will punish the world for their evil, And the wicked for their iniquity; I will cause the arrogancy of the proud to cease, And will lay low the haughtiness of the terrible…Every one that is found shall be thrust through." (Isaiah 13.11-15)

"Come, my people, enter thou into thy chambers, and shut thy doors about thee: hide thyself as it were for a little moment, until the indignation be overpast. For, behold, the YHVH *cometh out* of his place to punish the inhabitants of the earth for their iniquity: the earth also shall disclose her blood, and shall no more cover her slain." (Isaiah 26.20-21)

"The indignation of the YHVH is upon all nations, and his fury upon all their armies: he hath utterly destroyed them, he hath delivered them to the slaughter. Their slain also shall be cast out, and their stink shall come up out of their carcasses, and the mountains shall be melted with their blood." (Isaiah 34.2-3)

"The brightest star, (in the bull's eye), has a Chaldee name—*Al Debaran*, and means the leader or governor. The star (at the tip of the left horn) has an Arabic name—*El Nath*, meaning wounded or slain." ~Bullinger

All the ancient Zodiacs show the Bull charging ahead furiously, with elongated horns readied for goring. A red-giant star, *Al Debaran* (the leader), gives the Bull's eye its diabolical glint. With the God-man gone, the Devil-man follows like cause and effect. As sacred as Sirius was to Egypt, the Pleiades (the Bull's shoulder—*the congregation of the judge*) was "home" to the Maya. When Cortez arrived to conquer the Aztec Empire, the submissive Indians thought he was the return of their Ba'al, *Quetzalcoatl* from the Pleiades. ["According to Ptolemy (the Pleiades) are of the nature of the Moon and Mars. They are said to cause blindness, disgrace and a violent death. Their influence is distinctly evil…" ~Vivian E. Robson] The tip of the northern horn, *El Nath*, wounded, slain, denotes the rending of the Church, the mass slaughter of innocent bystanders as cunning Cain consummates his depraved destiny. Vile vengeance has a rip-snorting field day, absolute (Dark) God-given power for three and a half years…

---

[62] We saw how, *at their very moment of redemption*, the Twelve Tribes reverted to Ba'al worship. History is about to repeat itself as millions of anxious parents—with taxes to pay and kids to feed—prepare to bow down to the AC when he takes control. Even some of the righteous (or self-righteous?) are seduced by the king of Bullshit. **"For false Christs and false prophets shall rise, and shall show signs and wonders,** *to seduce, if it were possible, even the elect.*" (Mark 13.22)

Book IV: Supraliminality

Latin: GEMINI, twins
Hebrew / Arabic: THAUMIM / AL TAUMAN,
  the united
Coptic: PI-MAHI, the united,
  as in Brotherhood

"The name in the ancient Denderah Zodiac is *Clusus*, or *Claustrum Hor*, which means the place of *Him who cometh*. It is represented by two human figures walking, or coming. The second appears to be a woman. The other appears to be a man." ~Bullinger

The Great Purification complete, the Prince returns "to consummate the effort He made 2000 years ago in Palestine." [63] Yet *Him who cometh* is represented by two human figures, male and female.[64] It is *They who cometh*, the new Elohim, Jeshua and Mariah inaugurating the Kingdom of heavens on Earth. One comes as king—the other acting prime minister... the twin gods Castor and Pollux.[65]

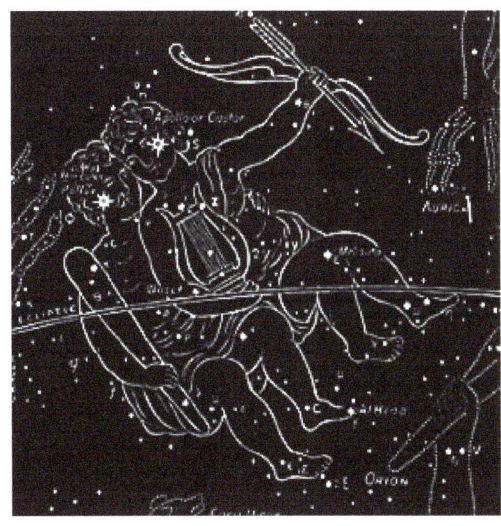
Fig. 26   Gemini Ⅱ

"The name of the star (in the head of one) is called (*Castor*) Apollo, which means ruler, or judge; while (in the head of the other) is called (*Pollux*) Hercules, who cometh to labour, or suffer. Another star, (in his left foot), is called *Al Henah*, which means hurt, wounded, or afflicted." ~Bullinger

Mariah, the very embodiment of Kuan Yin, actively engages in the day-to-day politics during the righteous **Eighth Week**, laboring on behalf of Her blessed children. A necessary sacrifice since her entheogenic awakening and subsequent rape by the Dark Lord in the garden produced the antagonists—our half-brothers and sisters, Ba'al's bastards, *aka* the Sons of Darkness. The Queen of Heaven's Herculean task is to unite men and women in their common uphill battle to Individuation (Godhood) within an egalitarian society. Jeshua remains the Hidden God, available only to those of the inner circle. The Prince *who comes to rule* is indicated by the now familiar 1st magnitude star in the second decan of Gemini, *Sirius*...

Fig. 27   Denderah Zodiac, Egypt circa 30 BC

Hebrew: SIRIUS, the prince
Arabic: AL SHIRA / AL JEMENIYA, the prince, or chief of the right hand
Egyptian: SEIR, the prince

"The English and French Sire, and English Sir, are obvious derivatives
  from the primitive root of *Sirius*, which means *to rule*." ~Rolleston

---

63 "The Hierarchy waits. It has done all that is possible from the angle of the present opportunity. The Christ stands in patient silence, attentive to the effort that will make His work materialize on Earth and enable Him to consummate the effort He made 2000 years ago in Palestine… Everything now depends upon the right action of the men of goodwill." ~*The Reappearance of the Christ*, A. Bailey
64 The famed stone ceiling in the Temple of Hathor—hand-copied by Egyptologist Schwaller de Lubicz—shows the twelve *zoidia* in red. [*See* **Fig. 27**] Gemini is at the six o'clock position, a man and woman in Pharaonic headdress, holding hands.
65 After his previous shipwreck on Malta, Paul felt comforted by the twin figureheads on the bow of the new ship. **"And after three months we departed in a ship of Alexandria, which had wintered in the isle, whose sign was Castor and Pollux."**   (Acts 28.11)

Latin: CANCER, the crab
Hebrew / Arabic: SARTAN / AL SARTAN,
  who holds, or binds
Coptic: KLARIA, the cattle-folds

"Cancer, the crab or beetle, holding fast its prey or its nest, well conveys the image of tenacious possession by Him who has assured us, as to His purchased flock, that no man can pluck them out of His hand... The Scarabaeus is thought to have been the original emblem in Cancer. *Sartan*, who holds, would well apply to the 'sacred beetle' of the Egyptians, who holds its 'progeny' fast even in death. The Scarabaeus was placed here in the Persian sphere." ~Rolleston

"But upon mount Zion shall be deliverance, and there shall be holiness; and the house of Jacob shall possess their possessions." (Obadiah 1.17)

Fig. 28 Cancer ♋

"The brightest star, (in the tail), is called *Tegmine*, holding. The star in the lower large claw, is called *Acubene*, which, in Hebrew and Arabic, means *the sheltering* or *hiding-place*. Another is named *Ma'alaph* (Arabic), assembled thousands; *Al Himarein* (Arabic), the kids or lambs." ~Bullinger

A true brotherhood of Man is realized as the downsized Human Race bonds into a functional family under the guidance of the **Utterly Trustworthy Parental Spirit**. [*See* **Book I**, footnote 9] Secure in the unconditional love of the High Priest-King and the Holy Mother, the children of God thrive, reaching ever new levels of luminous liberty within the shelter of their Heart. The **Ninth Week**.

Latin: LEO, the lion
Hebrew: ARIEH, the lion, rending[66]
Arabic: AL ASAD, the lion,
  who rends, who wasteth

"Leo, the majestic lion, rending the prey, represents irresistible strength, and final separation between good and evil. *His foot is over the head of the prostrate serpent*, closing the series as we are told by the Apostle that the dispensation must be closed: **'For He shall reign till His has put all things under His feet.'** The lion rends apart whatever he seizes, as at the last awful day the Judge will separate good from evil." ~Rolleston

Fig. 29 Leo ♌

"The brightest star, (on the Ecliptic), marks the heart of the Lion (hence sometimes called by the moderns, *Cor Leonis*, the heart of the Lion). Its ancient name is *Regulus*, which means *treading under foot*." ~Bullinger

---

66 "The Hebrew name of the sign is *Arieh*, which means the Lion. There are six Hebrew words for Lion, and this one is used of the Lion hunting down his prey: 1. *Gor*, a lion's whelp. 2. *Ciphir*, a young lion when first hunting for himself.
3. *Sachal*, a mature lion in full strength. 4. *Laish*, a fierce lion. 5. *Labia*, a lioness.
6. *Arieh*, an adult lion, having paired, in search of his prey."   ~Bullinger

Book IV: Supraliminality

*"And when the thousand years are expired, Satan shall be loosed out of his prison,
And shall go out to deceive the nations which are in the four quarters of the earth, Gog and Magog,
to gather them together to battle: the number of whom is as the sand of the sea."* (Revelation 20.7-8)

The ancient Dragon's submarine seal is broken. Freed from the deep blue sea, He mobilizes all His Sons of Darkness for a final, futile stand against the Law. An angry Lord, the Lion of Judah[67] *rends his prey*, Leviathan—the world's oldest living creature kept alive for the express purpose of consumption and transformation. Another comet's comeuppance extinguishes physical life for those who have not perfected their astral (energy) bodies. The entire Human Family (including reptilian relatives, angels and aliens) is marshaled for the Last Judgment[68], followed by the *Second* Death—supraliminal shift into a new *Kosmos* (Gk. orderly arrangement) vibrating 7^7 (823,543) times faster than this lower world. The luminescent Sons of Light rule their own turf as Lion Kings.[69]

Frances Rolleston concludes her remarkable thesis...

"**As the Jews have kept the word of prophecy, the Arabs have preserved the names of the stars which so remarkably correspond with it, while the Greeks and Egyptians have transmitted the figures to which they belong.** These independent but concurring testimonies not only witness to the purpose of the long misunderstood emblems, but to the existence of a revelation anterior to their formation; for if their purport be prophetic, He who seeth the end from the beginning had already given to man that knowledge of future events which He alone can impart. It is not doubted that about eighteen centuries ago there arose a remarkable person claiming to have no father but Him in heaven, who was put to death at the time of the slaying of the paschal lamb at Jerusalem.

His death, the time and manner of it, were not of his own power. If predicted by the prophets, prefigured in these ancient emblems, and indicated in their primitive names—that death, its manner and its time, must have been revealed by Him who by the mouth of Isaiah appeals to prophecy as the proof of His power and His Godhead, saying to the idols of the heathen, **'Show the things that are to come hereafter, that we may know that ye are gods.'** (Isaiah 41.23) *By prophecy and its fulfillment God speaks to man, at once displaying His foreknowledge and His sovereignty.* So He spake to our first parents in Eden; and the echo of that voice was in the ears of the fathers of mankind, when these emblems were framed in memorial of the revelation."

It must be remembered that both Rolleston and Bullinger were strict 19th century Christians, and therefore horrified at the thought of promoting astrology—the worship of pagan gods that brought down the Roman Empire. Dedicated to Mother Church, they carefully steered clear of *any* astrological references. Yet there can be no denying that the fathers of Mankind—perceiving the inherent attributes of the archetypes—deliberately yoked the Divine Plan to the dozen demigods

---

[67] "And one of the elders saith unto me, Weep not: behold, the Lion of the tribe of Judah, the Root of David, hath prevailed to open the book, and to loose the seven seals thereof." (Revelations 5.5)

"As for the lion whom you saw rousing up out of the forest and roaring and speaking up to the eagle and reproving him for his unrighteousness, and as for all his words that you have heard, this is the Messiah whom the Most High has kept until the end of days, who will arise from the offspring of David, and will come and speak with them. He will denounce them for their ungodliness and for their wickedness, and will display before them their contemptuous dealings. For first he will bring them alive before his judgment seat, and when he has reproved them, then he will destroy them. But in mercy he will set free the remnant of my people, those who have been saved..." ~*Jewish Apocrypha* (2 Esdras 12.31-34)

[68] "The wicked who had died from the time of Adam to Christ's second advent, and all the righteous and wicked who had died during and after the millennium, shall then have their eternal portion assigned to them...God's omniscience will not allow the most insignificant to escape unobserved, and His omnipotence will cause the mightiest to obey the summons." ~JFB Bible Commentary

[69] "Man's soul is redeemed by regeneration through the Holy Spirit now; man's body shall be redeemed at the resurrection; man's dwelling-place, His inheritance, the earth, shall be redeemed perfectly at the creation of the new heaven and earth, which shall exceed in glory the first Paradise, as much as the second Adam exceeds in glory the first Adam before the fall, and as man regenerated in body and soul shall exceed man as he was at creation." ~Ibid.

that grid the planet—the primary twelve Elohim *Judges* (Thrones) that empower the subtrilateral vortex of Dominions, Divine Virtues and Powers. [*See* **Book II**, *The Celestial Hierarchy*]

Since the restless *wanderers*, the Planets, never vary their appointed rounds, relative angles (aspects) to one another and celestial positions to Mazzaroth could be calculated years in advance. The incredible life spans of the ancient fathers, six hundred to nine hundred years, enabled them to observe how the seven spirits'[70] horizon coordinates coincided with phenomena down here. Within a few short centuries an elaborate science of *astroanthropology* was accumulated. This priceless gift of knowledge was handed down to Noah's sons, the Egyptians and subsequently the Chaldeans. By Abraham's time, however, the Babylonians had already corrupted the grandfathers' gleanings into an ignorant idolatry. The first messiah stayed up all night to record the angulations of the seven orbs.

"And in the sixth week, in the fifth year thereof, Abram sat up throughout the night on the new moon of the seventh month to observe the stars from the evening to the morning, in order to see what would be the character of the year with regard to the rains, and he was alone as he sat and observed. And a word came into his heart and he said: 'All the signs of the star and the signs of the moon and of the sun are all in the hand of the Lord. Why do I search (them) out? If He desires, He causes it to rain, morning and evening; And if He desires, He withholds it, And all things are in his hand.'

And he prayed that night and said, '**My God, God Most High, Thou alone art my God, And Thee and Thy dominion have I chosen.** And Thou hast created all things, And all things that are the work of thy hands. Deliver me from the hands of evil spirits who have dominion over the thoughts of men's hearts, And let them not lead me astray from Thee, my God. And establish Thou me and my seed for ever That we go not astray from henceforth and for evermore.'

And he said, 'Shall I return unto Ur of the Chaldees who seek my face that I may return to them, am I to remain here in this place? The right path before Thee prosper it in the hands of Thy servant that he may fulfill (it) and that I may not walk in the deceitfulness of my heart, O my God.' And he made an end of speaking and praying, and behold the word of the Lord was sent to him through me, saying: 'Get thee up from thy country, and from thy kindred and from the house of thy father unto a land which I will show thee, and I shall make thee a great and numerous nation'." (Book of Jubilees 12.16-22)

Abraham recognized the demonic influence that had crept over him, putting the star science ahead of the Almighty. From that point on, he resisted the temptation to rely upon the consistently unerring science and its apparent magic to predicate his actions. His complete subjugation to the YHVH ascertained the inauguration of the Messianic line. Yet Enoch knew a little knowledge could be a dangerous thing, and foretold the bastardization of the majestic mother science...

"Wisdom found no place where she might dwell; then a dwelling-place was assigned her in the heavens.
Wisdom went forth to make her dwelling among the children of men, and found no dwelling-place:
Wisdom returned to her place, and took her seat among the angels.
And unrighteousness went forth from her chambers:
Whom she sought not she found, and dwelt with them,
as rain in a desert, And dew on a thirsty land." (1 Enoch 42)

---

[70] The seven spirits of God—Sun, Moon, Mercury, Venus, Mars, Jupiter and Saturn—function as mutable transducers within the immutable Mazzaroth. (Likewise, the *kinetic* energy released from the supramundane Powers of Uranus, Neptune and Pluto is also entirely subject to, and dependent upon the *potential* energy of the fixed *Thrones*.)

"And out of the throne proceeded lightnings and thunderings and voices: and there
were seven lamps of fire burning before the throne, which are *the seven Spirits of God."* (Rev. 4.5)
"Then I saw a Lamb, looking as if it had been slain, standing in the center of the throne,
encircled by the four living creatures and the elders. He had seven horns and seven eyes,
which are *the seven spirits of God sent out into all the earth."* (Revelations 5.6)

Book IV: Supraliminality

The wisdom of the antediluvians had degenerated considerably during the 6,480-year Bronze Epoch (*Dvapara Yuga*). By 2100 BC—well into the dark *Kali Yuga*—the Chaldeans (present day Iran), including Abram, inherited but a superstitious remnant of Seth's sacred science. Another 1,300 years and the irresponsible fortunetelling, with its runaway powertripping, led to its condemnation by the sarcastic seer Isaiah...

> "Keep on, then, with your magic spells and with your many sorceries, which you have labored at since childhood. Perhaps you will succeed, perhaps you will cause terror. All the counsel you have received has only worn you out! Let your astrologers come forward, those stargazers who make predictions month by month, let them save you from what is coming upon you." (Isaiah 47.12-13)

Fig. 30 The Almagest, ca. 150 AD

Over *two more millennia* and the twisted wisdom teachings have returned full force. With all the puffed-up superiority and trendy atheism of the times, 21st century's neo-astrology has reared its ugly head. Most of today's astrologers kowtow to the indubitable religion endemic in our society—scientism—a mechanistic paradigm that requires no God. Conversely, New Age fledgling witches and apprentices to Magickal schools of homoerotic fellowship embrace a neo-pagan pantheon of multitudinous goddesses, devas and devils. It was this dread of reverting to Roman paganism that kept Mother Church silent for 2,000 years, while her hefty coffers overflowed with rare astrological treatises collected throughout the centuries.[71]

Chapter Six: Olam Haba, the World to Come

Learning the lawful motions and properties of the subtle Forces (*i.e.* mysteries of the Kingdom of seven Heavens) authorizes the wise ones to open the sacred texts and re-educate the populace. Since day one, the compilation and repository of holy Scriptures has been the responsibility of the Hebrew nations—especially the Book of Life, or Torah. Examination of the scriptural vestiges of Jewish eschatology may provide a stimulating glimpse into the Messianic Era and the long-promised *Olam Haba*, the World to Come.

It wasn't until Father Abraham's initiation as an Anointed One by the Lotus-Born Melchizedek that the Jewish legend of an avenging Messiah (*Mashiach*) materialized. Soon a Davidic *Day of the Lord* would smite all the enemies of Israel, bringing peace and prosperity to the chosen people.

---

[71] "Claudius Ptolemy, who lived in the second century A.D., did work of enormous importance in astronomy and geography in which the Vatican Library has particularly rich holdings. The *Almagest*, written about A.D. 150, is a comprehensive treatise on all aspects of mathematical astronomy—spherical astronomy, solar, lunar, and planetary theory, eclipses, and the fixed stars. It made all of its predecessors obsolete and remained the definitive treatise on its subject for nearly fifteen hundred years. This, the most elegant of all manuscripts of the *Almagest*, is one of the oldest and best witnesses to the text, and is very rich in notes."
~Library of Congress Exhibition, 1993   [*See* **Fig. 30**]

Hardly the patriotic warrior-king they were expecting, a humble, heretical preacher popped the ethnic bubble of the pompous priests by declaring the religion of Moses corrupt and kaput since the stiff-necked Sanhedrin acknowledged neither the forerunner, Elijah nor the long-predicted "Real Deal" Himself. Clear up to the 13th century, the Hebraic masters of ignorance refuse to admit their obvious obstinacy—ever vigilant should an avenging *Anointed One* appear. The Spanish edict of expulsion in 1492 ended a golden age of Jewish culture, over six centuries of stress-free worship under Islamic rule. One of the last scholars of the period, Maimonides (Moshe ben Maimon) revised the vengeful Hebrew messianic prophecy with a more humble, toned-down prognostication...

"Our sages and prophets did not long for the Messianic age in order that they might rule the world and dominate the gentiles, the only thing they wanted was to be free for Jews to involve themselves with the Torah and its wisdom."

With amazing correlations to 21st century skepticism, Maimonides completely rejected any phenomenal possibility of an Avatar (God-man). The expected Messiah would merely be a great king, a wise and righteous man respected by all, gentile and Jew alike...

"The Messiah will be a very great king, he will achieve great fame, and his reputation among the gentile nations will be even greater than that of King Solomon. His great righteousness and the wonders that he will bring about will cause all peoples to make peace with him and all lands to serve him..."

By the Dark Ages, any belief in the Divinity of Mankind was long buried, the degenerative effects of dwelling in denial for twelve centuries. Like *Mashiach*, the Messianic Age was overrated and will no doubt be a big disappointment[72] ...just like everything else.

"Nothing will change in the Messianic age, however, except that Jews will regain their independence. Rich and poor, strong and weak, will still exist. However it will be very easy for people to make a living, and with very little effort they will be able to accomplish very much... it will be a time when the number of wise men will increase... war shall not exist, and nation shall no longer lift up sword against nation..."

He goes along with Isaiah until the latter stretches credibility by declaring that the wolf shall dwell with the lamb, the calf with the lion, and so on... Certainly the great prophet is speaking allegorically! Pessimistic Maimonides was hopelessly resigned to never-ending drudgery.

> "Do not think that the ways of the world or the laws of nature
> will change, this is not true. The world will continue as it is."

---

[72] The first century Talmud ("Oral Law") drew a clear distinction between the earthly **Messianic Era** and the **World to Come**, or *Olam Haba*, the latter being the indescribable results of the Eternal Judgment, permanent shift into the incorruptible body. Evolution of the corporeal body is limited to the next thousand years of miracle and wonder, on Earth.

"R. Hiyya b. Abba said in R. Johanan's name: 'All the prophets prophesied [all the good things] only in respect of the Messianic era; but as for the world to come **'the eye hath not seen, O Lord, beside thee, what he hath prepared for him that waiteth for him'**." ~Babylonian Talmud: Tractate Sanhedrin, Folio 99a

The upright rabbis despised the self-righteous, lazy Pat Robertson types that talked the talk, but never walked the walk...

"Anyone who decides to be engaged in Torah [study] and not to work, and will be supported by *Tzedaqa*—this person desecrates God's name (*Chillel et Hashem*), degrades the Torah, extinguishes the light of our faith, brings evil upon himself and forfeits life in *Olam haBa* (The world to come); since it is forbidden to derive benefit from the words of Torah in this world. The Rabbis said (Avot 4:5): Anyone who derives benefit from the words of Torah in this world, forfeits his life in *Olam haBa*. They further commanded and said: (Avot 4:5) Do not make them [the words of Torah] a crown to magnify yourself or an axe with which to chop. They further commanded, saying: (Avot 1:10) Love work and despise positions of power (Rabbanut). And: (Avot 2:2) Any Torah which is not accompanied by work will eventually be nullified and will lead to sin. Ultimately, such a person will steal from others." **"Richer is one hour of repentance and good works in this world than all of life of the world to come; and richer is one hour's calm of spirit in the world to come than all of life of this world."**
~Pirkei Avot: *Ethics of the Fathers*

Book IV: Supraliminality

Nevertheless, he was adamant about the promised king-messiah, declaring such faith as the 12th of his thirteen "commandments"[73]... "I believe with a full heart in the coming of the Messiah, and even though he may tarry I will still wait for him." —last words uttered by Jews marching into Nazi gas chambers.
~ Jewish Virtual Library

Among His thirty incarnations, the Son of Man's noblest, next to the Redeemer Himself, was surely Isaiah.[74] Far and away the most accurate prophecies in the OT rolled off his 8th century BC tongue, yet like Daniel he is relegated to 2nd class seer status because the bulk of his prophecies precognize a supernatural Being, the archetype of which the Jews had no prior conception.[75]

> "For unto us a child is born, unto us a son is given: and the government shall be upon his shoulder: and his name shall be called Wonderful, Counselor, *The mighty God, The everlasting Father*, The Prince of Peace." (Isaiah 9.6)

Serrated in half with a wooden saw, a prophet's life was never very profitable. Isaiah's status improved considerably when the 20th century's Dead Sea scroll bonanza resurrected a pristine copy of his book that was 1,000 years older than any version extant. Although the holy scroll is housed in the most elegant setting imaginable[76], one chapter in particular remains a thorn in the Jew's side. The acclaimed *man of sorrows* in Chapter 53 is so precisely prescient it's hard to believe it was written 700 years before the Lamb's sacrifice. Imagine reading *your* own dire destiny as a kid growing up at the spartan Essene monastery in Qumran...

"He is despised and rejected of men; a man of sorrows, and acquainted with grief and we hid as it were our faces from him; he was despised, and we esteemed him not.

Surely he hath borne our griefs, and carried our sorrows: yet we did esteem him stricken, smitten of God, and afflicted."
(Isaiah 53.3-4)

Fig. 31   Shrine of the Book, Israel Museum, Jerusalem

---

73 The Thirteen Articles of Maimonides:
1. The existence of God; 2. His unity; 3. His spirituality; 4. His eternity; 5. God alone the object of worship; 6. Revelation through his prophets; 7. the preeminence of Moses among the Prophets; 8. God's law given on Mount Sinai; 9. the immutability of the Torah as God's Law; 10. God's foreknowledge of men's actions; 11. retribution; **12. the coming of the Messiah;** 13. Resurrection.
74 One can discern a definite etymological pattern in the Messiah's most formidable incarnations: Joshua, Josiah, Isaiah (Ysha'yah) and Jeshua (Latin: Jesus) all stem from Hbw. *Yehoshua*: "the YHVH is salvation"   ~Strong's
75 They couldn't even cognize, yet alone recognize the paradoxical God-man in their presence. [*See* **Book II**, *The Trinity*, pp. 68-69]
76 "The photograph [**Fig. 31**] is of the central showcase inside the **Shrine of the Book** at the Israel Museum in Jerusalem. The Shrine of the Book houses the famous Dead Sea Scrolls, possibly the most important archaeological discovery ever made in Israel. The first of the 2,000 year old scrolls were discovered in 1947 by a young Bedouin shepherd. From the eleven caves around the Qumran area scholars have recovered the manuscripts of almost 700 works, both Biblical and sectarian. Some of the works are complete scrolls, while others are only fragments containing a few sentences. The texts of the books of the Hebrew Bible number more than 170, and each Biblical book (with the sole exception of the book of Esther) can be found among the Dead Sea Scrolls.

From the outside the Shrine looks like the lid of a clay jar—like the ones many of the scrolls were found in. The display case pictured is in the form of an ancient scroll. The most prized exhibits at the Shrine are the two oldest copies of the book of Isaiah in existence. **These Isaiah scrolls are 1,000 years older than any other known Hebrew Biblical text**—they were written only six centuries after Isaiah first penned his marvelous words, as he looked forward to the Messiah!"   ~David Padfield, Church of Christ, Ill.

> "He was wounded for our transgressions, he was bruised for our iniquities: the chastisement of our peace was upon him; and with his stripes we are healed." (Isaiah 53.5)

This mind-boggling chapter gained even more attention when the late Yacov Rambsel found "YESHUA IS MY NAME" by skipping every 20th letter of the above Scripture. Recently, Bible code researcher Dr. Nathan Jacobi expanded Rambsel's ELS find into an incredible string of 22 letters [*See* below, **Red Box**]—a prodigious root sprouting mega-clusters!

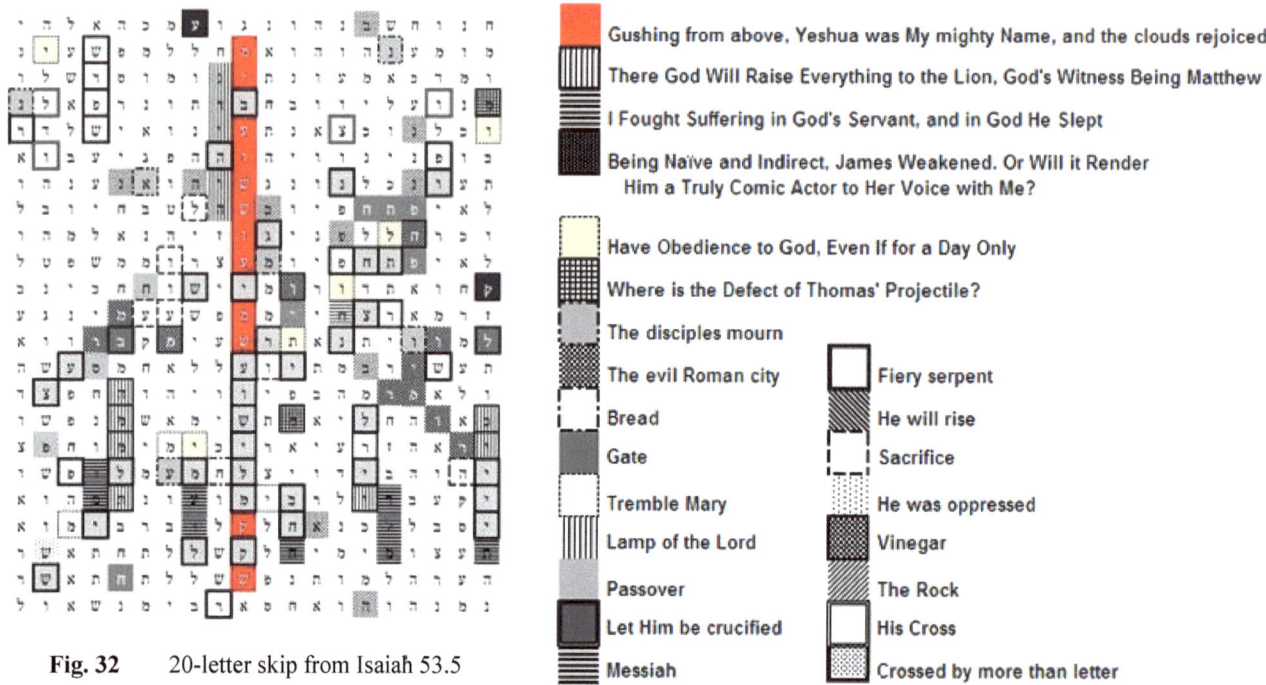

Fig. 32   20-letter skip from Isaiah 53.5

Contrary to Talmudic pie-in-the-sky speculations and later day skepticism of the Spanish Jews, Isaiah spoke reverently to the faithful about the incredible splendor of the Messianic Era...

> "For since the beginning of the world men have not heard,
> nor perceived by the ear, neither hath the eye seen, O God, beside thee,
> what he hath prepared for him that waiteth for him." (Isaiah 64.4)

As upright Mankind reclaims the shining countenance of Elohim, the awe-inspiring similitude forsaken in *eden* (Hbw. pleasure), the prophet presages a radical shift in Mother Nature—a return to the magical mystery of matriarchal tranquility—serene co-existence within a *Paradise Regained*.[77]

> "The wolf also shall dwell with the lamb, and the leopard shall lie down with the kid;
> and the calf and the young lion and the fatling together; and a little child shall lead them."[78]
> (Isaiah 11.6)

---

77   "I, WHO erewhile the happy Garden sung by one man's disobedience lost, now sing.
        Recovered Paradise to all mankind, by one man's firm obedience fully tried.
        Through all temptation, and the Tempter foiled in all his wiles,
           defeated and repulsed, and Eden raised in the waste Wilderness."   ~*Paradise Regained*, John Milton

78 "Each animal is coupled with that one which is its natural prey. A fit state of things under the 'Prince of Peace' (Is 65.25; Eze 34.25; Ho 2.18) **Still a literal change in the relations of animals to man and each other, restoring the state in Eden, is a more likely interpretation.** Compare Ge 2.19, 20 with Ps 8.6-8, which describes the restoration to man, in the person of 'the Son of man,' of the lost dominion over the animal kingdom of which he had been designed to be the merciful vicegerent under God, for the good of his animal subjects (Ro 8.19-22)."   ~Jamieson Fausset Brown Bible Commentary

Book IV: Supraliminality

Chapter Seven: The Pure Land

**"And other sheep I have, which are not of this fold:
them also I must bring, and they shall hear my voice;
and there shall be one fold, and one shepherd."**
(John 10.16)

Oddly enough, the intellectual religion-without-a-god has maintained a sect with not only a God but also Heaven. After witnessing centuries of degrading principles and morals, Asian Buddhist monks hit upon the idea of salvation-in-numbers wherein everyone is eventually enlightened.[79] They realized that the austere path of (Zen) Buddhism was too strict, leaving the average person behind. Instead, it was necessary to postulate a living Buddha that people could rely upon until they acquired the Siddhis (Skt. attainments) necessary for complete "re-integration".[80] Contrary to fundamental Buddhist *Dharma* (Skt. Law), personal responsibility and effort to eradicate Karma are minimized, co-dependence upon a Savior brought to bear on the equation. Renowned scholar/translator of East Asian religions, J.C. Cleary describes the slippery slope these maverick monks strode upon…

"Pure Land theorists were faced with the task of clarifying their teaching of salvation through faith in Amitabha, given the mainstream scriptural Buddhist view of salvation as the reward for eons of diligent effort at self-discipline and purification and refinement of perceptions. By holding out the prospect of rebirth in the Pure Land through buddha-name recitation even to sinners, the Pure Land teaching appears to depart from a strict rule of karmic reward, which emphasizes the individual's own efforts as the decisive factor in spiritual attainment. The Pure Land teachers explained this apparent anomaly by appealing to the infinite compassion of *Amitabha Buddha* (as an expedient embodiment of the infinitely pervasive *Dharmakaya Buddha*), who promises that all who invoke his name will attain birth in his Pure Land.

The pioneers of the Pure Land teaching indeed took the position that for people in the later ages, the arduous path of self-restraint and purification proposed in the old Buddhist scriptures was no longer feasible. For average people, the only hope of salvation would be to rely on another power than their own, the power of *Amitabha Buddha*. [in addition to their own personal effort]."

---

79 Not exactly an original idea, yet this is how the Far East acknowledged the higher Judeo-Christian path without losing face.
80 "Gradually through the training of yoga, the adept transcends the elements of appearance, conquers the laws of Nature and is able to perform extraordinary feats. The supra-human powers he thus acquires are called the 'Attainments', the Siddhis. These Attainments are of two kinds: (1) Those which are connected with the apparent laws of Nature are called the 'Physical Attainments' or the 'Attainments of Illusion' (Maya) for they belong to the physical world which is but the display of the Divine power of Illusion. These Attainments are the greatest obstacles of the adept in his journey towards re-integration. **Nature herself, in a final effort to keep the adept within her bonds yields him magic powers; if he uses them for any worldly end, he is apt to fall back into the arms of worldly enjoyments.** All true seekers, therefore, are careful not to perform miracles except in very special circumstances. (2) Those Attainments which are not of physical nature, but refer to spiritual realization, are called the 'Attainments of the intrinsic form (*svarupa siddhis*)', and are the stages through which the individual being travels on his way towards re-integration." ~Danielou

Without the Tathagata to give us a reality check, the Attainments (supernatural powers) are truly the greatest temptation on the Path. With the Omnipotent Father and Mother to emulate, we'll learn to be Power brokers rather than Power trippers. As the children of God mature and re-claim their inheritance, they'll learn, like Peter Parker, that great power brings great responsibility… and great glory.

"We need not shun the siddhis and cannot shun them. There is a stage reached by the yogin when, unless he avoids all action in the world, he can no more avoid the use of the siddhis of power and knowledge than an ordinary man can avoid eating and breathing; for these things are the natural action of the consciousness to which he is rising, just as mental activity and physical motion are the natural action of man's ordinary life. All the ancient rishis used these powers, all great avatars and yogins have used them, nor is there any great man… who does not use them continually in an imperfect form, without knowing clearly what are these supreme faculties that he is enjoying." ~*The Collected Works*, Aurobindo

The Pure Land/Heaven-on-Earth school (*Shin Buddhism*) is a radical departure from today's Buddhist Modernism, the chic, nihilistic religion that has every practitioner chanting the endless mantra, "Emptiness". Yet it remains true to the historical Buddha's fundamental dogma of *Mystery* at the very heart of Reality, inscrutable Suchness (awe) at the highest level of cognizance.[81]

> "Although he knows that Buddha lands are void like living beings,
> He goes on practicing the Pure Land (Dharma) to teach and convert men."
> ~*Vimalakirti Sutra*

---

[81] The 2nd century Indian sage, Nagarjuna founded moral Mahayana Buddhism by establishing the archetype of the *Bodhisattva*—whose selflessness and compassion surpassed the Hinayana *Arhat*—but misconstrued the Buddha's already ancient (6th century BC) and most ambiguous teachings on *sunyata* (emptiness), inextricably tying the salvational Vehicle to a *deadly doctrine of nothingness*.

Stemming from *Advaita Vedanta*, the Hindu school of non-duality, Nagarjuna's Buddhism further "refined" the primary tenets of *maya* (Skt. illusion) to claim that even Brahman, the impersonal Absolute, was a misnomer. Composing the *Prajnaparamita Sutra in 8,000 Lines* to reflect his own complete denial of *any* true Reality, Nagarjuna's *Madhyamaka* (Middle Way) teachings of unqualified *sunyata*—a precursor to Nietzsche's nihilism—infected the very core of the noble new philosophy, Mahayana.

In the early 6th century, Bodhidharma brought Nagarjuna's Buddhism—redacted a second time with his own idiosyncratic focus on just 1/8th of the Buddha's Noble Eightfold Path, *dhyana* (meditation)—to China, where it naturally took root by grafting onto the supramundane philosophy of Taoism. As in the subsequent Tibetan transmission, Nagarjuna's pernicious sutras were taken as Holy Writ—the Taoist Buddhist hybrid spreading rapidly throughout East Asia, crystallizing in Japan as the *religion of no religion*: Zen.

The corrupt Buddhism finally reaches the Tibetan highlands when Guru Padmasambhava initiates the Bonpo shamans into the forbidden Hindu *Tantras*, a necessary step to forcibly deal with demonic influences opposing the introduction of Mahayana Buddhism. **Thus the entire edifice of Tibetan Buddhism rests upon principals espoused within Nagarjuna's pseudepigrapha, reinforced by Dzogchen shamanism and modified by Tantric counter-measures transmitted to Tibet as Buddhism in the 8th century.**

A Hindu contemporary of Nagarjuna, Asvaghosa correctly understood that Gautama Buddha was neither denying existence nor affirming it, as *any conceptualization of the Absolute was heresy*; and emptiness (*sunyata*) is a concept. He carefully interpreted Buddha's highest doctrine to reveal an inconceivable suchness (*tathata*) as the closest description possible of our Indescribable Reality.

"The Mind in terms of the Absolute is the one World of Reality (Dharmadhatu) and the essence of all phases of existence in their totality. That which is called 'the essential nature of the Mind' is unborn and is imperishable. It is only through illusions that all things come to be differentiated. If one is freed from illusions, then to him there will be no appearances (*lakshana*) of objects regarded as absolutely independent existences; therefore all things from the beginning transcend all forms of verbalization, description, and conceptualization and are, in the final analysis, undifferentiated, free from alteration, and indestructible.

They are only of the One Mind; hence the name Suchness. All explanations by words are provisional and without validity, for they are merely used in accordance with illusions and are incapable of denoting Suchness. The term Suchness likewise has no attributes, which can be verbally specified. **The term Suchness is, so to speak, the limit of verbalization wherein a word is used to put an end to words.** But the essence of Suchness itself cannot be put an end to, for all things in their Absolute aspect are real; nor is there anything which needs to be pointed out as real, for all things are equally in the state of Suchness. It should be understood that all things are incapable of being verbally explained or thought of; hence the name Suchness."   ~*The Awakening of Faith*, Asvaghosa

Revered 4th century BC Taoist philosopher Chuang-Tzu came to the same conclusion as the historical Buddha, substituting the sacred word *Tao* for *tathata*…

> "The mind remains undetermined in the great Void. Here the highest knowledge is unbounded. That which gives
> things their thusness cannot be delimited by things. So when we speak of 'limits', we remain confined to limited things.
> The limit of the unlimited is called 'fullness'.
> The limitlessness of the limited is called 'emptiness'.
> Tao is the source of both
> **But it is itself neither fullness nor emptiness**."
> ~*Way of Chuang-Tzu*, Verse 22.6

Modern Taoist wizards of internal alchemy learned to distinguish between **relative voidness** and **absolute voidness** which radiates from the *Ajna Chakra* (Third Eye) while meditating within the microcosmic orbit…

"Seeing the void as not empty is right and seeing the void as empty is wrong, for failure to return to the (*tsu ch'iao*) center (which is not empty) prevents the light of vitality from manifesting. Under the heart and above the genital organ is an empty space where spiritual vitality manifests to form a cavity. When spirit and vitality return to this cavity, spiritual vitality will soar up to form a circle (of light) which is not void. Voidness which does not radiate is relative but voidness which radiates is absolute. Absolute voidness is not empty like relative voidness. Voidness that is not empty is spiritual light which is spirit-vitality that springs from the yellow hall center (*huang ting* or middle *tan t'ien*, in the solar plexus). My master Liao K'ung said: 'When the golden mechanism (of alchemy) begins to move and gives out flashes of light, that hall of voidness (*hsu shih*, i.e. the heart devoid of feelings and passions) will be illuminated by a white light which reveals the mysterious gate (*hsuan kuan*), the presence of which does not mean emptiness'."

~*Taoist Yoga*, Lu K'uan Yu   Cont. →

Book IV: Supraliminality

Even the Pure Land/Messianic Era itself is only a pit stop to full Enlightenment, absolute Buddhahood. Though we remain trapped in illusion, we are in a safe haven with much better odds of perfecting our faith... "Suppose there is a man who learns this teaching for the first time and wishes to seek the correct faith but lacks courage and strength. Because he lives in this world of suffering, he fears that he will not always be able to meet the Buddhas and honor them personally, and that faith being difficult to perfect, he will be inclined to fall back. He should know that the Tathagatas have an excellent expedient means by which they can protect his faith: that is, through the strength of wholehearted meditation-recitation on the Buddha [Amitaba], he will in fulfillment of his wishes be able to be born in the Buddha-land beyond, to *see the Buddha always, and to be forever separated from the evil states of existence...*" ~The Awakening of Faith

"I vow that when my life approaches its end, all obstructions will be swept away; I will see Amitabha Buddha, And be born in his land of Ultimate Bliss and Peace. When reborn in the western land, I will perfect and completely fulfill, without exception, these great vows, To delight and benefit all beings. The assembly of Amitabha Buddha is completely pure; When from a matchless lotus I am reborn, I will behold the Buddha's Measureless light as he appears before me to bestow a prediction of Buddhahood." ~Flower Ornament Scripture

Interestingly enough, the "Buddha-land beyond" is located *here*, in the "materialistic" West. The revered *Amida Sutra* declares: "The Buddha then said to the Elder Shariputra: 'If you travel westwards from here, passing a hundred thousand kotis of Buddha-lands, you come to the land called 'Utmost Bliss,' where there is a Buddha named 'Amida'. He is living there now, teaching the Dharma.'"

Of the many marvels to be encountered in the wonderful West, we can look forward to the steady evolution of song begun in the stellar sixties—the sublime licks of Clapton, poignant poetry of Dylan and heavenly harmonies of Lennon/McCartney... merely rehearsal for a *golden age of music*.

"Again, Shariputra, in that Buddha-land heavenly music is played continually. The ground is made of gold. Six times during the day and night *mandarava* flowers rain down from the sky.
Every day, in the serenity of early morning, the people of that land fill their baskets with exquisite flowers and go to make offerings to a hundred thousand kotis of Buddhas dwelling in the worlds of other directions. Then they return for their morning meal. After the meal they enjoy a stroll. Shariputra, the Land of Utmost Bliss is filled with such excellence and splendor."

---

81 *Continued*

As the *Madhyamaka* school gained ground, its Dharmic correction soon arose in the form of the *Yogacara* (Mind Only) school. Saint Asanga's *Bodhisattvabhumi* deftly deconstructed the disingenuous, ontological ramifications imputed by the impudent Middle Way: "According to them, the bare [real] substance that is the [underlying] basis of a designation does not exist, [it must also be the case that] the designation itself does not exist at all. On the basis of this method [of reasoning], these [individuals] have repudiated both [ultimate] reality and [nominal] designations. And because of this repudiation of both [nominal] designations and [ultimate] reality, it should be understood that this is [the position of] a preeminent nihilist. Those intelligent persons who are pursuing a pure, spiritual life should not converse or associate with such a nihilist. Doing so not only brings ruin upon oneself, misfortune will also befall any region where the views of such a person are looked upon with approval. How, then, does emptiness become correctly grasped? One realizes both of the following things as they truly are: (1) the bare substance and (2) the mere [nominal] designation that exists in relation to that bare substance. *There is a true realization of the genuine suchness* [of things] *and the ineffable essential nature* [of things]."

By combining Eastern Apophatic theology with Judeo-Christianity's theism and an enlightened (anthropic) superstring theory of resonant (vibrating) frequencies creating an Akashic Field [*See* footnote 29] binding ten dimensions, we can formulate a Grand Unified Theory of Reality: Everything that exists is relatively real due to their intrinsic connection with the Absolute (*Dharmadhatu*). A doubled, supreme Being is responsible for maintaining the cohesiveness of the Universal Akasha (integrity of the DNA morphic field) and as such He/She is sole governor of any given Galaxy. Every multi-dimensional Universe functions interdependently within an interface of modulated, hierarchical Worlds—each living *through* its own anthropomorphic Lord (countenance)—an interlaced Empire with one *Omnipotent*, subsistent Countenance (Godhead) per 10-Unit Mandala. Each component's akashic connection to its higher archetype imbues it with a degree of reality—the faster their vibratory rate (proximity to the dynamic Lord and His static Counterpart), the more real (solid) they become. However, only the **Tathagata Elohim** (Most High Suchness Beings) are the real deal. True Individuals, *They alone are Real* in His and Hers own local Universe; a seven-tiered, I-land playground for Brahman. Above the 7th level, only the Lonely can access the three primary levels of superessential Reality. [*See* **Fig. 42**]

The *Amida Sutra* ends with praise and acknowledgement from fellow Buddhas of not only Shakyamuni's complete Enlightenment, but also His supreme sacrifice of staying in the lower world to preach something too incredible to be believed during a time of rampant immorality, the Kali Yuga—to have faith in a sovereign savior, an *occidental* Tathagata who will usher in a magical Kingdom of love, a virtual Disneyland, the happiest place on earth...

"Shariputra, just as I now praise the inconceivable virtue of other Buddhas, they also praise my inconceivable virtue, saying, 'Shakyamuni Buddha, you have accomplished an extremely difficult and unprecedented task. In this Saha world, during the evil period of the five defilements—those of time, views, passions, sentient beings, and life-span—you have attained the highest, perfect Enlightenment and, for the sake of sentient beings, have delivered this teaching, **which is the most difficult in the world to accept in faith.**'

Fig. 33   Amida welcoming devotees

Shariputra, you must realize that I have accomplished this difficult task during the period of the five defilements. That is to say, having attained the highest, perfect Enlightenment, I have, for the sake of all the world, delivered this teaching, which is so hard for them to accept. This is indeed an extremely difficult task!"

~*The Amida Sutra*

Another Mahayana sutra focusing upon soteriological events is the venerated *Lotus Sutra*, where Amida (Jpn. *Infinite Light*) reigns in an *already* perfected, blissful world. Sangharakshita (Dennis Lingwood), the distinguished English scholar/monk and founder of the Western Buddhist Order (WBO), comments upon the eighth chapter of the *White Lotus Sutra*...

"...But it seems from what the Buddha goes on to say that in those days the world will be a very different place from what it is now. Indeed, it will have changed so much that it will be a 'pure world', to use the technical term—a world free from certain imperfections, an ideal world...

The sutra goes on to say—and some people find this a very interesting feature indeed—that in those days divine vehicles will be stationed in the sky. Does this have a familiar ring? Not only that, but the division between the world of men and the world of the gods will be completely broken down, so that there is no barrier between the ordinary human world and the world of the gods, which we might call the archetypal realm. Human beings on the Earth will be able to look up and see the gods, and the gods will be able to look down on them. There will be regular contact between them. And there will be no places of suffering in the world of those days, nor even the sound of any torment and distress.

The sutra also says that at that time in the world there will be no women—a provocative-sounding statement, to say the least. But of course it doesn't mean that the world will contain men but not women; what it means is that there will be no distinction of sex among the beings of the earth—neither men nor women, but just human beings. And those human beings will be born (or rather reborn) not by the present rather crude arrangements but by what is called apparitional birth.

People will just spring into existence, blossom naturally out of thin air. Having been born in that way, it is not surprising to find that they will live—according to the sutra—a purely spiritual life. They will have no gross physical bodies but what are called mental bodies, spiritual bodies, and they will be self-luminous, brilliant, and able to fly through the air at will. With no gross physical bodies, they will have no need for gross physical food, but will feed on just two things: delight in the Buddha's teaching and delight in meditation."

Book IV: Supraliminality

Chapter Eight: Millennium, Heaven on Earth

"Angels can fly because they take themselves lightly."   ~G.K. Chesterton

What Sangharakshita and the *Lotus Sutra* suggest is supraliminal existence which cannot occur until after the Eternal Judgment, and energetic shift. For an entity to exist in this lower, purgatorial world, he/she must don a corporeal body, including our Lord and His coregent—yet how rewarding for the Parental Pair to once again enjoy tender rack of lamb with a bottle of Cabernet Sauvignon.[82] The joy of conviviality was clearly implied when Jeshua said, **"Fear not, little flock; for it is your Father's good pleasure to give you the kingdom."** (Luke 12.32) Thus we shall savor the carnal kingdom together[83], even as we work to overcome pesky physical limitations like gravity and other seemingly unbendable laws of physics. Attendance at the "Hogwarts schools" of the new Golden Age promises inconceivable thrills as we develop our God-given *siddhis* in a natural and controlled environment. Without doubt, the most popular class will be flying. Sporadic levitations have been recorded throughout history, mostly connected with an overpowering euphoric vision: rapture.

"...often it comes like a strong, swift impulse, before your thought can forewarn you of it or you can do anything to help yourself; you see and feel this cloud, or this powerful eagle, rising and bearing you up with it on its wings... Occasionally I have been able to make some resistance, but at the cost of great exhaustion, for I would feel as weary afterwards as though I had been fighting with a powerful giant. At other times, resistance has been impossible: my soul has been borne away, and indeed as a rule my head also, without my being able to prevent it: sometimes my whole body has been affected, to the point of being raised up from the ground."
~*The Autobiography of Teresa of Avila*, Chapter XX

---

82   **"Verily I say unto you, I will drink no more of the fruit of the vine,
         until that day that I drink it new in the kingdom of God."**   (Mark 14.25)
83   **"Then shall the King say unto them on his right hand, Come, ye blessed of my Father,
         inherit the kingdom prepared for you from the foundation of the World."**   (Matthew 25.34)
According to Bishop Eusebius' (260-339) quite rare, candid account of the neophyte Church, St. John's *Book of Revelation* came under attack because it predicted 1,000 years of peace here on Earth. Due primarily to heretical Gnostic influences, this world and every pleasure in it was considered evil. For 2,000 years, Mother Church maintained her merciful dogma of postmortem Heaven or Hell, reincarnation's quagmire—the Eternal Return (to Earth)—not a problem for either the "saved" or the "damned"! The truth of self-salvation through spiritual/physical evolution was deemed unnecessary (and harmful) information.
    ["Father McKenzie, wiping the dirt from his hands as he walks from the grave, *no one was saved.*
     All the lonely people, where do they all come from?"   ~Paul McCartney]
    Chapter XXV. The Revelation of John
    Afterward he (Dionysius) speaks in this manner of the Revelation of John:
    "Some before us have set aside and rejected the book altogether, criticizing it chapter by chapter, and pronouncing it without sense or argument, and maintaining that the title is fraudulent. For they say that it is not the work of John, nor is it a revelation, because it is covered thickly and densely by a veil of obscurity. And they affirm that none of the apostles, and none of the saints, nor any one in the Church is its author, but that Cerinthus, who founded the sect which was called after him the Cerinthian, desiring reputable authority for his fiction, prefixed the name.
    For the doctrine which he taught was this: that the kingdom of Christ will be an earthly one. And as he was himself devoted to the pleasures of the body and altogether sensual in his nature, he dreamed that that kingdom would consist in those things which he desired, namely, in the delights of the belly and of sexual passion; that is to say, in eating and drinking and marrying, and in festivals and sacrifices and the slaying of victims, under the guise of which he thought he could indulge his appetites with a better grace.
    But I could not venture to reject the book, as many brethren hold it in high esteem. But I suppose that it is beyond my comprehension, and that there is a certain concealed and more wonderful meaning in every part. For if I do not understand I suspect that a deeper sense lies beneath the words; I do not measure and judge them by my own reason, but leaving the more to faith I regard them as too high for me to grasp. And I do not reject what I cannot comprehend, but rather wonder because I do not understand it."
~*The History of the Church*, Eusebius

A hundred years later in 17th century Italy, a Franciscan ecstatic did more than levitate, as has been carefully documented.[84]

"While the Lord High Admiral of Castille, Ambassador of Spain at the Vatican, was passing through Assisi in the year 1645, the custodian of the convent commanded Joseph to descend from the room into the church, where the Admiral's lady was waiting for him, desirous of seeing him and speaking to him; to whom Joseph replied, 'I will obey, but I do not know whether I shall be able to speak to her.' And, as a matter of fact, hardly had he entered the church and raised his eyes to a statue... situated above the altar, when he threw himself into a flight in order to embrace its feet at a distance of twelve paces, passing over the heads of all the congregation; then, after remaining there some time, he flew back over them with his usual cry, and immediately returned to his cell. The Admiral was amazed, his wife fainted away, and all the onlookers became piously terrified." But his most remarkable flights took place at Fossombrone, where once "detaching himself in swiftest manner from the altar with a cry like thunder, he went, like lightning, gyrating hither and thither about the chapel, and with such an impetus that he made all the cells of the dormitory tremble, so that the monks, issuing thence in consternation, cried, 'An earthquake! An earthquake!'" Here, too, he cast a young sheep into the air, and took flight after it to the height of the trees, where he "remained in kneeling posture, ecstatic and with extended arms, for more than two hours, to the extraordinary marvel of the clergy who witnessed this." This would seem to have been his outdoor record—two hours without descent to earth." ~*Old Calabria*, Norman Douglas

Fig. 34 The Flying Friar

Between Teresa's levitations and Joseph's wild flights, we'll learn the art of flying by taking baby steps, coupled with proper diet and meditation. The millennial premiere of *Crouching Tiger, Hidden Dragon* captured the imagination of the Western public;[85] its gravity-defying antics seemed to resonate on an unconscious level with viewers, no doubt primed by *The Matrix* the previous year. *Siddhis* exhibited in both films were the "magical" results of intense martial arts training.

Niched high up a mountain cliff, breathtaking Wudang monastery [*See* **Fig. 35**] was *alma mater* to flying Taoist masters (priests) in *Crouching Tiger*. China's renowned Shaolin Temple, popularized by David Carradine in the 70's, refined the original *18 hands of Lo Han* techniques—legacy of Hindu hermit and First Patriarch of Ch'an Buddhism, Bodhidharma circa 540 AD—into *Kung-Fu* (Chn. Skill).

---

84 "His life was now one long succession of visions and other heavenly favors. Everything that in any way had reference to God or holy things would bring on an ecstatic state: the sound of a bell or of church music, the mention of the name of God or of the Blessed Virgin or of a saint, any event in the life of Christ, the sacred Passion, a holy picture, the thought of the glory in heaven, all would put Joseph into contemplation. Neither dragging him about, buffeting, piercing with needles, nor even burning his flesh with candles would have any effect on him—only the voice of his superior would make him obey. These conditions would occur at any time or place, especially at Mass or during Divine Service. Frequently he would be raised from his feet and remain suspended in the air. Besides he would at times hear heavenly music. Since such occurrences in public caused much admiration and also disturbance in a community, Joseph for thirty-five years was not allowed to attend choir, go to the common refectory, walk in procession or say Mass in church, but was ordered to remain in his room, where a private chapel was prepared for him.

Evil-minded and envious men even brought him before the Inquisition, and he was sent from one lonely house of the Capuchins or Franciscans to another, but Joseph retained his resigned and joyous spirit, submitting confidently to Divine Providence. He practiced mortification and fasting to such a degree, that he kept seven Lents of forty days each year, and during many of them tasted no food except on Thursdays and Sundays. His body is in the church at Osimo. He was beatified by Benedict XIV in 1753, and canonized 16 July 1767 by Clement XIII; Clement XIV extended his office to the entire Church. His life was written by Robert Nuti (Palermo, 1678). Angelo Pastrovicchi wrote another in 1773, and this is used by the Bollandist 'Acta SS.', V, Sept., 992."

~The Catholic Encyclopedia, 1907-1912

85 In 2000, it was unprecedented for a foreign language film to be nominated in the top three categories, **Best Picture, Director and Screenplay**. The film took home four **Academy Awards:** Best Foreign Language Film (Taiwan); Best Cinematography (Peter Pau); Best Music, Original Score (Dun Tan); Best Art Direction-Set Decoration (Timmy Yip)

Book IV: Supraliminality

Fig. 35   Wudang Temple, Hubei Province, China

Fundamental to both schools of higher learning is the rigorous priesthood, the spiritual technology remaining occulted to laymen. Only after years of discipline and dedication to both sensei and the Way (Tao), would the *siddhis* manifest.

Telekinesis, the ability to move objects with intent, will be a natural side-effect of harnessing *Ch'i* (Qi), the life force. The 14th century travels of Marco Polo yielded some very interesting tales; one from Mongolia demonstrates TK powers Polo promptly attributed to the Devil...

"Here is another remarkable fact about these enchanters, or *Bakhshi** as they are called. I assure you that, when the Great Khan is seated in his high hall at his table, which is raised more than eight cubits above the floor, and the cups are on the floor of the hall, a good ten paces distant from the table, and are full of wine and milk and other pleasant drinks, these *Bakhshi* contrive by their enchantment and their art that the full cups rise up of their own accord from the floor on which they have been standing and come to the Great Khan without anyone touching them. And this they do in the sight of 10,000 men. What I have told you is the plain truth without a word of falsehood. Those skilled in necromancy will confirm that it is perfectly feasible."   *["...a corruption of *Bhikshu*, the proper Sanskrit term for a religious mendicant." ~Yule]

The physical body will evolve as the *doppelganger* (energy double) changes—the former a devolutionary encrusting of the latter.[86] Extreme paranormal powers such as telepathy, teleportation, bilocation and the like will correspond with a *sixth* digit mutation—the extra finger manifesting mental abilities achieved from the extended right-brain capacity bestowed by Uranus, the transcendental power broker.[87]

Fig. 36   Godfrey Hill

"Britain's Godfrey Hill (b.1928) has the condition super numerary, with 10 fingers and two thumbs. Godfrey found his hands an advantage at school—he topped the class at adding in the days when 12 pennies made a shilling. His condition has won him attention around the world, especially in Tunisia, where he was mistaken for a descendant of Allah."   ~The British Council

---

[86] Thousands of Out-of-Body Experiences amassed by Dr. Raymond Moody confirmed the existence of a duplicate "energy" body.
     "I kept getting in and out of my physical body, and I could see it from directly above. But, while I did, I was still in a body—not a physical body, but something I can best describe as an energy pattern. If I had to put it into words, I would say that it was transparent, a spiritual as opposed to a material being. Yet, it definitely had different parts."   ~*Life After Life*, Raymond Moody
     Yoga training reduces stress by its holistic approach to the mind/body connection. Ignoring one "body" harms the other...
     "We should not move the body without the soul or the soul without the body, and thus they will be on guard against each other, and be healthy and well-balanced. And therefore the mathematician or anyone else whose thoughts are much absorbed in some intellectual pursuit must allow his body also to have due exercise, and practice gymnastic; and he who is careful to fashion the body, should in turn impart to the soul its proper motions, and should cultivate music and philosophy, if he would deserve to be called truly fair and good."   ~*Timaeus*, Plato

[87] As with levitating/flying lessons, we learn everything in baby steps. In Alfred Bester's sci-fi classic, *The Stars My Destination*, everybody learns to teleport short distances called *jaunting*. A true instance of teleportation is recorded in the NT's *Book of Acts*...
     "And he commanded the chariot to stand still: and they went down both into the water, both Philip and the eunuch; and he baptized him. And when they were come up out of the water, the Spirit of the Lord caught away Philip, that the eunuch saw him no more: and he went on his way rejoicing. But Philip was found at Azotus: and passing through he preached in all the cities, till he came to Caesarea."   (Acts 8.38-40)

Another physical transmutation directly linked to psychic abilities involves decalcification of the pineal gland, manifesting in startling, ephemeral apparitions of the *Ajna Chakra* or Third Eye. The 16th century neurophysiologist/philosopher René Descartes regarded *common sense as soul* and believed it must correspond to a physical component of the brain—the most likely candidate being an anomalous singularity precariously perched centermass in the skull.

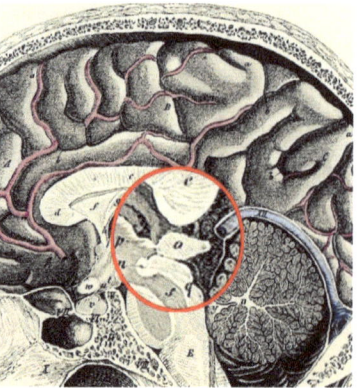

Fig. 37   (o) Pineal Gland

"Since we see only one thing with two eyes, and hear only one voice with two ears, and in short have never more than one thought at a time, it must necessarily be the case that the impressions which enter by the two eyes or by the two ears, and so on, unite with each other in some part of the body before being considered by the soul. Now it is impossible to find any such place in the whole head except this gland; moreover it is situated in the most suitable possible place for this purpose, in the middle of all the concavities; and it is supported and surrounded by the little branches of the carotid arteries which bring the spirits into the brain."

"Since it is the only solid part in the whole brain which is single, it must necessarily be the *seat of the common sense, i.e., of thought, and consequently of the soul*; for one cannot be separated from the other. The only alternative is to say that the soul is not joined immediately to any solid part of the body, but only to the animal spirits which are in its concavities, and which enter it and leave it continually like the water of river. That would certainly be thought too absurd."   ~*Passions of the Soul*, Descartes

Though modern science has added little to Descartes' metaphysical theories, contemporary physiological research reveals the gland's alchemical role in transmuting serotonin[88] to melatonin.

"The pineal gland (3rd Eye) is a light-sensitive organ which requires stimulation from electromagnetic impulses from the optic nerves. Sunlight enters the eye and triggers retinal nerve impulses which travel to the pineal gland. From there, the resulting nerve impulses from the pineal gland are fed to the hypothalamus and pituitary, which control, mediate or affect many of the vital functions of the body. Additionally, only the pineal gland makes melatonin from serotonin, a process which operates strictly according to day-night cycles. Melatonin formation is stopped by light and proceeds in darkness. So, we find the pineal gland, because of its sensitivity to light, has a profound effect on the biorhythm of the body. It is a kind of biological clock that affects the timing of certain physiological functions.

Melatonin works together with tryptophan in the brain to regulate the sleep/wake cycle. We find that alpha is the healing state of conscious, awakened mind, while sleep interspersed with vivid dreams is known to be a wonderful restorative. The pineal gland, in other words, may be called the 'peace gland' because of its biochemical role in rest, relaxation, and healing."   ~*The Complete Book of Chinese Health & Healing*, Daniel Reid

---

88 "Serotonin is one of the four main neurohumors or neurotransmitters in higher vertebrate nervous systems. I have mentioned the location of serotonin production and note here that the serotonin is transported via the bloodstream to the nerve cells throughout the body, but most especially in the neurons of the brain. Here they accumulate in the their minutest molecular form. The molecule serotonin is utilized by the nerve cells for the complete execution of electrical impulses across the synaptic gap (which is the micro-gap between every connection of every nerve cell in the entire nervous system). The impulses come along the nerve cell going through the electro-chemical processes with the ionic forms of calcium and potassium (the two vitals of the nervous system) until they reach the terminal end of the cell's dendrites. Upon reaching the end of the electrical impulse it is translated into the neurochemical serotonin. This is then 'squeezed' out into intercellular space only to connect and meet the other side which is the beginning of the next nerve soma (lining of the nerve cell).

Few molecules can penetrate what is known in biology as the 'blood brain barrier'. Those that do go directly to the neuron. After that it becomes a matter of their ability to imitate one of the neurotransmitters. Our neurons have a safety device for this type of situation. The neurotransmitters have a unique molecular shape and can only fit in a specific slot on the synaptic surface. Mind-altering drugs all operate on mimicking one of the neurotransmitters. (Most all drugs work internally, one exception is alcohol. Alcohol's effect is caused by altering the sensitivity of the soma or cell wall.)   *Cont.* →

Book IV: Supraliminality

Taoist yoga's internal alchemy (*Nei Dan*) agrees with Descartes' brain topography that the Soul ("prenatal vitality") rests directly behind the eyes, "a pearl of the size of a grain of rice..."

"It is (in the center of the brain behind) the spot between the eyes. Lao Tzu called it 'the gateway to heaven and earth'; hence he urged people to concentrate on the center in order to realize the oneness (of all things). In this center is a pearl of the size of a grain of rice, which is the center between heaven and earth in the human body (i.e., the microcosm); it is the cavity of prenatal vitality. To know where it lies is not enough, for it does not include the wondrous light of (essential) nature which is symbolized by a circle which fatherly Confucius called virtuous perfection (*jen*); the Book of Change (*I Ching*) calls it the ultimateless (*wu chi*), the Buddha perfect knowledge (*yuan ming*) and the Taoists, the elixir of immortality or spiritual light; which all point to the prenatal One True Vitality. He who knows this cavity can prepare the elixir of immortality."

~*Taoist Yoga*, Lu K'uan Yu

"The light of the body is the eye: therefore when thine eye is single, thy whole body also is full of light; but when thine eye is evil, thy body also is full of darkness." (Luke 11.34)

More than Descartes dreamed, this tiny organ, the *seat of the soul*, is also the key to a quasi third eye—a sublime reflex action of the gross physical body's pineal gland...

"It is not to be confounded with the pineal gland, which is distinctly a physical center or gland. The third eye exists in etheric matter, and is an etheric center of force, being made of the substance of the ethers, whereas the pineal gland is formed of matter of the three lower subplanes of the physical plane. The latter, nevertheless, has to be functioning more or less before the *Eye of Shiva* becomes in any degree active, and it is this fact that has led writers of occult books in the past purposely to confound the two, in order to protect the knowledge. The third eye is formed through the activity of three factors:

First, through the direct impulse of the Ego on its own plane. During the greater part of evolution the Ego makes its contact with its reflection, physical plane man, through the center at the top of the head. When man is more highly evolved, and is nearing or treading the Path, the indwelling Self takes a more complete grasp of its lower vehicle, and descends to a point in the head or brain which is found approximately in the center of the forehead. This is its lowest contact. [*See* **Fig. 37**]

Second, through the coordinated activity of the major head center, the many petalled lotus above the top of the head. This center directly affects the pineal gland, and the interplay of force behind the two (correspondence, on a tiny scale, of the pairs of opposites, spirit and matter), produces the great organ of consciousness, the *Eye of Shiva*. It is the instrument of wisdom, and in these three centers of energy we have the correspondence of the three aspects within the head of man.

Major head center →	Will aspect →	Spirit →	Father in Heaven
Pineal gland →	Love-Wisdom aspect →	Consciousness →	Son
Third eye →	Activity aspect →	Matter →	Mother

---

88 *Continued*

LSD happens to be one of the more famous antagonists. It not only penetrates the blood brain barrier but slips slyly into the transmission site inside the nerve cells themselves. It can mimic serotonin to the point where the body thinks it's serotonin and consequently shoots it across the synaptic gap. When LSD reaches the other side it is accepted but the LSD doesn't carry the message any further. The impulse of electricity is redirected down less familiar pathways, pathways which have not been highly conditioned. Specifically LSD affects the oldest parts of the brain first (e.g. upper end of the spinal cord, medulla oblongata, cerebrum, pineal gland and hypothalamus region) then the bloodstream takes it forward into the immediate back brain (location of sight interpretation) up through the area of hearing, the cerebellum, other sense interpretive centers, and the motor areas.

Using radioactive molecules traced with LSD, science has been able to follow the course of LSD through the various channels and avenues of the body. It has been found that after selecting certain areas of the various parts of the brain it then migrates to sections with fewer imprints, for instance the right of the hemisphere, the so-called creative center. By redirecting consciousness, as it were, into the unimprinted areas of the cortex, one hypothetically experiences the world anew, hence the variety of interpretations which arise upon questioning psychedelic voyagers about their 'trip'. Because of LSD's antagonistic effect on serotonin and the pineal gland itself, it would seem quite likely there is a chemical relationship between mental illness and deficiencies of serotonin."

~*The Pineal Gland, LSD and Serotonin*, Russ McClay

Third, the reflex action of the pineal gland itself. As these three types of energy, or the vibration of these three centers, begin to contact each other, a definite interplay is set up. This triple interplay forms in time a vortex or center of force, which finds its place in the center of the forehead, and takes eventually the semblance of an eye looking out between the other two."   ~*A Treatise on Cosmic Fire*, Alice Bailey

The shocking flash of an extra eye appearing between the binocular pair becomes more and more a frequent occurrence as the soul evolves, loosening the physical body's hold on the double. The psychic Eye corresponds to the Kabbalah's enigmatic, eleventh sefirah *Daath*, an endless abyss of knowledge governed by the Power, Uranus—a good place to visit, but you wouldn't want to live there.[89] The deliberate awakening of the etheric third eye depends upon decalcification and growth of the atrophied pineal gland through a discipline of diet, exercise, meditation and upright living…

"The pineal gland is subject to two lines of stimulation: First, that which emanates from the Ego itself via the etheric force centers. This downflow of egoic energy (the result of the awakening of the centers through meditation and spirituality of life), impinges upon the gland and in the course of years gradually increases its secretion, enlarges its form, and starts it into a new cycle of activity.

The second line of stimulation affecting the pineal gland is that which is the consequence of the discipline of the physical body, and its subjugation to the laws of spiritual unfoldment. As the disciple lives a regulated life, avoids meat, nicotine and alcohol, and practices continence, the pineal gland becomes no longer atrophied, but resumes its earlier activity."   ~Ibid.

As an adjunct to the disciplined life, ethnobotanists discover a remarkable species of flora that prevents pineal gland calcification—*doubling* our current lifespan.[90] Anyone dying at a mere 100 years old will be but a child, the result of a freak accident. All our love (and work) in vain *no longer*, families and Nations become self-sustaining, living in harmony with Nature's Way—her graceful, laidback conditions conducive to reaching the ripe old age of California's towering redwoods.

"There shall be no more thence an infant of days, Nor an old man that hath not filled his days;
For the child shall die an hundred years old, but the sinner being an hundred years old shall be accursed.

They shall build houses and inhabit them; and they shall plant vineyards and
eat the fruit of them. They shall not build and another inhabit; they shall not
plant and another eat; *For as the days of a tree, are the days of my people,*
and mine elect shall long enjoy the work of their hands.
They shall not labor in vain…"   (Isaiah 65.20-22)

---

89 "It is the eye of the inner vision, and he who has opened it can direct and control the energy of matter, see all things in the Eternal Now, and therefore be in touch with causes more than with effects, read the akashic records, and see clairvoyantly."   ~Bailey

90 "The pineal gland undergoes a gradual process of calcification throughout life. Calcification actually begins in childhood. By early adulthood, it can be seen on radiograph in about 53% of the population and is evident in approximately 80% of elderly individuals. Degree of calcification has also been correlated to daytime tiredness and sleep disturbance (Kunz et al., 1998). There is one remarkable study by the *British Medical Journal* over 15 years ago that indicates a correlation between pineal calcification in humans and a poor sense of direction (Bayliss et al., 1985). This report is intriguing when compared with studies on homing pigeons, whose pineal gland is paramount to survival, indicated by a brain weight of 10% (compared with 1% for humans). When homing pigeons have extensive calcification, they too lose their sense of direction. Perhaps, researchers should begin to study the correlation between pineal calcification and senility."   ~*The Scientific Basis of Integrative Medicine*, Leonard A. Wisneski, Lucy Anderson

A robust pineal gland continues to produce adequate serotonin/melatonin—a potent antioxidant and free radical scavenger that prevents skin aging (tissue degeneration), Alzheimer's and insomnia—keeping us young at heart… body and soul.

"..the power of the *tree of life* could not go so far as to give the body the prerogative of living for an infinite time, but only for a definite time… since the power of the tree of life was finite, man's life was to be preserved for a definite time by partaking of it once; and when that time had elapsed, man was to be either transferred to a spiritual life, or had need to eat once more of the *tree of life*."
~*Summa Theologica*, Thomas Aquinas

Book IV: Supraliminality

At the end of the day all these paranormal powers pale in comparison with the indispensable bestowment of perpetually saving Grace, the astonishing influx of the Spirit. Since Israel's original purpose was to become a nation of Priests, all the Elect must someday be *born again* as Chosen Ones.[91] To be reborn in the flesh is no easy task, the phenomenal process not even acknowledged today, much less 2,000 years ago. Prominent Pharisees of the time had uncensored access to sacred wisdom texts and carefully guarded oral tradition spanning millennia, yet the educated Nicodemus couldn't comprehend Jesus' off-the-wall response to his back-handed compliment...

"There was a man of the Pharisees named Nicodemus, a ruler of the Jews. This man came to Jesus by night and said to Him, 'Rabbi, we know that you are a teacher come from God; for no one can do these signs that you do unless God is with him.' Jesus answered and said to him, 'Most assuredly, I say to you, *unless one is born again, he cannot see the kingdom of God.*' [92]

Nicodemus said to Him, 'How can a man be born when he is old? Can he enter a second time into his mother's womb and be born?' Jesus answered, 'Most assuredly, I say to you, *unless one is born of water and the Spirit, he cannot enter the kingdom of God.* That which is born of the flesh is flesh, and that which is born of the Spirit is spirit.

Do not marvel that I said to you, *You must be born again.* The wind blows where it wishes, and you hear the sound of it, but cannot tell where it comes from and where it goes. So is everyone who is born of the Spirit.' Nicodemus answered and said to Him, 'How can these things be?' Jesus answered and said to him, 'Are you the teacher of Israel, *and do not know these things?*'" (John 3.1-10)

The Kingdom of God is to be distinguished from the one down here, the latter a training ground for those candidates who have successfully undergone shamanic initiation and received the gift of Grace from above. The martial art curriculum carefully hones the physical body until it is one with the mental body. In concert with advanced meditation techniques which accelerate the gross body's vibratory rate, the spiritual apprentice is soon capable of shifting states of awareness, something he has speculated upon his whole adult life.

---

91 The Elect's **x-variable** will include a great number of scribes and Pharisees, "stiff-necked" Hasidic Jews whose eyes were finally opened at the *Parousia* (Grk. Presence). Regrafted onto their own tree, Messianic Jews will become our greatest spiritual Elders...

"As the Church began at Christ's ascension, so the kingdom shall begin at His second advent. This is the humiliation of the modern civilized nations, that nations which they despise most, Jews and uncivilized barbarians, the Negro descendants of Ham who from the curse of Noah have been so backward, Cush and Sheba, *shall supplant and surpass them as centers of the world's history*.

The Jews are our teachers even in New Testament times. Since their rejection revelation has been silent. The whole Bible, even the New Testament, is written by Jews. If revelation is to recommence in the millennial kingdom, converted Israel must stand at the head of humanity." ~Jamieson Fausset Brown Bible Commentary

"Therefore consider the goodness and severity of God: on those who fell, severity; but toward you, goodness, if you continue in His goodness. Otherwise you also will be cut off. And they also, if they do not continue in unbelief, will be grafted in, for God is able to graft them in again. For if you were cut out of the olive tree which is wild by nature, and were grafted contrary to nature into a cultivated olive tree, *how much more will these, who are natural branches, be grafted into their own olive tree.* For I do not desire, brethren, that you should be ignorant of this mystery, lest you should be wise in your own opinion, that blindness in part has happened to Israel until the fullness of the Gentiles has come in."
(Romans 11.22-25)
"And I will pour on the house of David and on the inhabitants of Jerusalem the Spirit of grace and supplication; then they will look on Me whom they pierced. Yes, they will mourn for Him as one mourns for his only son, and grieve for Him as one grieves for a firstborn." (Zechariah 12.10)

92 "This blunt and curt reply was plainly meant to shake the whole edifice of the man's religion, in order to lay a deeper and more enduring foundation. Nicodemus probably thought he had gone a long way, and expected, perhaps, to be complimented on his candor. Instead of this, he is virtually told that he has raised a question which he is not in a capacity to solve, and that before approaching it, his spiritual vision required to be rectified by an entire revolution on his inner man. Had the man been less sincere, this would certainly have repelled him; but with persons in his mixed state of mind—to which Jesus was no stranger (John 2.25)—such methods speed better than more honeyed words and gradual approaches." ~Jamieson Fausset Brown Bible Commentary

A Divine entheogen[93] ingested at this time, in a proper sacred setting, gives incontrovertible proof of the eternal Mystery—unknowable Self as immortal God. It is this epiphany that encourages the initiate to dare ask for, and receive, the Power; a gift that once bestowed, cannot be rescinded within that incarnation. This special grace, this *awareness*, is what the Master alluded to when He put the Question to His disciples. He knew the secret desire burning in their hearts was to emulate the miraculous Messiah, in *every* way.

> "Hitherto have ye asked nothing in my name: ask, and ye shall receive, *that your joy may be full.* These things have I spoken unto you in proverbs: but the time cometh, when I shall no more speak unto you in proverbs, but I shall show you plainly of the Father. At that day ye shall ask in my name: *and I say not unto you, that I will pray the Father for you:* For the Father himself loveth you, because ye have loved me, and have believed that I came out from God." (John 16.24-27)

> "Ask, and it shall be given you; seek, and ye shall find; knock, and it shall be opened unto you: For every one that asketh receiveth; and he that seeketh findeth; and to him that knocketh it shall be opened." (Matthew 7.7-8)

> "He who seeks shall not cease until he finds, *and finding he shall marvel*, and having marveled, he shall reign, and having reigned, he shall rest."
> ~fragment of the *Gospel according to the Hebrews* from Clement of Alexandria, *Miscellanies* 5.14; and the *Oxyrhynchus Papyrus* 654, Logion 1

When the child of God becomes a Son of God, it is *his* decision, a sacred pact between him and the Father (Oversoul). With the apostles, it was the Christ's constant presence that acted as a consuming catalyst upon their psyche, an "entheogenic entity" that mirrored their own evolutionary future. Exposure to Perfection planted a holy seed.[94] Truth-seekers of the Messianic Era will use a psychoactive Sacrament to experience the true Communion: fusion with the Father—the penultimate accomplishment of Self-realization previously achieved after a lifetime of discipline and struggle.[95]

---

93 "In 1978 R. Gordon Wasson convened an informal committee of researchers interested in the ethnopharmacognosy of shamanic inebriants, to look for a substitute for inadequate terms like 'hallucinogenic' (which implied delusion and/or falsity, besides suggesting pathology to psychotherapists), 'psychotomimetic' (implying also pathology) and 'psychedelic' (besides being a pejorative term prejudicing shamanic inebriants in the eyes of persons unfamiliar with the field, this term had become so invested with connotations of 1960s western 'counterculture' as to make it incongruous to speak of a shaman ingesting a psychedelic plant). We finally settled on the neologism *entheogenic*, from the Greek *entheos*, a term used in the classical world to describe prophetic or poetic inspiration. The term means literally 'becoming divine within', and can be seen as the user realizing that the divine infuses all of the creation, or specifically that the entheogenic plant is itself infused with the divine. It is not a theological term, makes no reference to any deity, and is not meant to be a pharmacological term for designating a specific chemical class of drugs (psychedelic, for example, has come to be seen by some *sensu strictu* as a term to designate mescaline-like B-phenethylamines or DMT-like tryptamines). Rather, it is a cultural term to include all of the shamanic inebriants—sacraments, plant teachers, the stock-in-trade of shamans the world over."
~*The Age Of Entheogens*, Jonathan Ott

94 "Whosoever is born of God doth not commit sin; for His seed remaineth in him: and he cannot sin, because he is born of God." (1 John 3.9)

95 "Only a few blessed people spontaneously attain the mystical vision which can effect this transformation. As a result, mankind has repeatedly sought paths and evolved methods to evoke deeper perception and experience.... An especially important aid in the induction of mystical-ecstatic states of consciousness, discovered in the earliest times, is decidedly the use of certain plant drugs... *I have made it quite clear that their use must proceed within the scope of religious ceremony.*" ~Dr. Albert Hofmann

"Positive mystical experience with psychedelic drugs is by no means automatic. It would seem that the 'drug effect' is a delicate combination of psychological set and setting in which the drug is itself the trigger." ~Walter Pahnke, M.D., *Good Friday Experiment*

The entheogen, administered in a Vision Quest ceremony capping years of physical, mental and spiritual preparation, *need be taken one time only* to experience Mahasamadhi, breakthrough to complete Ego transcendence. The drug merely acts as a catalyst, a booster rocket igniting the dormant *kundalini* as the initiate's own desire takes over, climbing the last upper rungs of Jacob's Ladder (seven chakras). Initiation complete as permanent contact with the Oversoul is established—the aka cord connected. [**Book I, Fig. 1**]

The experiential seed engenders a new mind-set, the metanoia (Grk. change, mind)[96] igniting the soul of the initiated—now ready to claim his God-given inheritance. As a fervent, wholehearted prayer sends a strong surcharge of prana (kundalini) to the Father, He reciprocates, amplifying the energy and returning it straight back down to the crown *chakra*. A tingling at the top of the cranium snakes down, exploding the lower *chakras*, visibly shaking the candidate—Spirit's physical confirmation that his wish has been granted, instantaneously! Metamorphisized, the applicant is accepted, *chosen* as a Son and *reborn* as an agent of change—hence, a slave of Power. [*See* **Book I**, p.13]

Past the point of no return, the Great Spirit now dictates his every move as the wind blows the trees. Like a newborn, his tentative actions, good and bad, define his character for twenty-one years until "adulthood" when the promise of Power is fully realized. The sum goodness of all past lives' moral modalities determines the direction of his new life as Saint or Sorcerer.[97]

Esoterica scholar Rudolf Steiner believed that eventually *everybody* will become Chosen Ones, consequently polarizing into positive and negative *mahasiddhas* due to an invariable, insidious slide towards "black magic" that will set the stage for the final conflict between the Sons of Light and Sons of Darkness.

"Thus there appears on our horizon, so to speak, the division of mankind in the far distant future; the chosen of Christ, who finally will be the white magicians, and the adversaries, the terrible wizards, the black magicians, who cannot escape from matter… and thus in the far future we see two powers confronting each other; on the one hand those who swell the population of the great Babylon, and on the other hand those who rise above matter, who as man unite with the principle represented as the Lamb."

Chapter Nine: The Kingdom of Heavens

> "Then after that in the ninth week the righteous judgment shall be revealed to the whole world. All the deeds of the sinners shall depart from upon the whole earth, and be written off for eternal destruction; and all people shall direct their sight to the path of uprightness."
> (1 Enoch 91)

During Enoch's "ninth week", with our eyes on the prize we apply ourselves to the evolutionary task of releasing the carnal body. Since *flesh and blood cannot inherit the Kingdom*, we work day and night to perfect the astral body. Simply living upright (practicing as much sexual and substance abstinence as the mind/body allows), while immersed in a field of inspirational thoughts and images, organically transforms our energy bodies—the metabolization process entirely unconscious...[98]

---

96 "Whereas, our argument shows that the power and capacity of learning exists in the soul already; and that just as the eye was unable to turn from darkness to light without the whole body, so too the instrument of knowledge can only by the movement of the whole soul be turned [*metanoia*, turning around] from the world of becoming into that of being, and learn by degrees to endure the sight of being, and of the brightest and best of being, or in other words, of the good."   ~*The Republic*, Plato

97 Rabbi Bob taught us: **"It may be the Devil or it may be the Lord, but you're gonna have to serve somebody."** The only free will we truly have is the choice between Life (evolution) or Death (stagnation): Good or Evil. When the student's ready, powerful teachers—good and bad—appear from previous lives' karmic ties to nurture the "babe". These spiritual midwives become role models for the impressionable child of God.

98   "So is the kingdom of God, as if a man should cast seed into the ground; and should sleep, and rise night and day, and the seed should spring and grow up, *he knoweth not how*. For the earth bringeth forth fruit of herself; first the blade, then the ear, after that the full corn in the ear. But when the fruit is brought forth, immediately he putteth in the sickle, because the harvest is come."   (Mark 4.26-29)

   "It is sown a natural body; it is raised a spiritual body."   (1 Corinthians 15.44)

"Let us take man in his waking state… Let us suppose that in addition to his professional work and duties he devotes a short time to higher considerations in order to make his own, for instance, the great impulses which flow from the *Gospel of St. John*… the *Bhagavad Gita* or the *Dhammapada*…

Let us suppose that during the day a man fills his soul with pictures and ideas such as these, then his astral body is laid hold of by these thoughts, feelings and pictures, and they produce various effects in it. Then when man withdraws from his physical and etheric bodies at night, these effects remain in the astral body… In this way man works today during the waking consciousness upon his astral body." ~Rudolf Steiner

The real evolutionary work, however, will take place during sleep. Lucid dreaming techniques, over time, stabilize the energy double until it is as solid as, and identical to, the physical.[99] A Dream Yoga program will advance us, step-by-step through the seven gates of *Dreaming*, the last level embodying a permanent shift (awakening) into the original star-body. The covert methodology involved has been bequeathed to us from an ancient lineage of sorcerers, the Toltec, through the last of their line—the late anthropologist/warlock Carlos Castaneda.[100] When the astral self evolves to the degree where we can reach down deep enough into our psyche to effect the *etheric* body, we near the end of our transformations.[101] Yet, unlike the Egoic energy body, we need Divine assistance to penetrate the densest layer of our compounded Soul… the unconscious self, the Id (iot).

"No man cometh unto the Father, but by me." (John 14.6)

"Man cannot yet of himself work into this **etheric body**… Today he still has to leave both the physical and etheric bodies every night and emerge from them. But in order that the etheric body may receive its effects, so that man shall gradually learn to work into it, he needs a helper. And the helper who makes this possible is none other than Christ…Had Christ not united himself with the Earth as a living being, had he not come into the aura of the Earth, then what is developed in the astral body would not be communicated to the etheric body."

Making friends with our Inner Child—the etheric self—is key to the final metamorphosis: abandoning the physical body. It is the steady encouragement of, and inspiration from, the Role Model in the lower world that enables us to live more fully in the *conscious* etheric, to rise above the endless ephemeral pleasures and false security of Mother Earth. As all the priests of Christ[102] thoroughly train their lower etheric ego to collaborate with the noetic *metanoia* imprinted upon the astral self, former earthly obsessions now seem childish and simply fall away…

"The etheric body has now become important to them for, with the help of Christ, it has become so organized that it is for the time being adapted to the astral body and no longer desires and longs for what is below in the physical world." ~RS

---

99 "…when you fashion eyes in the place of an eye, and a hand in place of a hand, and a foot in place of a foot, and a likeness in place of a likeness; then will you enter [the Kingdom]." (*Gospel of Thomas*, Logion 22)

"A dream in which one is watching oneself asleep is the time of the double… The self dreams the double. Once it has learned to dream the double, the self arrives at this weird crossroad and a moment comes when one realizes that it is the double who dreams the self. Your double is *dreaming* you. No one knows how it happens. We only know that it does happen. That's the mystery of us as luminous beings. You can awaken in either one." ~*Tales of Power*, Carlos Castaneda

100 See **Book III**, *Necessary Evil*, for an *apologia* explaining the necessity of treading into areas angels may fear to. "You will find out for yourself that the true goal of dreaming is to perfect the energy body. A perfect energy body, among other things of course, has such control over the dreaming attention that it makes it stop when needed. This is the safety valve dreamers have. No matter how indulging they might be, at a given time, their dreaming attention must make them surface." ~*The Art of Dreaming*, Castaneda

101 "It must be possible for man during his Earthly evolution to imprint ever and again at least in the etheric body, what he has taken into himself. It is necessary for this etheric body also to receive effects from what man develops in his astral body…" ~Steiner

102 "Blessed and holy is he that hath part in the first resurrection: on such the second death hath no power, but *they shall be priests of God and of Christ*, and shall reign with him a thousand years." (Revelation 20.6)

Book IV: Supraliminality

Meanwhile, all the losers that flunked the final exam in the 21st c. eventually reincarnate and, returning dog-like to their vomit, shun *Mashiach* and His saving Grace.[103] The black magicians are consumed by uncontrollable carnal desires, torturing them on the subconscious (etheric) level.

"They are the souls who will feel hot fires of desire for physical sensuality… unable to change anything in the etheric body, for they could not find the helper, Christ."   ~RS

The Sons of Darkness instead turn to another ancient Power, the original Dark Lord Himself, Dagon[104], lying dormant at the bottom of the Sea for 26,000 years. Like His sycophant sorcerers, He has gained nothing at all from Earth's evolution…

"It has acquired the tendencies of other world periods and will feel deep satisfaction when it meets with beings such as those evil ones who have refused to take up inwardly the good which can flow from the Earth.

This being has been unable to receive anything from the Earth; it has seen Earth evolution come but has said: I have not progressed with the Earth in such a way that I can gain anything from Earthly existence.

This being could only have got something from the Earth by being able to gain the rulership at a certain moment, namely when the Christ-principle descended to the earth. If the Christ-principle had been strangled in the germ, if Christ had been overcome by the adversary, **it would have been possible for the whole Earth to succumb to the 666-principle.**

This, however, did not take place, and so this being has to be content with the refuse of mankind who have not inclined towards the Christ-principle, who have remained embedded in matter; they in the future will form his cohorts." ~*The Apocalypse of St. John* (1908), Steiner

Dreaming beneath the deep blue sea in suspended animation, the monster has not evolved one iota since the second Creation. Out of action for the entire *Mahayuga*, the sleeping giant makes a shocking comeback when the necromancers' incantations shatter the supernatural seal set over His subterranean crypt.[105] Horror writer H.P. Lovecraft is renowned in occult circles for "inventing" the world's most infamous grimoire, the *Necronomicon* or *R'lyeh Text*…

Fig. 38   Cthulhu (Dagon)

---

[103] **"But the rest of the dead lived not again until the thousand years were finished."** (Revelation 20.5) It is only towards the end of the Messianic Era that the population growth rate (PGR) once again spikes out of control. For untold centuries the human lifespan increases exponentially, dramatically decreasing the death/birth cycles—the vulnerable newborn more and more a rarity!

Matthew 18.10 reads, **"Take heed that ye despise not one of these little ones; for I say unto you, that in heaven their angels do always behold the face of my Father which is in heaven."** The critical follow-up is strangely eliminated from both *Codex Vaticanus* and *Codex Sinaiticus* (and subsequently all Revised KJV Bibles). **Matthew 18.11** is preserved only in *Codex Alexandrinus*: **"Ye and the Son of Man is come to save that which is lost."** Another subtle clue from the Redeemer: that which is lost is our original immortal soul—death and reincarnation the result of folly. When the entity reincarnates, it must survive 29 years (the Saturn Return) before its Soul can be fully reincorporated. Until that time the adult astral body remains in the presence of the Lord, acting as guardian angel to himself. Another ancient fragment puts it bluntly—"When Salome asked, **'How long will death have power?'** the Lord answered, **'So long as ye women bear children.'**—not as if life was something bad and creation evil, but as teaching the sequence of nature." ~*Gospel of the Egyptians*, commented by Clement of Alexandria in *Stromateis III*, 1st century

[104] *See* footnote 52. "Dagon in Hebrew is spelled: *Daleth, Gimel, Vav* and *Nun* = DAG + ON. Dagon means the Might of the Fish (Human Sperm). Dagon is the Nun-Force, the might of the human seed. Fornicators worship the lustful passional fires of their own particular, individual Dagon or Leviathan; they expel the fish (Human Sperm), their sexual strength through the orgasm or sexual spasm. They are slaves of Dagon, the Leviathan."   ~Samael Aun Weor

[105] **"Oh, may that night be barren! May no joyful shout come into it!
May those curse it who curse the day, those who are ready to arouse Leviathan."**
(Book of Job 3.7-8)

"Know ye that he hath slept death's dream for ages unnumbered—he who has slumbered long before the birth of man; He who is dead yet waits dreaming: SHALL RISE, and His time draws near. The worm shall not corrupt the corrupted; time is naught to His continuation; the aeons shall not lay waste that which is not of earth's flesh. In R'lyeh He dwells, bound in timeless sleep by Those who would hold back the darkness of Outer Hells and stem the fate of Man. Yet the darkness shall prevail, the destiny of man is sealed and graven. The stars shall mark the time of His coming, and when the spheres intersect: HE SHALL RISE. Great Cthulhu shall return, and armed with vengeful talons He shall smite the Elder Lords and rend the soul of Man. The earth shall know the night without cease.

His minions dwell amongst you, Beware O Man, they come in servile stealth; like thieves in the night. They heed not Man and his frail gods, blind in the will of their master. Great Cthulhu sleeps in His house and shapes the dream of what shall be, dead Cthulhu waits dreaming… Lament thy fate O Man, for the earth shall be void and cast for eternity into the abyss of perdition." ~H.P. Lovecraft

> **"And when the thousand years are expired, Satan shall be loosed out of his prison,
> And shall go out to deceive the nations which are in the four quarters of the earth,
> Gog and Magog, to gather them together to battle: the number of whom is as the
> sand of the sea. And they went up on the breadth of the earth, and compassed
> the camp of the saints about, and the beloved city: and fire came down
> from God out of heaven, and devoured them."** (Revelation 20.7-9)

> **"In that day the YHVH with his sore and great and strong sword shall
> punish leviathan the piercing serpent, even leviathan that crooked serpent;
> and he shall slay the dragon that is in the sea."** (Isaiah 27.1)

Fig. 39   The First Death—30?? AD

The last war of Man, **WW IV** is terminated by what has likely become a cliché except this comet's catastrophic course will *not* be interrupted. Slaying YHVH's pet nemesis and His henchmen in the Earth's penultimate mass extinction event leads directly to the Last Judgment as a *second resurrection*[106] rouses the damned and departed back to life. An unprecedented transition to the essential energy body leaves the Sons of Light unscathed.

Mitochondrial Eve's sundry, prodigious progeny are summoned to a Supreme Court of twelve celestial Elohim (*Thrones*)—the Holy Tribunal presided over by our Lord and a grand jury of peers, the brotherhood of Bodhisattvas.[107]

> **"Elohim has taken His place in the divine Council; in the midst of the Elohim He holds judgment."**
> (Psalm 82.1)

---

[106] "When John says that death and Hades gave up the dead that were in them (v. 13), he means the graves were opened and the dead were raised. This is the language of resurrection, the 'second' resurrection if you like…"   ~JFB Bible Commentary

[107]   "Do ye not know that the saints shall judge the world? and if the world shall be judged by you,
are ye unworthy to judge the smallest matters?"   (1Corinthians 6.2)

"In the next moment the space behind the podium was filled with Beings of Light. They faced the benches where I was sitting and radiated a glow that was both kindly and wise. I sat back on the bench and waited. What happened next was the most amazing part of my spiritual journey. I was able to count the Beings as they stood behind the podium. There were thirteen of them, standing shoulder to shoulder and stretched across the stage. I was aware of other things about them, too, probably through some form of telepathy. Each one of them represented a different emotional and psychological characteristic that all humans have. For example, one of these Beings was intense and passionate, while another was artistic and emotional. One was bold and energetic, yet another possessive and loyal. In human terms, it was as though each one represented a different sign of the zodiac. In spiritual terms, these Beings went far beyond the signs of the zodiac. They emanated these emotions in such a way that I could feel them."   ~*Saved by the Light*, Dannion Brinkley

Book IV: Supraliminality

The Akashic Records are opened, each Soul judged by the incontrovertible evidence therein. The sum total of all our past lives—all our deeds, good and bad—are weighed in the balance; shaming or glorifying every entity, including the Celestial and Diabolical Intelligences.[108]

A righteous banquet is set for all the Sons of Light whose names are found written in the Book of Life. The blue plate special at this Last Supper is BBQ Leviathan, the aged power meat just the jolt we need to permanently drop the ballast of both etheric and physical bodies[109], thus escaping Old Earth—the *Second Death*. As Mother Earth jettisons along with us, she leaves behind a steaming, sulfuric carcass of compact material excrement…

"A special cosmic body splits off that contains all the beings who have resisted evolution, a so to speak 'irredeemable moon', which now moves toward an evolution, for the character of which no expression can be found because it is too dissimilar to anything that man can experience on earth."   ~Steiner

Fig. 40   The Last Judgment (1535-41)   Michaelangelo

The refuse of Mankind, the wicked wizards of Darkness whose names *are not encoded in the holy Torah*, are left to their own devices when they find themselves stranded on a dwarf planet, a netherworld (Lake of Fire)—*undead* and enslaved to a primeval monstrosity, the Dark Lord Dagon.[110]

"After the sea gave up the dead that were in it, and death and Hades gave up the dead that were in them, and after all the dead were judged, says John, Death and Hades were thrown into the lake of fire.

The notion that death and the grave are thrown into the lake of fire characterizes the lake here not as a place of torment (contrast 19:21 and 20:10), *but as a place of destruction or nonexistence*. Death and Hades are not tortured or punished, *they simply cease to exist*."   ~Jamieson Fausset Brown Bible Commentary

As it was in the Beginning, so it shall be in the End as all the Galactic Lords (*Tathagatas*) congregate for the *third* Creation of a supernal Universe (*Olam Haba*)—the New Earth, formerly a footstool, now Her crowning jewel…

> "Then, after this matter, on the tenth week in the seventh part,
> there shall be the eternal judgment, and it shall be executed
> by the Watchers of the eternal heaven—
> the great (judgment) which emanates from all of the angels.

---

108 "Know ye not that we shall judge angels? How much more things that pertain to this life?" (1Corinthians 6.3)
109   "But to Leviathan you gave the seventh part, the watery part;
    and you have kept them to be eaten by whom you wish, and when you wish." (2 Esdras 6)
  "Behold, I show you a mystery; We shall not all sleep, but we shall all be changed, in a moment, *in the twinkling of an eye*,
    at the last trump: for the trumpet shall sound, and the dead shall be raised incorruptible, and we shall be changed.
    For this corruptible must put on incorruption, and this mortal must put on immortality." (1 Cor. 15.51-53)
110 "And they shall go forth, and look upon the carcasses of the men that have transgressed against me:
for their worm shall not die, neither shall their fire be quenched; and they shall be an abhorring unto all flesh." (Isaiah 66.24)

Fig. 41   The New Jerusalem   Doré

The first heaven shall depart and pass away;
a new heaven shall appear;
and all the powers of heaven
shall shine forever sevenfold.

Then after that there shall be many weeks
without number forever; it shall be (a time)
of goodness and righteousness, and sin
shall no more be heard of forever."
(1 Enoch 91.15-17)

The City of God, the *New Jerusalem* pulsates amidst the pristine Paradise[111]... a true Brotherhood of God-men once again dressed of light at play in the fields of a resplendent 7th level, supraliminal Cosmos.

In the egalitarian Theocracy of Heavens, the King of kings relinquishes His autonomous authority as "all the morning stars sing together" and neophyte "Sons of God shout for joy." Forever awakened (Skt. *buddh*) from those who sleep[112], *suffering has come to an end—* saved with a little help from our Friend.

"Then cometh the end, when he shall have delivered up the kingdom to God, even the Father; when he shall have put down all rule and all authority and power. For he must reign, till he hath put all enemies under his feet. The last enemy that shall be destroyed is death. For he hath put all things under his feet. But when he saith all things are put under him, it is manifest that he is excepted, which did put all things under him. And when all things shall be subdued unto him, then shall the Son also himself be subject unto him that put all things under him...
that God may be all in all."   (1 Corinthians 15.24-28)

"You and I have memories longer than the road that stretches out ahead.
Two of us wearing raincoats, standing solo... in the sun.

You and me chasing paper, getting nowhere... on our way back home.
We're on our way, home; we're on our way, home...
We're going home... We're going home."
(Better believe it.)

---

111 In *Saved by the Light*, Dannion Brinkley describes his OBE visitation to a Crystal City: "Like wingless birds, we swept into a city of cathedrals. These cathedrals were made entirely of a crystal substance that glowed with a light that shone powerfully from within. We stood before one. I felt small and insignificant next to this architectural masterpiece. Clearly this was built by angels to show the grandeur of God, I thought. There were spires as high and pointed as those of the great cathedrals of France, and walls as massive and powerful as those of the Mormon Tabernacle in Salt Lake City. The walls were made of large glass bricks that glowed with a life inside them. These structures were not about a specific religion of any kind. They were there as a monument to the glory of God."

112 Also the gospel which is named according to the Hebrews, and which was recently translated by me into Greek and Latin, which also Origen often used, refers after the resurrection of the savior:

"But the Lord, when he had given the shroud to the servant of the priest, went to James and appeared to him. James indeed had sworn that he would not eat bread from that hour when he had drunk the chalice of the Lord until he saw him risen from among those who sleep. And again after a little bit: Bear forth, said the Lord, a table and bread. And immediately is added: He bore bread and blessed it, and broke it, and gave it to James the just, and said to him:

My brother, eat your bread, because the son of man has resurrected from among those who sleep."
~*Gospel according to the Hebrews*, quoted from Jerome, *On Famous Men 2,* 4th century

"You think it's the end, but it's just the beginning..."
~Ethiopian prophet Bob Marley

Fig. 42   The Jeshua Mandala

I think I have now, by God's help, discharged my obligation in writing this large work. Let those who think I have said too little, or those who think I have said too much, forgive me; and let those who think I have said just enough join me in giving thanks to God. Amen.

Bibliography

Abelar, T. (1993). *The Sorcerer's Crossing.* Penguin Books.
Apuleius. (1999). *The Golden Ass.* Penguin Classics.
Aquinas, S. T. (1981). *The Summa Theologica of St. Thomas Aquinas.* Christian Classics.
Arguelles, J. (1987). *The Mayan Factor.* Bear & Company.
Atkinson, W. W. (1907). *Mystic Christianity.* Yogi Publication Society.
Augustine. (2004). *City of God.* Penguin Classics.
Aurobindo, S. (1972). *The Collected Works, Vol. 27.* Sri Aurobindo Ashram Trust.
Aurobindo, S. (1990). *The Life Divine.* Lotus Press.
Aurobindo, S. (1995). *Essays on the Gita.* Lotus Press.
Avila, T. (1988). *The Life of Saint Teresa of Avila by Herself.* Penguin Classics.
Babbitt, I. (1965). *The Dhammapada.* New Directions.
Bailey, A. A. (1973). *A Treatise on Cosmic Fire.* Lucis Publishing Company.
Bailey, A. A. (2006). *The Reappearance of the Christ.* Lucis Publishing Company.
Bander, P. (2005). *The Prophecies of St Malachy & St Columbkille.* Colin Smythe.
Bauval, R. (1995). *The Orion Mystery.* Broadway Books.
Begley, W. (1903). *Biblia Cabalistica.* University of Michigan Library.
Bentov, I. (1988). *Stalking the Wild Pendulum.* Destiny Books.
Bentov, I. (2000). *A Brief Tour of Higher Consciousness.* Destiny Books.
Berossus. (1832). *Ancient Fragments.* (I. P. Cory, Trans.) William Pickering.
Bialik, H. N. (1992). *The Book of Legends/Sefer Ha-Aggadah.* Schocken Books.
Blomquist, R. D. (2013). *Integrated Theory of Consciousness.* Millington House Publishing.
Bodhi, B. (2006). *The Noble Eightfold Path.* Pariyatti Publishing.
Brinkley, D. (2008). *Saved by the Light.* HarperOne.
Bryant, E. F. (2009). *The Yoga Sutras of Patañjali.* North Point Press.
Budge, E. A. (2009). *Legends of the Gods.* Book Tree.
Budge, E. A. (2011). *The Egyptian Heaven and Hell.* Dover Publications.
Bulgakov, S. (1993). *Sophia: The Wisdom of God.* Lindisfarne Books.
Bullinger, E. W. (2003). *The Witness of the Stars.* Kregel Classics.
Cashford, J. (1993). *The Myth of the Goddess.* Penguin Books.
Castaneda, C. (1985). *The Teachings of Don Juan.* Washington Square Press.
Castaneda, C. (1991). *Tales of Power.* Washington Square Press.
Castaneda, C. (1991). *The Eagle's Gift.* Washington Square Press.
Castaneda, C. (1993). *The Art of Dreaming.* Harpercollins.
Cayce, E. (1976). *Edgar Cayce's Story of Jesus.* Berkley Books.
Cayce, E. E. (1988). *Edgar Cayce on Atlantis.* Grand Central Publishing.
Chardin, P. T. (1976). *The Phenomenon of Man.* Harper Perennial.
Charlesworth, J. H. (1983). *The Old Testament Pseudepigrapha, Vol. 1, 2.* Doubleday.
Chinmoy, S. (1974). *Astrology, the Supernatural and the Beyond.* Aum Publications.
Cleary, J. (1994). *Pure Land, Pure Mind.* Sutra Translation Committee.
Cleary, T. (1993). *The Flower Ornament Scripture.* Shambhala Books.

Cohen, A. (1995). *Everyman's Talmud.* Schocken Books.
Collin, R. (2006). *The Theory of Celestial Influence.* Mercury Publications.
Crane, J. (2007). *Astrological Roots.* The Wessex Astrologer Ltd.
Daniélou, A. (1987). *While the Gods Play.* Inner Traditions.
Daniélou, A. (1991). *Yoga: Mastering the Secrets of Matter and the Universe.* Inner Traditions.
Dass, B. H. (1981). *Ashtanga Yoga Primer.* Sri Ram Publishing.
Dawood, N. J. (2015). *The Koran.* Penguin Classics.
Descartes, R. (2016). *The Passions of the Soul.* Oxford University Press.
Dionysius, P. (1988). *Pseudo-Dionysius: The Complete Works.* Paulist Press.
Doniger, W. (2005). *The Rig Veda.* Penguin Classics.
Donner, F. (1992). *Being-in-Dreaming.* HarperOne.
Douglas, N. (1915). *Old Calabria.* London: Martin Secker.
Drosnin, M. (1998). *The Bible Code.* Touchstone.
Drummond, W. (1866). *The Oedipus Judaicus.* Reeves and Turner.
Eagle, F. (2004). *Atlantis Motherland.* Cosmic Vortex.
Eckhart, M. (1981). *Meister Eckhart.* Paulist Press.
Elliott, J. K. (2005). *The Apocryphal New Testament.* Oxford University Press.
Erdoes, R. (1985). *American Indian Myths and Legends.* Pantheon Books.
Erdoes, R. (1994). *Lame Deer, Seeker of Visions.* Simon & Schuster.
Eusebius. (1990). *The History of the Church.* Penguin Classics.
Faulkner, R. O. (1996). *The Ancient Egyptian Book of the Dead.* British Museum Press.
Fideler, D. (1993). *Jesus Christ, Sun of God.* Quest Books.
Fleming, G. (1987). *Hitler and the Final Solution.* University of California Press.
Friedman, R. E. (1997). *Who Wrote the Bible?* HarperOne.
Garcia, K. (1996). *Uncovering the Secrets of the Mayan Calendar.* Atlantis Rising Magazine.
Gibran, K. (1923). *The Prophet.* Alfred A. Knopf.
Gimbutas, M. (1989). *The Language of the Goddess.* Harper and Row.
Godwin, J. (1989). *Cosmic Music.* Inner Traditions.
Goodspeed, E. J. (1989). *The Apocrypha.* Vintage Books.
Green, J. (1985). *Pluto: The Evolutionary Journey of the Soul.* Llewellyn Publications.
Gregory, A. (Ed.). (2017). *The Gospel according to the Hebrews.* Oxford University Press.
Guenon, R. (2004). *The King of the World.* Sophia Perennis.
Hakeda, Y. S. (2005). *The Awakening of Faith.* Columbia University Press.
Hancock, G. (1993). *Sign and the Seal.* Touchstone.
Hancock, G. (1997). *The Message of the Sphinx.* Broadway Books.
Hayden, D. (1981). *Mesoamerican Sites and World-Views.* Dumbarton Oaks.
Heraclitus. (2003). *Fragments.* Penguin Classics.
Hofmann, A. (2008). *The Road to Eleusis.* North Atlantic Books.
Hua, H. (2003). *The Buddha Speaks of Amitabha Sutra.* Buddhist Text Translation Society.
Jamieson, R. (1999). *Jamieson, Fausset, and Brown's Commentary.* Zondervan.
Jeffrey, J. (1997). *Prophecy and the Great Pyramid.* New Dawn Magazine No. 40.
Jenkins, J. M. (1998). *Maya Cosmogenesis 2012.* Bear & Company.
Jochmans, J. R. (1980). *Rolling Thunder: The Coming Earth Changes.* Sun Publishing Co.
Josephus. (1999). *The New Complete Works of Josephus.* Kregel Academic.
Kaplan, A. (1997). *Sefer Yetzirah.* Weiser Books.
Kato, B. (1989). *The Threefold Lotus Sutra.* Kosei Publishing Company.

Keepin, W. (1993). *Lifework of David Bohm.* ReVision Magazine.
Kingsborough, E. K. (1830). *Antiquities of Mexico.* A. Aglio.
Kühlewind, G. (1985). *Becoming Aware of the Logos.* Lindisfarne Books.
Kühlewind, G. (1992). *The Logos-Structure of the World.* Lindisfarne Books.
Lamott, A. (2000). *Traveling Mercies.* Anchor Books.
Lau, D. (1963). *Tao Te Ching.* Penguin Classics.
Lemesurier, P. (1996). *The Great Pyramid Decoded.* Element Books.
Leoni, E. (2000). *Nostradamus and His Prophecies.* Dover Publications.
Long, M. F. (1948). *Secret Science Behind Miracles.* Devorss & Co.
Lovecraft, H. P. (2008). *Necronomicon.* Gollancz.
Lubicz, R. A. (1982). *Sacred Science.* Inner Traditions.
Luk, C. (1999). *Taoist Yoga: Alchemy & Immortality.* Red Wheel/Weiser.
Luk, C. (2002). *Ordinary Enlightenment: The Vimalakirti Nirdesa.* Shambhala Books.
MacKenna, S. (1992). *Plotinus: The Enneads.* Larson Publications.
MacLaine, S. (1986). *Out on a Limb.* Bantam Books.
Mails, T. E. (1997). *The Hopi Survival Kit.* Penguin Books.
Maimonides, M. (2000). *The Guide for the Perplexed.* Dover Publications.
Martin, E. L. (1991). *The Star That Astonished the World.* Associates for Scriptural Knowledge.
McClay, R. (1976). *The Pineal Gland, LSD and Serotonin.* Pharmacology Paper.
McDermott, R. A. (2001). *The Essential Aurobindo.* Lindisfarne Books.
McKenna, T. (1994). *The Invisible Landscape.* HarperOne.
Meeks, D. (1996). *Daily Life of the Egyptian Gods.* Cornell University Press.
Mendis, N. (1993). *The Questions of King Milinda.* Buddhist Publication Society.
Merton, T. (2010). *The Way of Chuang Tzu.* New Directions.
Meyer, M. (2004). *The Gospel of Thomas.* HarperOne.
Meyer, M. (2009). *The Nag Hammadi Scriptures.* HarperOne.
Milton, J. (2010). *Paradise Lost and Paradise Regained.* Signet Classics.
Montfort, S. L. (1995). *Jesus Living in Mary.* Montfort Publications.
Moody, R. (2015). *Life After Life.* HarperOne.
Myer, I. (1970). *Qabbalah: The Philosophical Writings of Solomon Ibn Gebirol.* Weiser Books.
Nikhilananda, S. (1979). *The Bhagavad Gita.* Ramakrishna-Vivekananda Center.
Nikhilananda, S. (1984). *The Gospel of Sri Ramakrishna.* Ramakrishna-Vivekananda Center.
Nikodimos, S. (1981). *The Philokalia (Volume 2).* Faber & Faber.
Noah, M. (2013). *The Book of Jasher.* Artisan Publishers.
O'Flaherty, W. D. (1992). *The Laws of Manu.* Penguin Classics.
Oldfather, C. H. (1933). *Diodorus Siculus.* Harvard University Press.
Ott, J. (1995). *The Age of Entheogens.* Natural Products Co.
Oudh, A. T. (2009). *The Matsya Purana.* Sri Satguru Publications.
Pagels, E. (1989). *Adam, Eve, and the Serpent.* Vintage Books.
Plato. (2003). *The Symposium.* Penguin Classics.
Plato. (2007). *The Republic.* Penguin Classics.
Plato. (2008). *Timaeus and Critias.* Penguin Classics.
Plutarch. (1936). *Plutarch: Moralia, Volume V, Isis and Osiris.* Harvard University Press.
Polo, M. (1993). *The Travels of Marco Polo.* (H. Yule, Trans.) Dover Publications.
Rambsel, Y. (1997). *His Name is Jesus.* Frontier Research Publications.
Ravenscroft, T. (1982). *The Spear of Destiny.* Samuel Weiser, Inc.

Redfield, J. (1998). *The Tenth Insight.* Grand Central Publishing.
Reid, D. (1994). *The Complete Book of Chinese Health & Healing.* Shambhala Books.
Rendsburg, G. (1986). *Redaction of Genesis.* Eisenbrauns.
Rigor, J. E. (1979). *The Power of Fixed Stars.* Astrology and Spiritual Center.
Robson, V. E. (2005). *The Fixed Stars and Constellations in Astrology.* Astrology Classics.
Roland, P. (2001). *Investigating the Unexplained.* Berkley Books.
Rolleston, F. S. (2001). *Mazzaroth.* Weiser Books.
Santillana, G. (1977). *Hamlet's Mill.* David. R. Godin.
Schneemelcher, W. (1990). *New Testament Apocrypha, Vol. 1.* Westminster John Knox Press.
Schwarzwaller, W. (1990). *The Unknown Hitler.* Berkley Books.
Shallis, M. (1983). *On Time.* Penguin Books.
Shanks, H. (1993). *Understanding the Dead Sea Scrolls.* Vintage Books.
Shastri, J. L. (1998). *The Linga Purana.* Motilal Banarsidass.
Smith, M. (2005). *The Secret Gospel.* Dawn Horse Press.
Stearn, J. (1985). *Soulmates.* Bantam Books.
Stearn, J. (1989). *Edgar Cayce: The Sleeping Prophet.* Random House.
Steiner, R. (1993). *The Apocalypse of St. John.* SteinerBooks.
Stent, G. S. (1969). *The Coming of the Golden Age.* Doubleday.
Strong, J. (2009). *Strong's Exhaustive Concordance to the Bible.* Hendrickson Publishing.
Summers, M. (1971). *The Malleus Maleficarum.* Dover Publications.
Tacitus, C. (2008). *Annals of Imperial Rome.* Oxford University Press.
Taylor, T. (1994). *Proclus: On the Theology of Plato.* Prometheus Trust.
Tedlock, D. (1996). *Popol Vuh.* Touchstone.
Temple, R. (1998). *The Sirius Mystery.* Destiny Books.
Timms, M. (1993). *Beyond Prophecies and Predictions.* Ballantine Books.
Tishby, I. (1989). *The Wisdom of the Zohar, Vol. 1-3.* Littman Library.
Unger, M. F. (2006). *The New Unger's Bible Dictionary.* Moody Publishers.
Various. (1982). *The Holy Bible King James Version 1611.* Thomas Nelson Publishers.
Various. (1990). *The Catholic Encyclopedia.* Nelson Reference.
Various. (1993). *The Oxford Companion to the Bible.* Oxford University Press.
Various. (2000). *The Columbia Encyclopedia.* Columbia University Press.
Various. (2007). *The Geneva Bible: 1560 Edition.* Hendrickson Publishers.
Various. (2008). *Encyclopedia Britannica.* Encyclopedia Britannica Inc.
Vermes, G. (2012). *The Complete Dead Sea Scrolls in English.* Penguin Classics.
Waite, A. E. (2003). *The Holy Kabbalah.* Dover Publications.
Waters, F. (1977). *Book of the Hopi.* Penguin Books.
White, T. (2006). *Catch a Fire.* Holt Paperbacks.
Whitehead, A. N. (1979). *Process and Reality.* Free Press.
Wilhelm, R. (1967). *The I Ching.* (C. F. Baynes, Trans.) Princeton University Press.
Williams-Heller, A. (1990). *Kabbalah: Your Path to Inner Freedom.* Quest Books.
Wisneski, L. A. (2009). *The Scientific Basis of Integrative Medicine.* Routledge.
Wolf, L. (1999). *Practical Kabbalah.* Harmony Books.
Yogananda, P. (1998). *Autobiography of a Yogi.* Self-Realization Fellowship.
Yukteswar, S. S. (1977). *The Holy Science.* Self-Realization Fellowship.
Zimmermann, F. (2011). *Jungle and the Aroma of Meats.* Motilal Banarsidass.
Zlotowitz, M. (1984). *Ethics of the Fathers: Pirkei Avos.* Mesorah Publication.

Glossary of Terms

ABSOLUTE	God. The transcendental Unity, the Good (of Plato) or the One *beyond* Intellect as defined by Plotinus in the 3rd c. and explicated by his Christian contemporary, Tertullian as the FATHER coexisting within a *consubstantial* TRINITY. *See* SINGULARITY.
AGE	One Platonic Month of 2,160 Years. One-third of a Platonic Season (6,480-year EPOCH or YUGA). *See* GREAT YEAR.
AKA	"The shadowy body or *aka* is 'sticky'. It sticks to anything we contact or see. The idea of an *aka* thread or cord is closely related to the idea of a flow of MANA or vital force. The root *ka* means a cord, and also a vine which branches out." (Max Freedom Long) *See* HUNA.
AKASHA	"A primary substance, or tenuity beyond conception, filling all space, the *Akasha* or luminiferous ether, which is acted upon by the life giving PRANA or creative force, calling into existence, in never ending cycles all things and phenomena." (Nikola Tesla) *See* SPIRIT.
AKASHIC RECORDS	"The record that the individual entity itself writes upon the skein of time and space, through patience — and is opened when self has attuned to the infinite, and may be read by those attuning to that consciousness." (Edgar Cayce)
AMITABHA	"Sanskrit: *Infinite Light*, Japanese *Amida*. In Mahayana Buddhism, and particularly in the so-called Pure Land sects, the great savior BUDDHA. All who had faith in him and who called upon his name would be reborn in his paradise and would reside there in bliss until they had attained ENLIGHTENMENT." (Encyclopedia Britannica)
ANGELS	"Fill up and complete the lowest choir of all the Hierarchies of the CELESTIAL INTELLIGENCES since they are the last of the Celestial Beings possessing the angelic nature." (Dionysius) *See* ARCHANGELS, PRINCIPALITIES.
ANOINTED ONE	Hebrew: *mashiach*, Greek: CHRIST, a high priest in the clandestine Order of MELCHIZEDEK, an exclusive line of genetically engineered INITIATEs, beginning with Abraham and culminating with the Chosen One, JESHUA.
ANTEDILUVIAN	": of or relating to the period before the FLOOD described in the Bible" (Merriam-Webster)

ANTHROPOMORPHIC	"1 : described or thought of as having a human form or human attributes 2 : ascribing human characteristics to nonhuman things" (Merriam-Webster)
ANTICHRIST	"The polar opposite and ultimate enemy of CHRIST. The Christian conception of Antichrist was derived from Jewish traditions, particularly the Book of Daniel in the Hebrew Bible. He will come at a time of a general apostasy, sit in the temple of God, and claim to be God himself." (Ency. Britannica)
APOCALYPSE	Revelation, from Greek: *apokalypsis*. "The expectation of an imminent cosmic cataclysm in which God destroys the ruling powers of evil and raises the righteous to life in a messianic kingdom" (Merriam-Webster) *See* ARMAGEDDON.
ARCHANGELS	"It is joined with the Princedoms because it is turned in a princely way to the superessential Principality and, as far as it can attain, moulds itself in His likeness, and it is seen to be the cause of the union of the Angels with its own orderly and invisible leadership." (Dionysius) *See* ANGELS, PRINCIPALITIES.
ARCHETYPE	": the original pattern or model of which all things of the same type are representations or copies" (Merriam-Webster)
ARK OF THE COVENANT	"Constructed during the Israelites' wanderings in the desert and used until the destruction of the First Temple, the Ark was the most important symbol of the Jewish faith, and served as the only physical manifestation of God on earth." (Jewish Virtual Library)
ARMAGEDDON	"Hebrew: *Hill of Megiddo*. In the New Testament, place where the kings of the earth under demonic leadership will wage war on the forces of God at the end of history. The Palestinian city of Megiddo, located on a pass commanding a road connecting Egypt and Syria, was probably chosen as a symbol for such a battle, because it had been the scene of many military encounters owing to its strategic location." (Encyclopedia Britannica) *See* APOCALYPSE.
ASHERAH	"This was the name of a sensual Canaanitish goddess Astarte, the feminine of the Assyrian Ishtar. Its symbol was the stem of a tree deprived of its boughs, and rudely shaped into an image, and planted in the ground." (Easton's Bible Dictionary)
ASSIAH	"The World of Action: (lit. *deed*); in Kabbalistic terminology, this refers to the lowest of the four spiritual worlds, the final level in the creative process which includes the physical universe." (Chabad.org) *See* ATZILUT, BERIAH, YETZIRAH.

ASTRAL BODY	"The third member of the human body is what is called the Sentient or Astral Body. It is the vehicle of pain and pleasure, of impulse, craving, passion, and the like — all of which are absent in a creature consisting only of physical and ETHERIC bodies." (Rudolf Steiner)
ATLANTIS	"Plato describes how Egyptian priests, in conversation with the Athenian lawgiver Solon, described Atlantis as an island larger than Asia Minor and Libya combined, and situated just beyond the Pillars of Hercules (the Straits of Gibraltar). About 9,000 years before the birth of Solon, the priests said, Atlantis was a rich island whose powerful princes conquered many of the lands of the Mediterranean until they were finally defeated by the Athenians and the latter's allies. The Atlantians eventually became wicked and impious, and their island was swallowed up by the sea as a result of earthquakes." (Encyclopedia Britannica) See FLOOD.
AUMAKUA	"In HUNA, the superconscious part of the mind is the 'older, parental, *utterly trustworthy spirit.*' As it takes two to be a 'parent', the Aumakua was considered to be a spirit composed of a male and female pair." (Max Freedom Long) See HIGH SELF, NESHAMAH, ELOHIM.
ATZILUT	"The World of Emanation: (lit. *emanation*); in Kabbalistic terminology, the highest of the four spiritual worlds, the realm of spiritual existence which, although encompassing attributes which have a specific definition, is in a state of infinity and at one with the Infinite Divine Light." (Chabad.org) See BERIAH, YETZIRAH, ASSIAH.
BA'AL (SAMAEL)	"He and his demonic host descended from heaven to seduce the first human pair. He himself was the serpent, whose form he assumed, and was the leader of the angels who married the daughters of men, thus being partially responsible for the FALL OF THE ANGELS. Samael is the *chief of the Satans*, quite in the sense of the *prince of the devils* mentioned in Matt 9.34. All legends associated with Satan refer equally to him, while as a miscreant he is compared to Belial (Hbw. *without a yoke*). In the Book of Jubilees, Belial is, like Satan, the accuser and father of all idolatrous nations." (Jewish Encyclopedia 1901-1906) See WATCHERS, DARK LORD.
	A second Fish-Lord from Sirius B descends to subdue DAGON, and breaches the Creation by raping Eva (MARIAH), begetting CAIN —thus Samael stakes His claim as proprietary owner (Hbw. *ba'al*) per His prodigious progeny, the pernicious Sons of Darkness.
BARDO	For three days the soul oscillates its level of vibration to plane. "Lamaism : the intermediate or astral state of the soul after death and before rebirth" (Merriam-Webster)

BERIAH	"The World of Creation: (lit. *creation*); more specifically creation *ex nihilo*; in Kabbalistic terminology, the second of the four spiritual worlds, the realm of spiritual existence which represents the first beginnings of a consciousness of self." (Chabad.org) See ATZILUT, YETZIRAH, ASSIAH.
BEHEMOTH	"A form of the primeval monster of chaos, defeated by YAHWEH at the beginning of the process of creation; in fact, frequently identified with the hippopotamus, she is represented as tamed by him and with a ring through her lip, so that like LEVIATHAN she has become a divine pet. According to later Jewish tradition, at the end time Behemoth and Leviathan will become food for the righteous." (Oxford Companion to the Bible)
BHAKTI	"Sanskrit: *devotion*. In Hinduism, a movement emphasizing the mutual intense emotional attachment and love of a devotee toward a personal god and of the god for the devotee." (Encyclopedia Britannica)
BIBLE CODE	"There is an old Jewish tradition about a *hidden text* in the Hebrew Pentateuch (the Five Books of Moses), consisting of words or phrases expressed in the form of equidistant letter sequences (ELS's)—that is by selecting sequences of equally spaced letters in the text. We developed a methodology for systematic and rigorous studies of the same nature; namely, for attempts to show objectively the existence of the *hidden text* in the Hebrew Pentateuch. This methodology was applied to study the *hidden text* of the Book of Genesis... It has been noted that when the Book of Genesis is written as two-dimensional arrays, equidistant letter sequences spelling words often appear in close proximity with portions of the text which have related meaning. Quantitative tools for measuring this phenomenon are developed." (Statistical Science 1994, Doron Witztum, Eliyahu Rips, and Yoav Rosenberb) See TORAH.
BINAH	"It is the uppermost feminine element in the GODHEAD, and is symbolized as the mother of the SHEKHINAH. Many of the symbols associated with *Binah* are therefore identical to those of the *Shekhinah*." (Jewish Virtual Library) See KABBALAH, SEFIRAH.
BODHISATTVA	"Sanskrit: *one whose goal is awakening*. In Buddhism, one who seeks awakening (*bodhi*)—hence, an individual on the path to becoming a BUDDHA." (Encyclopedia Britannica)
BORN AGAIN	Upon breakthrough contact with the OVERSOUL, (complete Ego transcendence and fusion with the FATHER), the candidate is *born again* into a spiritually ordained life— becoming what used to be called an INITIATE.

BOOK OF ENOCH	"In the old Jewish and Christian literatures (for example, in the New Testament Epistle of Jude, verse 14) a Book of Enoch is quoted, and is undoubtedly often used without special reference being made to it. But about 300 the Christian Church began to discredit the book, and after the time of the Greek fathers Syncellus and Cedrenus, who cite it (ninth century), it was entirely lost until (1773) the traveler Bruce discovered in Abyssinia two manuscripts of the book. In the nineteenth century several editions and translations were made, and many critical inquiries into its contents published." (Jewish Encyclopedia 1901-1906)
BUDDHA	"Sanskrit: *awakened one.* An enlightened being, one who has awakened from the sleep of ignorance and achieved freedom from suffering. *Buddha* is one of the many epithets of a teacher who lived in northern India sometime between the 6th and 4th centuries before the Common Era. His followers, known as Buddhists, propagated the religion that is known today as Buddhism." (Encyclopedia Britannica) See ENLIGHTENMENT, TATHAGATA.
CAIN	"While the pious men all descended from SETH, there sprang from Cain all the wicked ones who rebelled against God and whose perverseness and corruption brought on the FLOOD: they committed all abominations and incestuous crimes in public without shame. The daughters of Cain were those 'fair daughters of men' who by their lasciviousness caused the fall of the SONS OF GOD." (Jewish Encyclopedia 1901-1906) See BA'AL, ANTICHRIST, MABUS.
CELESTIAL INTELLIGENCES	"*The Celestial Hierarchies* of Dionysius the Areopagite is based on passages from the Old and New Testaments, but like the other writings of this great mystic it embodies the essential principles of the Neoplatonic teachings. The Celestial Intelligences are constituted in three triads, forming nine Orders, whose names represent the Divine Attributes which they manifest to all below them." (Shrine of Wisdom) See KINGDOM OF HEAVENS.
CHAKRA	"Sanskrit: *wheel,* conceived of as focal points where psychic forces and bodily functions merge with and interact with each other. Six major ones located roughly along the spinal cord and another one located just above the crown of the skull are of principal importance." (Encyclopedia Britannica) See KUNDALINI.
CHRIST	"Septuagint translation of Hebrew *Mashiah* (MESSIAH = The Anointed), applied by Christians exclusively to Jesus as the Messiah." (Jewish Encyclopedia 1901-1906) See ANOINTED ONE, LIGHT LORD.

CREATIVE	"The first hexagram is made up of six unbroken lines. These unbroken lines stand for the primal power, which is light-giving, active, strong, and of the spirit. The hexagram is consistently strong in character, and since it is without weakness, its essence is power or energy. Its image is heaven." (Wilhelm/Baynes) See I CHING, RECEPTIVE.
CHERUBIM	"Denotes their power of knowing and beholding God, their receptivity to the highest Gift of Light, their contemplation of the Beauty of the GODHEAD in Its First Manifestation, and that they are filled by participation in Divine Wisdom, and bounteously outpour to those below them from their own fount of wisdom." (Dionysius) See SERAPHIM, THRONES.
DAATH	"The fear of the LORD is the beginning of *daath*: but fools despise wisdom and instruction." (Proverbs 1.7) Adam *knew* Eve. Sexual intercourse opens the quasi-quantum eleventh SEFIRAH, a bottomless abyss of knowledge. The outlawed Tantric practices of Dravidian India were devised to prolong the orgasmic ecstasy, and access this no-man's land. The Kabbalah's most dire warnings concern the tricky Uranian dimension known as *Daath* (Hbw. *knowledge*). The rabbis describe a very dangerous door that, once opened, is hard to close again. With good reason, the ancient seers even denied its existence! They warned one another to beware of direct knowledge — use wisdom to understand, become wise through understanding.
DAGON (OANNES)	"Unlike the BA'ALs, who, among the Canaanites, were essentially local deities, Dagon seems to have been considered by the Philistines as a national god. To him they attributed their success in war; him they thanked by great sacrifices, before him they rejoiced over the capture of Samson; into his temple they brought the trophies of their victories, the Ark, the armour, and the head of Saul." (The Catholic Encyclopedia 1907-1912)
	The original DARK LORD was historically known as OANNES, the first Fish-Lord from Sirius B who taught the antediluvians the arts of agriculture—barley for beer and grape vines for wine. Mythologized as OSIRIS by the Egyptians, this LEVIATHAN defeated by Ba'al awaits His subterranean release as Cthulhu.
DARK LORD	Twin streams of Mankind, each with their own Lord, feed the amalgamative Wholly SPIRIT with their deeds—good and bad. However, when the LIGHT LORD moves into the FATHER, He becomes *Ein-Sof* (Without End, Infinite), the Inscrutable Source of *everything*, good and evil. The Dark Lord and His Demons exist *solely* through the will of the Father and function as executors or Lords of Karma. See BA'AL, DAGON.

DELUGE	"When Noah was four hundred and eighty years old all the righteous sons of men were dead, except Methuselah and Noah himself. At God's command they both announced that one hundred and twenty years would be given to men for repentance; if in that time they had not mended their evil ways, the earth would be destroyed." (Jewish Encyclopedia 1901-1906) See FLOOD.
DEVA	"Sanskrit: *divine*. In the Vedic religion of India and in later Hinduism, one of many gods, often roughly divided into sky, air, and earth divinities on the basis of their identification with the forces of nature. In the pantheistic systems that emerged by the Late Vedic period, the *deva*s became subordinate to the one supreme being." (Encyclopedia Britannica) See GROUP-SOUL.

DHARMA	"1 *Hinduism* : an individual's duty fulfilled by observance of custom or law
	2 *Hinduism & Buddhism*
	    a : the basic principles of cosmic or individual existence : divine law
	    b : conformity to one's duty and nature" (Merriam-Webster)

DHARMADHATU	"The Mind in terms of the ABSOLUTE is the one World of Reality (*Dharmadhatu*) and the essence of all phases of existence in their totality. That which is called 'the essential nature of the Mind' is unborn and is imperishable." (Asvaghosa) See SUCHNESS.
DOMINIONS	"Signifies a certain unbounded elevation to that which is above, freedom from all that is of the earth, and from all inward inclination to the bondage of discord, a liberal superiority to harsh tyranny, an exemptness from degrading servility and from all that is low: for they are untouched by any inconsistency." (Dionysius) See VIRTUES, POWERS.
ELOHIM	"Plural of *eloah*. *Gods* in the ordinary sense; but specifically used (in the plural thus, especially with the article) of the supreme *God*; occasionally applied by way of deference to *magistrates*; and sometimes as a superlative." (Strong's Exhaustive Concordance) See AUMAKUA.
ENOCH	"Name of the seventh progenitor of the race in the 'book of the generations of Adam'; he was the son of Jared and the father of Methuselah. He lived 365 years, and is described as 'walking with God', his end being told in the words 'and he was not; for God took him.' Enoch was a pious worshiper of the true God, and was removed from among the dwellers on earth to heaven, receiving the name (and office) of METATRON." (Jewish Encyclopedia 1901-1906) See JESHUA.

ENNEADS	"Plotinus must thus be regarded as the first Neoplatonist, and his collected works, the *Enneads* (from the Greek *enneas*, 'set of nine'—six sets of nine treatises each, arranged by his disciple Porphyry), are the first and greatest collection of Neoplatonic writings." (Encyclopedia Britannica)
ENLIGHTENMENT	Redemption of the compounded Soul. Dropping the weight of virtual ego and id reveals the *true ego* of no ego. "Buddhism : a final spiritual state marked by the absence of desire or suffering" (Merriam-Webster) *See* KINGDOM OF HEAVENS.
EPOCH	One Platonic Season composed of 6,480 Years. One quarter of a MAHAYUGA (25,920 years). *See* YUGA, PRECESSION.
ESCHATOLOGY	"The doctrine of the last things. It was originally a Western term, referring to Jewish, Christian, and Muslim beliefs about the end of history, the resurrection of the dead, the LAST JUDGMENT, the MESSIANIC ERA, and the problem of theodicy." (Encyclopedia Britannica) *See* SOTERIOLOGY.
ESSENES	"A branch of the Pharisees who conformed to the most rigid rules of Levitical purity while aspiring to the highest degree of holiness. They lived solely by the work of their hands and in a state of communism, devoted their time to study and devotion and to the practice of benevolence, and refrained as far as feasible from conjugal intercourse and sensual pleasures, in order to be initiated into the highest mysteries of heaven and cause the expected Messianic time to come." (Jewish Encyclopedia 1901-1906)
ETERNAL JUDGMENT	"On the tenth week in the seventh part, there shall be the eternal judgment, and it shall be executed by the WATCHERS of the eternal heaven the great judgment which emanates from all of the angels. The first heaven shall depart and pass away; a new heaven shall appear; and all the powers of heaven shall shine forever sevenfold." (1 Enoch)
ETHERIC BODY	"Man has this etheric or life-body in common with the plants and animals. The life-body works in a formative way upon the substances and forces of the physical body, thus bringing about the phenomena of growth, reproduction, and inner movement of the saps and fluids. It is therefore the builder and molder of the physical body, its inhabitant and architect." (Rudolf Steiner) *See* ASTRAL BODY.
FALL OF THE ANGELS	"The angels were depicted as rebels against God: lured by the charms of women, they 'fell' (Heb, *nfl.* נפל), defiled their heavenly purity, and introduced all manner of sinfulness to earth. Their giant offspring were wicked and violent; the FLOOD was occasioned by their sinfulness." (Jewish Virtual Library) *See* NEPHILIM, WATCHERS.

FATHER	An anthropomorphic ABSOLUTE, the GODHEAD acting as dynamic Creator within His mandalic Galaxy by oscillating from SON OF GOD or LOGOS to the incandescent Source, generating His living SPIRIT. *See* TRINITY, ELOHIM.
FLOOD	"There occurred portentous earthquakes and floods, and one grievous day and night befell them, when the whole body of your warriors was swallowed up by the earth, and the island of ATLANTIS in like manner was swallowed up by the sea and vanished; wherefore also the ocean at that spot has now become impassable and unsearchable, being blocked up by the shoal mud which the island created as it settled down." (Plato) *See* DELUGE.
GALACTIC ALIGNMENT	"It will take the December solstice sun 36 years to precess through the Galactic equator. The precise alignment of the solstice point (the precise center-point of the body of the sun as viewed from earth) with the Galactic equator was calculated to occur in 1998 (Jean Meeus, *Mathematical Astronomy Morsels*). Thus, the Galactic Alignment 'zone' is 1998 +/- 18 years = 1980 - 2016. This is *era-2012*. This Galactic Alignment occurs only once every 26,000 years, and was what the ancient Maya were pointing to with the 2012 end-date of their Long Count calendar." (John Jenkins) *See* PRECESSION, MAYA CALENDAR.
GEMATRIA	"A cryptograph which gives, instead of the intended word, its numerical value, or a cipher produced by the permutation of letters. As the essence of things is number, the identity of things in number demonstrates their identity in essence." (Jewish Encyclopedia 1901-1906)
GODHEAD	Like the lower choirs of triune CELESTIAL INTELLIGENCES, the Godhead also participates in His own evolution. The SON OF GOD *purifies* himself to ascend to the FATHER whereupon He receives nourishment or *illumination*, which is then digested and radiated throughout the entire Galactic body as the *perfecting* SPIRIT of cognition. *See* TRINITY.
GREAT PYRAMID	"The Hall of the Initiates... This, then, receives all the records from the beginnings of that given by the priest... to that period when there is to be the change in the earth's position [POLE SHIFT] and the return of the Great Initiate to that and other lands for the folding up of those prophecies that are depicted there. All changes that came in the religious thought in the world are shown there, in the variations in which the passage through same is reached, from the base to the top or to the open tomb and the top. These are signified by both the layer and the color [and] in what direction the turn is made." (Edgar Cayce) *See* PILLARS OF ENOCH, ZIGGURAT.

GREAT YEAR	"The complete number of Time fulfills the Complete Year when all the eight circuits, with their relative speeds, finish together and come to a head, when measured by the revolution of the Same and Similarly-moving." (Plato) "The period of one complete cycle of the equinoxes around the ecliptic, about 25,800 years. Also called *platonic year*." (NASA) See MAHAYUGA, PRECESSION.
GROUP-SOUL	Even with our superior, compounded Soul, Humans are still members of a Group-Soul and without the God-man above, we'd have no existence *whatsoever*. — "A single human being has no reality, the existence of man begins with the word that floats between I and you. The LOGOS connects human beings through the Word — all else is temptation or a temporary connection." (Georg Kuhlewind) See DEVA.
HIGH SELF	"The High Self, which is connected to the body by a thread of the AKA (*kino mea*) or invisible 'shadowy body stuff' is under some compulsion to let the lower selves exercise free will and learn by experience unless they desire and request guidance and help from the High Self, in which case the AUMAKUA takes a hand in the affairs of the man." (Max Freedom Long) See LOW SELF, MIDDLE SELF.
HOMOOUSION	"Greek, from *homos*, same, and *ousia*, essence; the word used by the Council of Nicaea (325 AD) to express the Divinity of CHRIST. Arius had taught that the SON, being, in the language of Philo, the Intermediator between God and the world, was not eternal, and therefore not of the Divine substance, but a creature brought forth by the will of God. Homoousion was indeed used by philosophical writers to signify *of the same or similar substance*; but as the unity of the Divine nature wasn't questioned, the word carried the fuller meaning: *of one and the same substance*." (The Catholic Encyclopedia 1907-1912)
HOPI INDIANS	"The 15,000 or so Hopis are a small nation, but their sense of burden is great. According to a 900-year-old religious tradition, the Great Spirit *Maasau'u*, Guardian of the Earth, assigned them the duty of preserving the natural balance of the world and entrusted them with a series of ominous prophecies warning of specific threats and providing guidance on how to avoid them. The prophecies remained a secret oral tradition until 1948, when Hopi religious leaders, alarmed by reports of the atomic bomb's mushroom cloud, which they saw as the destructive 'gourd of ashes' foretold in the prophecies, appointed Mr. Banyacya and three others as messengers to reveal and interpret the prophecies to the outside world." (New York Times, Feb. 15, 1999) See HOPI PROPHECIES.

HOPI PROPHECIES	"My people await Pahana, the lost White Brother, [from the stars]. The Fourth World shall end soon, and the Fifth World will begin. This the elders everywhere know. These are the Signs that great destruction is coming. The world shall rock to and fro. The white man will battle against other people in other lands—with those who possessed the first light of wisdom. There will be many columns of smoke and fire such as White Feather has seen the white man make in the deserts not far from here. Only those which come will cause disease and a great dying. Many of my people, understanding the prophecies, shall be safe. Those who stay and live in the places of my people also shall be safe. Then there will be much to rebuild. And soon—very soon afterward—Pahana will return." ~Hopi Elder White Feather, 1958
HUNA	The revolutionary work that revealed "the three voltages of vital force (MANA) used by the three spirits of man." Max Freedom Long coined the word Huna (Hwn. *secret*) to scientifically explain the magic used by the early Polynesians for healing, changing the future for the better, control of winds and weather, fire-walking, etc. *See* KAHUNA.
I CHING	"Chinese: *Book of Changes.* An ancient Chinese text, one of the Five Classics (*Wujing*) of Confucianism. Though the book was originally used for divination, its influence on Chinese minds and its universal popularity are due to a cosmology that involves humans and nature in a single system. The uniqueness of the *Yijing* consists in its presentation of 64 symbolic hexagrams that, if properly understood and interpreted, are said to contain profound meanings applicable to daily life." (Encyclopedia Britannica)
INITIATE	Once the candidate is "singled-out" by SPIRIT (many are called, few are chosen) and his KUNDALINI (*i.e.,* MANA) ascends to the seventh CHAKRA (*i.e.,* Most High God), the BORN AGAIN *Initiate* then assumes the role *agent of change* for either Good or Evil — henceforth retaining the AKA cord connection with the FATHER. Past the point of no return, the Great Spirit now dictates his every move as the wind blows the trees. The sum goodness of all past lives' moral modalities determines the direction of his new life as Saint or Sorcerer.
ISVARA	"The Lord is a special soul. He is untouched by the obstacles [to the practice of *yoga*], *karma*, the fructification [of *karma*], and subconscious predispositions." ~Meditative Absorption: 1.24 The ARCHETYPE of a personal God was first introduced to the pious Hindus by the anomalous manisfestation of a blue entity, Krsna. The ABSOLUTE (Brahman) had emanated its LOGOS who descended (Avatar). The BUDDHA inadvertently exasperated this dichotomy upon His ENLIGHTENMENT as *another* Isvara. "In him, the seed of omniscience is unsurpassed." ~Ibid. 1.25

JESHUA	Cayce was asked to list the names of the previous incarnations of the CHRIST — "First, in the beginning, of course as Adam; Then as ENOCH, MELCHIZEDEK in the perfection. Then in the earth as Joseph, Joshua, Jeshua (Jesus)." (Edgar Cayce)
KABBALAH	"*Kabbalah* (= 'Tradition') is distinguished by its theory of ten creative forces that intervene between the infinite, unknowable God (*Ein Sof*) and our created world. The most famous work of Kabbalah, the ZOHAR, was revealed to the Jewish world in the thirteenth century by Moses De Leon." (Jewish Virtual Library) *See* SEFIRAH.
KAHUNA	"There were several kinds of Kahunas (*Keeper of the Secret*) in Hawaii before they ceased almost entirely to understand the ancient lore. Some were hardly more than spiritualistic mediums. Some were prophets. Some labored to control wind and weather. A few were able to perform almost any part of the magic, be it healing or controlling the elements." (Max Freedom Long) *See* HUNA.
KALI YUGA	"The age of conflict. Righteousness has dwindled to one quarter of its original substance. Spiritual efforts slacken off, knowledge is forgotten, evil dominates. Disease, fatigue, anger, hunger, fear and despair gain ground; humanity has no goal." (Linga Purana) *See* EPOCH, YUGA.
KINGDOM OF HEAVENS	The superconscious, supraliminal state of existence that remains when one has *consciously* released the ETHERIC BODY as well as the physical, thereby achieving the final spiritual state of full ENLIGHTENMENT. *See* NIRVANA.
	"Heaven" (Hbw. *Shamayim*, plural form of the unused singular *Shameh*) is always translated in the plural, Heavens. In the Greek NT, JESHUA always refers to the kingdom of *heavens*—mistranslated as *Ouranos* (sing.), a mistransliteration of *Shamayim*. A kingdom is a natural hierarchy of designated authority like the Armed Forces. As everything in our world originates in the upper Dimensions (*Sefirot*), all secular governments are natural, subconscious imitations of relegated power structures in the higher Worlds. *See* CELESTIAL INTELLIGENCES.
KUNDALINI	"In ordinary thinking only a small quantity of psychic energy is is utilized. The rest of the PRANA lies 'coiled' or dormant as a a store of reserve energy called the kundalini. The rousing of the kundalini is the one and only way of attaining divine wisdom, superconscious perception, realization of the Spirit. The rousing may come in various ways, through love for God, through the mercy of perfected sages, or through the power of the analytic will of the philosopher." (Vivekananda) *See* MANA.

LAKE OF FIRE	"After the sea gave up the dead that were in it, and death and Hades gave up the dead that were in them, and after all the dead were judged, says John, Death and Hades were thrown into the lake of fire. The notion that death and the grave are thrown into the lake of fire characterizes the lake here not as a place of torment (contrast 19:21 and 20:10), but as a place of destruction or nonexistence. Death and Hades are not tortured or punished, *they simply cease to exist*." (Jamieson Fausset Brown Bible Commentary)
LAST JUDGMENT	"The Last Judgment precedes the Resurrection... at the close of the MESSIANIC ERA." (Jewish Encyclopedia 1901-1906) See ETERNAL JUDGMENT.
LEFT-HAND PATH	"The Tantrists of the Vamachara (*the left-hand practice*) sought to intensify their own sense impressions by making enjoyment, or sensuality (*bhoga*), their principal concern: the adept pursued his spiritual objective through his natural functions and inclinations, which were sublimated and then gratified in rituals in order to disintegrate his normal personality." (Encyclopedia Britannica) See TANTRA.
LEVIATHAN	"His defeat by God is a prelude to creation. According to apocalyptic literature, that battle will be rejoined in the end time when the evil Leviathan will be finally defeated (Isaiah 27.1; Revelation 12.3; Revelation 17.1-14; Revelation 19.20; Revelation 21.1). In Job 41, Leviathan is described as fully under God's control, a divine pet. Many commentators have equated the Leviathan of Job 41 with the crocodile, and some elements of the description seem to fit this identification." (Oxford Companion to the Bible) See BEHEMOTH, DAGON.
LIGHT LORD	The Light Lord is Self-limited through a *quid pro quo* "Prime Directive" not to interfere with Mankind's actions, since any miraculous intervention on the CHRIST's part automatically justifies equal and opposite interference from the DARK LORD — a Yang/Yin law of moral metaphysics. Yahweh's empowerment of His Son for 3½ years will be counter-balanced by BA'AL's Son for the 3½ year tribulation and unholy desecration of the Church. See SON OF GOD.
LILITH	The only mention of Adam's first wife in the entire Bible is a *coded* reference in Isaiah's apocalyptic prophecy of a decimated Rome, reinhabited with the dregs of nature: "The wild beasts of the desert shall also meet with the wild beasts of the island, and the satyr shall cry to his fellow; the *screech owl* also shall rest there, and find for herself a place of rest." "A female demon assigned a central position in Jewish demonology. She appears briefly in the Sumerian Gilgamesh epic and is found in Babylonian demonology." (Jewish Virtual Library)

LOGOS	"It is in Heraclitus that the theory of the Logos appears for the first time, and it is doubtless for this reason that, first among the Greek philosophers, Heraclitus was regarded by St. Justin (Apol. I, 46) as a Christian before CHRIST. For him the Logos, which he seems to identify with fire, is that universal principle which animates and rules the world. This conception could only find place in a materialistic monism. The philosophers of the fifth and fourth centuries before Christ were dualists, and conceived of God as transcendent, so that neither in Plato (whatever may have been said on the subject) nor in Aristotle do we find the theory of the Logos." (The Catholic Encyclopedia 1907-1912) *See* SON OF GOD, LIGHT LORD.
LOW SELF	"Remembers but has defective reason. Creates all emotions; handles the vital force of the body. It does its work with secrecy and silent care, but it is stubborn and disposed to refuse to obey. It refuses to do things when it fears the gods (holds a complex or fixation of ideas), and it intermingles or tinctures the MIDDLE SELF to give the impression of being one with it." (Max Freedom Long) *See* UNIHIPILI.
MABUS	Nostradamus' anagram for the name of the final, culminating incarnation of the DARK LORD's son, the ANTICHRIST. "Mabus then will soon die, there will come of people and beasts a horrible slaughter: Then all of a sudden vengeance will be seen coming, a hundred-hand, thirst, famine when the comet will run." (CII-62) *See* CAIN.
MAHAYUGA	One Platonic Year (25,920 Years) composed of four Platonic Seasons or YUGAS. *See* GREAT YEAR, PRECESSION.
MALKHUT	"The last SEFIRAH, Malkhut or Kingdom, the abode of the SHEKHINAH, does not represent any new attribute, but symbolizes the harmony of all the others, and the kingdom of that harmony, over the entire universe. Here is the idea of an Ideal Perfect Kingdom, which is in perfect prototype in the highest world and which is to come on earth in the future, in perfection; and in which, the MESSIAH or CHRIST, is to govern over all the just or pious." (Isaac Meyer) *See* KABALLAH.
MANA	"Known to us as vital force. It is electrical in its nature and shows strong magnetic qualities. The invisible substance through which the vital force acts is called AKA, or 'shadowy body stuff.' *Mana-mana* means to branch out and move upward or outward as a growing vine. It symbolizes the vital force when raised in voltage and used by the MIDDLE SELF. *Mana loa* translates strongest vital force and represents the high voltage of force used by the HIGH SELF." (Max Freedom Long) *See* HUNA, PRANA, KUNDALINI.

MANDALA	"Sanskrit: *circle*. In Hindu and Buddhist Tantrism, a symbolic diagram used in the performance of sacred rites and as an instrument of meditation. The mandala is basically a representation of the universe, a consecrated area that serves as a receptacle for the gods and as a collection point of universal forces. Man (the microcosm), by mentally 'entering' the mandala and 'proceeding' toward its centre, is by analogy guided through the cosmic processes of disintegration and reintegration. Similar ritual drawings have been found in cultures other than Hindu and Buddhist—for example, in the sand paintings of the North American Indians. The Swiss psychologist Carl Jung published studies of mandala-like drawings executed by his patients. In his view, the spontaneous production of a mandala is a step in the individuation process—a central concept in Jung's psychological theory—and represents an attempt by the conscious self to integrate hitherto unconscious material." (Encyclopedia Britannica)
MARIAH	The Anthropomorphic Daughter, the Female Countenance or LOGOS: *Beauty*, second person of the Female GODHEAD. *See* SHEKHINAH, SOPHIA, QUEEN OF HEAVEN.
MAYA CALENDAR	"Dating system of the ancient Mayan civilization and the basis for all other calendars used by Mesoamerican civilizations. The calendar was based on a ritual cycle of 260 named days and a year of 365 days. Taken together, they form a longer cycle of 18,980 days, or 52 years of 365 days, called a *Calendar Round*. The original name of the 260-day cycle is unknown; variously referred to as the TZOLKIN (*Count of Days*). Within the *Tzolkin* are two smaller cycles of days numbered from 1 to 13 and an ordered series of 20 named days. To describe a given date more accurately, the Maya instituted the *Long Count*, a continuous marking of time from 4 *Ahau* 8 *Cumku* (August 11, 3114 BC)—the base date used by the Maya for the first *Great Cycle*, a period of 5,125 years that ends on December 21, 2012 AD." (Encyclopedia Britannica) *See* GALACTIC ALIGNMENT.
MESSIAH	"Though the name is of later origin, the idea of a personal Messiah runs through the Old Testament. It is the natural outcome of the prophetic future hope. The first prophet to give a detailed picture of the future ideal king was Isaiah. The ideal king to whom Isaiah looks forward will be a scion of the stock of Jesse, on whom will rest the spirit of God as a spirit of wisdom, valor, and religion, and who will rule in the fear of God, his loins girt with righteousness and faithfulness. He will not engage in war or in the conquest of nations; the paraphernalia of war will be destroyed; his sole concern will be to establish justice among his people." (Jewish Encyclopedia 1901-1906) *See* CHRIST, ANOINTED ONE.

MESSIANIC ERA	"The reign of peace, lasting one thousand years, which will precede the LAST JUDGMENT and the future life. The concept has assumed especial importance in the Christian Church, where it is termed also *chiliasm*, designating the dominion of Jesus with the glorified and risen saints over the world for a thousand years. Chiliasm or the idea of the MILLENNIUM is, nevertheless, older than the Christian Church; for the belief in a period of one thousand years at the end of time as a preliminary to the resurrection of the dead was held in Parseeism." (Jewish Encyclopedia 1901-1906)
MELCHIZEDEK	"(*King of righteousness*): King of Salem and priest of the Most High in the time of Abraham. He brought out bread and wine, blessed Abram, and received tithes from him. Reference is made to him in Psalm 110.4, where the victorious ruler is declared to be *priest forever after the order of Melchizedek*." (Jewish Encyclopedia 1901-1906) See JESHUA.
METANOIA	"The instrument of knowledge can only by the *movement of the whole soul be turned* from the world of becoming into that of being, and learn by degrees to endure the sight of being, and of the brightest and best of being, or in other words, of the good." (Plato) See BORN AGAIN, INITIATE.
METATRON	"Greatest of angels in Jewish myths and legends, variously identified as the Prince (or Angel) of the Presence, as Michael the archangel, or as ENOCH after his ascent into heaven. He is likewise described as a celestial scribe recording the sins and merits of men, as a guardian of heavenly secrets, as God's mediator with men, as the *lesser Yahweh*, and as the ARCHETYPE of man." (Jewish Encyclopedia 1901-1906) See JESHUA.
MIDDLE SELF	"The conscious mind, spirit or entity. It is a separate spirit and not a permanent part of the LOW SELF. The conscious (UHANE) cannot remember a thought once it has let it go out of its center of attention. It has to depend on the subconscious to give back any thought needed as a memory. The conscious mind has two powers which are its very own, however. One is the power to use will of the hypnotic kind (more potent than the elementary will of the subconscious self). The second power is that of using the highest known form of reason, the inductive, which sets man apart as a superior animal in the animal kingdom." (Max Freedom Long) See HUNA.
MIDRASH	"Designates an exegesis which, going more deeply than the literal sense, attempts to penetrate into the spirit of the Scriptures, to examine the text from all sides, and thereby to derive interpretations which are not immediately obvious." (Jewish Encyclopedia 1901-1906)

MILLENNIUM	"Millennialism or *chiliasm*, the belief, expressed in the book of Revelation to John, the last book of the New Testament, that CHRIST will establish a 1,000-year reign of the saints on earth (the millennium) before the LAST JUDGMENT. More broadly defined, it is a cross-cultural concept grounded in the expectation of a time of supernatural peace and abundance on earth." (Encyclopedia Britannica) *See* MESSIANIC ERA.
MOLOCH	"Hebrew: *Molech*, king. A deity to whom child sacrifices were made throughout the ancient Middle East. Often used in the Old Testament as a variant name for the popular god BA'AL (Lord)." (Encyclopedia Britannica) *See* DARK LORD.
NEFESH	"There are three levels that comprise the soul, and therefore the soul has three names, on the pattern of the mystery above: *nefesh*, RUAH and NESHAMAH. The *nefesh* is the lowest stimulus. It is close to the body and nourishes it. The body depends upon it, and it depends upon the body." (Zohar) *See* LOW SELF, UNIHIPILI.
NEPHILIM	"An extinct race, inhabitants of the earth before the FLOOD, the progeny of the *Bene Elohim* and the daughters of men." (Jewish Encyclopedia 1901-1906) *See* WATCHERS.
NESHAMAH	"The prevailing view in the ZOHAR is that the soul consists of three parts, called NEFESH, RUAH and *neshamah*. The *neshamah* is a matter of true intellect. It is hewn from the source of life, and from the well-spring of intelligence and wisdom. Glory comes to dwell in the body in order to sustain everything for the service of the Creator, in order to provide him with substance (a Soul)." (Moses de Leon) *See* HIGH SELF, AUMAKUA.
NIRVANA	": the state of perfect happiness and peace in Buddhism where there is release from all forms of suffering" (Merriam-Webster) *See* ENLIGHTENMENT.
OANNES	"In Mesopotamian mythology, an amphibious being who taught mankind wisdom. Oannes, as described by the Babylonian priest Berosus, had the form of a fish but with the head of a man under his fish's head and under his fish's tail the feet of a man. In the daytime he came up to the seashore of the Persian Gulf and instructed mankind in writing, the arts, and the sciences." (Encyclopedia Britannica) *See* OSIRIS, DAGON, LEVIATHON.
OLAM HABA	"The term *olam ha-ba* (literally, 'the coming world') refers to the hereafter, which begins with the termination of man's earthly life. The final order of things beginning with the general resurrection and the LAST JUDGMENT." (Jewish Virtual Library) *See* ETERNAL JUDGMENT.

OMEGA POINT	"Teilhard aimed at a metaphysic of evolution, holding that it was a process converging toward a final unity that he called the Omega point." (Encyclopedia Britannica) See KINGDOM OF HEAVENS.
OSIRIS	"One of the most important gods of ancient Egypt. According to the Greek author Plutarch, Osiris was slain or drowned by SETH, who tore the corpse into 14 pieces and flung them over Egypt. Eventually, Isis and her sister Nephthys found and buried all the pieces, except the phallus, thereby giving new life to Osiris, who thenceforth remained in the underworld as ruler and judge." (Encyclopedia Britannica) See OANNES.
OVERSOUL	": the ABSOLUTE reality and basis of all existences conceived as a spiritual being in which the ideal nature imperfectly manifested in human beings is perfectly realized" (Merriam-Webster) See ENLIGHTENMENT, HIGH SELF.
PAROUSIA	"*Second Coming*. In Christianity, the future return of CHRIST in glory, when it is understood that he will set up his kingdom, judge his enemies, and reward the faithful, living and dead." (Encyclopedia Britannica) See MESSIANIC ERA.
PILLARS OF ENOCH	"The children of SETH were the inventors of that peculiar sort of wisdom which is concerned with the heavenly bodies, and their order; and that their inventions might not be lost before they were sufficiently known, upon Adam's prediction, that the world was at one time to be destroyed by the force of fire, and at another time by the violence and quantity of water, *they made two pillars, the one of brick, the other of stone*." (Josephus) See GREAT PYRAMID, ZIGGURAT.
POLE SHIFT	"Earth's Impending Magnetic Flip. Earth's magnetic north and south poles have flip-flopped many times in our planet's history — most recently, around 780,000 years ago. Geophysicists who study the magnetic field have long thought that the poles may be getting ready to switch again, and based on new data, it might happen earlier than anyone anticipated." (Scientific American, 2014)
POWERS	"An orderly and unconfined order in the divine receptions, and the regulation of intellectual and supermundane power which never debases its authority by tyrannical force, but is irresistibly urged onward in due order to the Divine." (Dionysius) See DOMINIONS, VIRTUES.
PRANA	"As AKASHA is the infinite, omnipresent material, so is Prana the infinite, omnipresent manifesting power. Out of this Prana is evolved everything that we call energy, that we call force. At the end of a cycle everything becomes Akasha, and all the forces resolve back into Prana." (Vivekananda) See MANA.

PRANAYAMA	"The fourth of the eight rungs of Yoga is Pranayama, which is regulating the breath so as to make it slow and subtle, leading to the experience of the steady flow of energy (PRANA), which is beyond or underneath exhalation, inhalation, and the transitions between them." (Yoga Sutras)
PRECESSION	"Precession of the equinoxes; motion of the equinoxes along the ecliptic (the plane of Earth's orbit) caused by the cyclic precession of Earth's axis of rotation. Such a motion is called precession and consists of a cyclic wobbling in the orientation of Earth's axis of rotation with a period of 25,772 years. Precession was the third-discovered motion of Earth, after the far more obvious daily rotation and annual revolution." (Encyclopedia Britannica) See MAHAYUGA.
PRINCIPALITIES	"Godlike princeliness and authoritativeness in an Order which is holy and most fitting to the princely POWERS, and that they are wholly turned towards the Prince of Princes, and lead others in princely fashion, and that they are formed, as far as possible, in the likeness of the Source of Principality, and reveal Its superessential order by the good Order of the Princely Powers." (Dionysius) See ANGELS, ARCHANGELS.
PURANA	"Sanskrit: *Ancient*. Traditionally, a Purana is said to treat five subjects, or 'five signs': the primary creation of the universe, secondary creation after periodic annihilation, the genealogy of gods and patriarchs, the reigns of the Manus (the first humans), and the history of the solar and lunar dynasties." (Encyclopedia Britannica)
QUEEN OF HEAVEN	Isis replaced all the minor goddesses in the pantheon as an existential ARCHETYPE was acknowledged for the first time in known history — a supreme Female Being, the *Queen of Heaven*. Until the next Queen, full of grace, took her place... "In Holy Writ, concerning the Son whom Mary will conceive, We read this sentence: 'He shall be called the Son of the most High, and the Lord God shall give unto him the throne of David his father, and he shall reign in the house of Jacob forever, and of his kingdom there will be no end,' and in addition Mary is called 'Mother of the Lord'; from this it is easily concluded that she is a Queen, since she bore a son who, at the very moment of His conception, because of the hypostatic union of the human nature with the Word, was also as man King and Lord of all things. So with complete justice St. John Damascene could write: 'When she became Mother of the Creator, she truly became Queen of every creature.' Likewise, it can be said that the heavenly voice of the Archangel Gabriel was the first to proclaim Mary's royal office." (*Ad Caeli Reginam*, Pope Pius XII, 1954) See MARIAH.

QUETZALCOATL	"The Feathered Serpent, one of the major deities of the ancient Mexican pantheon. With the immigration of Nahua-speaking tribes from the north, Quetzalcóatl's cult underwent drastic changes. The subsequent Toltec culture (9th through 12th centuries), centered at the city of Tula, emphasized war and human sacrifice linked with the worship of heavenly bodies." (Encyclopedia Britannica) *See* BA'AL.
RECEPTIVE	"This hexagram is made up of broken lines only. The broken lines represents the dark, yielding, receptive primal power of yin. The attribute of the hexagram is devotion; its image is the earth." (Wilhelm/Baynes) *See* I CHING, CREATIVE.
REINCARNATION	"In religion and philosophy, rebirth of the aspect of an individual that persists after bodily death — whether it be consciousness, mind, the soul, or some other entity — in one or more successive existences." (Encyclopedia Britannica)
RUAH	"The prevailing view in the ZOHAR is that the soul consists of three parts, called NEFESH, *ruah*, NESHAMAH. The *ruah* is the home of the sensual desires... it controls both good and evil moral conduct — the *ruah* is the power that enables the *nefesh* to maintain itself in the body." (Moses de Leon) *See* MIDDLE SELF, UHANE.
SAMADHI	"In Indian religion, particularly in Hinduism and Buddhism, the highest state of mental concentration that a person can achieve while still bound to the body and which unites him with the highest reality. *Samadhi* is a state of profound and utterly absorptive contemplation of the ABSOLUTE that is undisturbed by desire, anger, or any other ego-generated thought or emotion." (Encyclopedia Britannica)
SEFIRAH	"Hebrew: *number,* plural *Sefirot.* In the speculations of esoteric Jewish mysticism (KABBALAH), any of the 10 emanations, or powers, by which God the Creator was said to become manifest. The concept first appeared in the *Sefer Yetzira* ('Book of Creation'), as the 10 ideal numbers." (Encyclopedia Britannica)
SERAPHIM	"The name Seraphim clearly indicates their ceaseless and eternal revolution about Divine Principles, their heat and keenness, the exuberance of their intense, perpetual, tireless activity, and their elevative and energetic assimilation of those below, kindling them and firing them to their own heat, and wholly purifying them by a burning and all-consuming flame; and by the unhidden, unquenchable, changeless, radiant and enlightening power, dispelling and destroying the shadows of darkness." (Dionysius) *See* CHERUBIM, THRONES.

SETH — "Seth was the third son of Adam. He was born after CAIN had murdered Abel and when Adam was 130 years old. Seth lived to the age of 912." (Jewish Encyclopedia 1901-1906)

"Jewish, Persian, and Arabian ancient writers preserve the tradition, that *the family of Seth*, Adam, Seth, and ENOCH, invented astronomy, the Egyptians attributing it to Seth or *Thoth*, said to be the same as *Hermes Trismegistus*, the thrice-great. Plutarch mentions Seth, to whom the third day of the five of the epact was dedicated, as worshipped in Egypt. He was said to be the third son of Set and Netpthe, the father and mother of the gods." (Mazzaroth, Rolleston)

SHEKHINAH — The Holy SPIRIT of quickening Evolution, Truth and Compassion: *Grace*, second person of the Female GODHEAD.
"The *Shekhinah* is a Talmudic concept representing God's dwelling and immanence in the created world. According to a Rabbinic tradition, the *Shekhinah* shares in the exiles of the Jewish people." (Jewish Virtual Library)
See MARIAH, SOPHIA, BINAH.

SIDDHIS — "Gradually through the training of yoga, the adept transcends the elements of appearance, conquers the laws of Nature and is able to perform extraordinary feats. The supra-human powers he thus acquires are called the 'Attainments', the *Siddhis*." (Alain Danielou)

SINGULARITY — God. The ABSOLUTE of Plotinus. In the final analysis, there is only the One, a Singularity *beyond* number or scrutability —*absolutely* beyond any anthropomorphic conceptualization.

SIRIUS — "Also called *Alpha Canis Majoris* or the Dog Star, brightest star in the night sky, with apparent visual magnitude −1.44. It is a binary star in the constellation *Canis Major*. Sirius was known as *Sothis* to the ancient Egyptians, who were aware that it made its first heliacal rising of the year at about the time the annual floods were beginning in the Nile River delta. The companion star, *Sirius B*, is about as massive as the Sun, though much more condensed, and was the first white dwarf star to be discovered." (Encyclopedia Britannica)

SITRA AHRA — (Aramaic: *the other side*) "The Gerona kabbalists tended to deny the independent existence of evil. They state quite explicitly that evil is nothing but absence of good. In the ZOHAR, we find precise and detailed descriptions that present evil *as an array of powerful forces*." (Isaiah Tishby)

"Just as there are ten crowns (SEFIRAH) of faith above, so there are ten crowns of sorcery of uncleanness below. All the crowns that are not comprised within a body are abominable and unclean." (Zohar) *See* LEFT-HAND PATH, TANTRA.

SON OF GOD	The LIGHT LORD. The hypostatic, anthropomorphic Entity within the GODHEAD, the living LOGOS is the omnipotent ARCHETYPE, therefore supreme ELOHIM of His Galaxy. An ephemeral echelon, the ABSOLUTE continually renews Itself through the metamorphosis of the next BODHISATTVA. JESHUA superseded the previous *Son of God*, YAHWEH.
SONS OF GOD	The Elect, the faithful destined to full ENLIGHTENMENT, the KINGDOM OF HEAVENS. "The Apostles caught 153 fish, a number Augustine and other Church Fathers found significant. 153 is cabalistically the number of the Sons of God. This expression, *Sons of God* (Hebrew: *Bene Elohim*) occurs several times in scripture, and per GEMATRIA it counts up 153." (Biblia Cabalistica)
SON OF MAN	"Jesus did not simply transfer to himself the promise of heavenly *Son of man*, as it was articulated in the apocryphal First BOOK OF ENOCH. Instead, he gave this expectation of the Son of man an entirely new interpretation. Pious Jewish circles, such as the ENOCH community and other pietist groups, expected in the coming Son of man a figure of light from on high, a heavenly conquering hero, with all the marks of divine power and glory. Jesus, however, linked expectations of the Son of man with the figure of the suffering servant of God (as in Isaiah, chapter 53). He would return in glory as the consummator of the Kingdom." (Encyclopedia Britannica) *See* MESSIAH.
SOPHIA	The Unknowable, Transcendental, All-encompassing Mother of Wisdom: *Faith,* first person of the Female GODHEAD. *See* MARIAH, SHEKHINAH.
SOTERIOLOGY	"Salvation, in religion, the deliverance of humankind from such fundamentally negative or disabling conditions as suffering, evil, finitude, and death. The term *soteriology* denotes beliefs and doctrines concerning salvation in any specific religion, as well as the study of the subject. Christianity adds a further requirement in this context: because human nature is basically corrupted by sin, God's prevenient (antecedent, activating) grace is needed before the human will can be disposed even to desire salvation." (Encyclopedia Britannica) *See* ESCHATOLOGY.
SOULMATE	"All the souls of the world, which are the fruit of the deeds of the Holy One, blessed be He, are all one, and originate in a single mystery. When they descend into the world they all become separated into male and female forms... When the souls emerge, they emerge as male and female together. After this, when they descend, they become separated, one on one side and one on the other, and the Holy One, blessed be He, unites them subsequently." (Zohar)

SPIRIT	The third mysterious modulation of GODHEAD, the World Soul or Spirit (Greek: *Pneuma*) seems to be an independent force of the Inconceivable One (FATHER), yet is intimately tied to the LOGOS. "And I believe in the Holy Ghost, the Lord and Giver of Life; who proceeds from the Father and the SON; who with the Father and the Son together is worshipped and glorified; who spoke by the prophets." (Council of Constantinople, 381 AD) See AKASHA.
SUCHNESS	In the *Cula-suññata Sutta: The Lesser Discourse on Emptiness,* Siddhartha delineates *sunyata*'s hierarchical levels of relative Reality that ultimately lead to the quagmire of Suchness... "There is only this *non-emptiness*: the singleness based on the perception of the dimension of nothingness. Thus he regards it as empty of whatever is not there. Whatever remains, he discerns as present: 'There is *this*.' And so *this*, his entry into emptiness, accords with actuality, is undistorted in meaning, pure—superior and unsurpassed." This *this-ness* or *thus-ness* (tathata) that remains is inconceivable, unknowable—neither empty nor full, it is an ineffable SINGULARITY. "The term *Suchness* (tathata) is, so to speak, the limit of verbalization wherein a word is used to put an end to words." (The Awakening of Faith)
TANTRA	"Sanskrit: *Loom*. Because tantric practices typically represent teachings of relatively late development and incorporate elements of different traditions, they are often eschewed by orthodox practitioners. In Hinduism, *tantras* deal with popular aspects of the religion, such as spells, rituals, and symbols. Buddhist tantric literature, believed to date from the 7th cent. or earlier, has reference to numerous practices, some involving sexual activity, that have no basis in canonical literature." (Encyclopedia Britannica) See LEFT-HAND PATH.
TATHAGATA	"One of the titles of a BUDDHA and the one most frequently employed by the historical Buddha, Siddhartha Gautama, when referring to himself. The most generally adopted interpretation is 'one who has thus (*tatha*) gone (*gata*)' or 'one who has thus (*tatha*) arrived (*agata*),' implying that the historical Buddha was only one of many who have in the past and will in the future experience ENLIGHTENMENT and teach others how to achieve it." (Encyclopedia Britannica)
THIRD EYE	"It is not to be confounded with the pineal gland, which is distinctly a physical center or gland. The third eye exists in etheric matter, and is an etheric center of force, being made of the substance of the ethers, whereas the pineal gland is formed of matter of the three lower subplanes of the physical plane. The latter, nevertheless, has to be functioning more or less before the *Eye of Shiva* becomes in any degree active." (Alice Bailey) See CHAKRA.

THRONES	"Denotes that which is exempt from and untainted by any base and earthly thing, and the supermundane ascent up the steep. For these have no part in that which is lowest, but dwell in fullest power, immovably and perfectly established in the Most High, and receive the Divine Immanence above all passion and matter, and manifest God, being attentively open to divine participations." (Dionysius) See SERAPHIM, CHERUBIM.
TORAH	"God's revealed teaching or guidance for mankind. The meaning of *Torah* is often restricted to signify the first five books of the Old Testament, also called the Law or the Pentateuch. These are the books traditionally ascribed to Moses, the recipient of the original revelation from God on Mount Sinai." (Encyclopedia Britannica) See BIBLE CODE.
TRINITY	"The fundamental dogma of Christianity; the concept of the union in one God of FATHER, SON, and Holy SPIRIT as three infinite persons. It was the Nicene Council and even more especially the Athanasian Creed that first gave the dogma its definite formulation: 'And the Catholic Faith is this: That we worship one God in Trinity, and Trinity in Unity; Neither confounding the Persons; nor dividing the Substance.' Equalization of the Son with the Father marks an innovation in the Pauline theology: 'Yet to us there is one God, the Father, of whom are all things, and we unto him; and one Lord, Jesus CHRIST, through whom are all things, and we through him', while in another passage the Holy Ghost is added, thus rapidly developing the concept of the Trinity." (Jewish Encyclopedia 1901-1906) See GODHEAD.
TZOLKIN	": a period of 260 days constituting a complete cycle of all the permutations of 20 day names with the numbers 1 to 13 that constitutes the Maya sacred year" (Merriam-Webster) See MAYA CALENDAR.
UHANE	"Middle spirit or self: the conscious mind, spirit or entity. It is a separate spirit and not a permanent part of the LOW SELF. Uses a middle voltage of vital force: *mana-mana*. Used as will, it can be mesmeric or hypnotic force, provided that a thought form is introduced into the mind of the subject." (Max Freedom Long) See MIDDLE SELF, RUAH.
UNIHIPILI	"Low spirit or low self: the subconscious. A separate spirit. Low MANA or low voltage of vital force used by the subconscious can flow over threads of shadowy body substance. A large discharge of this low voltage vital force, commanded by the 'will' can exert a paralyzing effect, or a mesmeric effect resulting in unconsciousness, sleep and the rigid or cataleptic state." (Max Freedom Long) See LOW SELF, NEFESH.

VIRTUES	"Signifies a certain powerful and unshakable virility welling forth into all their Godlike energies; not being weak and feeble for any reception of the divine Illuminations granted to it; mounting upwards in fullness of power to an assimilation with God; never falling away from the Divine Life through its own weakness, but ascending unwaveringly to the superessential Virtue which is the Source of virtue." (Dionysius) See DOMINIONS, POWERS.
WATCHERS	"Like Beelzebub, or Lucifer, two hundred 'Irin' or 'watchers' fell, attracted by the beauty of the daughters of men. These fallen angels became 'the evil spirits' who taught mankind all the arts of deception, witchcraft, and sin. But their children (the NEPHILIM), the offspring of this mixture of an earthly and a celestial race, became, when slain, the hybrid race of disembodied spirits or demons doing the work of destruction until the Day of Judgment." (Jewish Encyclopedia 1901-1906)
YAHWEH	"Of the names of God in the Old Testament, that which occurs most frequently (6,823 times) is the so-called Tetragrammaton, Yhwh (יהוה), the distinctive personal name of the God of Israel. The meaning is 'He who is self-existing, self-sufficient,' or, more concretely, 'He who lives,' the abstract conception of pure existence being foreign to Hebrew thought." (Jewish Encyclopedia 1901-1906)
YETZIRAH	"The World of Formation: (Kabbalistic term; lit. *formation*); the third of the four spiritual worlds, the realm of spiritual existence in which the limited nature of the created beings takes on form and definition; the abode of the lower classes of angelic beings." (Chabad.org) See ATZILUT, BERIAH, ASSIAH.
YUGA	"In Hindu cosmology, an age of humankind. Each *yuga* is progressively shorter than the preceding one, corresponding to a decline in the moral and physical state of humanity." (Encyclopedia Britannica) See EPOCH, MAHAYUGA.
ZIGGURAT	"Pyramidal stepped temple tower that is an architectural and religious structure characteristic of the major cities of Mesopotamia from approximately 2200 until 500 BC. The ziggurat was always built with a core of mud brick and an exterior covered with baked brick." (Encyclopedia Britannica)
ZOHAR	"Sefer ha-Zohar, (Hebrew: *Book of Splendor*). 13th-century book, mostly in Aramaic, that is the classic text of esoteric Jewish mysticism, or KABBALAH. Though esoteric mysticism was taught by Jews as early as the 1st century AD, the *Zohar* gave new life and impetus to mystical speculations through the 14th and subsequent centuries. The *Sefer ha-Zohar* should be credited to Moses de León (1250–1305) of Spain." (Encyclopedia Britannica)

Afterword

"I will arise at Midnight to give thanks to you..."   ~Psalms 119.62

Believe it or not, but the *penetration*, the comprehension of sacred[1] texts depends upon both time and space — or what Drs. Timothy Leary and Richard Alpert deemed *Set and Setting*. Similar to psychoactive agents, truly *sacred* literature will move your spirit, your state of consciousness. You will get high. But timing is everything because the Spirit of truth, the shy Shekhinah, *cannot* descend until Midnight. Amazingly, higher concepts that were once obscure and even obscene become crystal clear and profound:

> *"While one is deeply engaged in study of the Torah, one inevitably draws the Shekhinah. It was the custom of many Kabbalistic mystics to rise at midnight and study till dawn, during which time they could cleave to Her in a special way."*
> ~*Safed Spirituality*, trans., Lawrence Fine

The anointed (initiated) King David instituted the practice of rising at Midnight for Torah study, Spirit Herself gently striking the Midnight Hour:

> *"The Talmud states that every night at midnight a northern wind would blow through King David's bedroom window and strike the strings of his harp, hanging above him; the instrument would sound, waking him up, and he would spend the rest of the night singing to G-d and learning Torah."*
> ~*Up at Midnight*, Baruch Emanuel Erdstein

Nevertheless, hierophantic revelations are *for such men as receive the truth with joy,* thus the manuscript will remain incredible to the general public no matter what precautions are taken. **Truth is stranger than fiction**, and only a *twice-born* Initiate can fully penetrate our paradoxical Reality. When you come across ideas that are alien to your mind-set, realize that you are not yet ready to hear some things, instead of dismissing such information as nonsense. Space is equally important as Time and one should have a chair, cushion or corner of the couch devoted to sacred study. Light the candle, ring the bell, and read this book, again. At Midnight.

---

[1] According to the rules of Jewish *Gematria*, two words that share the same letters also share the same vibration, numerologically. The words *sacred* and *scared* are therein intimately connected, and one should search for a common theme behind the two disparate words. Since sacred literature must be approached with respect (**"The fear of the LORD is the beginning of knowledge."**   ~Proverbs 1.7), we can determine a cautionary attitude is advised.

About the Author

Born in Palo Alto, 1952, Daniel Briggs was a late bloomer, youthful folly taking him down a number of disparate paths. From Nature's Way, the first avocado & sprouts, smoothie & carrot juice bar in Northern California to an ill-fated career as a movie producer (*Sextette*, Mae West) in the hedonistic 70's of Los Angeles, Briggs kept searching for his true calling.

In between projects, the road of excess led to the palace of wisdom when shamanic allies like Psilocybin Mushrooms, Peyote and Lysergic acid diethylamide opened the doors of perception—triggering a graceful *samadhi* awakening on a white sand beach in the Bahamas.

Daniel stumbled upon his destiny when he opened a humble bookshop in pre-Silicon Valley. The venerable spiritual oasis in Menlo Park, East West Books had been bought by a slick New Age cult, Ananda, and this was an ideal opportunity to offer an unbiased metaphysical bookstore to sincere seekers being seduced by an incursion of Hindu gurus, superseded by the diaspora of Tibetan Buddhists in the 90's.

For 10 years, Daniel Briggs managed Mandala Books, one of the finest collections of religious, spiritual and esoteric books on the West Coast.

He painstakingly built and now operates their Website, mandalabooks.com, an eclectic selection of wisdom literature, jealously guarded to preserve the most luminous works in Human literacy.